SCOTTISH LITURGICAL TRADITIONS
AND RELIGIOUS POLITICS

Scottish Religious Cultures *Historical Perspectives*

Series Editors: Scott R. Spurlock and Crawford Gribben

Religion has played a key formational role in the development of Scottish society shaping cultural norms, defining individual and corporate identities, and underpinning legal and political institutions. This series presents the very best scholarship on the role of religion as a formative and yet divisive force in Scottish society and highlights its positive and negative functions in the development of the nation's culture. The impact of the Scots diaspora on the wider world means that the subject has major significance far outwith Scotland.

Available titles

George Mackay Brown and the Scottish Catholic Imagination
Linden Bicket

Poor Relief and the Church in Scotland, 1560–1650
John McCallum

Jewish Orthodoxy in Scotland: Rabbi Dr Salis Daiches and Religious Leadership
Hannah Holtschneider

Miracles of Healing: Psychotherapy and Religion in Twentieth-century Scotland
Gavin Miller

George Strachan of the Mearns: Seventeenth-century Orientalist
Tom McInally

Scottish Liturgical Traditions and Religious Politics: From Reformers to Jacobites, 1540–1764
Edited by Allan I. Macinnes, Patricia Barton and Kieran German

Forthcoming titles

Dissent after Disruption: Church and State in Scotland, 1843–63
Ryan Mallon

The Scot Afrikaners: Identity Politics and Intertwined Religious Cultures
Retief Muller

Dugald Semple and the Life Reform Movement
Steven Sutcliffe

Scottish Presbyterianism: The Case of Dunblane and Stirling, 1687–1710
Andrew Muirhead

The Catholic Church in Scotland: Financial Development 1772–1930
Darren Tierney

The Dynamics of Dissent: Politics, Religion and the Law in Restoration Scotland
Neil McIntyre

William Guild and Moderate Divinity in Early Modern Scotland
Russell Newton

edinburghuniversitypress.com/series/src

SCOTTISH LITURGICAL TRADITIONS AND RELIGIOUS POLITICS

From Reformers to Jacobites, 1540–1764

Edited by ALLAN I. MACINNES,
PATRICIA BARTON and KIERAN GERMAN

EDINBURGH
University Press

To the Reverend Donald Macintosh, the non-juror who out-fiddled the College of Bishops

Edinburgh University Press is one of the leading university presses in the UK. We publish academic books and journals in our selected subject areas across the humanities and social sciences, combining cutting-edge scholarship with high editorial and production values to produce academic works of lasting importance. For more information visit our website: edinburghuniversitypress.com

© editorial matter and organisation Allan I. Macinnes, Patricia Barton and Kieran German, 2021, 2023
© the chapters their several authors, 2021, 2023

Edinburgh University Press Ltd
The Tun – Holyrood Road
12 (2f) Jackson's Entry
Edinburgh EH8 8PJ

First published in hardback by Edinburgh University Press 2021

Typeset in 10/12 ITC New Baskerville by
Servis Filmsetting Ltd, Stockport, Cheshire

A CIP record for this book is available from the British Library

ISBN 978 1 4744 8305 6 (hardback)
ISBN 978 1 4744 8306 3 (paperback)
ISBN 978 1 4744 8307 0 (webready PDF)
ISBN 978 1 4744 8308 7 (epub)

The right of the contributors to be identified as authors of this work has been asserted in accordance with the Copyright, Designs and Patents Act 1988 and the Copyright and Related Rights Regulations 2003 (SI No. 2498).

Contents

	List of Contributors	vii
	List of Abbreviations	viii
	Introduction: Liturgical Continuities and Denominational Differences *Allan I. Macinnes*	1
1	Liturgy in Scotland before 1560 *Stephen Mark Holmes*	19
2	Jesuits, Mission and Gender in Post-Reformation Scotland *Patricia Barton*	36
3	Liturgical Problems on the Catholic Mission: Franciscan Mission to the Highlands in the Seventeenth Century *Thomas McInally*	54
4	Liturgical Reform during the Restoration: The Untold Story *John M. Hintermaier*	70
5	Henry Scougal and the Move Away from Calvinism in the Later Seventeenth Century *Isaac M. Poobalan*	86
6	Worship and Devotion in Multiconfessional Scotland, 1686–9 *Alasdair Raffe*	96
7	The Episcopalian Community in Aberdeen in the Jacobite Period *Kieran German*	112
8	Jurors and Qualified Clergy: Adopting the Liturgy at Home and Abroad *Tristram Clarke*	126
9	Devoted Episcopalians, Reluctant Jacobites? George and James Garden and their Spiritual Environment *Marie-Luise Ehrenschwendtner*	138
10	The Liturgical Tradition of the English Non-jurors *Richard Sharp*	154

11	Archibald Campbell: A Pivotal Figure in Episcopalian Liturgical Transition *A. Emsley Nimmo*	172
12	Clerics Behaving Badly: Ecclesiastical Commitment in the Jacobite Rising of 1745–6 *Darren S. Layne*	189
13	Bishop Thomas Rattray: His Eucharistic Doctrine, *The Ancient Liturgy of the Church of Jerusalem* and its Influence on the Scottish Liturgy of 1764 *W. Douglas Kornahrens*	205

Index   222

Contributors

Patricia Barton is subject leader in History, School of Humanities, University of Strathclyde.

Tristram Clarke worked for thirty-four years as an archivist at the National Records of Scotland.

Marie-Luise Ehrenschwendtner is a lecturer in Church History at the University of Aberdeen.

Kieran German is a teaching fellow at the University of Dundee.

John M. Hintermaier is instructor in Social Studies at Mount de Sales Academy, Macon, GA.

Stephen Mark Holmes is an Honorary Fellow at Edinburgh University and Rector of Holy Cross Episcopal Church, Edinburgh.

W. Douglas Kornahrens retired as Rector of Holy Cross Episcopal Church, Edinburgh and is Honorary Canon of St Mary's Cathedral, Edinburgh.

Darren S. Layne is curator of the Jacobite Database of 1745.

Allan I. Macinnes is Emeritus Professor of History at the University of Strathclyde.

Thomas McInally is an Honorary Research Fellow at the University of Aberdeen.

A. Emsley Nimmo is Rector of St Margaret of Scotland Episcopal Church, Aberdeen and Dean Emeritus of the Episcopal Diocese of Aberdeen and Orkney.

Isaac M. Poobalan is Provost of St Andrews Cathedral, Aberdeen.

Alasdair Raffe is a Chancellor's Fellow in History at the University of Edinburgh.

Richard Sharp retired as a Senior Research Fellow at Worcester College, Oxford.

Abbreviations

ACA	Aberdeen City Archive
APPF	Archivio del Palazzo di Propaganda Fide
ASV	Archivio Segreto Vaticano
AUL	Aberdeen University Library
BL	British Library
BLO	Bodleian Library, Oxford
CHR	*The Catholic Historical Review*
CUAP	Catholic University of America Press
CUP	Cambridge University Press
EHR	*English Historical Review*
ELCA	East Lothian Council Archive
ESTC	English Short Title Catalogue
EUL	Edinburgh University Library
EUP	Edinburgh University Press
HL	Huntington Library, San Marino, California
HMC	Historical Manuscripts Commission
IR	*Innes Review*
LPL	Lambeth Palace Library
NLS	National Library of Scotland
NRS	National Records of Scotland
ODNB	*Oxford Dictionary of National Biography*
OUP	Oxford University Press
RIAL	Royal Irish Academy Library
RPCS	*Register of the Privy Council of Scotland*
RPS	*Records of the Parliaments of Scotland to 1707* [http://www.rps.ac.uk/]
RPSS	*Register of the Privy Seal of Scotland*
RSCHS	*Records of the Scottish Church History Society*
SCA	Scottish Catholic Archives
SHR	*Scottish Historical Review*
SHS	Scottish History Society
TNA	The National Archives (Kew)
TSES	*Transactions of the Scottish Ecclesiological Society*
YUP	Yale University Press

INTRODUCTION

Liturgical Continuities and Denominational Differences

Allan I. Macinnes

Much has been made of the polity, the doctrine and the discipline of the churches in Scotland. Relatively little has been done on modes of worship, and even less on liturgical practices.[1] Historical writing has been weighted towards the preaching of the word in comparison to the administration of the sacraments. To redress this imbalance, this collection of essays examines the essence of liturgical practices for Roman Catholics and Episcopalians from Reformation to Enlightenment.

Roman Catholicism was ousted as the national faith at the Reformation in the mid-sixteenth century, but continued and consolidated in Edinburgh and the Borders, in the Highlands and the north-east. By the mid-eighteenth century, the faith had reached a plateau from which there was limited movement until the continuous influx of Irish Catholics in the nineteenth century. Originally sharing a commitment to the Reformed tradition identified with Calvinism, Episcopalianism vied with Presbyterianism in constituting the established Kirk between 1560 and 1690. Episcopalianism was finally overthrown at the Revolution which forced James VII & II into exile in France. The Presbyterian re-establishment was confirmed subsequently by the Treaty of Union in 1707. Episcopalianism retained a considerable presence beyond the confines of the central belt, and, in association with the Catholic minority, became the sacramental life force behind Jacobitism which sought to restore the exiled house of Stuart and terminate the Anglo-Scottish Union.

I

By 1540, the Roman Catholic Church, a multi-national corporation trading in souls, was facing a sustained challenge from clerical and lay protestors unconvinced that fundamental reforms could be accomplished from within. The two main influences promoting a Protestant Reformation were initially Lutheranism in Germany and Scandinavia and, subsequently, Calvinism in Switzerland, France and the Netherlands. Lutheranism argued for justification by faith alone, not by good works or the purchase of indulgences. Salvation was to be attained by graceful living and reliance solely on the Bible translated into vernacular languages. Calvinism also stressed the primacy of scripture over all ecclesiastical authority. Salvation was a matter not of free will but of predestination. Calvinism prioritised preaching of the word over administering the sacraments. Particular emphasis was placed on ecclesiastical discipline to promote godly communities. In England, where a Reformation initiated by the monarchy in the 1530s was eventually accomplished by the 1560s, Anglicanism under Episcopal directions strove for a national accommodation between the prevailing Protestant influences from the continent. However, sects mainly inclined to Calvinism and known as Puritans for their asceticism and austerity, preferred loosely gathered congregations.[2]

In Scotland, the initial inroads made by Lutherans from the late 1520s were to be superseded by Calvinists in the 1550s. Anti-clericalism was rampant in Scotland as evident from Sir David Lyndsay of the Mount's theatrical staging of *Ane Satyre of the Thrie Estaitis* before the royal court at Linlithgow in 1540. But the Catholic Church was still a mainstay of civility in Scotland. As Stephen Homes affirms, the Church in Scotland was no stagnant backwater having borrowed liturgical practices extensively from England and then France before according precedence in the course of the fifteenth century to Roman standards, tweaked to accommodate Scottish intercessions to saints.[3] John Hamilton, archbishop of St Andrews, summoned provincial councils from 1549 to 1559 to promote reform from within the Church through improved preaching, better education and restored discipline in religious houses. He was even prepared to move in a Lutheran direction with regards to justification by faith. But doubts remained, especially at Rome, that the Church in Scotland was capable of meaningful reform. Hamilton made no attempt to harmonise internal reforms with the Council of Trent, which met fitfully in northern Italy from 1547 to 1563, to establish clerical, doctrinal and liturgical standards for Counter-Reformation under papal direction. Pre-Tridentine liturgical practices, however, were to find a ready welcome within Episcopalian worship.[4]

Reformation was accomplished in Scotland in defiance of the monarchy with military backing from England, by equating Protestantism with patriotism and by condoning the destruction of religious houses, paintings and ornaments. Parliament at Edinburgh in 1560 abolished the mass, rejected papal authority and accepted a distinctly Protestant confession of faith that leaned more towards Calvinism than Lutheranism.[5] Constant harassment by the Protestant Kirk reinforced by threats of civil sanctions against regular clergy, practising Roman Catholics and those who aided them, certainly restricted the scope for Counter-Reformation in Scotland. Catholicism was a declining, if lingering, force in the later sixteenth century, its laity much given to compromising on matters of church attendance and partaking of communion as a Protestant sacrament. Its practice tended to be confined to aristocratic households in town and country where occasional masses were held for families, friends and servants. Barely a handful of priests were active in Scotland by 1603, when the union of the crowns coincided with the death in exile of the last of the pre-Reformation hierarchy, James Beaton, archbishop of Glasgow, ambassador for James VI in France and principal benefactor of the Scots College, whose work included training priests in Paris.[6]

Before James VI of Scotland became James I of England, his queen, Anna, had openly converted to Catholicism. James was personally tolerant towards the leading Catholic nobles despite their covert dealings with France, Spain and the papacy before 1603. Thereafter, as an absentee monarch, he condoned the regular application of fines, sufficient to stifle the development of Catholicism. Leading Catholics were made to feel uncomfortable, but never desperate, far less rebellious. The composite enactment of penal laws by the Scottish Parliament in 1609, which brought together legislation against Roman Catholics passed piecemeal since 1573, was undoubtedly draconian in tenor. Catholics, and those who aided and abetted them, were liable in the first instance to have their goods and gear confiscated. Catholics refusing to participate in Protestant communions were to be excommunicated and liable to have all rents and revenues sequestrated. Contumacious offenders ultimately faced charges of treason, and, if convicted, capital punishment. If members of the landed classes their estates were forfeited. The enforcement of the penal laws was not comprehensive, however. A handful of Catholic gentry had moveable goods confiscated and were forced temporarily into exile. No attempt was made to forfeit them.[7] None the less, Catholics lacking the backing of lordship or strong kin networks faced ritualised humiliation when obliged to make public recantations before kirk sessions in town and country.[8]

The Scottish bishops of the first Episcopate deployed comprehensive judicial commissions to search out Catholic clergy and laity and those who harboured and protected them. The most intemperate prosecutor was John Spottiswood, archbishop of Glasgow (later translated to St Andrews), who contrived unity among Protestants by enforcing the penal laws against Roman Catholics.[9] His principal target was a Jesuit priest captured in Glasgow after working clandestinely in Edinburgh and Renfrewshire as well as in his native north-east. After three months of exhaustive questioning and torture by protracted sleep deprivation, John Ogilvie was tried for treason in Glasgow in February 1615. Ogilvie was convicted less for his Jesuit ministry than for his uncompromising stance in upholding the spiritual supremacy of the papacy over James VI & I.[10]

Far from presaging wholesale prosecutions of all deemed recusants, the trial and execution of John Ogilvie revitalised Catholicism in the Lowlands, the ground rules for which were laid down from 1617 by the Jesuits. Especially targeted were landed families, particularly those with heritable jurisdictions able to protect priests and encourage conversions within their territorial spheres of influence. Catholic families were encouraged to intermarry, both to consolidate their faith and to bridge their geographical isolation. From 1623, with the exception of the Jesuits, oversight of all regular and secular clergy on the Scottish Mission was exercised spiritually, if not always financially, by Propaganda Fide at Rome. The Jesuits remained reluctant to co-operate with other missionaries, particularly the secular clergy: not just because their order had pioneered and continued to bear the brunt of missionary work but because the secular clergy were perceptively less well equipped intellectually, administratively and materially to endure a life of personal privation and constant movement to spread the faith.[11] By focusing on the religious rather than the political aspects of their mission, Patricia Barton explores the Jesuits' relationship with the laity and their liturgical practices. In Highlands as well as Lowlands, the Jesuit mission was notably furthered by devout women as catechists, poets and protectors of priests.[12] At the same time, reinvigorated missions, sponsored by Propaganda Fide deepened the sacramental experience of Scottish Catholics. As with the Jesuits, the various covert missions mounted by secular clergy as by religious orders, most notably the Franciscans, Vincentians and Dominicans, faced practical problems that were not just logistical but also doctrinally at odds with Tridentine decrees, especially for the open celebration of the new Roman liturgy. However, as Tom McInally makes clear, such problems were not insurmountable and were tackled through imagination as well as dispensation.[13]

Catholicism thrived within geographic pockets, most notably in the north-east within the extensive territorial bounds of the Gordons of Huntly and in the south-west among the kin and associates of the Maxwells of Nithsdale and Herries. Catholicism sustained a peripheral presence in the households of nobles and gentry in Tayside, the Lothians and west-central Scotland. Catholicism within the Highlands can be identified not just with landed households but with clans. The Highlands, no less than the Lowlands, were in direct competition for finite missionary resources with vastly more fertile areas for conversion in Asia and the Americas. Optimistic accounting of Scottish converts by missionaries can in part be attributed to their need to attract funding from Propaganda; but was also grounded in lingering Catholic practices condemned by uncompromising Protestants as superstitious or more malevolently as witchcraft.[14]

People continued to visit wells for their reputed healing powers for humans and livestock. Most wells had a firm religious connection, being located near chapels dedicated to saints or the Holy Family, as did annual fairs in rural and even some urban localities. Well into the eighteenth century, perennial pilgrimages to chapels had not been entirely eradicated; nor had the seasonal observance of festival days, carol singing, bonfires and guising.[15] Lingering Catholicism in the Highlands was further evident in Gaelic hymns and incantations that can be traced back to the Celtic Church in the early Middle Ages. The bulk of spiritual material reproduced in the later nineteenth century as *Carmina Gadelica* was drawn from the mid-fourteenth to the mid-eighteenth centuries and passed on through oral tradition by Episcopalians as well as Catholics. Religion infused the whole fabric of life with blessings for everyday activities by the laity. In addition to intercessions to saints and the Holy Family, prayers eased distress, facilitated travel and celebrated victories.[16]

Catholicism was given a unifying focus and the Scottish Mission a more cohesive organisation following the appointment of Thomas Nicholson as vicar-apostolic in 1697. James Gordon joined him as coadjutor bishop in 1705. Two years later, the bishops on the Scottish Mission, the overseas Colleges, prominent laity and their associates in the exiled Jacobite court refused to contemplate clerical union with England or promote shared British missions. Instead, the bishops established training colleges for priests that made the Highlands markedly less dependent on Irish missionaries who had worked there intermittently since 1619 and cut the costs of sending trainee priest to the Scots Colleges on the continent. Hugh MacDonald from Morar, the first native bishop trained in Scotland since the Reformation, was given charge of the newly created Highland mission in 1731. Priests reporting back to Propaganda became ever hopeful of winning over Episcopalians in Jacobite heartlands throughout the Highlands. None the less, missionary work was severely hampered by internal rivalries between Lowlands and Highland districts that mirrored the tensions and divisions between the Scots Colleges at Rome, Douai and Valladolid with Paris. Only the latter was not under Jesuit control. These domestic and international rivalries led to charges of Jansenism against the Lowland district and the College at Paris that owed more to perceived inequalities of funding than receptiveness to heretical teaching or to deviations in sacramental practice. Catholicism in Scotland was debilitated but not despondent.[17]

II

Notwithstanding the break with Rome, Scottish Protestants had no common liturgical standards until 1636–7, when their introduction was highly contentious. Bishops who had not conformed to Protestantism in the 1560s were replaced by superintendents. At best they facilitated rather than commanded the use of either the Anglican *Book of Common Prayer* or the indigenous *Book of Common Order*. The initial *Book of Common Prayer* produced in 1549 was Lutheran-influenced but moved in a more Reformed direction when modified in 1552 and then reissued in 1559. From 1571, the *Book of Common Prayer* incorporated the Thirty-Nine Articles, the defined standards of doctrine and practices for the Church of England.[18] In Scotland, the *Book of Common Order* of 1562 remained distinct from the Confession of Faith authorised by parliament in 1560. Both had a more pronounced Calvinist influence than their English equivalents. In 1567, the *Book of Common Order* was translated into Gaelic, as *Foirm na n-Urrnuidheach* by John Carswell, superintendent of Argyll (later bishop of the Isles); not in the vernacular language of the people but in the common classical version used by the learned orders in Scotland and Ireland. The forms of prayer in this far from literal translation emphasised clerical direction more than lay participation. Whilst upholding Calvinist justification by faith and predestination, Carswell does not dismiss the importance of good works. He rejects the Catholic mass and transubstantiation (the conversion of wine and bread into the blood and body of Christ), papal authority, invocations to saints and prayers for the dead. But he does allude to saints and archangels and includes responses for the blessing of a ship.[19]

The Kirk under bishops and superintendents of the stamp of John Carswell – like Anglicans in England, Wales and Ireland, and Lutherans in Germany and Scandinavia – sought to adapt rather than throw over Catholic sacramental practices; the favoured option for the Puritan and the Presbyterian. However, this Calvinist position was strengthened from the 1570s by the growth of Presbyterianism, initially through the universities of Glasgow and St Andrews. No concessions were made to the monarchy in exercising spiritual jurisdiction over the Kirk. Ecclesiastical authority was to be exercised through a series of courts, commencing with weekly kirk sessions for every parish, then regular presbyteries for every district, occasional synods for every region and annual general assemblies for the whole kingdom. The areas most receptive to Presbyterianism were in the central Lowlands and eastern Borders. Although Presbyterianism became the established faith of Scotland in 1592, the autonomy of the Kirk from the State was not conceded by James VI. The king retained the right to choose the time and place of general assemblies, which he used to bring back bishops from 1597.[20]

After the union of the crowns, James VI & I viewed bishops as essential to his exercise of imperial power in Scotland as in England and Ireland. His Stuart dominions were subordinate to no spiritual or temporal power by land or sea. When James restored bishops in full to their spiritual office and temporal estates in 1610, he also expelled leading Presbyterians from Scotland. Episcopal authority was grafted on to the Presbyterian framework operative in the Kirk since the 1590s. The consecration of three Scottish bishops at Westminster in October 1610 did not subordinate the Kirk to the Anglican Church. No consecrated bishops in Scotland were still alive. Yet the publication of the *King James Version* of the Bible in 1611 underscored the Anglican character of the king's drive for religious uniformity. This Bible promoted Standard English, a confirmation that Scots, like Gaelic, was not an authorised language for salvation in the Stuart dominions. With ready assistance from his bishops, James imposed liturgical innovations on the Kirk that became known as the Five Articles of Perth, where they were promulgated at a general assembly in 1618. By far the most controversial Article was that which required all partakers of communion to kneel before the bishop or minister; a provocative return to the pre-Reformation role of priests as intermediaries between God and humanity. By judiciously managing proceedings and votes, James VI & I secured parliamentary ratification for the Five Articles in 1621. A substantial dissenting minority obliged James to drop plans for a draft liturgy to facilitate convergence between the Scottish and Anglican churches.[21]

Such pragmatism was missing from the religious policies pursued by his son Charles I, markedly averse to any constitutional limitations enacted by parliaments or general assemblies. Again, the bishops were his willing helpers, albeit the Scottish Episcopacy was notably more ecumenical than its English counterparts. The leading Episcopalian theologians, celebrated as the Aberdeen Doctors, favoured an accommodation with Lutheranism, explored the Central European Reformed tradition and even flirted with Greek Orthodoxy to reinvigorate their Protestantism in ways that were spiritually as well as doctrinally distinct from Presbyterianism. They endorsed the endeavours of John Durie, an itinerant intellectual from Edinburgh, for an irenicist accommodation between the Calvinist and Lutheran traditions. Throughout the 1630s, Durie strove unflinchingly to gather support for confessional union in Germany, Poland-Lithuania and Sweden. His claim to speak for 'the British Churches' was a subtle, but none the less subversive, challenge to the hegemonic Anglican agenda then being pursued throughout the Stuart dominions by William Laud, as archbishop of Canterbury. A committed Arminian, he favoured salvation through the exercise of free will rather than by election; a stance that provoked confrontation with Scottish Calvinists.[22]

As Durie's ecumenical endeavours were unravelling, so was Charles I's hold over Scotland, primarily but not exclusively due to his determination to impose religious uniformity aided and abetted by Laud and his acolytes among the Scottish bishops. The *Book of Canons*, published in Aberdeen at the outset of 1636, made no compromise with Presbyterianism, upholding the royal supremacy in ecclesiastical affairs. Bishops were no longer accountable to general assemblies. It served notice of radical liturgical innovations in a Service Book that was published in Edinburgh in spring 1637. It did accommodate Scottish sensibilities. Presbyter replaced priest or minister; Pasche was inserted instead of Easter. Most lessons from the Apocrypha in the Anglican *Book of Common Prayer*, which had been introduced for use in all five Scottish universities in 1633, were removed for scriptural unsoundness. For the first time biblical texts were drawn from the *King James Version* of the Bible. There was no attempt to include the Thirty-Nine Articles or a revised Scottish Confession of Faith. None the less, the Service Book was perceived by lay as well as clerical opponents as moving the Kirk beyond Anglicanism to threaten the very reception of Protestantism at the Reformation. The Service Book's prescription for communion prayers included oblation, denoting the sacrificial offering of bread and wine, and epiclesis, elevating the host when the presbyter held up the chalice, paten or other receptacles while facing the congregation: practices commended by the Aberdeen Doctors. In this respect, the Service Book was not so much following the more muted formula in the 1549 *Book of Common Prayer* as the Scottish pre-Tridentine mass, albeit in English not Latin.

The introduction of the Service Book by royal decree was greeted by premeditated rioting in Edinburgh and Glasgow and thereafter by nationwide petitioning which led to the emergence of the Covenanting Movement by 1638, intent on imposing fundamental limitations on monarchy in Kirk and State. The first stage was concluded at Glasgow when a general assembly, in defiance of Charles I, abolished Episcopacy and rescinded all liturgical innovations from the Five Articles. After the Covenanters defeated the Royalists loyal to Charles I in the Bishops' Wars of 1639–40, their revolution was ratified in parliament in 1641, when the power of the king was reduced to that of a cipher. Presbyterianism, bolstered by sporadic iconoclasm, reigned triumphant.[23]

The varying degrees of enthusiasm with which the Covenanting revolution was received in central and south-west Scotland were not necessarily replicated in the rest of the country. The more reflective Covenanters were also aware that Episcopacy was not deemed anathema to the Reformed tradition in continental Europe. A case can also be made for many lay and clerical Episcopalians trimming towards Covenanting to avoid swingeing fines and to retain their livings.[24] Nevertheless, the theological defence of Episcopacy mounted by the Aberdeen Doctors was swept aside. All thirteen bishops and well over a hundred clergy were deposed for adherence to Episcopacy as the Covenanting Movement exported revolution to Ireland and then England by 1643: an agenda that led to civil war, sectarianism and ultimately regicide in 1649, when Charles I was executed in London at the behest of Oliver Cromwell and his New Model Army. In their push for confessional confederation, the Covenanters accepted both the Confession of Faith of 1646 and the Public Directory of Worship of 1645 produced by the Westminster Assembly of Divines following the abandonment of Episcopacy in England. The Westminster Confession of Faith confirmed that the doctrinal standards of the Kirk were firmly Calvinist. Not only was the Roman Catholic mass reaffirmed to be a form of idolatry but the pope was denounced as Anti-Christ. The Westminster Directory, which was based on the Scottish *Book of Common Order*, prescribed minimalist standards of worship that were explicitly based on scripture. Effectively it was a pastoral handbook that prioritised preaching. At the same time, irreconcilable splits between radical and conservative Covenanters were compounded by political purges that undermined efforts for a patriotic accommodation with Royalists in favour of Charles II. Cromwell and his New Model Army went on to impose their armed occupation of Scotland, which was forced into an incorporating union with England from 1652. General assemblies ceased to function for the whole Kirk. The qualified measure of religious toleration accorded to Episcopalians was not extended to Catholics.[25]

Episcopalianism regained establishment status following the Restoration of Charles II in 1660. Presbyterianism, in the guise of Covenanting, went underground as a movement of protest no longer of power. Bishops, who included former Covenanters as well as the occasional survivor from the first episcopate, were restored to their temporal as well as their spiritual estates. The second Episcopate was not answerable to general assemblies but it did retain synods and presbyteries under diocesan control. The Westminster Confession of Faith and Public Directory of Worship were rescinded. No effort was made to reimpose liturgical innovations although the new Scottish bishops were consecrated according to the Anglican ordinal of 1661. The use of the Anglican *Book of Common Prayer* as revised in 1662 was encouraged but not prescribed. The Thirty-Nine Articles did not become the accepted confessional standards for the Kirk. Oblation and epiclesis, excluded since 1552, did feature, albeit more implicitly than explicitly. Biblical readings, as in the Service Book of 1637, now followed the text of the *King James Version* (1611).[26]

North of the Tay, Episcopalianism was generally accepted. But the subordination of the Kirk to the State provoked significant dissent south of the Tay. All ministers were to be confirmed by a bishop. Those who refused to do so in 1662–3 were outed from their parishes. Fewer than a third of ministers (around 262) were forcibly separated from their former congregations from whom they were required to live at least twenty miles distant. Some chose exile in the Dutch Republic. Members of congregations who absented themselves from services held by their replacements faced punitive fines. Despite being subject to military reprisals, illicit conventicles in houses and in fields flourished. In 1674, outed ministers were offered conditional toleration under indulgence. They were allowed to return and receive full stipends if they accepted episcopal confirmation and attended presbyteries and synods. As just under half of the outed ministers accepted indulgence, this left no more than a sixth of the Scottish clergy implacably opposed to Episcopalianism. However, toleration was an ineffective check on conventicling, which now protested against indulged ministers as well as the Episcopal establishment. By way of contrast, when William of Orange agreed to replace Episcopalianism by Presbyterianism in 1690, he remained opposed to the persecution of Episcopalians. Fewer than a fifth of their clergy were deprived. Indulgences were given to those prepared to swear allegiance to the new monarchy in 1693 and 1695. Around a hundred Episcopalian clergy took the oath as jurors. The majority of Episcopalians remained Jacobite, as supporters of the exiled house of Stuart. As late as 1707, at least 165 ministers who had not sworn the oath of allegiance held out as non-jurors in rural and urban parishes.[27]

The subjection of Presbyterians to regular repression and occasional conciliation in the Restoration era and of Episcopalians to reprisals at the Revolution underplays the latter's quest for renewed liturgical reform, distinct from but in harmony with Anglican practices.[28] Episcopal proposals for a new prayer book were debated but never implemented in 1665–6. Nevertheless, sacramental innovations, based firmly on Greek patristic readings, were notable in the writings of Robert Leighton, bishop of Dunblane (and intermittently archbishop of Glasgow). Leighton rebuilt the basic structure of devotion, states John Hintermaier, by emphasising the importance of set prayer and personal piety in preparing to receive the sacraments. His practical mysticism, which gained some traction in Fife and the Lothians, was worldly affirming in seeking to reach an accommodation with Presbyterians, few of whom were open to reconciliation with Episcopacy.[29] This emphasis on prayer and piety was carried further by Henry Scougal, professor of Divinity at King's College, Aberdeen, who argued for frequent communion sacraments in which epiclesis was broadened from a call to the congregation to the whole of Scotland. As Isaac Poobalan affirms, Scougal's advocacy of a plain life of justice and charity laid the groundwork for the spread of practical mysticism into the north-east of Scotland.[30] Although Leighton and Scougal were leading figures in the move away from Calvinism in the later seventeenth century, this did not lead to resurgence in Arminianism or to greater liturgical observance. The Episcopal establishment specified no more than yearly communion at Easter when clergy were instructed to preach obedience and social order from their pulpits.[31] Differences in worship and devotion between Episcopalians and Presbyterians were not necessarily substantial; albeit Episcopalians knelt for communion and uttered responses to more prayers than the Lord's Prayer common to both denominations. Alasdair Raffe explores, with reference to architecture and publishing, how religious pluralism under James VII in the late 1680s stimulated devotion and worship and fostered a Catholic revival centred on Edinburgh.[32] The Revolution, which drove Catholicism underground, paved the way for a clear confessional break among Protestants. With the Westminster Confession of

Faith restored as the doctrinal standard, subordinate only to the Bible, Calvinist orthodoxy, propagated through extempore prayer and preaching, was reaffirmed by Presbyterians but eschewed by Episcopalians.

III

The removal of James VII in favour of his daughter Mary and son-in-law William of Orange at the Revolution was castigated by William MacRae, an Episcopalian clergyman from Wester Ross, as an abnegation of patriarchal duty that breached the fifth commandment. Other Gaelic poets subsequently underpinned their Jacobitism by their religious faith.[33]

However, Episcopalians divided in the wake of the Revolution. A minority, particularly career-minded politicians and merchants engaged in the colonial trade, were prepared to seek an accommodation first with William of Orange, then Queen Anne and the Hanoverians, in order to secure religious toleration. Meeting houses of these Episcopalians – the jurors – effectively became outposts of the Church of England. The refusal of the vast majority of Episcopalians to abjure the exiled Stuart led them to reject not only accommodation with the Presbyterian establishment in the 1690s but also toleration from the British government in 1712. The Toleration and the associated Patronage Acts in 1712 followed on from a celebrated judicial appeal by an Episcopalian clergyman, James Greenshields, an Ulster-Scot. His preaching and use of the Anglican liturgy in Edinburgh in defiance of the local presbytery led to his imprisonment by the town council; a decision upheld in the Court of Session but lost on appeal to the House of Lords in 1711. This legislation was the first substantive breach in the Act for securing the Protestant Religion and Presbyterian Church Government as embodied within the Treaty of Union. As such, the acts were more a cause of tension for Presbyterians than Episcopalians. Nevertheless, Greenshields, 'a vain, senseless fellow' in the eyes of the Scottish judiciary, had relocated to London, where he was particularly active in seeking to foist the 1662 Anglican *Book of Common Prayer* on Scotland, for use by all Episcopalians; an endeavour which ran counter to the desire of non-jurors to reinstate the Scottish Service Book of 1637, which was reprinted in 1712 and 1724. Non-jurors thereby signified they were not aligned confessionally with the Thirty-Nine Articles.[34]

Clergy in the town of Aberdeen were already noted for their flexibility in reading prayers from the Anglican liturgy, but preferring prayers at communion from the Scottish Service Book.[35] Notwithstanding penal laws restricting non-juring clergy from communicating with more than five associates from 1719, non-juring laity pragmatically took oaths abjuring Jacobitism for political preferment as civil magistrates during the 1720s. Kieran German shows that jurors in Aberdeenshire were as remiss as non-jurors either in omitting or ignoring the legislative requirement for prayers for the incumbent British royal family, especially after the Hanoverians succession in 1714. Rarely if ever, did jurors go so far as to pray for the Jacobite Court in exile.[36] Tristram Clarke affirms that divisions between jurors and non-jurors on the Anglican liturgy were not set in stone. Juring and non-juring clergy assisted each other in Glasgow. Although use of the 1662 Anglican *Book of Common Prayer* was readily adopted by juring congregations in Edinburgh and Dundee, non-jurors there were not averse to its use.[37] This was particularly the case in the American colonies. Scottish Episcopalians recruited into the service of the Church of England in the Caribbean were noted for their incorruptible rectitude and their reliance on support networks of fellow countrymen regardless of denominational or liturgical difference.[38] These support networks in New York, New Jersey, Pennsylvania and Massachusetts were also utilised to promote charity for clergy, predominantly non-jurors, in straightened circumstances. In turn, legacies from the Americas, especially from slave plantations producing tobacco, sugar and rum, sustained spiritual and material support for Episcopalians from Perthshire to Shetland. A generous bequest from John Anderson, a former Episcopalian priest and plantation owner in St Kitts, for hospitals, schools and clerical support allowed considerable latitude to his trustees, mainly drawn from lords and gentry in Aberdeenshire. Anderson's instruction in 1735 that clergy in the university towns be supported in their use of the Anglican liturgy was set aside by 1744 in favour of supporting non-juring schools and clergy.[39]

Non-juring Episcopalianism was grounded in a spirit of obedience and submission to rightful royal authority. Nevertheless, the political allegiance of many clergy to Jacobitism was undertaken reluctantly and ritually. They had come to see the loss of establishment status at the Revolution as a gateway to liturgical liberation. They not only desired to distinguish themselves doctrinally from the Presbyterians, but they were also averse to becoming adjuncts of Anglicanism. As Marie-Luise Ehrenschwendter explains, some non-jurors in their emphatic rejection of Calvinism were given more to pietism than political action.[40] The brothers James and George Garden, academic colleagues and followers of Henry Scougal, who went on to minister in Aberdeenshire post-Revolution, were inclined to move in the direction of Flemish mysticism. Others flirted with Coptic Christianity or Greek and Russian Orthodoxy.[41]

Archibald Campbell, along with James Gadderar, his successor as non-juring bishop of Aberdeen, were to the fore in a group of Scottish and English non-jurors in London, who described themselves as the 'Orthodox and Catholic Remnants of the British Church'. They began a rapprochement with Greek and Russian Orthodoxy from 1716. Despite backing from Peter the Great of Russia, there was limited unity among the English non-jurors. Before negotiations collapsed by 1728, Scottish endeavours had been increasingly directed to returning their English colleagues to 'the usages of the primitive church'.[42] Both non-juring communities had split by the 1720s over the usages, primarily the mixing of water with wine in the communion chalice. Also controversial were prescription of oblation and epiclesis, reservation of the communion elements and prayers for the sick and dying. Although the non-jurors had a more considerable presence in Scotland than in England, the latter had their own distinctive dynamic that Richard Sharp explores.[43]

Cross-border collaboration was particularly evident on sacramental matters in the rejection of a single Confession of Faith and in the production of the non-juring rite as an alternative liturgy in 1718. This liturgy borrowed heavily from the Scottish Service Book of 1637, not least in its prescription of oblation and epiclesis. But in the aftermath of the split on the usages, Bishop Campbell came to view the Scottish bishops as being in league with their Anglican counterparts to make the Scottish Episcopal Church entirely dependent on the Church of England.[44] The failure of the exiled Stuarts to appoint to Scottish sees had led the formation of a college of bishops which perpetuated itself from 1720 by consecrating bishops to 'ad hoc' territories rather than to established diocese. The college's resolve from 1731 to override elections – whether territorial or diocesan – that favoured 'usagers' for episcopal vacancies was a further cause of dissent in Scotland.[45] Non-jurors in both Scotland and England subsequently sought to regroup in 1744 by subscribing to new spiritual paths in *The Ancient Liturgy of the Church of Jerusalem* that sacramentally united them as the true apostolic heirs to the primitive purity of the Universal Catholic Church. Essentially this was the work of Bishop Thomas Rattray of Brechin who broke ranks with the college of bishops on such issues as the appointment of usagers and diocesan elections.

Liturgical innovation and theological debates on the intermediate state between heaven and hell, as on prayers for the dead, came to be viewed as a spiritual aspect of Enlightenment based on rigorous patristic scholarship and forensic historical enquiry that also drew strength from sacramental continuity since the Reformation.[46] The non-jurors, with Bishop Rattray taking up the mantle of Bishops Campbell and Gadderar, were advocating a distinctively, but not exclusively, Scottish approach to salvation. This approach, as Emsley Nimmo articulates, promoted an intermediate or middle state that was not so much a revamped purgatory for sinners as a place of reflection and light for departed souls.[47] Like the Covenanters in the Restoration era, they did so by covert conventicling in the houses of landed and mercantile patrons, and by open preaching in fields.

A spy for the British government reported that, over four days in May 1731, John MacLachlan, non-juring clergyman in Appin, had preached in a field at North Ballachulish from Friday, 16 to Monday, 19 April.

As well as preaching to over five hundred people drawn from the MacLachlans of Ardgour, the Camerons of Lochaber, the MacDonalds of Glencoe and the Stewarts of Appin, he administered the sacrament of communion to over 240 and examined another hundred persons. This was allegedly the largest meeting of Jacobites in the Highlands since the Fifteen. They took the sacrament to affirm they held steadfast to the exiled 'James VIII & III'.[48] MacLachlan administered communion with a chalice and paten made in Edinburgh that were presented to his parish of Appin in 1723. On Culloden field, fifteen years to the day after his field preaching in North Ballachulish, the chalice and paten were again deployed to administer communion, using oatcakes and whisky rather than bread and wine, to many of the same clansmen about to confront the superior military forces of a vengeful British Army. As Darren Layne enumerates, MacLachlan was by no means the only Episcopalian or Jacobite priest active in the Forty-Five.[49] He and his fellow clergy were particularly targeted in the field and the hills by the British Army in the years after Culloden, where the broad confessional divide in battle was between non-jurors and Anglicans. Sermons against the Jacobite clergy in particular and the cause in general were the least of their worries as the Presbyterian clergy reverted to being the Revolution interest at prayer.[50]

Although Jacobitism was brutally crushed in the aftermath of the Forty-Five, clergy and poets in the Jacobite heartlands of the Highlands and the north-east of Scotland had created a liturgy of commemoration for the Stuarts that featured the regicide of Charles I, the Restoration of Charles II, the deposition of James VII & II, royal birthdays of the princes in exile and Jacobite victories in the major risings in the Fifteen and the Forty-Five as well as the final trauma of Culloden.[51] Catholics and non-jurors were extirpated and their churches, chapels and meeting houses destroyed. Yet their liturgical traditions continued.

The non-juring tradition was far from eradicated from liturgical practices of Episcopalians not just in Scotland but in America. The liturgy of 1764, which Douglas Kornaherns scrutinises, built on the Service Book of 1637, the non-juring Prayer Book of 1718 and, above all, *The Ancient Liturgy of the Church of Jerusalem* of 1744. It consolidated a Eucharistic perspective that can be traced back beyond the Revolution to the Aberdeen Doctors.[52] It also reaffirmed liturgical continuity with the Roman Catholic pre-Tridentine tradition. By permitting the reserving of sacramental elements, the new liturgy enabled non-jurors to circumvent reimposed penal laws that restricted the Eucharist to a handful of communicants in one room or meeting place. This liturgy was testament to the growing rapprochement between the jurors who adhered to Anglicanism and the non-jurors who remained committed to a universal, Catholic and Orthodox Church. This Jacobite tradition was exported to America after the surviving non-juring hierarchy consecrated Samuel Seabury at Aberdeen in 1784 as the first Episcopalian bishop of the fledgling United States. His *Communion Office*, published in New London, Connecticut, in 1786 drew on the Scottish liturgy of 1764. Within Scotland this liturgy was not necessarily in force beyond the Jacobite heartlands in the Highlands and the north-east. The Anglican liturgy was not replaced or subordinated elsewhere.[53] When not totally discounted by the reconstituted college of bishops following the formal reunification of jurors and non-jurors in the Scottish Episcopal Church by 1804, non-juring tradition has not been served well. Compulsory acceptance of the Thirty-Nine Articles was a bitter pill for non-jurors to swallow.

Notes

1. A notable exception to denominational writing is that by the late Audrey-Beth Fitch, *The Search for Salvation: Lay Faith in Scotland, 1480–1560* (Edinburgh: John Donald, 2009).
2. E. Duffy, Saints, *Sacrilege and Sedition: Religion and Conflict in the Tudor Reformation* (London: Bloomsbury Publishing, 2012), pp. 15–32.
3. See Chapter 1.
4. Psalters used by clerical choirs were adapted for communal singing by congregations and contributed to the distinctive metrical tradition in Scotland from that in England (Timothy Duguid, *Metrical Psalmody in Print and Practice: English 'Singing Psalms' and Scottish 'Psalm Books', c.1547–1640* (London and New York: Routledge, 2016), pp. 141–64).
5. J. E. A. Dawson, *Scotland Reformed 1488–1587* (Edinburgh: EUP, 2007), pp. 155–239.
6. M. H. B. Sanderson, 'Catholic Recusancy in Scotland in the Sixteenth Century', *IR*, 21 (1970), 87–107; A. Ross, 'Reformation and Repression' in D. McRoberts (ed.), *Essays on the Scottish Reformation, 1513–1625* (Glasgow: Burns, 1962), pp. 371–414; *Narratives of Scottish Catholics under Mary Steward and James VI*, ed. W. F. Leith, 2 vols (Edinburgh: W. Paterson, 1885), I, pp. 1-40, 269–74.
7. J. J. La Rocca, 'James I and His Catholic Subjects, 1606–1612: Some Financial Implications', *Recusant History*, 18 (1987), 251–62; A. I. Macinnes, 'Catholic Recusancy and the Penal Laws, 1603–1707', *RSCHS*, 23 (1987), 27–63.
8. R. Burns, 'Enforcing Uniformity: Kirk Sessions and Catholics in Early Modern Scotland, 1560–1650', *IR*, 69 (2018), 111–30; P. Goatman, 'Religious Tolerance and Intolerance in Jacobean Scotland: The Case of Archibald Hegate revisted', *IR*, 67 (2016), 159–81.
9. M. V. Hay, *The Blairs Papers (1603–1660)* (London and Edinburgh: Sands & Co., 1929), pp. 187, 242.
10. W. J. Anderson, 'A Jesuit that Calls Himself Ogilvie', *IR*, 15 (1964), 56–65; R. Pitcairn, *Ancient Criminal Trials in Scotland*, 3 vols (Edinburgh: Maitland Club, 1833), III, pp. 252–7, 330–54.
11. Hay, *The Blairs Papers*, pp. 52–221; Peter F. Anson, *Underground Catholicism in Scotland 1622–1878* (Montrose: Standard Press, 1970), pp. 8–17, 47–56, 60–77, 85–7.

12. See Chapter 2.
13. See Chapter 3.
14. J. Kirk, 'The Jacobean Church in the Highlands, 1567–1625' in L. Maclean (ed.), *The Seventeenth Century Highlands* (Inverness: Inverness Field Club, 1985), pp. 24–51; C. Giblin, 'The "Acta" of Propaganda Archives and the Scottish Mission, 1623–1670', *IR*, 5 (1954), 39–6.
15. A. I. Macinnes, 'John Ogilvie: The Smoke and Mirrors of Confessional Politics', *Journal of Jesuit Studies*, 7 (2019), 34–46.
16. A. Carmichael, *Carmina Gadelica: Hymns and Incantations Collected in the Highlands and Islands of Scotland* (Edinburgh: Floris Books, 1992), *passim*.
17. APPF, Congregazione Particolari, Scozia, vol. 34A (1707–12), ff. 128–31; vol. 86 (1736), ff. 119–20; vol. 87 (1737–41), ff. 401—7, and Scritture referite nei Congressi Scozia, I (1623–1700), ff. 27–50; II (1701–60), ff. 49–54; J. MacMillan, 'Jansenists and Anti-Jansenist in Eighteenth-Century Scotland', *IR*, 39 (1988), 112–45.
18. D. MacCulloch, *The Later Reformation in England, 1547–1603* (Basingstoke: Palgrave Macmillan, 1990), pp. 24–37.
19. *Foirm na n-Urrnuidheadh*, ed. R. L. Thomson (Edinburgh: SGTS, 1970), pp. 5–6, 16–17, 19, 110–11, 175; D. E. Meek and J. Kirk, 'John Carswell, Superintendent of Argyll: A Reassessment', *RSCHS*, 19 (1975), 1–22.
20. A. R. MacDonald, *The Jacobean Kirk, 1567–1625: Sovereignty, Polity and Liturgy* (Aldershot: Ashgate, 1998), pp. 6–99, 184–7; J. Kirk, 'The Politics of the Best Reformed Kirks: Scottish Achievements and English Aspirations in Church Government', *SHR*, 59 (1980), 22–53.
21. A. I. Macinnes, *The British Revolution, 1629–1660* (Basingstoke: Palgrave Macmillan, 2005), pp. 8–39; D. Mullan, *Episcopacy in Scotland: The History of an Idea 1560–1638* (Edinburgh: John Donald, 1986), pp. 171–83.
22. Rigsarkivet Copenhagen, TKUA, Alm.Del. I Indtil 1670, no. 141, Breve med Bilag fra engelsk Praest Johannes Duraeus, 1634–39; BL, J. Dury, Epistolae Pace Ecclesiastica, Sloane MS 654, ff. 216–17; J. Dury, *A Summary Discourse concerning the work of peace ecclesiastical, how it may concure with the aim of a civill confederation amongst Protestants* (Cambridge, 1641).
23. A. I. Macinnes, *Charles I and the Making of the Covenanting Movement, 1625–41* (Edinburgh: John Donald, 1991), pp. 155–213; G. Donaldson, *The Making of the Scottish Prayer Book of 1637* (Edinburgh: EUP, 1954), pp. 41–58, 127–8.
24. L. A. M. Stewart, *Rethinking the Scottish Revolution: Covenanted Scotland, 1637–51* (Oxford: OUP, 2016), pp. 87–121; A. D. Campbell, 'Episcopacy in the Mind of Robert Baillie', *SHR*, 93 (2014), 29–55; J. McDougall, 'Episcopacy and the National Covenant', *RSCHS*, 47 (2018), 3–30.
25. S. Spurlock, *Cromwell and Scotland: Conquest and Religion 1650–1660* (Edinburgh: John Donald, 2007), pp. 39–99; K. M. MacKenzie, *The Solemn League and Covenant of the Three Kingdoms and the Cromwellian Union, 1643–1663* (London and New York: Routledge, 2018), pp. 97–107, 128–36, 180–3.
26. J. Spur, *The Restoration Church of England, 1646–89* (New Haven and London: YUP, 1991), pp. 29–43.
27. A. I. Macinnes, *A History of Scotland* (London: Red Globe Press, 2019), pp. 97–8, 103.
28. M. B. Riordan, 'The Episcopalians and the Promotion of Mysticism in North-East Scotland', *RSCHS*, 47 (2018), 31–56.

29. See Chapter 4.
30. See Chapter 5.
31. NRS, Synod Records of Moray (1668–86), CH2/271/3/123 & Records of the Presbytery of Aberlour, 1671–88, CH2/6/1/62-5.
32. See Chapter 6.
33. *Lamh Sgriobhainn Mhic Rath: The Fernaig Manuscript*, ed. M. Macfarlane (Dundee: MacLeod, 1923), p. 187; *Highland Songs of the 'Forty-Five*, ed. J. L. Campbell (Edinburgh: SGTS, 1984), pp. 312–45, 658–92.
34. HL, Loudoun Scottish Collection, box 18/LO8351 & box 45/LO9439; NRS, Papers of the Maule Family, earls of Dalhousie, GD45/14/349/1-18 & /14/355; J. Stephen, 'English Liturgy and Scottish Identity: The Case of James Greenshields' in A. I. Macinnes and D. J. Hamilton (eds), *Jacobitism, Enlightenment and Empire, 1680–1820* (London: Pickering & Chatto, 2014), pp. 59–74.
35. AUL, Records of the Scottish Episcopal Church: Diocesan Office – See of Aberdeen and Orkney, MS 3320/6/5.
36. See Chapter 7.
37. See Chapter 8.
38. S. Barber, '"Let him be an Englishman": Irish and Scottish Clergy in the Caribbean Church of England, 1610–1720' in Macinnes and Hamilton (eds), *Jacobitism, Enlightenment and Empire*, pp. 75–91.
39. NRS, Records of the Episcopal Church of Scotland: Episcopal Chest, CH12/12/398, /846, & /1231 & Records Collected by Bishop Alexander Jolly, CH12/14/22; AUL, MS 3320/4/6 & 6/75 & Duff of Meldrum Collection, MS2778/12/2/6/1 & /36.
40. See Chapter 9.
41. A. E. Nimmo, 'Liturgy: The Sacramental Soul of Jacobitism' in A. I. Macinnes, K. German and L. Graham (eds), *Living with Jacobitism, 1690–1788: The Three Kingdoms and Beyond* (London: Pickering and Chatto, 2014), pp. 39–54; AUL, Pitsligo Papers, MS 2740/18/1/18; Dundee University Archives, Brechin Library Manuscripts, Br MS 3/DC 89, pp. 7–9.
42. NRS, CH12/19/3, /6.
43. See Chapter 10.
44. NRS, CH12/12/291.
45. B. S. Sirota, *The Christian Monitors: The Church of England and the Age of Benevolence, 1680–1730* (New Haven and London: YUP), pp. 154–5; K. German, 'Non-Jurors, Liturgy, and Jacobite Commitment, 1718–1746', *RSCHS*, 47 (2018), 74–99.
46. M. McGill, 'A Protestant Purgatory? Visions of an Intermediate State in Eighteenth Century Scotland', *SHR*, 94 (2018), 153–86; A. E. Nimmo, 'Archibald Campbell: Aberdeen's Absent Bishop?', *RSCHS*, 47 (2018), 100–27.
47. See Chapter 11.
48. TNA, Secretary of State: State Papers Scotland, SP54/20/48.
49. See Chapter 12.
50. C. A. Whatley, '"Zealous in the Defence of the Protestant Religion and Liberty": The Making of Whig Scotland, c.1688–c.1746' in Macinnes, German and Graham (eds), *Living with Jacobitism*, pp. 55–69.
51. A. Robertson of Struan, *Poems on Various Subjects and Occasions, mostly taken*

from his own original manuscripts (Edinburgh, 1749), pp. 140–1; W. Meston, *Old Mother Grim's Tales, Found in an Old Manuscript, dated 1527, Never before published: Decadem Alteram* (London, 1738), pp. 30–2, 36–47.
52. See Chapter 13.
53. AUL, MS 3320/6/71; N. Taylor, 'Liturgy and Theological Method in the Scottish Episcopal Church', *RSCHS*, 47 (2018), 143–54.

CHAPTER ONE

Liturgy in Scotland before 1560

Stephen Mark Holmes

The important thing about liturgy in Scotland before the Protestant Reformation of 1559–60 is that it is simply a series of variants of the Latin liturgy of the West adapted in various ways for local use.[1] These liturgical variants, uses or rites were taken from places or groups outside Scotland such as Salisbury, Rome and the religious orders. When James IV's 1507 licence to print the Aberdeen Breviary and other liturgical books speaks of 'our awin Scottis use', this sounds more like a wish than a description, unless it simply means the local reception and adaptation of these rites from elsewhere.[2] This reception and diversity are the subject of this chapter, which gives a sketch of the forms of public worship in Scotland before the overthrow of the Latin liturgy, based primarily on surviving liturgical books and fragments. This subject has certainly been neglected. In 1957, David McRoberts published a survey of the evidence which he said 'should be regarded merely as a preliminary report' but little has been done since beyond more studies of the surviving books and material culture.[3] I have edited and brought up to date McRoberts's important 1970 Rhind Lectures on the furnishings of late medieval Scottish churches and produced a new edition of his 1953 *Catalogue of Scottish Medieval Liturgical Books and Fragments*.[4] Although the materials are there, there is not yet an analytical survey of Scottish medieval liturgy comparable to Richard Pfaff's magisterial 2009 *The Liturgy in Medieval England*.[5] This chapter offers another 'preliminary report', demonstrating that a major study is possible and would be richly rewarding.

I

First, some definitions. Liturgy is the public official worship of the Church. It is a communal thing even if a solitary person celebrates it, as Peter Damian emphasises in his *Liber Dominus Vobiscum* where he responds to the question of whether a hermit should use the plural in his liturgical prayers.[6] The great liturgical scholar Cyprian Vaggagini defined liturgy as 'a complexus of verbal and physical signs ordered to the worship of God and the sanctification of humanity'.[7] This shows that liturgy is more than just words and more than just the books, buildings and artefacts used in this ritual performance. The gestures and words, however, disappear when done, said or sung; but the books and objects, the architectural spaces and the descriptions and interpretations of the rites remain. It is these, particularly the books, which form the basis of this chapter that is concerned with liturgy in Scotland. While the shadowy figure of Ninian traditionally brought Christianity to the south-west, it is likely that the Christian story was first heard through contact with the Romans.[8]

The first evidence of Christianity in Scotland comes from the early fifth century when a stone was erected in Whithorn to Latinus and his daughter which includes the phrase *te laudamus Dominum*.[9] This may just be 'a generalised Christian sentiment', 'we praise you Lord', with the accusative 'Dominum' as a mistake, but it recalls a chant, *Te laudamus Domine*, which became part of the Ambrosian liturgy of Milan and is sung as a 'transitorium' during communion.[10] This chant is older than the stone as it is quoted by Jerome (c.347–420) in his letter to Damasus and in his commentary on Isaiah.[11] The Latinus inscription also recalls another ancient communion chant, this time in the Mozarabic liturgy of Spain, *Refecti Christi corpore et sangunie, te laudamus, Domine, Alleluia*. A variant of this was known in the British Isles at a later date, as the chant *Refecti Christi corpore et sanguine, tibi semper, Domine, dicamus, Alleluia*, which is found in some of the earliest Scottish and Irish liturgical books: the Bangor Antiphonary (Northern Ireland, late seventh century); Book of Dimma (Ireland, eighth century); Book of Mulling (Ireland, late eighth century); Stowe Missal (Ireland, late eighth or early ninth century); Book of Deer (north-east Scotland, tenth century).[12] Both these texts refer to Holy Communion which is particularly relevant if the Latinus stone is indeed a memorial to the dead because the sacrament was a promise of eternal life. It is significant for the study of Christian worship that the first Christian artefact from Scotland should have a Latin liturgical text inscribed on it. It suggests that the liturgy of the first Christians in northern Britain was part of a community of liturgical practice in Latin shared with the rest of Latin Europe. The earliest Christian worship in Scotland was thus Roman, not in the sense of following the practice of the city of Rome but rather being a local variant of the Latin liturgy of the Empire. The fifth-century bishop Patrick wrote to a warlord called Coroticus who was probably a Christian ruling at Alt Clud (Dumbarton) speaking of 'fellow citizens of the holy Romans' meaning not subjects of the Empire but followers of the same religion as Rome.[13] Christianity and *Romanitas* clearly went together. This may even, perhaps, be seen in building style as Richard Fawcett suggests that the early fifth-century structures with apses found at Traprain Law in East Lothian and Dod in Roxburghshire were churches.[14]

After the original sub-Roman evangelisation, Lothian and the Borders were settled by Anglo-Saxons and became part of the kingdom of Bernicia which itself became Christian in the early seventh century. This Northumbrian Christianity, with its liturgy influenced by Rome and Iona, held sway in this area until the second Christian millennium although

Edinburgh was taken by the Scots c.960. In the west there was Irish influence and the earliest liturgical book of probable Scottish provenance is the *Cathach* of St Columba, an incomplete Latin psalter with directions for liturgical use written between 560 and 630, probably on Iona whence it came to Ireland.[15] It is a mistake to speak of a 'Celtic rite' in Scotland and Ireland as there was no 'Celtic' identity at that time and Irish evidence suggests that local Christians probably used a liturgy from the Gallican family with Roman influences.[16]

II

There are over 120 extant liturgical books and about a hundred liturgical fragments from Scotland in the period before 1560, of which forty-eight are printed texts.[17] In the four centuries before 1560, Scotland had over a thousand parishes. Medieval canonical legislation generally said that a parish should have at least these liturgical books: a missal, gradual and troper for mass; a breviary, antiphonal and psalter for the office; a manual for the occasional offices; an ordinal with rules for the services; and probably also gospel and epistle books for mass; a hymnal, legendary and collectar for the office; and the obituary and processional.[18] These are practical books (see Appendix 1.1) and at least some would be absolutely required in every parish, otherwise there would be no worship, with some parishes having considerably more. It is interesting to note from these lists that parish liturgy was expected to include a sung divine office. Even allowing for very poorly equipped churches, this gives us a minimum of eight thousand liturgical books in Scotland, even before we include the thirteen cathedrals, about sixty monasteries, about forty-five friaries, fifteen nunneries and various colleges, chapels and hospitals.

Examples of the number and type of books in a church are given by the thirty extant inventories, such as Aberdeen Cathedral, with sixty-two books, and St Salvator's College Chapel, St Andrews, with fifty-nine books.[19] Many churches had more than one altar, each of which often had its own books, as in the case of the altar of the Visitation in St John's parish church, Perth, in 1544 with three missals.[20] There were at least thirty-six other altars in the church, as Scottish burghs tended to multiply altars rather than churches as in England. Compared to these examples, the books surviving today would hardly equip one cathedral: thirteen missals, one gradual, thirteen psalters, twenty breviaries, three pontificals and a manual. At very best, this is a 0.5 per cent survival rate. The largest category among the survivals are the twenty-nine para-liturgical prayer books and books of hours, often owned by the laity and perhaps surviving for this reason.

If the study of worship in North Britain in this period of this study begins in uncertainty with hints on stones, it ends in devastation: the cessation of the Latin liturgy in large parts of Scotland after 1560, the destruction of the material culture of this liturgy and its replacement by a simple reformed order of worship in English or Scots and, after 1567, Gaelic. The Latin Catholic liturgy was not only prevented from being celebrated in most places, it was outlawed by the Scottish Parliament in 1560–7, and Protestant Reformers such as John Knox saw the mass as positively evil, claiming that 'one mass ... was more fearful to him than if ten thousand armed men were landed in any part of the realm to suppress true religion'.[21] It was not just the mass that was feared, the whole complexus of the medieval liturgy, in as far as it was not directly demanded by scripture, was held to be offensive to God and liable to call down his curse upon Scotland as did idolatry upon Israel in the Old Testament.[22] Knox wrote to his friend Anne Locke from St Andrews on 23 June 1559, 'The Abbey of Lindores a place of black monks was reformed, their altars overthrown, their idols, vestments of idolatry and mass books were burnt in their own presence', and James Gordon of Rothiemay wrote of the books of Aberdeen Cathedral being burnt in 1560.[23] This ideological devastation should not, however, cause modern bibliophiles to blame all destruction on the Protestant. In his edition of Scottish medieval library catalogues John Higgitt has shown how invading English armies burnt many churches together with the books they contained.[24] Some books were deliberately preserved, a number of extant volumes have recusant Catholic provenance and have been preserved in the Blairs and Preshome collections now in Aberdeen University Library. A 1559 list of books and church furnishings from St Salvator's Collegiate Church, St Andrews, shows that they were taken to St Andrews Castle for safekeeping in 1559.[25] Marcus Wagner, a German book collector working for the Protestant theological historian Matthias Flacius Illyricus, was in Scotland in 1553 and obtained various volumes including liturgical items from St Andrews and Arbroath which ensured their survival.[26] If individual Protestants may not be blamed for the totality of the destruction of almost all the liturgical books that were in Scotland before 1560, it was the success of the Protestant Reformation that was responsible for so few books surviving.

Just as recent research has shown that more of the fabric of medieval Scottish churches has survived than previously thought, incorporated in rebuilt churches, the same instinct not to waste resources led to parchment from liturgical books being reused in bindings.[27] Forty liturgical fragments have been removed from the bindings of Scottish books in the National Records of Scotland in Edinburgh and other examples have been found recently in the burgh records of Haddington.[28] Despite the limited amount of material that has survived, there is much that can be learned about what type of liturgy was used in medieval and Renaissance Scotland.

III

In 1736, a question was asked at the exiled Jacobite court which began the modern study of medieval Scottish liturgy. It was whether a statement in

Blind Harry's fifteenth-century poem *The Wallace* was true: that Scotland used Roman liturgical books until Edward I burnt them all and the clergy started using the English use of Salisbury or Sarum. In his answer, the Scottish Roman Catholic priest Thomas Innes showed that this was false and that Sarum came to Scotland at the request of the Scottish cathedral chapters. He claimed that all Scotland used Sarum and avoided the liturgical use of York because of its archbishop's claims to jurisdiction over Scotland.[29] Nineteenth- and early twentieth-century antiquarianism saw editions of some of these liturgical books, and in the articles of Francis Eeles and David McRoberts, based on their unrivalled knowledge of the sources, Innes's view of the dominance of Sarum was accepted but modified. This new consensus has been repeated in more recent works.[30]

When did the Sarum liturgy come to Scotland? McRoberts claimed that Glasgow used it under Bishop Herbert in the mid-twelfth century, but the 1172 papal bull confirming this actually refers to the Salisbury Cathedral constitution or customary (which has a liturgical element) rather than liturgical rules of its ordinal (although later fragments do show that Glasgow did come to follow the Sarum use in worship).[31] Richard Pfaff notes that the first recorded use of the Sarum ordinal outside Salisbury was at St David's in 1223 and the first explicit Scottish evidence is at Elgin where the Moray chapter had used the Lincoln constitution since c.1210 but the 1242 statutes state that, in addition to this, the divine office, psalmody, reading, singing and other liturgical matters would follow the order established at Salisbury.[32] Slightly earlier is the earliest extant Sarum liturgical book copied in Scotland, the St Andrews Antiphoner and diurnal produced in that city in the 1230s by the same scribe as the Pontifical of David de Bernham.[33] It seems that the St Andrews/Wolfenbüttel Choir Book (known as W_1) was at least in part written at St Andrews at this time and the impressive repertoire of French polyphony it contains shows that Sarum liturgical books existed together with liturgical items from elsewhere in Europe, although in the case of the alleluia for the vigil of Christmas the words of a piece were adapted to fit Sarum custom.[34] Most Scottish secular cathedrals adopted the Sarum constitution, as Dunkeld and Ross did about 1250, and the predominance of Sarum use books among those surviving from Scotland suggests that, like Elgin, they also followed Sarum liturgical practice.

Richard Pfaff has done much to sort out the complicated origin and nature of the Sarum use, but we should remember that before printing there was no absolute uniformity in liturgical texts. Pfaff's comparison of printed Sarum books has revealed a similar diversity between editions, which is obscured by modern editions of 'the Sarum rite' like Dickinson's 'Sarum missal'.[35] 'Sarum use' was thus not monolithic and the variations found in Scottish books may be typical of the use rather than reflecting peculiar Scottish customs. It must be remembered that English books, like English clerics, would have come north before the mid-thirteenth century.

In the twelfth century Glasgow Pontifical the name of the English diocese for which it was written was erased and 'Glasgow' substituted. There is the puzzle of the Anglo-Saxon pontifical found in the stables of Brodie Castle in 1970 which had been in Scotland since at least the seventeenth century and may have come from Elgin Cathedral or the Benedictine priory of Urquhart.[36] Imported books were adapted for Scottish use principally by adding Scottish saints to their calendars, and sometimes their propers were added to the sanctoral (liturgical prayers for the celebration of the individual saint added to the section of the liturgical book which contains these types of prayers). These books were then sometimes copied.

Despite Blind Harry's anti-Sarum propaganda, the wars with England did not end the use of Sarum books, which was encouraged later by the import of Sarum books printed on the continent. This even continued after the ban on their import in James IV's 1507 licence.[37] Liturgists like to work out what type of liturgy a book represents by searching for distinctiveness in saints, rubrics or texts, but for most Scots clergy at the time, apart from those with a special interest in liturgy, there were almost certainly simply 'books that enabled them to celebrate the liturgy'. James Sibbald, priest of St Ternan's, Arbuthnott, produced such books when he wrote a psalter, office of Our Lady and missal for his church.[38] In his 1491 missal we can see various distinctive features, such as omitting sequences in Lent, in a book that follows a basic Sarum plan.[39] The Aberdeen Breviary seems to be on the same lines: a basic Sarum plan with certain modifications and with its distinctiveness in calendar, feasts, lessons, prayers and hymns.[40] This is the 'our awin Scottis use' of the licence, but, if we take heed of Pfaff's recognition that 'Sarum' was not monolithic, then the 'Scottish use' or 'Scottish Sarum liturgy' was just a series of variations of the common pattern of liturgy in Britain, Ireland and their offshore islands.

Beyond Sarum it is said that Galloway diocese used the York use, Orkney and Shetland the Norwegian customs of Nidaros (as they were under its archbishop until 1472) and the Isles had survivals of so-called Celtic customs.[41] Extant evidence supports the first of these. Three fourteenth-century York use fragments have been found in Scotland: a page from an antiphoner used in a binding at Sweetheart Abbey; some pages from a breviary, exhibited at the 1911 Glasgow exhibition but now lost, which were used by a Lanarkshire fisherman to hold his hooks; and a fragment from a missal with both York and Sarum elements found in a book in Dumfries.[42] It is probably that these are all from Galloway diocese and, although from the mid-fourteenth century the bishops of Galloway were not in practice subject to York, it does suggest that York use was influential in the area. Although there is no material evidence, it is probable that Orkney and Shetland, which did not become part of Scotland until 1472, followed Norwegian customs which were eclectic. In the preface to the Nidaros Missal, which has links to Sarum use and was printed in 1519, Archbishop Walkendorf noted that, owing to the scarcity of books, the Norwegian secular clergy were using a variety of liturgical books including Cistercian ones. There would probably have been the same eclecticism in the Western Isles which, as part of the diocese of Sodor, were also part of the province of Nidaros but had close ties to Ireland. From the Gaelic-speaking west, including the Western Isles, there are a number of survivals including a series of semi-liturgical Gaelic calendars and a fragment of a fifteenth-century Sarum antiphoner with Gaelic interlinear annotations, but more work needs to be done to interpret the surviving books and fragments.[43] There is also one fragment of a liturgical book associated with Dundee from the Ambrosian rite of Milan.[44] This possibly comes from the library of a liturgically minded cleric rather than being a book for use in worship; but it does remind one of the diversity of liturgical influences in pre-1560 Scotland.

Some of the religious orders had their own rites which added to this liturgical diversity in bringing elements from France and elsewhere in Europe to Scotland. These included the Dominicans, Carmelites, Cistercians, Premonstratensians and Carthusians, whilst those following the Benedictine rule had a distinctive distribution of psalms at the office. Sadly, the only proper inventories of liturgical books to survive from a religious house are those from Coldingham Priory, but we have eight Benedictine, eleven Cistercian, fourteen Augustinian, two Premonstratensian, three Franciscan and two Dominican books and fragments, together with a book of prayers from the brothers of St Anthony's hospital, Leith. There are no liturgical books from the three Scottish houses of the Valliscaulian Order which fused Cistercian and Carthusian elements on a Cistercian framework, nor any from Scotland's only Charterhouse at Perth. Both of the Dominican books and two of the Augustinian are from nunneries. More work needs to be done on these, for example do the Augustinian books reflect Pfaff's conclusion about English Augustinian liturgy: that there was no such thing as an 'Augustinian use'? It was certainly true that the Augustinian canons of St Andrews in the mid-sixteenth century were enthusiasts for the reformed Roman liturgical books of Cardinal Quiñones, and the fourteenth-century antiphoner fragment from the Augustinian abbey of Inchcolm includes liturgical texts and music from the Sarum and Roman uses and probably from earlier native Scottish traditions.[45] The Cistercians, however, do seem to have valued their distinctive liturgy. A breviary from Sweetheart Abbey, lost since 1764, was recently obtained by the National Library of Scotland.[46] In addition, two ordinals survive, one printed in Paris in 1531; a monk of Kinloss had a Cistercian breviary which was printed in Paris in 1542; and another monk of Kinloss copied the Cistercian private mass order into his notebook. Looking at the calendars in the Scottish Cistercian books, each has a small number of Scottish saints added, more than was officially allowed but fewer than the 'fairly liberal inclusion of unauthorised English saints' noted by Pfaff in his study of extant English Cistercian liturgical books.[47] Franciscans generally used the Roman rite and, apart from an obituary, the only extant Franciscan book is a Roman breviary of 1549.

The religious orders thus brought their own traditions to Scotland but, as shown by the Cistercian calendars and Inchcolm Antiphoner, domesticated it in a Scottish context in a similar way to the use of Sarum books by the secular clergy.

IV

The important East Lothian burgh of Haddington gives a good example of the problems and opportunities encountered by the Scottish liturgical scholar. The birthplace of John Knox, Haddington was also a centre of Catholic devotion and religious life. The burgh kirk of St Mary's was a large structure and its clergy were constituted as a College c.1540 The Cistercian convent, founded in the twelfth century by Ada countess of Northumberland and Huntington, had a taxable income of £226 sterling a year and was one of the wealthiest convents in medieval Britain and Ireland. The chapel of St Martin's in the nungate was probably in the precinct of the nunnery. There was also a significant Franciscan friary founded before 1242, a probable Dominican friary which lasted only a few years and four hospitals: John Haliburton's almshouse, noted around the year 1478; a leper house noted in the 1470s; the hospital of St Mary mentioned in 1319; and the hospital of St Laurence, an Augustinian house dependent on St Andrew's Priory first noted in 1312 and by 1511 run by Observant Augustinians. If we add to the liturgical books required by these churches and chapels, other personal books probably owned by the various clergy of the town there would have been well over two hundred liturgical books in Haddington by 1560. No complete liturgical book is known to have survived from the burgh, but a number of liturgical fragments used as binding material for local government records from the town give some idea of the liturgical diversity of the time and illustrate the problems of interpreting the scattered remains.

Seven fragments, which seem to be of fifteenth-century origin, have been identified so far by the staff at the John Gray Centre in Haddington (see Table 1.1). Such fragments used in bookbinding could have been brought into the town from outside but it is probable that the binding was done in Haddington, which would have had many redundant liturgical books after 1560. The fragments do indeed seem to reflect the variety of religious foundations there.

Three are from three late medieval antiphonals or noted breviaries with parts of the Sarum night office. Fragment A, a single large page used to cover the Haddington Burgh Court Book 1585–97, has the fourth to the ninth noted responsories and third nocturn antiphons from Matins together with the first four antiphons of Lauds for the feast of St Mary Magdalene (22 July).[48] Fragment F, a bifolium used to cover the 1587–96 minute book of the presbytery of Haddington, has the second and third Matins responsories from the feasts of St Peter's chains (1 August) together with the seventh to ninth Matins responsories from the feast of the finding of the relics of

St Stephen (3 August).⁴⁹ Fragment G, a single damaged large page used to cover the 1596–1608 minute book of the Presbytery of Haddington, has the fifth and sixth responsories and the antiphons with the beginning of the gospel from Matins of Christmas Day.⁵⁰ As these appear to be Sarum, they are probably not from the Franciscan friary which used the Roman rite or from the Cistercian nunnery which used the Cistercian rite. They may well have come from St Mary's which, as a college of secular clergy, would have utilised the Sarum use and had a musical establishment capable of singing the daily office which would have needed such books.

Fragment C is another page from an office book, an un-noted breviary, used to cover the 1574–5 accounts of the Common Good of Haddington.⁵¹ It has Matins of the feast of the finding of the relics of St Stephen with the rubric from the Matins gospel, all as in the feast of St Stephen (26 December), followed by first Vespers and Matins of the feast of St Laurence (10 August) up to the second antiphon of the second nocturn. The texts are not from the Sarum use and broadly fit with the Cistercian breviary which only has a series of commemorations between these two twelve-lesson feasts. The feast of St Dominic with twelve lessons was added to the Cistercian Office in 1255 and it is strange that this is not found between the two feasts but it is also not in that position in the 1542 Paris Cistercian breviary owned by a monk of Kinloss Abbey.⁵² The antiphons and responsories are the same as the Cistercian use and the distinctive ancient hymn by St Ambrose 'Apostolorum supparem', which is prescribed at first Vespers and Matins, was used by the Cistercian Order as part of their policy of simplifying worship and going 'back to the sources'. St Benedict called a hymn an 'Ambrosianum', so the Cistercians tried to get as many authentic Ambrosian hymns as possible. The readings at Matins on both feasts, however, are either rearranged or not those of the Cistercian breviary (with the single exception of the first reading on the feast of St Laurence). It is possible that variations like this might be found in a Cistercian manuscript but there is another possibility. The Hospital of St Laurence, founded before 1300 and dependent on the Augustinian canons of St Andrews Cathedral Priory, would have had a special interest in its patron. Although little is known about liturgy in the Scottish Augustinian houses, English Augustinian liturgy was eclectic and they may well have used this Ambrosian hymn and would certainly have celebrated the feats of St Laurence with special texts. In the Iona Psalter, a thirteenth-century book made in England for the Augustinian nuns of Iona, there is only one English saint between the translation of the relics of Stephen and St Laurence. Thus, in a non-English book, the two would follow on from each other as here. The balance of evidence, however, suggests that it was from the Cistercian priory.

Fragment E, a page covering the Haddington Treasurers Accounts for 1558, is from a missal and has no musical notation.⁵³ It contains part of the lessons of the Easter vigil, three of the four lessons of the Sarum vigil in the right order: Genesis 1–2; Exodus 14–15 with the Canticle *Cantemus*,

Isaiah 4 with the tract *Vinea facta est*, but the last lesson is not the Sarum Deuteronomy 31 but rather from Isaiah 54–5 which is the fourth and last reading in the Cistercian and Dominican uses. The Roman and Franciscan Easter vigil had twelve lessons but these four readings suggest that the missal was from the well-established priory of Cistercian nuns, as the Dominican foundation was of short duration.

Fragment D, a page covering the Haddington Writ, Receipt and Delivery Book 1579–1656, is from a gradual.[54] It has chants from two of the Sundays after Trinity or after Pentecost. From one mass it has the introit *Miserere mihi* and references to the gradual *Timebunt gentes*, the offertory, *Domine in auxilium*, and the communion *Domine memorabor*, and from the other the introit *Iustus es*, a reference to the gradual *Beata gens*, and the beginning of the offertory *Oravi*. These are all in the Sarum missal as used in Scotland for the sixteenth and seventeenth Sundays after Trinity, but for both Sundays the Alleluia verse differs from the Sarum use; in the first mass it is *Cantate Domino* and in the second *Domine exaudi*. These are however found, with the other chants, in the Roman gradual on the sixteenth and seventeenth Sundays after Pentecost. This Roman gradual may have been owned by any priest or institution in Haddington. But there was one institution that explicitly used the Roman rite, the Franciscan friary, demolished in 1572, which was such a significant building that it was known as the 'Lamp of Lothian'. This may be a fragment from one of its liturgical books.

Fragment B, a bifolium from a missal, was used to cover the Haddington Burgh Court Book for the years 1581–5.[55] It has the sanctoral for 2–5 February and 4–17 March containing many Scottish saints and is a good example of the 'Scottish use'; that modification of the Sarum use by adding Scottish saints and removing others which culminated in Bishop Elphinstone's Aberdeen Breviary (1510).[56] The list of saints in these periods is the same as the calendar of the Arbuthnott Missal (1491) with the single omission of St Felix of Dunwich (9 March instead of the usual 8 March) and the same as the Aberdeen Breviary with the exception of St Kevoc (13 March) and the addition of St Longinus (15 March). This fragment gives mass formularies for all the saints, however, whereas the Arbuthnott Missal has masses only for SS Perpetua and Felicity and St Gregory the Great in the period 4–17 March. Whilst this fragment reflects the secular 'Scottish use', it also includes two local saints from islands in the Forth, St Baldred of the Bass and St Adrian of May, and has a number of divergences from standard Sarum texts, for example the mass of St Blaise has four elements in common with Sarum but six divergences. This is probably another example of that local modification which was more typical of medieval liturgical books than the uniformity more characteristic of the post-Tridentine era.

The Haddington fragments reflect how little has survived from the rich liturgical life of medieval Scottish burghs but they also show how much can be learned from the limited evidence. They hint at the strong musical culture which was maintained by the network of Scottish song schools

Table 1.1   Liturgical fragments

Fragment	Reference	Haddington book	Liturgical book	Liturgical texts	Use
A	NRS RH 12/21	Burgh Court Book 1585–97 ELCA HAD/4/2/3/6	Antiphonal	Matins of St Mary Magdalene	Sarum
B	NRS RH 12/28	Burgh Court Book 1581–5 ELCA HAD/4/2/3/5	Missal	Sanctoral for 2–5 February and 4–17 March	
C	ELCA HAD/4/6/76	Accounts of the Common Good 1574–5	Breviary	Relics of St Stephen and St Laurence	Cistercian
D	ELCA HAD/4/6/78	Writ, Receipt and Delivery Book 1579–1656	Gradual	Sixteenth and Seventeenth Sundays after Pentecost	Roman
E	ELCA HAD/4/6/73	Treasurers accounts 1558	Missal	Easter Vigil	Cistercian
F	NRS CH2/185.1	Presbytery Minutes 1587–96	Antiphonal	St Peter's Chains and Relics of St Stephen	Sarum
G	NRS CH2/185.2	Presbytery Minutes 1596–1608	Antiphonal	Christmas Day	Sarum

and show how the diversity of religious institutions led to a diversity of religious rites and uses, with the seven fragments reflecting Sarum, Roman-Franciscan, Cistercian and possibly even Augustinian customs.[57] Fragment B also provides more evidence of the attempt to construct 'our awin Scottis use' associated with James IV, Bishop Elphinstone and the Aberdeen Breviary and reflected in the Arbuthnott Missal. With the absence of any survivals of the polyphony that would have been sung in St Mary's burgh kirk, it is a reminder of how much has been lost.

V

The Scottish Church was no stagnant backwater, and the liturgical texts that survive show a rich diversity of liturgical forms influenced by liturgical developments in the rest of Britain and on the continent. This was true also of the adoption of new liturgical customs: elevating and censing the host after its consecration at mass are found in Scotland soon after they were introduced in France in the early thirteenth century; six candlesticks on the high altar and the use of altar cards at mass are attested in Scotland right at the start of the popularity of these customs in Europe.[58] Newly popular feasts and devotions such as the Compassion of Our Lady and the Holy House of Loreto also swiftly took root in Scotland.[59] This should not surprise us as there were close trading links between Scotland and the rest of Europe. Many Scottish clerics studied on the continent and brought home news of new developments.

From the fifteenth and sixteenth centuries there are examples of Roman liturgical books and of Scottish clerics petitioning to use the Roman rite. This might have been to ingratiate themselves with the Curia or just out of respect for Rome – the Scottish theologian John Mair noted at the time that an unbeneficed cleric could always use the Roman rite, 'because Rome is the common fatherland'.[60] Cardinal Quiñones produced a reformed and simplified Roman breviary for Pope Clement VII in 1535, which cut out most feasts, eliminated most non-scriptural material, and simplified and shortened the offices. Eight extant copies of various editions come from Scotland pre-1560, together with two Quiñones-influenced Roman missals, and most belonged to known Catholic reformers.[61] One was Canon John Watson of Aberdeen, and this symbolises the failure of the project for a uniform national use of which the Aberdeen Breviary was part. Flodden and its aftermath damaged the project but McRoberts argued that the conservative and unwieldy nature of Elphinstone's breviary was the real reason for its failure.[62] It should also be remembered that no Sarum missals were published in France between 1534 and 1555.

Even Quiñones's radical reform, which was replaced by the Tridentine breviary in 1568, was not enough for some and there is evidence for use of the 1552 English *Book of Common Prayer* in Scotland before 1560 when the old order was swept away.[63] Some books, however, remained in use and not only by recusant Roman Catholics. The twelfth-century Blantyre Psalter was marked with the divisions of the psalter used in the *Book of Common Prayer*, possibly in York, and a book of Epistles and Gospels from Dundee has a note in Latin recording changes in readings in the lectionary of the English *Book of Common Prayer*.[64] Even in the restrained world of the Genevan *Book of Common Order*, swiftly adopted by the Reformed Church of Scotland, there were still significant continuities with the pre-Reformation mass.[65]

This period thus sees the Latin liturgy brought in with the gospel; close early connections with Ireland; the rise and decline of the Sarum use in Scotland; a diversity of practice and rites; the failure to create a uniform national use; the rising popularity of Roman books; the destruction of the Latin liturgy after 1559 and its replacement in most places by a radically changed vernacular liturgy. This study of the Haddington fragments shows that much can be learned from sketchy remains. A full and detailed study of liturgy in Scotland in this period is still needed. A good way of doing this would be to use the method of Pfaff's book on English liturgy which is closely based on extant liturgical books. Whilst liturgy in Scotland pre-1560 was simply a variant of the Latin liturgy of the West, there was a specifically Scottish synthesis of uses. The size of the realm and extant sources means that a study of liturgy based on Scottish books and references could be set in a broader context of religious culture and devotion than was possible with Pfaff's work. Worship is far more than words and books.

Appendix 1.1: Guide to medieval liturgical books[66]

SACRAMENTARY: with all the prayers needed by the celebrant at mass.

MISSAL: with the celebrant's texts, but also readings and chants. From the twelfth century onwards the missal gradually replaced the sacramentary.

GRADUAL: with the proper chants of the mass arranged according to the liturgical year.

TROPER: compositions for festivals and saints' days which are sung before the traditional chant or are interpolated between the lines of the chants.

SEQUENTIARY: with sequences which are hymn-like chants that follows the epistle at certain masses.

BOOKS OF READINGS: lectionaries, gospel books and epistle books for mass.

PROCESSIONAL: with chant, texts and rubrics for liturgical processions.

BREVIARY: with all the texts required for the divine office.

ANTIPHONAL: with chants for the offices.

LITURGICAL PSALTER: with the psalms and canticles for the divine office and usually with a calendar and other texts such as hymns and readings.

HYMNAL: with hymns for the divine office. Other parts of the office also had their own books such as the LECTIONARY with readings from the Bible and fathers for the night office of Matins; LEGENDARY or PASSIONAL with lives of the saints; COLLECTAR with the readings and prayers for the celebrant at the office; and two books to be read after the morning office of Prime, the MARTYROLOGY with brief passages on the saints of the day and the OBITUARY or NECROLOGY with lists of the dead to be prayed for on the day.

PONTIFICAL: with occasional services for the bishop such as confirmation, ordination, excommunication, the dedication of churches and the coronation of a king.

MANUAL or RITUAL: with occasional services for the priest such as baptism, marriage and blessings.

ORDINAL: with rules for the services during the year.

Notes

1. This chapter has its origins in a paper given at the 2010 annual conference of the Scottish Catholic Historical Association, 'Liturgy and the Nation', held at Glasgow University.

2. *Register of the Privy Seal of Scotland*, ed. M. Livingstone, 8 vols (Edinburgh: H. M. General Register House, 1908), pp. 223–4, no. 1546,
3. D. McRoberts, 'The Medieval Scottish Liturgy Illustrated by Surviving Documents', *Transactions of the Scottish Ecclesiological Society*, 15 (1957), 24–40.
4. S. M. Holmes, 'Catalogue of Liturgical Books and Fragments in Scotland before 1560', *IR*, 62 (2011), 127–212; D. McRoberts and S. M. Holmes, *Lost Interiors: The Furnishings of Scottish Churches in the Later Middle Ages* (Edinburgh: Aquhorties Press, 2012).
5. Richard Pfaff, *The Liturgy in Medieval England: A History* (Cambridge: CUP, 2009).
6. Peter Damian, *Letters 1–30*, ed. O. J. Blum (Washington, DC: CUAP, 1989), pp. 255–89; P. Ranft, *Theology of Peter Damian: 'let Your Life Always Serve as a Witness'* (Washington, DC: CUAP, 2012), pp. 71–83.
7. C. Vagaggini, *Theological Dimensions of the Liturgy* (Collegeville: Liturgical Press, 1976), pp. 19–32. S. M. Holmes, *Sacred Signs in Reformation Scotland: Interpreting Worship, 1488–1590* (Oxford: OUP 2015), p. 14.
8. J. E. Fraser, *From Caledonia to Pictland: Scotland to 795* (Edinburgh: EUP, 2009), pp. 36–7, 68–72.
9. C. Tedeschi, *Congeries Lapidum. Iscrizioni Britanniche dei secoli V–VII* (Pisa: Edizioni della Normale, 2005), pp. 295–7. K. Forsyth, 'The Latinus Stone: Whithorn's Earliest Christian Monument' in J. Murray (ed.), *St Ninian and the Earliest Christianity in Scotland* (Oxford: Blackwell, 2009), pp. 19–41.
10. C. Thomas, 'The Early Christian Inscriptions of Southern Scotland', in *Glasgow Archaeological Journal*, 17 (1992), 1–10. The Milanese chant is *Te laudamus, Domine omnipotens, qui sedes super Cherubim et Seraphim . . . Hunc Sacrosanctum calicem sumentes, ab omni culpa libera nos semper*, AMM 81 in *Antiphonale Missarum juxta ritum Sanctae Ecclesiae Mediolanensis*, ed. G. M. Suñol (Rome: Desclée et socii, 1935).
11. *Hieronymus Commentariorum in Esaiam libri I–XI*, ed. M. Adriaen, *Corpus Christianorum Series Latina* 73, (Turnhout, 1963), pp. 85–6; *Hieronymus Epistularum Pars I Epistulae I–LXX*, ed. I. Hilberg, *Corpus Scriptorum Ecclesiasticorum Latinorum* 54 (Vienna, 1996), pp. 97–103; R. Gryson and D. Szmatula, 'Les commentaires patristiques sur Isaïe d'Origène à Jérôme', *Revue des Etudes Augustiniennes*, 36 (1990), 3–41.
12. A. Toniolo, F. M. Arocena and A. Ivorra, *Concordantia missalis hispano-mozarabici* (Rome and Toledo: Libreria Editrice Vaticana, 2009), O41cn; Bangor Antiphonary, Biblioteca Ambrosiana, Milan, C. 5 inf.; Trinity College Dublin Library, Book of Dimma, MS 59 & Book of Mulling, MS 60; RIAL, Stowe Missal, MS D ii 3; Cambridge University Library, Book of Deer, MS. Ii.6.32; F. E. Warren, *Liturgy and Ritual of the Celtic Church* (Oxford: Clarendon Press, 1881), pp. 165, 171, 173, 192, 225 (which show minor Variants in the text); *The Stowe Missal*, HBS 31 and 32, ed. G. F. Warner (London: Henry Bradshaw Society, 1906, 1915), pp. 1, 36; *The Antiphonary of Bangor*, ed. F. E. Warren (London: Henry Bradshaw Society, 1895), p. 31.
13. *Manu mea scripsi atque condidi uerba ista danda et tradenda, militibus mittenda Corotici, non dico ciuibus meis neque ciuibus sanctorum Romanorum sed ciuibus daemoniorum, ob mala opera ipsorum.* (With my own hand I have written and put together these words to be given and handed on and sent to the soldiers of Coroticus. I cannot say that they are my fellow-citizens, nor fellow-citizens of

the holy people of Rome, but fellow-citizens of demons, because of their evil works.) St Patrick, *Epistola ad Milites Corotici* 2, http://www.confessio.ie/etexts/epistola_latin#02 (accessed 26 November 2015).
14. R. Fawcett, *The Architecture of the Scottish Medieval Church* (New Haven: YUP, 2011), p. 2.
15. RIAL, MS 12 R 33 (Holmes 1). Each Scottish liturgical book is its number in S. M. Holmes, 'Catalogue of Liturgical Books and Fragments in Scotland before 1560', *IR*, 62 (2011), 127–212.
16. I. Bradley, *Celtic Christianity: Making Myths and Chasing Dreams* (Edinburgh: EUP, 1999).
17. In Holmes, 'Catalogue', there are 126 liturgical books but some are not of certain Scottish provenance; fragments of liturgical books are from time to time discovered as binding material as in the case of the Haddington fragments discussed.
18. Pfaff, *Liturgy in Medieval England*, p. 511. The lists quoted are from English sources but are said to be taken from standard lists. I have not encountered similar evidence from Scotland.
19. McRoberts and Holmes, *Lost Interiors*, pp. 214–19; *Registrum Episcopatus Aberdonensis*, 2 vols (Edinburgh: Spalding and Maitland Clubs, 1845), pp. 127–48; R. G. Cant, *The College of St. Salvator* (Edinburgh: Oliver & Boyd, 1950), pp. 107–63.
20. R. S. Fittis, *The Ecclesiastical Annals of Perth* (Edinburgh: James Gemmell, 1885), pp. 299–300.
21. *John Knox's History of the Reformation in Scotland*, ed. W. C. Dickinson, 2 vols (London, 1949), II, p. 12.
22. Holmes, *Sacred Signs*, pp. 161–5.
23. D. Laing (ed.), *The Works of John Knox*, 6 vols (Edinburgh, 1846–54), VI, p. 26; J. Higgitt, *Scottish Libraries, Corpus of British Medieval Library Catalogues* 12 (London: BL, 2006), p. lix.
24. Higgitt, *Scottish Libraries*, lvii–lx. See also D. McRoberts, 'Material destruction caused by the Scottish Reformation' in D. McRoberts (ed.), *Essays on the Scottish Reformation 1513–1625* (Glasgow, 1962), pp. 415–62.
25. Higgitt, *Scottish Libraries*, pp. 374–75. Cant, *The College of St. Salvator*, pp. 107–63.
26. Holmes, 'Catalogue', 34, 53, 54.
27. This is the conclusion of the University of St Andrews project 'A Corpus of Scottish Medieval Parish Churches', http://arts.st-andrews.ac.uk/corpusofscottishchurches/, accessed 14 November 2016, 'it is becoming increasingly clear that a majority of parish churches survived the Reformation, although many were subsequently rebuilt or abandoned'.
28. Holmes, 'Catalogue', 59.
29. EUL, MS La.111.346; J. Stuart (ed.), *Miscellany of the Spalding Club* (Aberdeen: Spalding Club, 1842), II, pp. 364–7.
30. L. MacFarlane, *William Elphinstone and the Kingdom of Scotland 1431–1514: The Struggle for Order* (Aberdeen: Aberdeen University Press, 1985), pp. 233–4. I. W. Preece, *'Our awin Scottis use': Music in the Scottish Church up to 1603* (Glasgow: The Universities of Glasgow and Aberdeen, 2000), pp. 55–6.
31. McRoberts, 'The Medieval Scottish Liturgy', p. 27. Bull of Pope Alexander III, cited *Registrum Episcopatus Glasguensis*, ed. C. Innes, 2 vols (Edinburgh: Maitland and Bannatyne Clubs, 1843), 1, p. 26. The fragments are Holmes 26,

50, 66, 67, 68, 69; see also the Sprouston Breviary, Holmes 39, and the liturgical instructions in the Blackadder Prayer Book, Holmes, 'Catalogue', 101.
32. Pfaff, *Liturgy in Medieval England*, 377–8; *Registrum Episcopatus Moraviensis*, ed. C. Innes (Edinburgh: Bannatyne Club, 1837), p. 109.
33. Holmes, 'Catalogue', 24 and 36.
34. Holmes, 'Catalogue', 34; Preece, *'Our awin Scottis use'*, pp. 225–71.
35. Pfaff, *Liturgy in Medieval England*, pp. 350–87, 412–23.
36. Holmes, 'Catalogue', 10 and 16.
37. A Sarum missal printed in Paris in 1534 was owned by John Stewart, Commendator of Coldingham and grandson of James IV.
38. Holmes, 'Catalogue', 94, 96, 97.
39. *Liber Ecclesie Beati Terrenani de Arbuthnott*, ed. A. P. Forbes (Burntisland, 1864).
40. *Breviarium Aberdonense*, ed. W. Blew (London: Toovey, 1854); Holmes, 'Catalogue', 135–44.
41. McRoberts, 'The Medieval Scottish Liturgy', p. 26.
42. Holmes, 'Catalogue', 47, 48, 4.1.2. The last fragment was discovered c.1950 but was not in previous catalogues.
43. Holmes, 'Catalogue', 62, 63, 65, 126, 127, 161.
44. Holmes, *Sacred Signs*, pp. 82–4, 107–8.
45. Holmes, 'Catalogue', 56. Preece, *'Our awin Scottis use'*, p. 71.
46. Holmes, 'Catalogue', 46.
47. Pfaff, *Liturgy in Medieval England*, p. 263. Holmes, 'Catalogue', 88, 95.
48. NRS RH 12/21, Holmes, 'Catalogue', 59xv; F. Procter and C. Wordsworth (eds), *Breviarii ad usum insignis ecclesiae Sarum*, [*Sarum Breviary*] (Cambridge: CUP, 1882–6), III, pp. 519–24. The Cistercian office is quite different, see EUL, De.2.23: Cistercian Breviary (Paris: 1542), owned by William Forsyth monk of Kinloss Abbey; Holmes, 'Catalogue', 165.
49. NRS, Records of Presbytery of Haddington, CH2/185/1; *Sarum Breviary*, III, pp. 567–8, 585–7.
50. NRS, CH2/185/2: *Sarum Breviary* I, pp. clxxx–clxxxii.
51. ELCA, HAD/4/6/76.
52. EUL, De.2.23, Holmes, 'Catalogue', 165. Waddell, Chrysogonus, *The Primitive Cistercian Breviary* (Fribourg: Academic Press, 2007), p. 96.
53. ELCA, Treasurers Accounts, HAD/4/6/73.
54. ELCA, Writ Receipt and Delivery Book, HAD/4/6/78.
55. NRS, Fragments of Manuscripts, RH 12/28.
56. The feasts are the Purification (2), St Blaise (3), St Agatha (5 February). St Adrian of May and companions (4), St Baldred of the Bass (6), St Thomas Aquinas (7), SS Perpetua and Felicity (7), St Duthac (8), St Kessog (10), St Constantine (11), St Gregory the Great (12), St Longinus (15), St Boniface (16), St Patrick (17 March). It uses the Sarum term for the introit at mass, 'Officium'.
57. S. M. Holmes, 'Education in the Century of Reformation' in R. Anderson, M. Freeman and L. Paterson (eds), *The Edinburgh History of Education in Scotland* (Edinburgh: EUP, 2015), pp. 57–78, 62–3.
58. McRoberts, 'Medieval Scottish Liturgy', 29–30, 32 n 1; McRoberts and Holmes, *Lost Interiors*, p. 52.
59. A.-B. Fitch, *The Search for Salvation: Lay Faith in Scotland 1480–1560* (Edinburgh: John Donald, 2009), pp. 65–6, 136–7, 147. A.-B. Fitch, 'Marian Devotion in

Scotland and the Shrine of Loreto' in E. J Cowan and L. Henderson (eds), *A History of Everyday Life in Medieval Scotland* (Edinburgh: EUP, 2011), pp. 274–88.
60. Preece, *'Our awin Scottis use'*, pp. 77–81. McRoberts, 'Medieval Scottish Liturgy', pp. 32–3.
61. Holmes, *Sacred Signs*, pp. 67–70, 152–3.
62. McRoberts, 'Medieval Scottish Liturgy', 37.
63. G. Donaldson, *The Making of the Scottish Prayer Book of 1637* (Edinburgh: EUP, 1954), pp. 3–26.
64. Holmes, 'Catalogue', 21, and Holmes, *Sacred Signs*, pp. 87–8.
65. These are explored in Holmes, *Sacred Signs*, pp. 176–205.
66. For further information on these books and how they changed over time, see: Pfaff, *The Liturgy in Medieval England*; E. Palazzo, *A History of Liturgical Books from the Beginning to the Thirteenth Century* (Collegeville, MN: Liturgical Press, 1998); C. Vogel, *Medieval Liturgy: An Introduction to the Sources* (Washington, DC: Pastoral Press, 1986).

CHAPTER TWO

Jesuits, Mission and Gender in Post-Reformation Scotland

Patricia Barton

Thomas McCoog commented that the history of Jesuits in Scotland at the beginning of the twenty-first century remained limited: 'On the most basic level, there is no general list of the Scottish Jesuits'.[1] The historiography that does exist has focused on politics rather than religion, reflecting the early Jesuit belief in 'trickle down' evangelisation: that winning over political and mercantile elites would provide legal and financial foundations upon which to re-establish the Catholic Church in Europe. Yet Reformation leaders obsessed about the Jesuit influence in Scotland.[2] Little has been written about Jesuits' relationships with the laity or their influence upon liturgical practice. Instead, grudging acceptance of their work in pockets of Scotland before the arrival of Irish missions under the aegis of Propaganda Fide often gives way to condemnation. Peter Anson, for instance, accepted most Jesuits as 'great lovers of their country', enduring hardships, poverty, imprisonment, exile and even martyrdom. However, this is countered by a litany of failures including consorting only with aristocracy, while feuding with popes, Propaganda, other orders and Scottish secular priests.[3] Few spoke Gaelic, distancing them from Highlanders and seemingly ensuring a severely circumscribed geographical missionary field. Fiona Macdonald's dismissive conclusion is typical: 'While Highlanders cannot be seen as even comparatively uncultured . . . a society based on the mercenary trade and tenant farming was unlikely to have the degree of refinement to which Jesuits had become accustomed in continental Europe'.[4] The clear understanding emerging is one in which elite politics dominated and proselytisation came distant second. Michael Yellowlees openly declares his political focus.[5] He is by no means alone. Another discourse recounts the unimportance of the Scottish Mission relative to more famous brethren such as Francis Xavier. This resounded through time: Yellowlees declaring his work the first full-length study of the Scottish Mission precisely 'due to its relatively low profile in modern Scotland'.[6] Most scholars ultimately discount their role: Alexander MacWilliam decreeing, 'From 1622 and for long years afterwards, the preservation of the faith in Scotland and any progress that was made in the conversion of the country must in the main be ascribed to [the Propaganda's] work'.[7]

All this, however, ignores the Jesuit activity that laid the foundations when Scotland was finally declared missionary territory by Rome. For Jesuits to have maintained some small flame of Catholicism, factors other than failed political ventures must have been at play. Recent scholarship on the order's global work contains a variety of issues relevant to Scotland, above all a new sense of what constituted priestly mission.[8] This chapter will assess the role of Jesuits in preserving liturgical and prayer life in an environment of increasingly virulent anti-Catholic legislation. It utilises Fr Robert Abercromby's 1580 Report that offered a common-sense approach to liturgical requirements in the context of mission-scape, the underground practice of faith. Further, Abercrombie singled out the importance of Scottish women as a missionary force, later exemplified by the dangers faced protecting Jesuits and trying to secure Catholic education for their sons. It concludes with an analysis of the early eighteenth-century Gaelic poet, Sìleas na Ceapaich, as an example of the enduring power of Jesuit contacts with Scottish women. From such examples a more nuanced picture of the Jesuit role in the Scottish mission emerges.

I

Papal authority in Scotland was destroyed in August 1560 with acceptance of the Reformed Confession of the Faith by the Scottish Parliament: 'Although many people appear to have remained nominally Catholic, there were no longer any bishops to coordinate or supervise the work of those priests who remained or to safeguard the recruitment of new priests'.[9] An early Jesuit report by Nicholas de Gouda was equally pessimistic: 'The monasteries are nearly all dissolved; some completely destroyed, churches and altars are overthrown: all things holy profaned; the images of Christ and the Saints are broken and cast down'.[10] Yet, despite papal statements recording worries about Scotland, it was not declared mission territory. The flight of bishops to the continent created a vacuum including difficulties creating seminaries vital for a new generation of Scottish priests. The latter resulted from problems reconciling Tridentine edicts on the foundation of national seminaries and the realities of the post-Reformation world.[11] Surviving remnants of Catholicism fractured further, caught in the machinations of kings, Episcopalian bishops and the Kirk's second generation of Presbyterian ministers. Above all, there would be deep divisions over what constituted missionary activity.[12]

Into this situation, Scottish Jesuits would re-enter their home country: this was no intrusion by foreigners. Persuasive evidence is readily found that the Jesuits focused too heavily upon 'trickle down' political missions. Most were sons of Catholic gentry, drawn to work where family connections offered protection.[13] Moreover, in the 1560s, Alphonsus Salmerón, the first Jesuit to visit Scotland, rejected it as missionary territory, not only for bleak prospects of success, but deeming it inappropriate 'to the honour of the Apostolic See for them to hide in forests and secret places'.[14] Evidence equally can be found in Abercromby's recommendations for the restoration of Catholicism. Fr Robert Abercromby came from the Scottish gentry. His father, Alexander, was Laird of Murthly, Perthshire, and kinsmen included lairds of Galbrideston and Gourdie, and Richard Abercromby, the last abbot of Inchcolm.[15] Having graduated from St Andrews in 1558, he accompanied de Gouda and Fr Edmund Hay to Europe. Hay was another kinsman, emphasising the importance of familial links among Scottish Jesuits. Abercromby entered the Society in 1563 and, recommended as 'an excellent man, not wanting in knowledge, even of theology, and prudent', was sent to Braunsberg (Braniewo). A pattern was established for early-generation Scots Jesuits, training in continental Europe before returning to their homeland. In Poland, as Robertus Scotus, he acted as novice master, confessor and examiner of candidates. Juan de Polanco, secretary to the Father General, regarded this period as preparatory for when the 'door' to Scotland might open: meaning financially supported by Rome. Vicar-General Francis Borgia rejected mission 'until arms have done their work ... having defeated the heretical rebels'. Therefore, they rejected requests for missionaries from Archbishop Beaton of Glasgow and Scottish Jesuits themselves as the order's hierarchy awaited invitation from Mary Queen of Scots or the pope.[16] After visiting Scotland in 1580, Abercromby would work in Danzig, before returning home in 1586. His health broken acting as Superior during the persecution after the Battle of Glenlivet, he returned to Braunsberg in 1606. He died there on 16 August 1613.[17]

Abercromby's report was based on a six-week expedition. It is often considered faulty, or at best naive, based on limited local knowledge. Martin Murphy, for instance, argues he was 'over-sanguine in his hopes of converting the king [whom he had met three times] and of turning the tide against the Calvinist reformers, and was over-reliant upon the good faith of the nobility'.[18] Some of Abercromby's writing does reflect this: 'God willing, provided I received also my expenses, to win over, by holy artifice, the King and a great part of the Court'.[19] This is similar to reports by de Gouda and Fr John Hay, entrenching the emphasis on politico-religious connections. Partly this resulted from Abercromby's audience. McCoog suggests he compiled the report in 1581 for his superiors in Rome. Its question-and-answer format emphasised the religious sentiments of the king and nobility and whether there were 'young men of noble birth who could be got into our colleges'.[20] This clearly reflected the priorities of the Jesuit hierarchy that potential students would come with financial support. Letters from college rectors disclosed an overriding financial concern alongside the religious formation of their students.[21] Nor was this emphasis on the nobility reflected by Scottish Jesuits alone. It was a fundamental objective of the *Constitutions* of Ignatius Loyola who identified those to be courted as men who 'through their own improvement become a cause which can spread the good accomplished to many others who are under their guidance'.[22]

Although trickle-down politics can be considered Abercromby's primary focus, his briefer contemplation of the religious is far more pragmatic.[23] Here were eminently sensible recommendations that religious working in Scotland should have dispensations to adopt secular clothes and celebrate mass in unconsecrated places. Fellow Jesuit Fr William Good also contributed on how such thoughts could become reality. Travelling cases should be provided carrying vestments and sacred liturgical objects constructed as small as possible to avoid discovery in a hostile environment. Vestments were to be of the finest materials to ease portability accompanied by small missals and portable altar stones. The latter were fundamental to Abercromby's belief that mass should be celebrated wherever and whenever possible in post-Reformation Scotland. Some missionaries accepted the practicality of such unorthodox liturgical ideas. The Franciscan Edmund McCann was arrested in 1620 with his portable mass pack including an altar stone.[24]

Alexander Collins's visualisation of 'altarscape', the living experience of presiding and participating in the pre-Reformation mass, paints an image of its profundity, religiously and liturgically, for clergymen. His definition of 'altarscape' includes the chalices, patens and sacred Eucharistic vessels, the beauty of the sanctuary and its missals illustrated by master craftsmen, all directing celebrants into the heart of the liturgical experience. In particular, missals represented an immediate recollection of mass as the recreation of the Last Supper and the sacrifices made by the Son of God for humanity. The iconography of Mary and the saints was also emphasised. Collins argues that 'altarscape' became even more important and prominent during crisis points in the pre-Reformation Church when challenge promoted increased pomp and liturgical display in major ecclesiastical centres of Western Europe.[25] Even Scotland, usually regarded as one of the wastelands of liturgical practice before 1559, provided similar evidence, for instance in Edinburgh, Aberdeen and Dunkeld. David McRoberts emphasised the richness of the pre-Reformation Scottish liturgy, the beauty of the furnishings, missals and breviaries.[26] Abercromby's and Good's suggestions represented a new, minimalist 'altarscape' of mission in which mass and other liturgical services could be prepared instantly, whenever and wherever the opportunity arose. The resulting mission-scape incorporated a hidden liturgy, but one no less powerful in maintaining the faith and preserving its folk memory in the face of public distaste and ridicule.[27] Indeed, a liturgy probably more pious and relevant, in which priest and congregation were no longer separated by the ostentation of the pre-Reformation Church but united in a now forbidden experience of worship of their faith. On his return to Scotland, Abercromby practised his own recommendations, including multi-confessionalism whereby Catholics publicly abjured their faith, only to practise in secret.[28] This met severe criticism in Rome, by papal and Jesuit authority alike, and, after Abercrombie a changed emphasis was notable. Fr John Leslie wrote in September 1633:

We have some advantages over our predecessors in our mode of teaching, explaining, and applying the dogmas of faith and precepts of the Christian doctrine, and we frequently hear it objected to that we are much stricter than they used to be, and excessively rigorous in our doctrine.[29]

Ann MacDonell's and McRoberts's description of artefacts used in later missions reveals again that some of Abercromby's and Good's suggestion would endure. Small brass chalices, between 3 and 4 inches long, discovered in Dumbarton, Cromdale and Rodel in Harris, served as individual clerical chalices: light objects in the pack of an itinerant priest.[30] However, from the numerous priests of all ilk, it is clear that the lightweight portable 'Mass bags' had largely been discounted. Instead, images were of cumbersome packs in travels through Scotland, of bulk not lightness, necessitating expense of mules and servants to carry the load.[31] The concept of portable consecrated altar stones became ones that 'must have added considerably to the weight of the "valise"'. Only later did 'curious "do-it-yourself" altar-stones appear – pieces of slate, scratched with five crosses and quite devoid of relics'.[32] Abercromby would have approved such belated recognition of the dangers faced in a hostile environment, even if it departed from the beautiful 'altarscapes' of Rome and wherever Catholicism still was practised openly and securely. Demands for Counter-Reformation liturgical and catechetic purity failed to meet the realities of mission. While Abercromby's recommendations were sensible, with genuine understanding of the practicalities and the protection required for the safety of missionaries, Rome prevailed. This raises an interesting question about the weakness of the influence of Annual Reports and letters relating the harshness of the Scottish Mission sent to Paris and Rome by priests. No doubt they were regarded as mere monetary pleading in a period of financial constraint for the Counter-Reformation Church. It reveals the limited understanding of missionary work by Church authorities, including the Jesuit hierarchy. All mission priests had to deal with the consequences of this failure to contemplate the difficulties facing the priests and laity of the mission lands. Abercromby's 1580 report explicitly recognised Scotland as missionary territory requiring external funding, something not in keeping with papal sensibilities. Maclean, therefore, could classify 1560 to 1610 as 'the period when the [Scottish] Church was silent and moribund'.[33]

That the Jesuit Mission in Scotland suffered from many problems was known only too well to its protagonists. Whilst some comment on the exaggerated bluster of the letters and Annual Reports to Rome, a more abiding image is the consistent portrayal of a troubled mission. Fr Robert Valens reported to Rome in June 1629 after the Countess of Abercorn had been excommunicated:

I am deprived of my two retreats, where I offered the solemnities of religion, and take refuge in times of peril, am obliged to live in an inn, at very great expense, which however I should not object to if I was safe. The searchers of the town visit the house monthly, or oftener, and on two occasions have come while I was saying office. I was in considerable danger, and still greater alarm. For they came close to my room, where I had some sacred furniture exposed to view. The hand of God stayed them from coming farther.[34]

Nor do the reports provide much evidence of the common assertion that the Jesuits enjoyed comforts lacking poorer secular priests. Instead, the impression is of no organised restitution but a grace-and-favour situation in which priests hoped other Jesuits would support them in need. Everyone was struggling for funds. In 1628, Fr John Macbreck proposed his own solution and made a heartfelt plea to the Vicar-General in Rome:

> Another absolutely necessary measure is that we should have some fixed place, in France or in Belgium, separately or in conjunction with others of the Society, it does not matter which, where our veteran workers can rest from their labours, and recover their strength, and where the new ones may be instructed for two whole years at least in their final studies, before they descend into the arena. For our Fathers, whether French or Belgian, are very reasonably unwilling and unable to attend to the wants of others, beyond their own numbers.[35]

Fr Abercromby would have concurred.

II

Abercrombie's proposed gifts to Scottish Catholics reveal clear gendered divisions. Gifts intended for men emphasised an outward political role in the offering of swords and other external signs of masculine importance. Alisdair Roberts has observed that historians tended to view Catholic survival as a masculine achievement: 'Indeed its clerical emphasis has caused the principal characters to emerge as men without women, or celibate priests'.[36] Yet Abercromby deliberated exactly on ways to appeal to women's faith and determination to ensure Catholicism's survival. For women, Abercromby's gifts are predominantly religious in nature: rosaries, Agnus Dei, statues 'carved or moulded in pottery', books on the Life of Christ and the Rosary 'beautifully bound', and catechisms, 'if there are any to be had', rings with 'Agnus Deis skilfully encased in crystal or gold', and relics 'which have touched the Chair of St. Peter'.[37] Whilst men were to focus on their governmental and courtly links, women were identified as repositories of the faith. They would be protectors of missionaries and, above all, those who maintained Catholicism into a new generation, their children providing the next wave of Scottish priests. In reality, Murphy noted that later Abercromby would become sceptical of the possibility of converting King James and his belief in the power of women is revealed best in his conversion of Queen Anna of Denmark in 1600.[38]

With no benefices, having kin connections determined the pathways of mission, and the role of women as protectors became paramount, as Abercromby had identified. The countesses of Abercorn, Linlithgow, and Atholl were prominent providers of safe accommodation for and financial support to Jesuits. The countess of Atholl protected three Jesuits according to Roberts, while Abercorn provided Fr Valens with a safe house for two years. In 1628, Fr Macbreck reported that the countess of Linlithgow hid Fr William Christie the Elder, even though 'The Earl is a most obstinate heretic, and the excellent Catholic lady keeps the Father in her house secretly without her husband's knowledge'. However, this led to Christie's imprisonment in the castle for six months, probably due to his fear of discovery.[39] Such fear was ever present, as Fr John Leslie decreed in his Annual letter for 1626:

> [A]ll members of our Society, are already proclaimed enemies of the State, traitors to our country, guilty of high treason, foes of God and religion, and are punished as such . . . The apprehension of imprisonment or death has perhaps made us, if anything, too timid, or at least, too cautious and solicitous.[40]

Communications by Jesuits emphasise their financial crises, yet also that they did not wish to burden their female benefactors lest they suffered pecuniary punishment for such actions as well as the practice of their faith.

McCoog argued that, after the disappointments of the first permanent Scottish mission, Vicar-General Claudio Acquaviva decided that resources should be concentrated upon educating the next generation. Thus, colleges in continental Europe became the focus of Scottish Jesuit energy: 'Throughout the seventeenth century, the Society would send fewer workers into the vineyard, but it would ensure that they were properly trained'.[41] Whilst this seems practical, it ignored the fundamental problem that Scotland needed priests in the field. Yet again, though, the desires of Catholic women seeking education for their sons and those of Jesuits to maintain a Scottish educational presence on the continent merged. Anson noted that students at Douai 'were nearly all sent there by the Jesuits in Scotland, and had been brought up in the country under their care'.[42] Hay decreed Jesuits at Douai 'particularly anxious to preserve the national characteristics of the college; they were determined to maintain it as a really Scottish school, staffed by Scottish teachers'. Scottish Catholic women helped such ventures. In 1629 the countess of Abercorn was excommunicated for trying to get her children to the continent to be educated.[43] In his Report of 1642–6, Macbreck bemoaned Lady Aboyne's death and the marchioness of Huntly's exile: Aboyne's 'house was a sort of asylum for Catholics for the celebration of divine worship . . . [Their loss] deprived the workers of the vineyard of a fortress and protection, and they were now less able to travel in safety.' Huntly's 'castle became a kind of miniature of the Church. Mass was said continually. More than one priest celebrating daily. Sermons were frequent and the Sacraments administered with great and encouraging results.'[44] Women's roles were undeniably predicated by Abercrombie and the Jesuits who followed upon contemporary gendered concepts of care, but they proved pivotal to mission. The life and work of the Scottish poet Sìleas na Ceapaich further illustrates the contacts fostered by Scottish Jesuits among the women of their homeland and the importance of the house of Gordon in preserving such links.

III

Sìleas na Ceapaich (Julia MacDonald of Keppoch) was declared by her biographer Colm Ó Baoill 'to be a dominant figure in the poetic transition between the seventeenth century and the eighteenth'.[45] Initially known for her Jacobite poetry, she is recognised now for her many hymns and religious poetry unabashed in their Catholic imagery, especially of sacramental devotion and Marian belief. She was the daughter of Gilleasbuig (Archibald), fifteenth chief of the Clan Ranald (MacDonald) of Lochaber. On his succession, her brother Colla was only eighteen and a student at St Andrews. The Marquis of Huntly became his adviser.[46] In 1685, Sìleas married Alexander Gordon of Camdell, near Tomintoul and moved to Banffshire. Gordon belonged to Huntly's extended family, acting as his factor in Lochaber. As such, he too would have spoken Gaelic: Allan Macinnes argues that the factors of the north-east landed families provided the bilingual conduit with their Gaelic-speaking tenants.[47] By 1700, Alexander and Sìleas owned Beldorney Castle, a few miles from Huntly in Aberdeenshire, locating them firmly within the Gordon ambit and the Jesuit contacts there. Sìleas's marriage joined two leading northern Scottish aristocratic families consistently linked with the fight to maintain Catholicism post-Reformation. James Stewart decreed that 'the Gordon Catholic establishment was central to the situation throughout the Highlands', sheltering some six Catholic schools as well as the secular seminary at Scalan. Both Gordons and MacDonalds of Keppoch appeared regularly in General Assembly and Presbytery records, accused of supporting Jesuits and secular priests on their lands.[48] Thus, whilst living in the era in which secular priests served the mission more regularly, through marriage Sìleas remained within the sphere of Jesuit influence.

Sìleas's love of poetry was lifelong. Her father, Gilleasbuig, was recognised as 'a cultured man ... and like so many of his family, he was a poet of considerable talent', while her brother, Angus Odhar, 'composed many Gaelic songs'.[49] During her husband's lifetime, their friend the famous harper Lachlan Mackinnon was a frequent visitor, 'bringing music and news of the family in the west'.[50] In turn through him, her hymns and songs reached back to Keppoch. Kenneth MacDonald has identified them sung in Lochaber generations after her death: two notably recovered this way reflected the depth of the loss of her eldest son, Gilleasbuig, and her daughter, Màiri.[51] Sìleas's poetry was part of, and survived due to, the Gaelic oral tradition, written down only after 1746.[52] Sarah Dunnigan suggests that the relative paucity of Catholic and nonconformist women's writing in this period resulted from their heretical and treasonable reputation.[53] In a world in which they were 'othered' as 'the enemy', this is highly plausible.[54] Therefore, it is through the strength of the Gaelic oral tradition as a tool against persecution that Sìleas's corpus survived: ironically preserved by eighteenth-century ministers transfixed by Gaelic oral verse considered criminal by earlier peers.[55]

Sìleas's work reveals a woman whose Catholic faith was her core, practised whenever possible and the support to which she turned in good times and bad. A corpus of twenty-three extant poems, songs and hymns remains. These are vibrant with biblical allegories and Catholic theology of the seven sacraments, including the 'five bastard sacraments' denounced by James in 1580.[56] For instance, in *An Eaglais*, 'The Church' becomes a castle:

> *They made stones from His crown of thorns and stairs from His passion cross; they welded it tightly together with fasting and prayer. Lady Mary is its floor. Twelve Apostles furnished it; they devoted much labour to it all their lives until they died.*[57]

Even her powerful political verse reflected her faith. Whilst many scholars have discussed the sophistication of her work, others have identified its utilisation of Jesuit theology. Barbara Hilliers analyses her Jacobite poem *Do Dh'Armm Righ Sheumais* (To King James's Army) and its incorporation of Aesop's fable of the dog, who seeking the illusion of more, loses what it already possessed, a tale 'which she evidently expected her audience to know and understand'.[58] It provides an example of the breadth of Sìleas's education, consistent with a family sending a brother to St Andrews. It raises questions about the discourse of the limited access to education for even aristocratic women in early modern Scotland and that it was the Protestant revolution that brought education to them.[59] Hilliers describes her poetry as that of a woman

> literate in Gaelic ... fully literate in English: she lived for the greater part of her life in a bilingual, bicultural world and her poetry shows abundant exposure to ... the political discourse of Jacobitism and the religious discourse of the Catholic Counter-Reformation ... Her religious poetry appears to be actively conversant and engaged with contemporary Catholic doctrine.[60]

Hilliers connects this interpretation of Aesop to the contemporaneous sermons of the German Counter-Reformation scholar Peter Hehel, SJ. Although Hilliers thinks that Sìleas's knowledge was 'probably mediated through English channels', more likely it resulted through her trilingual roots with the Scots-speaking Jesuits whom she encountered on Huntly lands.[61]

Ó Baoill sees in Sìleas's poetry the didactic formula of medieval religious verse. Further, in his assessment of 'Hymn to the Virgin Mary', in which Sìleas links the lives and suffering of Mary and Christ, this is shared by Peter Davidson. He argued that 'in this way it is reminiscent of texts for meditation in use among the early Jesuits, such as *The Mysteries of the Life of Christ our Lord* by Ignatius of Loyola. Sìleas, like Ignatius, is faithful to the Gospel narrative, though she tells it in her own informal words'. Ó Baoill posits that 'Songs of that kind may belong to an older tradition in which ordinary Catholics in Gaelic Scotland and Ireland, not having a Bible in central position in their church, derived some of their knowledge of biblical history from orally transmitted songs'.[62] This assumed even greater importance in post-Reformation Scotland when possession of a Catholic bible or missal merited severe punishment. Sìleas's words, thus, become sermons in verse, an important tool for a community with little recourse to mass and catechesis. According to McCoog, Salmerón, travelling in 1542 to see the Scottish Bishop Robert Wauchop in Armagh, spent two months in Edinburgh teaching the 'Spiritual Exercises' to Catholics there.[63] Nobles, in turn, took this knowledge back to their estate families to enter the oral tradition, both Scots and Gaelic, augmented when the Jesuit missionaries arrived.

Ó Baoill notes,

> We do not know nearly enough about the education available to Catholics in the seventeenth-century Highlands, but Sìleas's poetry suggests that she for one had a thoroughly traditional Catholic education. She might well have been taught by a priest, perhaps a chaplain, to the ruling Keppoch family; it is not surprising, of course, considering the official attitude to Catholicism at the time, that we have no evidence that there was such a chaplain.[64]

However, MacDonald suggests that no such chaplain existed as Lochaber was neglected until the Dominican Peter Cluan served between 1708 and 1714, long after Sìleas had left her birthplace. Instead, she argues, whilst

> the MacDonalds of Keppoch . . . were said by Royalists not to be averse to orthodox piety in the 1640s, they were derided by Devoyer and Lea [Irish missionaries] in 1687 as people without God and without religion because of their continuous cattle reiving. Clearly, little had been done to establish the spirit of Catholicism in Lochaber in the forty three years since the Royalists.

In between there was only one recorded visit pf a priest, Fr Francis White, in 1672.[65]

How, then, does this accord with the haunting spirituality of Sìleas's poetry so clearly rooted in understanding of Catholic theology and Jesuit spirituality, as suggested by Ó Baoill, Davidson and Hilliers? Her brother, as a declared Catholic, participated in the Jacobite risings of 1689–90 and

1715–16. In the interim, though, Colla was also recorded as swearing allegiance to the Kirk to obtain an Army commission for his brother Alasdair.[66] These, though, are recognisable examples of the politicised multi-confessionalism of Catholics participating in an underground faith, visible also in Colla's enrolment at St Andrews.[67] It reflected Fr Abercromby's earlier advice for Catholic survival. MacDonald's Irish missionaries, of course, were rivals to both Jesuit and secular priests and it is noteworthy that all were deeply critical of each other's work. Meanwhile, if Jesuits were loath to state exact dates and places they visited for fear of reprisals upon their supporters and parishioners, this was true of all priests operating underground in Scotland. It was accepted that communications were regularly intercepted, while news reaching Rome, spoken openly, fell easily into the hands of spies from the Reformed countries.[68]

Sìleas's early Catholic influence in Keppoch was probably Fr White. The Limerick Vincentian served Lochaber and Glengarry from 1651 until his death in February 1679 with only one year's absence in 1662 because of financial difficulties.[69] He emphasised education's importance, establishing schools wherever he served. Alexander Dunbar, the second Prefect-Apostolic, reported that White was in Lochaber with the secular priest, Mr Robert Munro, during the winter of 1672.[70] However, Dunbar continued that White faithfully 'visits the islands and the lands of Glengarry and all the mountain districts, as far as he is able, though he endures great fatigue and suffering'. This suggests that, before her marriage, Sìleas had an ongoing, if irregular, Catholic presence in her life, beyond MacDonald's one recorded visit by White.

Munro's presence in Lochaber provides another intriguing Jesuit link in Sìleas's early life. Though secular, Munro was trained by Jesuits at Douai and Scots College Rome. Abbé Macpherson apparently declared that the Society had hoped Munro would enter and 'the Jesuits laid all their snares to catch him for themselves, being a young man of uncommon sense and piety'. He was recommended as a missionary by Fr Adam Gordon, Rector at Douai, and by Fr Macbreck, who commended his fluency in Gaelic. Munro, therefore, is another possible channel for Sìleas's knowledge of Ignatian *Spiritual Exercises*. While MacDonald sees tales of reiving by the 'Lochaber Robbers' as a sign of loss of faith, MacWilliams argues that their secretive routes offered safety to White and other priests 'on a more peaceful mission'.[71]

Marriage into the Gordons brought Sìleas into not only one of the foremost Catholic families but one with a long record of supporting and providing priests for the Scottish Jesuit Mission. In November 1573, Fr William Crichton had recommended for training Thomas Gordon, brother of George, earl of Huntly.[72] Despite earlier reports that the family had abjured, the earl provided sanctuary for the first permanent Jesuit mission in 1584. This permitted Fr James Gordon and his nephew Fr Edmund Hay to work in Aberdeenshire and Banffshire. Gordon would become famous for his preaching, become Superior of the Mission in the 1590s and later important in the planning of John Ogilvie's mission.[73] Huntly also was involved in the affair of the Spanish Blanks in 1592, ostensibly to raise financial support for the Jesuits.[74] Other family members to serve as Jesuits included Fr Adam Gordon who worked in Scotland in between periods as Rector of the Scots College, Madrid and Douai, where he would die in 1665.[75] Fr Patrick Gordon served in the Highlands in the 1730s and also would become Jesuit Superior.[76]

Jesuit chaplains were a constant presence at Huntly and, later, Gordon Castles, including Fr Robert Stickell in the 1620s.[77] Chaplains resided in the castles during winter, leaving to preach to the Catholic community during the better weather. Fr Macbreck wrote in 1628 that Stickell 'labours actively, makes excursions mostly in the neighbourhood, and every year brings back many to the faith'.[78] He would be followed by Fr William Christie, who worked in Scotland for twenty years. In his last decade, he acted as chaplain to the marquis of Huntly, administering him the Last Rites in June 1636. Fr Christie's Scottish connection would continue when appointed rector at Douai in 1656.[79] Christie offers another example of Scots Jesuits entering the Society on the continent, serving the Scottish mission and 'retiring' from its stresses to become rector, in their turn, of the various European Jesuit colleges. In this way, new generations of Scottish Jesuits were trained by those experienced in the home mission. This reinforces John O'Malley's argument that the Society played a leading role in changing the concept of mission, breaking from the monasticism of the pre-Reformation Church and creating a new priest who shared the apostolic mission granted the first disciples to 'go out' and evangelise.[80]

It must be noted that the Gordons aided all missionaries who came their way, not only Jesuits. The marchioness of Huntly took the first Prefect-Apostolic, William Ballantyne, under her wing, between his appointment in 1653 and arrest and exile in 1656. Gordon Castle, thus, became a focal point for both Highland and Lowland missions.[81] Alexander Leslie's 1680 report on the Highland Mission suggests that Gordon hosted annual mission assemblies.[82] Similarly, the Barnabite Fr Hugh Ryan recorded a meeting there on 25 April 1687.[83] Huntly also acted as safe staging post for newly arrived missionaries. The Irish Vincentians Devoyer and Cahasay, the deriders of the faith of Sìleas's family, accompanied Leslie there in 1681 before going to the Highlands.[84] Similarly, Gordon offered a much-needed hospice for sick missionaries. Mr Burnet noted in 1687 that 'Mr Lea sickly come Downe to Gordon Castle just now to charge'.[85] In the Highlands at this time, ten missionaries were Irish and one the first Gaelic-speaking Scottish Jesuit, Fr Henry Forsyth, who worked Huntly lands between Glenlivet and Braemar. Thus, there was a greater level of fluidity in the Scottish Mission than delineations between Highland/Lowland or Jesuits/others have suggested. It would have been well known that the 4th marquis of Huntly was 'unwilling to put public promotions ahead of his personal adherence to the

Catholic faith'.[86] Under the stressful conditions of mission, Huntly acted as a necessary safe haven for all Catholic priests, also breaking down the paradigm of those who consorted only with the nobility and those only with the labouring classes. Hence, the understandable consternation in 1728 when Alexander Gordon died after a short illness and his widow abruptly ended their sons' Catholic education.[87] The loss of such protection was a major blow to all missionaries.

This reflects the turbulent era when Sìleas was composing her most religious and political works. Anson described it as an era of 'poverty and despair' for Scottish Catholics.[88] Six years after her death, it was reported to Rome that there were about nine thousand Catholics in Scotland.[89] Between 1689 and 1704, one-third of the Jesuit contingent in Scotland were arrested and imprisoned, including Fr Gordon, sent to the Edinburgh Tolbooth with Fr Mair and the future Bishop Thomas Nicolson.[90] Whilst Bishop Gordon reported in 1709 that Jesuits finally had accepted the authority of the Vicar-General in Scotland and that he was pleased with their obedience, he reiterated old ideas that they had access to finances from the Society and Scottish aristocrats not shared with their secular brethren.[91] He made similar claims about Irish clergy. If there were extra finances, they must have been minimal. In striking similarity to complaints reported by contemporary secular priests, in 1709 it was reported that in the summer months the four Jesuits in the Highlands

> are very badly off, having hardly a bed to sleep on, for they have no couch but the straw. They have neither wine nor beer to drink but only water and milk, and they eat barley bread, not well prepared. But they bear it all with unfailing good temper, giving all their attention to the care of the poor with no insignificant results.[92]

There is evidence that Sìleas still had contact with Jesuits despite the difficulties. Fr Charles Farquharson, SJ, revealed that in 1671 a Jesuit, Fr Forsyth (alias Forsay), converted his father, Lewis, and 'Mr Forsey departed the next night for Castle Gordon'. In turn, in 1706, Lewis permitted a priests' meeting on his land in Braemar, including Forsyth and Fr Stephen Maxwell, Jesuit Superior. This lasted several days and, according to the presbytery of Kincardine, some two hundred were confirmed by Bishop Nicolson. However, since Forsyth died in November 1699, it is more likely that it was another Jesuit working there: Robert Seton, John Innes or Hugh Strachan. Seton and Strachan operated while Sìleas was resident in the area. Moreover, the religious tenor of her poetry reflected their liturgical practices. Seton was devoted to Mary, using the rosary and Marian litanies as catechesis. Strachan wrote a Gaelic catechism, having accepted the need to learn the language to work effectively in the area.[93] This would place Sìleas's work firmly within the Jesuit Marianology disseminated in Post-Reformation Scotland including Abercromby's proposed gifts and the seventeenth-century rosary scenes painted at Provost Skene's House in

Aberdeen.[94] Such links help explain the strong Jesuit paradigms in Sìleas's work.

IV

There were undoubtedly serious problems in the various Jesuit missions undertaken in Scotland between the Reformation and the Society's dissolution. However, some assessments have concentrated too heavily on the political factors. Contemporary accounts were vehemently vocal in their dislike of Jesuits. No doubt tensions were fomented about priests Scottish in nationality, but owing allegiance to an international outwardly focused order. Yet it appears that searching for the spiritual footprints of Scottish Jesuits reveals an experience of mission more in common with their secular and orders brethren than previously suggested. They shared not only the same fears of discovery but also the poverty, disappointments and difficulties of finding safety inside and outside Scotland during the more intense periods of anti-Catholic activity. The division between Highland and Lowland missions was not as rigid as discourse suggested. Abercromby's 1580 recommendations provided an early recognition of the necessity to adapt Church liturgy to the conditions of mission. However, they fell foul of an established authority in Rome anxious to maintain the new Tridentine liturgy even under unsuitable conditions and determined to impose its missionary authority throughout Counter-Reformation Europe. Meanwhile, the interaction between members of the Jesuit missions and Scottish Catholic women reinforces their importance, as identified by Abercromby, from support for priests to protecting their children's education and maintaining knowledge of the faith. Jesuits certainly viewed women through the contemporary gendered lens, but this should not obscure the validity and importance of roles and responsibilities Scottish women adopted. It raises general questions about the lives of women in post-Reformation Scotland: their freedom of action, access to education and practice and preservation of their faith through oral rather than written forms. How many other Sìleas na Ceapaichs existed then? Educated women who understood not only the basic tenets of their faith, but also the sophistication of the spirituality espoused by contemporary Jesuits.

Notes

1. T. M. McCoog, SJ, ' "Pray to the Lord of the Harvest": Jesuit Missions to Scotland in the Sixteenth Century', *IR*, 53:2 (2002), 127.
2. James VI permitted the Countess of Sutherland a chaplain 'provided he was not a Jesuit'. A. Roberts, 'The Role of Women in Scottish Catholic Survival', *SHR*, 70 (1991), 132.
3. P. F. Anson, *Underground Catholicism in Scotland, 1622–1879* (Montrose: Standard Press, 1970), 67, 15.
4. F. A. Macdonald, *Mission to the Gaels: Reformation and Counter-Reformation in Ulster*

and the Highlands and Islands of Scotland 1560–1760 (Edinburgh: John Donald, 2006), p. 56.
5. M. Yellowlees, *'So Strange a monster as a Jesuiste': The Society of Jesus in Sixteenth Century Scotland* (Colonsay: House of Lochar, 2002).
6. Ibid., p. 3.
7. A. C. MacWilliam, 'A Highland Mission: Strathglass, 1671–1777', *IR*, 24 (1973), 5.
8. See special issue of the *Journal of Jesuit Studies*, 2015.
9. C. Johnstone, *Developments in the Roman Catholic Church, 1789–1829* (Edinburgh: John Donald, 1983), cited Macdonald, *Mission to the Gaels*, p. 14.
10. Cited Yellowlees, *So Strange a Monster*, 31.
11. A. D. Wright, 'Rome, the Papacy and the Foundation of National Colleges in the Sixteenth and Early Seventeenth Centuries' in R. McCluskey (ed.), *The Scots College Rome, 1600–2000* (Edinburgh: John Donald, 2000); M. Dilworth, 'Archbishop James Beaton II: A Career in Scotland and France', *RSCHS*, 23 (1989), 309–13.
12. A. I. Macinnes, 'Catholic Recusancy and the Penal Laws, 1603–1707', *RSCHS*, 23 (1987), 40.
13. R. E. Scully, 'Trickle Down Spirituality? Dilemmas of the Elizabethan Jesuit Mission', *Nederlandisch archief voor kerkgeschiedenis*, 85 (2005), 285–99.
14. *Monumenta Angliae III: England, Ireland, Scotland and Wales: Documents (1541–1562)*, ed. T. M. McCoog and L. Lukács (Rome: Institutum Historicum Societatis Iesu, 2000), p. lvii.
15. Yellowlees, *So Strange a Monster*, p. 35.
16. McCoog, 'Pray to the Lord', pp. 131–2, 140–1.
17. G. Martin Murphy, 'Robert Abercromby (1536–1613)', *ODNB;* McCoog, 'Pray to the Lord', p. 161. Abercromby declared after Glenlivet that he, Murdoch and Christie 'lived in caves, in secret and unfrequented places, perpetually moving from place to place ... Spies and officers are posted at all the inns, and in every parish, to discover our whereabouts, and give us up to the authorities'. In *Narratives of Scottish Catholics under Mary Stuart and King James VI*, ed. W. Forbes-Leith, 2 vols (Edinburgh: W. Paterson, 1885), I, pp. 226–9.
18. Murphy, 'Abercromby', *ODNB*.
19. W. J. Anderson, 'Narratives of the Scottish Reformation I: Report of Father Robert Abercrombie, S.J., in the Year 1580', *IR*, 7 (1956), p. 45.
20. McCoog, 'Pray to the Lord', pp. 140–2.
21. See M. Hay, *The Blairs Papers (1603–1660)* (London and Edinburgh: Sands & Co., 1929), pp. 58–9.
22. *The Constitutions of the Society of Jesus*, ed. and trans. George E. Ganss, SJ (St Louis: The Institute of Jesuit Sources, 1970), p. 275, cited McCoog, 'Pray to the Lord', p. 157.
23. Anderson, 'Narratives', p. 47.
24. A. MacDonell and D. McRoberts, 'The Mass Stones of Lochaber', *IR*, 17 (1966), p. 77.
25. A. D. Collins, 'Mass Magnified: The Large Missal in England and France, c.1350–c.1450' (Ph.D. Thesis, University of Edinburgh, 2017).
26. D. McRoberts, *Essays on the Scottish Reformation 1513 to 1625* (Glasgow: Burns, 1962).
27. J. Durkin, 'Sidelights on the Early Jesuit Mission in Scotland', *Scottish Tradition*,

13 (1984–5), pp. 34–5; M. A. Mullet, *The Counter-Reformation and the Catholic Reformation in Early Modern Europe* (London: Methuen, 1984).
28. Murphy, 'Abercromby', *ODNB*.
29. William Forbes-Leith, *Memoirs of Scottish Catholics: During the XVIIth and XVIIIth Centuries*, Volume 1 (London: Longmans, Green and Company, 1909), I, p.159.
30. MacDonell and McRoberts, 'Mass Stones', pp. 79–81.
31. Mary Purcell, *The Story of the Vincentians* (Dublin: All Hallows College, 1973), cited MacDonald, *Mission to the Gaels*, p. 144.
32. McDonell and McRoberts, 'Mass Stones', p. 77.
33. D. C. Maclean, 'Catholicism in the Highlands and Isles, 1550–1680', *IR*, 3 (1962), 5–6.
34. Forbes-Leith, *Memoirs*, I, p. 75.
35. Ibid., I, p. 11.
36. Roberts, 'Women in Scottish Catholic Survival', p. 129.
37. Anderson, 'Narratives', p. 42.
38. Murphy, 'Abercromby', *ODNB*; P. Anson, *The Catholic Church in Modern Scotland* (London: Burns, Oates & Washbourne, Ltd, 1937), p. 8.
39. Roberts, 'Women in Scottish Catholic Survival', pp. 14–141; Forbes-Leith, *Memoirs*, I, p. 10
40. Forbes-Leith, *Memoirs*, I, p. 13.
41. McCoog, 'Pray to the Lord', 159.
42. Anson, *Underground Catholicism*, p. 27.
43. Hay, *Blairs Papers*, p. 45.
44. Forbes-Leith, *Memoirs*, I, pp. 233–4.
45. C. Ó Baoill, 'Sìleas na Ceapaich' in T. O. Clancy and M. Pittock (eds), *The Edinburgh History of Scottish Literature*. Volume I (Edinburgh: EUP, 2007), p. 305.
46. N. H. Macdonald, *The Clan Ranald of Lochaber. A History of the MacDonalds or MacDonells of Keppoch* (Edinburgh: private, 1972), p. 24.
47. Macinnes, 'Catholic Recusancy', pp. 30–1.
48. J. Stewart, 'The Clan Ranald and the Catholic Missionary Successes, 1715–1745', *IR*, 45 (1994), 31–2.
49. Macdonald, *Clan Ranald*, pp. 21, 23.
50. C. Ó Baoill, 'NicDhomhnaill [MacDonald], Sileas [Sileas nighean Mhic Raghnaill] (c.1660–c.1729), Scottish Gaelic poet', *ONDB*.
51. K. Macdonald, 'Unpublished Verse by Sìlis Nu Mhic Raghnaill Na Ceapaich' in J. Carney and D. Greene (eds), *Celtic Studies. Essays in Memory of Angus Mathieson 1912–1962* (London: Routledge and Kegan Paul, 1968), pp. 78–9.
52. Ó Baoill, 'Sìleas na Ceapaich', p. 35.
53. S. Dunnigan, 'Introduction', in S. M. Dunnigan, C. M. Harker and E. S. Newlyn, *Women and the Feminine in Medieval and Early Modern Scottish Writing* (Basingstoke: Palgrave Macmillan, 2004), p. xxiv; M. B. Rowlands, 'Recusant Women, 1560–1640' in M. Prior (ed.), *Women in English Society, 1500–1800* (London: Routledge, 1985).
54. See Forbes-Leith, *Memoirs*, I, p. 151, for Jesuits' perception of this and their female protectors; C. Prunier, *Anti-Catholic Strategies in Eighteenth Century Scotland* (Frankfurt am Main: Peter Lang, 2004).
55. MacDonald, 'Unpublished Verse', p. 76.
56. Cited in Yellowlees, *So Strange a Monster*, p. 63.

57. Translation, C. Ó'Baoill, 'Neither In nor Out' in Dunnigan et al., *Women and the Feminine*, p. 144.
58. B. Hilliers, '"Cleas a'Choin Sholair? Aesop's Dog Fable in the Poetry of Sìleas na Ceapaich', in W. McLeod, A. Burnyeat, D. U. Stiùbhart, T. O. Clancy and R. Ó Maolalaigh (eds), *Bile ós Chrannaibh: A Festschrift for William Colliers* (Tigh a'Mhaide, Perthshire: Clann Tùirc, 2010), p. 195.
59. For instance, S. Nenadic, *Lairds and Luxury: The Highland Gentry in Eighteenth Century Scotland* (Edinburgh: John Donald, 2007), p. 112.
60. Hilliers, 'Aesop's Dog Fable', p. 195.
61. Ibid., pp. 205-7.
62. Ó Baoill, 'Sìleas na Ceapaich', p. 312.
63. McCoog, 'Pray to the Lord', p. 128.
64. Ó Baoill, 'Sìleas na Ceapaich', p. 312.
65. MacDonald, *Mission to the Gaels*, p. 250.
66. MacDonald, *Clan Ranald*, pp. 29–33.
67. A similar pattern is revealed in Paul Goatman, 'Religious tolerance and intolerance in Jacobean Scotland: The case of Archibald Hegate revisited', *IR*, 67 (2016), 159–81.
68. Forbes-Leith, *Memoirs*, I, pp. viii–ix.
69. MacWilliam, 'A Highland Mission', 80; MacDonald, *Mission to the Gaels*, p. 143.
70. C. Giblin, 'The Mission to the Highlands and the Isles, c.1670', *Franciscan College Annual* (Multyfarnham, 1954), p. 19, cited Macdonald, *Mission to the Gaels*, p. 148.
71. Catalogue of Missionary Priests' in J. F. S. Gordon, *The Catholic Church in Scotland* (Aberdeen, 1874), p. 584, cited MacWilliams, 'A Highland Mission', pp. 79–80.
72. McCoog, 'Pray to the Lord', p. 137.
73. Durkan, 'Sidelights', 35–6; W. Brown, *John Ogilvie* (London: Burns, Oates & Washbourne, Ltd, 1925), pp. 25–6.
74. McCoog, 'Pray to the Lord', 146–7; F. Shearman, 'Crichton and the Spanish Blanks', *IR*, 4 (1953), 60.
75. Anson, *Catholic Church*, p. 25.
76. B. M. Halloran, 'Jesuits in 18th Century Scotland', *IR*, 52 (2001), 83, 86–7.
77. Forbes-Leith, *Memoirs*, I, p. x.
78. Ibid., I, p. 5.
79. Ibid., I, pp. 80, 82, 179–80.
80. J. W. O'Malley, *Saints or Devils Incarnate? Studies in Jesuit History* (Leiden: Brill, 2013), pp. 3–10.
81. MacDonald, *Mission to the Gaels*, p. 141.
82. Anson, *Underground Catholicism*, p. 76.
83. SCA, CC1/8015, Canon William Clapperton, 'Memoirs of Missionary Priests', cited Macdonald, *Mission to the Gaels*, p. 156.
84. Macdonald, *Mission to the Gaels*, p. 158; Anson, *Underground Catholicism*, p. 80.
85. SCA Blairs Papers, BL1/118/16 cited Macdonald, *Mission to the Gaels*, p. 166.
86. B. Robertson, *Lordship and Power in the North of Scotland: The Noble House of Huntly, 1603–1690* (Edinburgh: John Donald, 2011), p. 181.
87. Stewart, 'Clanranald', p. 36.
88. Anson, *Catholic Church*, p. 89.
89. APPF, Congregazione Particolari Scozia, vol. 32 (1696–1707) Missioni di Scozia, 1733–36, f. 246, April 1735. Thanks to Allan Macinnes for this source.

90. Halloran, 'Jesuits', pp. 88–9; Anson, *Catholic Church*, p. 55
91. W. Doran, 'Bishop Thomas Nicolson and the Roman Catholic Mission to Scotland, 1694–1718', *IR*, 39 (1988), 109–32.
92. Forbes-Leith, *Memoirs*, II, p. 253.
93. AUL, Farquharson MSS 537 cited A. C. Macwilliam, 'The Jesuit Mission in Upper Deeside, 1671–1737', *IR*, 23 (1972), 22–39.
94. Fern Insh, 'Recusants and the Rosary: A Seventeenth Century Chapel in Aberdeen', *Recusant History*, 31 (2012), 195–218.

CHAPTER THREE

Liturgical Problems on the Catholic Mission: Franciscan Mission to the Highlands in the Seventeenth Century

Thomas McInally

In 1580, Robert Abercromby, in his annual report to General Claudio Acquaviva, the head of the Society of Jesus, stated that the situation in Scotland was inimical to Catholics in general and Jesuits in particular. He was writing from Braunsberg in what is now north-eastern Poland but had recently returned from Scotland where he had been recruiting students for the new Northern College which he and other Scottish Jesuits had helped set up as part of the University of Braunsberg. In his letter he stressed that any Jesuit visiting Scotland would have to go in disguise – that is, not wear clerical garb – and that any correspondence should be written in cipher since letters would be read by others. He made these points to Acquaviva because he was proposing that there should be a Jesuit mission to Scotland and the general needed to know that a mission there could not be conducted in the same fashion as those to the New World or the Far East. The reason for his concern was that the religious situation in Scotland was dominated by political issues as much as by confessional differences. Unlike in most European countries, the Reformation in Scotland had been established by act of parliament. The Reformation Parliament of 1560 promulgated the Calvinist Confession of Faith and enacted penal laws whereby Catholicism was outlawed and saying mass was punishable by death. Notwithstanding the dominance of the Protestant lords in parliament the question of the religion of the country was far from settled. The next two decades saw dissension and civil war. The defeat of the supporters of Mary Queen of Scots at the Battle of Langside in 1568 forced the queen to flee to England but did not end the conflict. The struggle between the Lords of the Congregation and the Catholic nobles continued for a further five years in what has been called the Marian Wars. The triumph of the Protestants was followed by political squabbling among the victors but a measure of peace was established in 1578 when James VI gained his freedom from the series of regents who had had custody of him from infancy. By then, however, Scotland was in the control of the Calvinist lords and the Kirk's position was dominant. The pre-Reformation Church had been largely destroyed. Priests and members of religious orders had either ascribed to the Confession of Faith, had gone into exile or had ceased performing any of their religious duties openly, if at all. Before the end of the century all of the Scottish provinces of the religious orders had been disbanded and the few secular priests who remained were in hiding.[1] Despite the unpromising situation Acquaviva agreed to establish a Scottish mission with Abercromby as its head and it was from this low point that he and his companions began a Counter-Reformation in Scotland in an attempt to restore Catholicism.

I

In the half century following the start of the Jesuit mission, seminaries were set up on the continent to train Scots for the priesthood. Initially their students joined the Jesuits who for a while ran the sole coherent mission in Scotland. The Jesuit mission was later joined by Franciscan and Dominican missionaries working among the Gaelic speakers of the Highlands and Islands. At that time, owing to their small numbers and lack of financial support, secular priests were unable to contribute much to these efforts. It was only in the 1660s, with increasing numbers of priests being ordained by the Scots colleges abroad and financial support from Propaganda Fide, that seculars were able to organise a mission of their own. Initially each of the different religious orders worked independently with little co-ordination of effort between them. The religious orders took fundamentally different approaches to the planning and operation of their missions. That was particularly true of the Jesuits and Franciscans. Given the origins and founding principles of these orders, that was perhaps inevitable. From its inception the Society of Jesus had seen its role as a missionary one with direct submission to the pope. It quickly became engaged in preaching and education and took on a pre-eminent role in the Catholic Reformation worldwide. The Franciscan order was already long established when the Church was faced with the upheavals of the Reformation. It had been founded in the thirteenth century as a mendicant order especially dedicated to poverty and preaching. In Scotland the Jesuit strategy was to engage with the elite in society by stationing priests in the households of those members of the nobility who were sympathetic to the Catholic religion. Even before the Franciscans began their work in Scotland, the Jesuit approach had succeeded to such an extent that Lord Burghley, Elizabeth of England's chancellor, in 1590 reported to the queen that:

> all the Northern part of the Kingdom, including the shires of Inverness, Caithness, Sutherland, and Aberdeen, with Moray, and the Sherrifdoms of Buchan, of Angus, of Wigton, and of Nithsdale, were either wholly or for the greater part, commanded mostly by noblemen who secretly adhered to that faith (Catholicism), and directed in their movements by Jesuits and priests, who were concealed in various parts of the country, especially in Angus.[2]

Burley's report was essentially correct. At the time he was making this observation the missionaries' annual reports to Rome confirmed that they were resident in the homes of Kirconnell, Munches, Terregles and Traquair in the south-west and south, also in the palace of Seton (the Scottish Lord Chancellor's residence) near Edinburgh and in the north-east in the castles of Gordon (Huntly), Letterfourie, Slaines and Strathbogie.[3] The overall Jesuit strategy was vindicated in 1598 when Robert Abercromby received James VI's queen, Anna of Denmark, into the Church. Their approach was, however, in complete contradiction to decrees of the Council of Trent. When Robert Abercromby wrote his letter to Acquaviva in 1580 he knew that it would present the Society's general with difficulties. Specifically the clandestine protocols he was recommending ran counter to the liturgical provisions laid down by the Council.

The Council had been called in 1545 in an attempt to reconcile the differences between the conservative and reforming factions in the Church and thereby avoid a permanent split between Catholics and Protestants. The alpine city of Trentino had been chosen to hold the meetings since it was deemed to be in neutral territory between the two confessional blocs. The discussions ranged over theological issues and the failings and abuses within the Church and, although they failed in their attempt to maintain unity, over eighteen years of intermittent sessions the Catholic delegates produced a series of canons and decrees which defined points of faith and liturgical observances. Their intentions were to clarify doctrine and purge the Church of the abuses which the reformers had identified and attacked. The Council's pronouncements were to represent the Catholic position on these matters for centuries. The published outcome of the Council also represented a master plan for Catholic efforts to counter the criticisms of the Protestant reformers. On completion of the Council's final session in 1563 implementation of the new canons and decrees became fundamental to the Counter-Reformation. These were vigorously applied by the reigning pope, Gregory XIII. As Cardinal Boncompagni, he had been a papal delegate at the opening of the Council and had helped formulate its findings. On being elected pope he became a driving force in the Catholic Reformation. Ignatius Loyola had founded the Society of Jesus as a religious order which reported directly to the papacy. Obedience to papal ordinance was critical to the Society's rule. Its adherence to the Tridentine canons and decrees was intended to be without question. The council had issued its final deliberations only seventeen years prior to Abercromby's letter, and compliance with them was still being closely scrutinised within the Church. Worthy though the intentions of the Council were, the strictures which it laid down were what in modern terms would be known as an attempt at 'micro-management' which fell foul of 'the Law of Unintended Consequences'. The canons which the council had drawn up were seen as eternal and universal truths but the decrees covered codes of behaviour and liturgical practices and had been drafted to suit situations where the Church was dominant.

Observing the council's decrees in hostile Protestant countries was often to present formidable problems to missionaries.

The twenty-second session of the Council of Trent which sat in 1562 stated, in its decree concerning the things to be observed and to be avoided in the celebration of mass, that priests should not 'suffer the holy sacrifice to be celebrated ... in private houses; or, at all, out of the church, and those oratories which are dedicated solely to divine worship'. This stipulation had been made to ensure that 'the mass be celebrated with all religious service and veneration'.[4] By using the homes of their protectors to say mass the Jesuits were breaking this Tridentine decree and violating papal ordinance. However, they argued that they were keeping not only to the spirit but also to the letter of the decree by designating an apartment within each house as a chapel and consecrating it as such. Outwith the times when services were held these chapels had the appearance of ordinary domestic rooms in order to avoid detection. This approach illustrates the Jesuits' pragmatism and the resourcefulness which they showed in overcoming the many liturgical problems with which they were faced.

Despite its success in Scotland, the Society of Jesus did not serve in the Western Highlands and Islands, regions which Rome designated *Montana Scotiae*. The Gaelic language presented them with a problem. The Scots Colleges abroad were not recruiting native Gaelic speakers as students and consequently there was a dearth of priests who could minister to these communities.[5] By 1611, a number of requests had been made by Catholic chieftains to Pope Paul V to send priests to Scotland to work among their clans.[6] The Irish and Scottish Gaelic languages were still mutually intelligible[7] and, in the absence of Scottish priests who could speak Gaelic, Irish priests from Ulster were considered for the mission. The problem was passed to the papal nuncio in the Spanish Netherlands, Lucio Morra, who in 1617 approached the Irish provinces of the Franciscan and Dominican orders to request that they establish a mission in *Montana Scotiae*. The Dominicans refused, saying that their resources were fully stretched in dealing with their responsibilities in Ireland.[8] Initially the Franciscans reacted in the same manner, stating that their Irish benefactors would not be so generous if they learned that part of their alms was being spent on a mission in Scotland. However, after some deliberation and especially the promise of financial support from the papacy they agreed to the request. The papal choice of the Irish Franciscans for the Scottish mission was due to a number of reasons other than the convenience of a common language. From the second half of the sixteenth century in many parts of Catholic Europe communities of Irish[9] had been established together with colleges for the education of Irish youth.[10] France was particularly attractive to many Irish students. By 1650 it was claimed that Paris had more Irish students than students from any other part of the world. Eminent Irish scholars such as David Rothe, bishop of Ossary, had based themselves in Paris and published theological works there. In Louvain, John Colgan, the Franciscan friar and intellectual, built networks of contacts particularly with Rome.[11] By the early seventeenth century, Irish intellectual life represented a significant part of the European Counter-Reformation. Many Irish students on completion of their studies remained in France and sought employment within the diocesan structures of the French Church or relied on the expatriate Irish communities for support. There were more Irish priests available in France than could be easily supported. The request for help in the Scottish Mission was directed to the Irish community in continental Europe because of their pre-eminence in numbers of priests available and commitment to Counter-Reformation work as well as their linguistic suitability for the mission in Gaelic-speaking Scotland.

There was another reason why the Irish Franciscans were suitable for the proposed mission. A small number of Scots were members of the Irish province of the order. Following the dissolution of the Scottish province of the Franciscan and Dominican orders which happened in the 1570s, any Scot wishing to join these orders was directed to their Irish province. Two of these recruits had earlier gone to Scotland to gather information on the state of affairs in their homeland. John Ogilvie, an ordained Franciscan, had gone as a missionary to Scotland in 1612 travelling by way of England. John Stuart, a lay brother, followed him a year later.[12] Ogilvie remained working in Scotland but Stuart reported back to their mother house in Louvain and although he could not give an encouraging account of conditions he was able to provide information on the best means of travelling from the Spanish Netherlands to the Highlands.

The challenges which the two friars faced in *Montana Scotiae* did, however, fit well with the Franciscan tradition of service. The order had been formed in the early thirteenth century by St Francis with a commitment to poverty and hardship along with chastity and obedience. Francis had obtained formal recognition for his fledgling order from Pope Honorius II who also approved the Franciscan's founding regulations in the document *Regula Bullata*. The rules were laid out in twelve short chapters and were intended to ensure that Francis's commitment to total poverty was maintained.[13] Despite the good intention, this proved impossible and the rules were continually amended to take account of the growing size and importance of the order. The Franciscans gained a reputation as preachers and were used in the fourteenth and fifteenth centuries by the Church as missionaries to non-Christian lands such as Syria and Africa and in the fifteenth and sixteenth centuries as missionaries to the New World and India. Over much of their early history, dissensions occurred between those committed to total poverty and others who were prepared to own possessions which they viewed as useful to their vocation. This led to the formation of differing branches of the order which, in turn, led to additional differences springing up particularly between the Italians (Cismontane) and their northern brethren (Tramontane). The Irish province kept to the strict vows of poverty as Friars Minor and followed the order's original *Regula Bullata*.

The principal house of the province was St Anthony's College in Louvain but in order to function as missionaries in Ireland and later Scotland the Irish Franciscans needed to seek dispensation from a number of the regulations of the *Regula Bullata*. Chapter five of the *Regula* laid a prohibition on friars handling money. Chapter six expanded on this prohibition by explaining the proper activities which could be undertaken to earn a living but any payment received was to be in the form of life's necessities, food, shelter etc. In addition friars were forbidden to ride a horse and were required to go everywhere on foot. These conditions were insisted upon to ensure that nothing would distract a Franciscan from his penitential obligations or lead to *otiositas* (a leisurely life).

II

Adherence to these particular requirements in most places in Britain would have marked the missionaries out as alien and made it impossible for them to adopt any kind of realistic disguise on their travels. When Lucio Morra's request to set up a mission in Scotland was made, the guardian of the Franciscans in Louvain, Hugh MacCaghwell, was able to present his missionaries with faculties which allowed them, among other things, to use money, ride horses and leave off their religious habit.[14] These concessions were not given lightly. The rules of the order were detailed even to the point of restricting the quality of the grey cloth to be used in the Franciscans' robes. Every aspect of their lives was determined to ensure a constant awareness of their vow of poverty. The financial negotiations between St Anthony's College and Rome lasted until 1619 and it was only when they were concluded that the mission was able to start. Two Irish friars, Patrick Brady and Edmund McCann, accompanied by John Stuart, in the guise of mercenaries returning from the European wars set out to work in the west of Scotland. They had each been given sixty florins[15] and the two priests had been provided with a chalice and everything necessary for saying mass. If these materials had been discovered by the authorities it would have meant immediate arrest. Missionaries in Britain had developed ingenious ways of disguising such items. The school archives at Stonyhurst College in Lancashire have preserved a set of mass vestments kept in a pedlar's pack. They were designed to have the appearance of cloth samples for a travelling draper. An unnamed Jesuit working in the north-west of England in the seventeenth century had used them without detection by the Protestant authorities. There is no record of how Brady and McCann camouflaged their mass equipment but they would have taken pains to make it fit with their personas as soldiers.

They travelled via Ireland and took over three months to reach the west of Scotland. On arrival Fr Brady began working in Morar and Lochaber in the Highlands while McCann travelled to the Hebrides. Br Stuart worked with both Irish priests as well as John Ogilvie who had remained behind when he had returned to Louvain. Stuart used his time teaching catechism. Highland society was for the most part illiterate but the people were not uneducated. Through their strong oral tradition there was a large stock of stories, poems, songs and family histories. Memorising these works was fundamental to Gaelic culture. In explaining and reciting the catechism Br Stuart was instructing not just those who heard him but others who would later hear reports of his work. The ability to memorise instruction was an important feature of Highland society that the Irish missionaries were to make particular use of. Before long, however, Fr McCann's activities attracted the attention of the Kirk and in 1620 he was arrested and taken to Aberdeen.[16] He was tried there in an ecclesiastical court and imprisoned. After two years, through the intervention of the French ambassador, he was released but exiled with the court's standard threat of execution if he returned to Scotland.[17] After Edmund McCann's capture, Brady, Stuart and Ogilvie remained as the only active Franciscan representatives of the Irish/Scottish Mission.

On returning to Louvain, McCann found that another party of Franciscans was being prepared for the Scottish Mission. While he had been imprisoned, a major change had occurred in the Church's organisation. During his brief reign, Pope Gregory XV had created a special department to oversee the Church's world mission, Congregazione per lEvangelizzazione dei Populi o 'Propaganda Fide'. It took precedence over all religious orders and was responsible for approving and directing all missionary activity. This innovation was not met with universal approval, especially by the Jesuits, but the Irish Franciscans complied with the papal directive. The Scottish Mission[18] was a low priority for Propaganda Fide. Greater opportunities for evangelisation existed in the New World and the Far East and it saw these lands as better choices for investing its limited resources. However, Pope Urban VIII, who as Cardinal Maffeo Barberini had been cardinal protector of Scotland, instructed the new department to fund another group of friars from St Anthony's to work in *Montana Scotiae*.[19] It was this group of new missionaries that Edmund McCann encountered on his return to Louvain. Despite the draconian terms of his sentence of exile, he immediately joined them to return to Scotland. The group, which in addition to McCann consisted of Paul O'Neill, Patrick Hegarty and Cornelius Ward, set off for Scotland in September 1623.[20] Working under the auspices of the newly created Congregation for the Propagation of the Faith they were required to follow its instructions on how the mission should be run. As paymaster the Congregation could insist on this condition even though as events transpired it was often remiss in its payments to the missionaries. One of its requirements was that the Franciscans should submit an annual report on the progress being made. It is from these reports together with letters of complaint to Rome that we have knowledge of the problems that the friars faced in adhering to the general liturgical procedures stipulated by Propaganda Fide. Before they left St Anthony's, the papal nuncio met with the group and instructed them on Rome's requirements. Lucio Morra made clear to the Franciscans that in all of their dealings with Propaganda Fide first they would have to communicate through him as its representative. Bound by their oath of obedience, the Franciscans had no choice but to agree. However, Edmund McCann had first-hand experience of the conditions to be faced in Scotland which he no doubt explained to his fellow missionaries. It is clear from their later behaviour that from the start the Irish had their own way of doing things. Where Rome's instructions proved impractical they wrote via the nuncio to ask for dispensation. While waiting for the inevitably delayed reply they acted as they thought the situation required. It was in matters of liturgy that the need to act in this manner was most pronounced and on occasion when they were denied, rather than comply with impractical instructions, they repeated their request in writing.[21]

The small party travelled first to Ireland in order to sail from Antrim to Kintyre where they met a prominent local clansman, Hector McNeill. McNeill provided them with guides to lead them to other chieftains whom he knew to be sympathetic to Catholicism. In this way, the party almost immediately separated and to took up mission stations in different parts of *Montana Scotiae*. Coll MacDonald of Colonsay and Roderick MacLeod of Harris were among the first chiefs the missionaries visited. By this time, the Franciscans were in breach of one of the strictures that the papal nuncio had placed on them. Their instructions were to meet together as a group at least once every three nights to confer on their work.[22] The distances involved made this impossible and the stipulation shows the level of ignorance that the Roman authorities had of the true nature of the conditions in Scotland. A liturgical issue soon arose regarding where the friars were to hold services. Often they had no choice but to conduct them in the open since there were no 'churches or oratories' available to them and the homes of their congregations were too small or otherwise unsuitable.[23] Occasionally they were able to use abandoned pre-Reformation churches such as the chapel dedicated to St Ninian on the island of Sanda (their first place of landing in Scotland) and similar derelict structures on the islands of Eigg and Oronsay but this was exceptional.[24] The scarcity of surviving pre-Reformation churches and chapels was not only due to them having fallen into disrepair through neglect: some were deliberately destroyed during the frequent bouts of clan warfare.[25] The islanders were conscious of their Catholic heritage and directed the missionaries to use the former churches wherever possible and it is clear that they viewed the ruins with respect. On at least one occasion – on Eigg – the people asked the Franciscans to reconsecrate their church and its small cemetery.[26]

Unorthodox places of worship did not present Propaganda Fide with a problem, and permission was granted to say mass in the most convenient space available, but when Cornelius Ward asked that the friars be allowed to omit using candles while saying mass the Roman authorities were unwilling to agree.[27] The impracticality of candles at an open air service in the west of Scotland was difficult for them to understand. Rome held to the decree that the Church 'employed ceremonies such as . . . lights . . . derived from an apostolic discipline and tradition'. The adherence to this point illustrates the bureaucratic mindset of Propaganda Fide. The Council of Trent's stipulation on the use of candles was driven principally by a desire to limit the number of candles used at services because an undesirable practice had grown up of filling churches with hundreds of candles. The decree on their use was to insist on moderation.[28] The Irish dispensed with candles anyway. Their attitude to Rome was that it was easier to obtain forgiveness than it was to get permission. They had run a mission in Scotland for five years before Propaganda Fide had become involved and they relied on their experience to determine how matters should be ordered. Attempts to control the Irish went as far as Rome trying to insist that they should write in Latin and use the ciphers with which they had been provided rather than write their reports in Gaelic. Propaganda Fide informed them that it was difficult for them to get anyone in Rome to translate their letters. The Irish continued to write in Gaelic, saying that the British authorities had the same problem which was why it was safer to write in Gaelic than in cipher.[29] Another liturgical practice from which they asked for dispensation was the use of servers at mass.[30] Their request arose because visits to some communities such as Bute and Kintyre had to be short and secretive. The friars had no time to train members of the congregation in the correct Latin responses. Where their visits were of longer duration there was no problem since, due to the oral tradition of Gaelic culture, congregations could easily memorise long passages of prayers such as the Pater Noster and Ave Maria. The friars would teach the prayers to a few who in turn would instruct the rest of the community. When the priest came to conduct services his time could be spent explaining the meanings and purposes of the prayers rather than teaching by rote.

    The Franciscan method of evangelising fitted well in other ways with the culture of their Gaelic hosts. Like the Jesuits they saw their ministry as one of preaching. One of the many stories surrounding St Francis concerns his sermons to the birds, animals and fish when people were unwilling to listen. The Franciscan order from its beginnings was open to unusual ways of reaching out to people. A tradition grew up in the order in Italy of telling Bible stories and illustrating moral principles in poetry and song. In their mission work in Ireland the Franciscans had created a repertoire of similar poems in Gaelic. Fr Ward was particularly gifted in this respect. He had grown up in a family versed in the bardic tradition using classical Gaelic poetry. Classical Gaelic was as respected in Scotland as it was in Ireland. In 1624 Ward posed as an itinerant bard to gain access to Sir John Campbell of Calder. He had composed a poem in praise of Calder and was allowed to stay and entertain his guests. After three days he had gained the laird's confidence and revealed his true identity to his host and was able convert him to Catholicism.[31] The Franciscans' sermons included poems and songs in contemporary Gaelic, which were memorised by the worshippers who had otherwise little access to such instruction. The friars' services thereby had an element of entertainment which was welcomed by their congregations. As well as their devotional purpose, these poems and songs could be used as part of the social fabric of the community when the priests were absent, as was often the case due to the size of their 'parishes' and the ever-present risk of discovery by the authorities, both Kirk and State.

The friars attempted to expand on the social integration of religion in another way by engaging their congregations in fraternities. In a letter dated 19 March 1626 they asked for the faculty (authority) to establish the 'Confraternity of the Cord' in *Montana Scotiae*. The Franciscan 'Confraternity of the Cord' was a post-Tridentine foundation. It was first approved by Pope Sixtus V in 1585 but was given additional privileges by Paul V in 1607.[32] Medieval confraternities had been essentially guild-based and largely parochial. Although religious observance was intended to be their *raison d'être* (the parish priest normally held their services and acted as spiritual guide), the exclusive nature of the guilds often meant that their social functions came to dominate. Tridentine reforms were intended to rectify this by making them more inclusive. In addition to parish confraternities, religious orders set up their own with membership open to all (even women!). Each branch was affiliated to the arch-confraternity which in the case of the Franciscans was based at Assisi.[33] In its reply to their request, Propaganda Fide referred the missionaries to their superiors in the Franciscan order at St Anthony's since Rome had no objection to make.[34] It is not known if permission was given but it is unlikely that the guardian of St Anthony's would have refused. The concept of confraternity would have been recognised by and would have appealed to the communities of the Highlands and Islands who identified themselves on the basis of kinship and clan membership. There is no evidence that the friars were successful in setting up any confraternities or that they even tried although the request for permission would not have been made if they had had no intention of acting on it. Successful implementation would have been difficult, however. Two major obstacles would have been the poverty of the population and the hostility of the Protestant authorities. The legacies of confraternities in Italy and elsewhere in Catholic Europe lie in the chapels and religious objects that they sponsored. In the seventeenth century people in the west of Scotland would have been as unable to afford such displays of devotion as the Kirk and State would have been unwilling to allow them to flourish. Any success that the Franciscans might have had in setting up confraternities would have been limited in public display and short-lived. Survival of confraternity activity would have been near impossible once the priests had left the community.

III

Attacks on the missionaries by ministers of the Kirk continued throughout the whole of their time in Scotland. They had to move frequently to avoid arrest. Fr McCann had been arrested in 1620 on his first visit and spent two years in prison. Br Stuart was arrested and sent to London in 1624. He was released on the orders of King James and exiled. His treatment during this period was harsh and on release he survived only a few months, dying at St Anthony's College in 1625.[35] In Caithness in 1627 Fr Brady was attacked by fourteen ministers of the Church of Scotland, thrown from his horse, robbed and left severely injured.[36] Cornelius Ward was arrested and sent to London where he spent two years in prison from 1630 to 1632. The other missionaries fared no better and each of them was arrested and imprisoned on at least one occasion.[37] These experiences gave rise to a continuous point of contention between them and Propaganda Fide. The Irish insisted on moving whenever danger threatened. The Roman authorities required them to stay within designated mission stations. The source of this disagreement came from another pronouncement of the Council of Trent. At one of the earliest sessions held in 1547, the council laid great stress on priests being attached to specific parishes and that they should not leave them without the permission of their bishop or the superior of their order.[38] The council's intention was to avoid dereliction of duties to parishioners and prevent doctrinally suspect priests or even pretenders being able to say mass in places where they were unknown. Their concerns in this matter continued throughout the whole period of the council. The third decree of the twenty-fourth session, the second last of the council, in 1563 stipulated that an annual visitation of each parish should be made by a bishop or authorised depute whose purpose was 'to lead to sound and orthodox doctrine, by banishing heresies'.[39]

These points clearly did not relate to the Irish Franciscans in Scotland but Propaganda Fide was influenced also by its desire that missionaries be supported by their congregations rather than by stipends from Rome. In its view, by continuously leaving his station the missionary prevented a bond of financial dependency being developed between him and his congregation. In their letters the Irish argued that the opposite was the case. The people of the west, they wrote, were so poor that the priest felt obliged to move on after a few weeks to avoid being too great a drain on their limited resources and straining their hospitality. Propaganda Fide appears to have had its misconceptions of conditions in Scotland reinforced by the advice being proffered by the Scottish principal of the Pontifical Scots College in Rome, Patrick Anderson, who was concerned that the Irish were usurping part of the role of the Scottish Church. This was in opposition to the rector of the Royal Scots College in Madrid, Hugh Semple, who argued strongly in their favour and even provided financial support when Propaganda Fide was remiss in meeting its commitments to the Irish. It would appear that the Roman authorities needed little encouragement to neglect the Scottish mission. A letter survives in the archives of Propaganda Fide written by Fr Ward in July 1634 shortly after he was released from prison which shows the extent of the neglect. The letter is addressed to the secretary of the Congregation of Propaganda Fide and in it the priest complains that he had received what he describes as the miserable allowance[40] decreed for the missionaries by Propaganda Fide on only three occasions in the twelve years he had been on the Scottish mission. He emphasises his dissatisfaction by writing that he obtained the payments only by travelling from Scotland to Belgium to deliver his annual report to the nuncio and collect the money in person. In the letter he makes clear that the fault lies with the Congregation and not the nuncio since there had been no response to the communications which the Irish had sent via the nuncio to Rome. The tenor of the letter is a mixture of anger and disappointment. The priest is anxious to stress the need to help the Scottish Mission but he is direct in expressing his frustration notwithstanding his opening address of '*Reverendissime domine*' (Most reverend lord).

Living conditions on the mission were harsh even for Franciscans dedicated to a life of poverty and hardship. Food and shelter were not easy to come by and were often of poor quality. In a report to Propaganda Fide in April 1625 they wrote that they had to sleep in the open for several nights at a time and on occasions they had to eat only shellfish which they had collected themselves from the seashore. Of the inhabitants of the western Highlands they wrote that they 'have a greater taste for military exploits than for food and are content with fare that would be scarcely sufficient for other people when fasting'.[41] Even so it is clear that the Irish were forced to rely heavily on their Scottish parishioners to survive. Their hardships were in keeping with the earliest rule of St Francis. Chapters five and six of the *Regula Bullata* insist that the friars work for their living and receive payment only in kind. The communities of the west of Scotland operated largely on a barter system and coins were in short supply. Payment of the priests in board and lodging was usually all that was possible. Additionally, the Highlanders on occasion provided protection from the authorities of the State and Kirk. In a testimonial sent to Rome in 1629, Coll Ciotach MacDonald, laird of Colonsay, commended Fr Ward, saying that he had visited the island three times converting almost all its inhabitants but had been attacked by a group of heretics and ministers. On that occasion, the laird had gone to his aid 'at risk to his life and the loss of his goods'. In rescuing the priest he had suffered severe injury.[42] MacDonald was probably exaggerating his losses, perhaps in the forlorn hope of receiving compensation from Rome. He had a formidable reputation and his appearance on the scene would mostly likely have been enough to make the attackers hand over their victim with little argument.

The Franciscans earned their keep by saying mass, conferring the sacraments and conducting religious ceremonies such as baptisms, marriages and funerals. The marriage provision was particularly valued since it legitimised unions and safeguarded inheritances by protecting against claims of illegitimacy which could disqualify the couples' offspring.[43] In ministering to their parishioners the missionaries moved continuously around *Montana Scotiae* serving communities as far north as Caithness and south to Kintyre. All of the Hebrides were included in their territories with Harris and Barra in the Outer Hebrides being particularly supportive along with many of the small isles (for example Colonsay and Canna) of the Inner Hebrides. On the mainland they regularly visited Lochaber and Morar as well as having a near-permanent presence in Caithness. Frequently, however, they had to flee Scotland for their own safety. This usually meant retreat to Ireland. The need for this had been recognised at the outset of the mission and Hugh MacCaghwell, the guardian of St Anthony's, had raised the matter of providing a safe house in Ulster for the first missionaries in 1618.[44] It took until 1626 before this point was conceded by the nuncio in Brussels by which time a number of the friars had been arrested and exiled. Rome gave the Franciscans permission to use the friary of Bonamargy on the Antrim coast.[45] This provided a refuge in times of persecution. Franciscans also regularly withdrew from their mission stations to Bonamargy to buy wheaten hosts and wine for the mass; items which were difficult to obtain in the west of Scotland. These trips were as much to recover their energies as they were to replenish stocks. The Franciscans' mission ended when they were forced to withdraw to Ireland for their own safety in 1637. Their eventual withdrawal was due to a number of factors but the principal one was the failure of Propaganda Fide to understand the true needs of the missionaries. The reports to Rome frequently pleaded for greater freedom from rules in order to minister to the spiritual needs of their congregations. They needed regular and reliable financial support as the country could not support them. The people were too poor to spare food especially in the hungry times of winter and early spring. Items such as wheaten bread and wine for use in the mass were difficult to obtain and always required payment in cash. Trips to Ireland and the Lowlands of Scotland were essential to replenish these supplies. All of these difficulties were poorly appreciated in Rome where the belief was that missions should be able to support themselves from the contributions of their congregations. This lack of understanding almost certainly contributed to Rome's tardiness in providing financial support. Communication with Propaganda Fide, which had never been easy, became more difficult as the political situation in Britain and Ireland deteriorated. Physically and financially exhausted, the missionaries withdrew to Ireland – O'Neill in 1626, Brady in 1630, Hegarty in 1631 and Ward in 1637. The date of McCann's final withdraw from the Scottish mission is unknown but he preceded Ward. There is no record of the Scottish Franciscan, John Ogilvie, after the early 1620s.[46] In Bonamargy they continued to serve the mission as Catholics from the Highlands and Islands regularly visited the friary to receive the sacraments. However, Ireland did not prove to be a permanent refuge: Patrick Hegarty was imprisoned in 1641 and not released until five years later. The others had already been forced to withdraw to St Anthony's in Louvain.[47] Despite the fact that their mission lasted less than twenty years and that at no stage were there more than six priests involved, they were able to make a lasting impact on the Western Highlands and Islands. They re-established Catholicism in many communities, a number of which have remained Catholic to the present day. The missionaries who followed them to *Montana Scotiae* in the second half of the seventeenth century – Lazarists, Dominicans, later Franciscans and eventually secular priests – were for the most part merely maintaining the achievements of the first Franciscans.

Notes

1. James Owen, priest in Braemar, managed to stay in his parish despite attacks from Protestant neighbours. Remarkably, his parishioners protected him from persecution by their landlord, the earl of Mar, who was strongly opposed to Catholicism. They were helped by the remoteness of the parish from central authority. *Memoirs of Scottish Catholics during XIIth and XIIIth Centuries*, ed. William Forbes-Leith, 2 vols (London: W. Paterson, 1909), p. 227.
2. J. F. S. Gordon, *The Catholic Church in Scotland* (Glasgow: J. Tweed, 1869), p. ii.
3. *Diccionario Historico de la Compañia de Jesus IHSI* (Rome, 2001), II, pp. 1259–62.
4. *Canons and Decrees of the Council of Trent*, trans. H. J. Schroeder (Rockford, IL: Tan Books and Publishers 1978), p. 151.
5. The annual report from the Jesuit mission to Rome in 1623 said that there were no Scottish priests in the country at that time who could speak Gaelic: *ex Scotis hucusque catholicis non fuerit sacerdos qui dicto idiomate utatur* (*Biblioteca Apostolica Vaticana*, Barb. Lat., vol. 8628, p. 83. See also: T. McInally, *The Sixth Scottish University, The Scots Colleges Abroad: 1575 to 1799* (Leiden and Boston: Brill, 2012), p. 182).
6. C. Giblin, 'The Irish Mission to Scotland in the Seventeenth Century', *Franciscan College Annual* (Multyfarnham, 1952), p. 9.
7. The superior of the Irish Franciscan College in Louvain wrote to Rome in 1618 stating: 'it is very true that the greater part of the Scottish nation uses the Irish language': *E molte ben vero che la detta nazione Scozzese per la maggiore parte usa della lingua irlandese*. ASV, Borghese II, CIV, p. 140).
8. Dominicans became involved when their General Chapter committed Scotland to the care of the Irish province in 1629. Attempts to send missionaries were made in 1632 and 1647 but they were refused permission by the Roman authorities. They wanted the order to send more missionaries to the Far East and the New World (APPF, Acta 1623–1670, cited in C. Giblin, 'The "Acta" of Propaganda Archives and the Scottish Mission, 1623–1670', *IR*, 5 (1954), 39–76). The Dominican mission to Scotland, set up in 1655, was led by a Scot, Thomas Primrose, and although there was some Irish involvement most of the missionaries were Scotsmen (*Archivium Generale Ordinis Praedicatorum* IV, ff. 85, 132. Archives held in the Priory of Santa Sabina, Rome).
9. C. O'Scea, 'The Irish Catholic Exile in early-modern Galicia, 1598–1666' in

T. O'Connor (ed.), *The Irish in Europe 1580–1815* (Dublin: Four Courts Press, 2001), pp. 27–48.
10. P. O'Connell, 'The Early-modern Irish College Network in Iberia, 1590–1800' in O'Connor (ed.), *The Irish in Europe*, pp. 49–64.
11. L. Chambers, 'A Displaced Intelligensia: Aspects of Irish Catholic Thought in Ancien Régime France' in O'Connor (ed.), *The Irish in Europe*, pp. 158, 160–3, 157.
12. APF, *Rif. nelle Cong. Gen.*, vol. 312, f. 99.
13. B. Roest, *Franciscan Literature of Religious Instruction before the Council of Trent* (Leiden: Brill, 2004), pp. 123–4.
14. *Irish Franciscan Mission to Scotland, 1619–1646: Documents from Roman Archives*, ed. C. Giblin (Dublin: Assisi Press), pp. 36–7.
15. The Irish provincial had asked Rome to provide them with at least 100 florins (ASV, *Fondo Borghese II*, vol. 104, 140–1).
16. *Register of the Privy Council of Scotland*, 1545–1625, ed. M. F. Graham, J. H. Burton and D. Masson, 14 vols (Edinburgh: Scottish Record Publications), XII, 47; APPF, *Rif. nelle Cong. Gen.*, vol. 312, ff. 66–71.
17. *Irish Franciscan Mission*, ed. Giblin, p. x.
18. Before Scotland was recognised by the Church as a missionary country in 1629, there were continuing problems regarding the authorisation of financial support for the missionaries.
19. ASV, *Fondo Borghese*, II, vol. , ff. 118–19; Giblin, 'Irish Mission to Scotland', pp. 10–12.
20. APPF, *Rif. nelle Cong. Gen.*, vol. 312, fo. 70.
21. APPF, *Rif. nelle Cong. Gen.*, vol. 312, fo. 299.
22. APPF, *Instruzioni diversi*, 1623–38, ff. 68–71.
23. When possible, houses of the gentry were used to say mass, one example being the home of an unnamed chieftain on Kintyre in 1624 (APPF, *Rif. nelle Cong. Gen.*, vol. 312, ff. 25–7).
24. On one occasion, Ward and O'Neill, fleeing arrest, used the deserted chapel of St Columba on the Island of Cara (off Kintyre). On another occasion Ward baptised in the roofless church of St Barr on the island of Barra. Giblin (ed.), *Irish Franciscan Mission*, pp. 51, 73.
25. The church on Canna was burned out during a feud between Clanranald and Maclean of Duart (D. Rixon, *The Small Isles: Canna, Rum, Eigg and Muck* (Edinburgh: Birlinn, 2001), p. 118).
26. *Irish Franciscan Mission*, ed. Giblin, p. 64.
27. APPF, *Rif. nelle Cong. Gen.*, vol. 312, ff. 15–16, 25–7.
28. The Council's position was ambiguous when viewed against previous practice. The tradition of candles was deemed to be apostolically ordained and therefore had to be observed. Lavish use was prohibited since it was considered to have originated in superstitious worship (*Canons and Decrees of the Council of Trent*, pp. 147, 151).
29. APPF, *Rif. nelle Cong. Gen.*, vol. 102, ff. 121–2.
30. The request was repeated in 1626 when it was granted at the second time of asking. Permission to dispense with candles at mass was again refused (APPF, *Rif. nelle Cong. Gen.*, vol. 312, ff. 299–300).
31. APPF, *Rif. nelle Cong. Gen.*, vol. 312, ff. 25–7.
32. The name was chosen from the cincture or cord worn by St Francis and his fol-

lowers. The cord was worn by all at the confraternity's ceremonies as a sign of membership.
33. C. F. Black, 'Early Modern Italian Confraternities', *Historein*, 2 (2000), 66, 77.
34. APPF, *Rif. nelle Cong. Gen.*, vol. 312, pp. 299–300.
35. *Irish Franciscan Mission*, ed. Giblin, p. x.
36. A. Bellesheim, *History of the Catholic Church in Scotland*, 4 vols (Edinburgh: Blackwood, 1890), IV, p. 68.
37. Ibid., pp. 66–72.
38. *Canons and Decrees of the Council of Trent*, pp. 46–7.
39. *Canons and Decrees of the Council of Trent*, p. 193.
40. APPF, *Rif. nelle Cong. Gen.*, vol. 134, f. 260.
41. APPF, *Rif. nelle Cong. Gen.*, vol. 312, ff. 15–16.
42. APPF, *Rif. nelle Cong. Gen.*, vol. 312, ff. 294–5.
43. Cornelius Ward reported in 1626 that Ranald MacDonald, the uncle of the chief of Clanranald, sought to have his marriage to his cousin legitimised and consecrated. The friars had no powers to agree but wrote to Rome for faculties which would allow them to decide in such cases. After a delay of two years the faculty was granted (APPF, *Rif. nelle Cong. Gen.*, vol. 312, ff. 27–34).
44. Giblin (ed.), *Irish Franciscan Mission*, p. 35.
45. Randal MacDonnell, 1st earl of Antrim, on whose land the deserted friary of Bonamargy stood, was Catholic and allowed the Franciscans to take possession of it (APPF, *Rif. nelle Cong. Gen.*, vol. 101, f. 155).
46. Giblin, 'The Irish Mission to Scotland', p. xv.
47. Ibid., p. xiv.

CHAPTER FOUR

Liturgical Reform during the Restoration: The Untold Story

John M. Hintermaier

Writing on the eve of the Restoration, James Durham, minister at St Mungo's in Glasgow, catalogued the various causes of religious scandal. Ranging across church history ancient and modern, he came to conclude that 'debates concerning Government seem most easie to be removed, yet often and almost ever, they have been most difficultly healed, and have been followed with great bitternesse and contention in the Church'.[1] As a voice for unity among Presbyterians, Durham was largely ignored, but his insistence that differences over church government were the most significant has been embraced by generations of scholars examining Scottish religion during the seventeenth and eighteenth centuries. From the authors of *Naphtali* to Robert Wodrow and Julia Buckroyd, the history of religion in Scotland has been dominated by church politics.[2] Earlier ages invested the difference in government with religious, even apocalyptic, significance, whilst modern historians have found that religious and secular politics can be analysed using some of the same tools.[3] What these scholars miss is that there is more to Scottish religion than the debate about how the Kirk should be governed. Some have attempted to address this through a shift of attention towards religious culture, but even here the temptation has been to see a religious culture that existed largely aloof from the religio-political rancour of much of the seventeenth century.[4] Recently Alasdair Raffe has suggested that the period from the Restoration to the end of Stuart rule should be seen as a time when separate 'confessional cultures' arose in Scotland.[5] Raffe's account rightly pays attention to all of the dimensions of religious life, especially theology, prayer and worship. Yet even his sophisticated analysis tends to argue that Episcopalian identity was largely a product of the post-Revolution period. In what follows, the efforts at liturgical reform during the 1660s and 1670s will be examined to demonstrate that influential Episcopalians had come to see liturgical worship as an essential feature of church life and made significant efforts to settle a liturgy in the Kirk. These efforts failed because they were caught in the crossfire between competing factions in the Kirk. It was this dispute that set Episcopalians on the path to developing the robust devotional and liturgical culture that has been a hallmark since the eighteenth century. This discussion is divided into four parts. First, we will consider what happened to both public worship and personal devotion during the Covenanting period. Then we will shift our attention to the period immediately after the restoration of Episcopacy. Moving on, we will examine the proposal for a liturgy debated in 1665 and 1666. We conclude with an examination of the arguments for set prayer and liturgy that emerged from the circle around Bishop Leighton in the early 1670s and the influence they had on future generations of Episcopalians.

I

It was well established in the minds of seventeenth-century Scots that 'Bishops and Books' went together.[6] In 1661, most observers of Scottish affairs were confident that the dream of Charles I would be fulfilled; worship and government would be the same throughout the three kingdoms. Yet conformity in worship never occurred. Gordon Donaldson, echoing the standard explanation, argued that Charles II's fear of meeting the same fate as his father doomed this effort.[7] Alasdair Raffe, echoing Brian Spinks, claimed that 'there were serious discussions in the 1660s about introducing a Prayer Book, but the proposal was aborted by the government's caution'.[8] What both contemporary observers and present-day scholars have minimised is the powerful influence of the Covenanting Movement on the way prayer was viewed and practised.

The period of the Covenants saw the dismantling of the conventions of public worship that had obtained since the Reformation. The agents of this destruction were primarily Presbyterians fleeing persecution in Ireland, who had often been forced to meet in private for prayer and preaching. This was in keeping with the pre-Reformation practice in Scotland, but adapted to the new circumstances of the 1640s.[9] Whilst this group was influential in bringing about the National Covenant, their idiosyncratic piety began to divide the Kirk in the early 1640s. In the 1641 General Assembly, they argued for 'omitting Glory to the Father [at the conclusion of a psalm], [opposed] kneeling in the pulpit, [and also] discountenanc[ed] read prayers [including the Lord's Prayer]'.[10] In the view of one of these ministers, John McLellan, read prayers should be rejected because there was no support for them in scripture, because they stinted the Holy Spirit and because Christ did not intend to tie his disciples to a particular set of words when he gave them the Lord's prayer.[11] McLellan went further, condemning those who used read prayers in family worship, going so far as to claim that pious breathing was better than a read prayer. In the 1642 Assembly, the matter of innovations in piety was raised again. The Assembly of that year worked very hard to prevent the matter from being debated publicly. Robert Baillie, professor of Divinity at Glasgow University, wrote, 'Our Northland brethren were much inflamed; and if it had come in face of Synod, would have made a violent act'. The ministers in the west of Scotland were able to get the matter referred to the local synod in Glasgow since 'the places of these evils being alone among us in the West'.[12]

Once the Solemn League and Covenant was formalised in 1643, English views came to impinge upon Scottish traditions. In an effort to appease English independents, the Scottish commissioners agreed to change the Scottish practice of requiring godparents to say the Apostles' Creed at baptisms. They abolished the office of reader because the office had no support, in their reading, from the New Testament. They also ended the practice of kneeling in the pulpit and singing the doxology at the conclusion of psalms sung by the congregation. Finally, they agreed to adopt the *Directory of Worship* and abandon the *Book of Common Order*. Under the influence of these changes, the order of service came to be reduced to singing psalms, extemporaneous prayer by the minister only, and preaching. Thus, by the time of the Restoration extemporaneous prayer in public and private was the norm and seen as furthering the progress of the Reformation. It was a commonplace that only spontaneous prayers could claim to be inspired by the Holy Spirit.

To the extent that there were those who were firm in their commitment to liturgical worship and set prayer before 1638, the Covenanting period saw them quietened or exiled. This is not to say that there were no defenders of set prayer. Baillie for his part was deeply troubled by the changes noted above, but acquiesced to them. Robert Leighton, while he was principal at Edinburgh University, addressed the issue of the proper way to pray in a way that pointed attention away from the method of prayer to its motivation and essence.

By temperament, Leighton inclined to gentleness and irenic arguments. This can be seen in his attitude towards set prayer. In his *Exposition of the Lord's Prayer*, Leighton tried to plot a middle way between extemporaneous prayer and set prayer. Starting from the premise that every person needed to pray, 'so there is a necessity of a direction how to perform it', he noted that:

> as for prescribing forms of prayer in general, to be bound to their continual use in private or in public, is nowhere practised. Nor is there, I conceive, on the other side, anything in the word of God, or any solid reason drawn from the word, to condemn their use.[13]

Leighton was wary of prescription in either direction and thus was able to survey the strengths and weaknesses of the various modes of prayer.

He also noted that always using set prayers could lead to 'coldness and formality; and yet, to speak the truth of this it is rather imputable to our dullness and want of affection in spiritual things, than to the forms of prayer that are used'. Leighton went on to condemn the need for continual novelty in prayer, saying:

> whereas some may account it much spiritualness to despise what they have heard before, and to desire continual variety in prayer, it seems

rather to be want of spiritualness that makes that needful, for that we find not our affections lively in that holy exercise, unless they be awaked and stirred by new expressions.[14]

For the spiritually minded person, prayer

> though it be in those words that it hath heard and uttered a hundred times, yet, still it is new ... And surely the desires that do move in that constant way, have more evidence of sincerity and true vigor in them, than those that depend upon new notions and words to move them, and can not stir without them.[15]

'The Spirit of prayer', he argued, 'hath not his seat in the invention, but in the affection'. Those who believed otherwise 'deceive themselves, in that they think the work of this Spirit of prayer to be mainly in furnishing new supplies of thoughts and words'. Instead real prayer consisted

> mainly in exciting the heart anew at times of prayer, to break forth itself in ardent desires to God, whatsoever the words be, whether new or old, yea, possibly without words; and then most powerful when it words it least, but vents in sighs and groans that can not be expressed.[16]

Leighton's aim here was to defend prayer, not necessarily any particular mode of prayer. Still, his argument clearly favours the constancy of a disciplined prayer life as opposed to searching for constant variety in prayer. Whilst not alone in seeing religious enthusiasm as tending towards instability and spiritual burnout, Leighton's willingness to see the benefit of set forms of prayer was unusual in the 1650s.

In the specific case of the Lord's Prayer, he again argued that prayer was an act of spiritual engagement with God marked by attention and an open heart. He condemned as 'a foolish, superstitious conceit' the notion 'that the rattling over these words is sufficient for prayer; but it is, on the other side, a weak, groundless scruple to doubt that the use of it, with spiritual affection, is both lawful and commendable'. For Leighton the disposition of the heart, not the words of the mouth, mattered most. Confronting the contention that using the Lord's Prayer verbatim fell under Jesus's condemnation of 'vain repetition', he argued 'in truth, where the matter is new, and the words still diverse and very rich in sense, yet, with God, it may be idle multiplying of words, because the heart stays behind'. For his own prayer he preferred to 'share with that publican in his own words, and say it often over, as if I had nothing else to say, "God be merciful to me a sinner"'.[17] Leighton's style of piety partook of elements of both extemporaneous and set forms of prayer, but in a way that clearly favoured the tried-and-true over the new-and-exciting.

The attention paid to Leighton's friendliness towards set forms may seem inordinate. Yet, given the context of what was happening to worship and piety in Scotland in the Covenanting period, Leighton's modest contention for the value of set forms marked a potential starting point for the construction of an alternative style of devotion and worship. The conviction that extemporaneous prayer was the only genuine species of prayer was so widespread that any movement towards liturgical reform had to begin with the conviction that set prayers were as spiritually efficacious as spontaneous ones and that the personal, political and religious benefits of set prayers were greater than those provided by the current practices in devotion and worship.

II

The Kirk in 1661–2 was even less open to liturgy and set prayers than it had been in 1637. Still, not all Scots shared the conviction that religious enthusiasm was an unmixed blessing and that adherence to the Covenants was the hallmark of fidelity. Although he rejected the English liturgy and episcopacy, Alexander Brodie of Brodie was

> not avers from a form of Liturgie. 1. Becaus albeit it be not soe livli as otherways; yet with som measure of affection may God be worshiped. 2. I hav sein, and dayli, much disordour in conceiv'd prayers of som, and extravagancie, which does afflict me.[18]

The 1650s had not been kind to Scotland. This fact was recognised even by Bishop Thomas Sydserff of Galloway, the only surviving Scottish bishop. He did not believe that there was a substantial Episcopalian party in Scotland, but noted that 'many of the Noblemen are young in years and aspire after his majesties favor. Others are thrald with debt, and will need his Majesties support'. Still others were open to prosecution for their actions. Sydserff urged Charles II to 'use this opportunity well, not knowing if the like may ever offer againe'.[19] Sydserff believed that Presbyterian government was incompatible with monarchy and that when the General Assemblies 'abolished the Liturgie out of the Church God', they deprived

> the people of that happy mean, to have preserved them in a pleasant harmonie of publict worship with all other Churches of Christ, and kept their heart in a constant dependence upon their dread Soveraigne under God.[20]

For Sydserff bishops and books were both necessary to preserve monarchy and prevent disorder.

Ironically, Presbyterians shared Sydserff's conviction that the return of bishops meant the return of a liturgy. In a letter to the earl of Lauderdale soon after the king's return to London, Robert Baillie wrote that he would never 'have dreamed that Bishops and Books, should have been so soon restored' in England.[21] Writing about the adjournment of the Scottish Parliament in 1661, Baillie feared that it 'was but for the ripening of the designes of bringing in books and bishops, either in whole or in part, as praeparatorie to all was in England'.²² Another minister, Alexander Cant, was deposed by the synod of Aberdeen for a number of inflammatory comments against the king and bishops and for saying

> we hear of a Service Book, which may be fitly called, *Liber Servitus*. Whoever will own or make use of that Book, KING, Nobleman, Minister, or whosoever he be, the curse of GOD will, and shall be upon him.²³

The fear that bishops would return with a liturgy was further stoked when Bishop Sydserff's son began publishing a newspaper, *Mercurius Caledonius*, in Edinburgh.²⁴

As the only sanctioned newspaper in the capital, Sydserff's publication had a monopoly. He used his privileged position to promote an anti-Covenanting, aristocratic pre-eminence in politics and culture, the return of bishops and ordered worship in religion. When Julia Buckroyd surveyed the paper, she stressed the political programme of *Mercurius Caledonius*. What she overlooked were the overt attacks on the piety of the Covenanters. This might take the form of a swipe at Robert Baillie:

> there was a little whistling Pedant . . . had the impudence to design it [the National Covenant] by the name of the Oath of God: But its no great matter what such a one says, that was so saucy as to brand the Piety and Learning of the Ancient Fathers, with the reproaches of Ignorance and Superstition.²⁵

Baillie's book comparing the 1637 Scottish prayer book with the mass had been reprinted in 1661 as an argument against the return of the *Book of Common Prayer* to England.²⁶ More personally, Bishop Sydserff had suffered bodily injury for his support of the 1637 liturgy. This was not an isolated comment either.

Commenting on the sermons before parliament by William Scrogie and James Ramsay in the 25 January to 1 February edition, Sydserff observed 'two remarkable things'. Scrogie 'instanced the Authority of the learned Fathers' and Ramsay 'restored us to Glory to the Father, to be sung at the end of the Psalms: both which, have been great strangers to our Kirk these many years'.²⁷ These reports clearly hit their mark: writing in February 1661, James Sharp, who would later become archbishop of St. Andrews, reported that 'They say they have discharged Thomas Sydserff. It is intolerable that a papist should bespatter the ministry of our Church'.²⁸ In another report, Sydserff praised Perth for being the site of 'a Venerable Assembly, that ornamented the Church with articles . . . etc'.²⁹

Sydserff also used his paper to report the consecration of new bishops in Ireland and England and a petitioning campaign in London to have the Prayer Book used.³⁰ His drumbeat for the return of bishops and liturgy seemed even more ominous when in February 1661 the commander of the English garrison in Edinburgh ordered that the *Book of Common Prayer* be used for services in the castle.[31] Sydserff would be forced not to publish his newspaper in March 1661, but he did not remain silent. In a series of pamphlets he continued to harass the Presbyterian clergy and advocate for his ideal of a Kirk ordered around bishops and set prayer.[32]

In a long pamphlet that largely recounted the feasting surrounding Charles II's coronation in England, Sydserff exulted in the enthusiastic and besotted celebration of the official return of the king. Yet he tucked in between tales of revelling news of an ecclesiastical import. As the citizens of Edinburgh danced in the streets

> the Provincial Synod of the Church of Aberdeen, hath made a solemn acknowledgement of all their rebellious Defections, Hypocrisies and Oppressions, by which they either misled the people against His MAJESTY, or trampled upon their Brethren who refused to commit Idolatry with either of the Dagons, National or League: They have ordained before the beginning of Sermon on Sundays, that the reading of the Holy Scriptures, and Prayers, be used as formerly before the Rebellion, that Glory to the Father shall be sung at the ends of Psalms, that the Lords Prayer be likewise said by the Ministers, either at their first or second Prayer: that Parents who presents their Children to be Christened repeat the Creed, and be obliged to educate their Children in the Christian Faith, and no more mention to be made of the Articles of the Covenant.[33]

Whilst many of these changes were in the direction of the status quo pre-1637, even this modest return of some set forms could be seen as laying a foundation for further reform. In fact, when David Mitchell, the Restoration bishop of Aberdeen, first met with his synod in 1662, these directives were repeated and expanded.[34]

The synod of Aberdeen's directions were mentioned again in another of Sydserff's pamphlets, where they were contrasted with what happened in St Andrews. He noted that

> One would think (at least a good Protestant) that the reading of holy Scripture, singing Psalms before Sermons, the using of the Lords Prayer, rehearsing the Apostolic Creed at Baptism, giving glory to God at the end of the Psalms, and using of Prayer morning and evening in Congregations, were good and bonny works.[35]

In Fife, however, 'the good Synod (which is none of the learned'st) where Blew-beard is a member, hath rejected such works, when tendered to them by a noble Person. For which he dissolved their Synod, and so their work went scurvily on'.[36] To further inflame worries, Sydserff inserted a story from England about the preparation of bonfires to celebrate the 29 May holiday. The story pointed out that the king's birthday was also 'the day (1549) that the Book of Common Prayer was first established'. The kind reference to the Prayer Book was especially worrying at a time when leading

Presbyterians were being told they were in danger of having a liturgy imposed upon them. Relaying a message from Archbishop Sharp, Patrick Drummond wrote that if they kept talking 'after the old mode', they would bring 'hurt to yourselves' and bring the English into Scotland, who would 'reduce you to a service: for if you will justify the lawfulness of extirpating them [the Scottish bishops] they must seek themselves preservation by the most lively means'.[37] Sydserff's advocacy for changes in worship plus the news coming from London suggesting moves to bring the English service to Scotland made many Presbyterians nervous that 'Bishops and Books' were in the near future.

When the first synods met after the return of episcopacy, there were moves made to dignify worship. The Synod of Dunblane in September 1662 garnered the attention of later Episcopalians for its exemplary pronouncements on worship.[38] Bishop Leighton's synod was the picture of order with most ministers present and most of those absent having sent excuses. Instead of rancorous debate, the synod listened to the bishop discuss his priorities, 'which by the unanimous vote of the synod, were approved and enacted'. With this, the synod 'having no further to do at this meeting' adjourned. The written copy of Leighton's speech then was entered into the record and the synod adjourned. The fact that his address drew no protest is slightly surprising given its content.

On the face of it, Leighton's proposals seem minor, but, given what we know about the preferred style of piety in Scotland, they represent a deviation. Leighton began with an admonition 'that all diligence be used for repressing of profaneness, and the advancement of solid piety and holiness'. This meant 'that not only scandals of unchastity, but drunkenness, swearing and cursing, filthy speaking and mocking of religion, and all other gross offences be brought under Church-censure'. He also advocated that offenders be required to show true repentance before absolution and that ministers examine would-be communicants 'not only into the knowledge but the practice and tract of life'. Leighton urged that 'all profane and evidently impenitent persons be secluded till their better Conversation & obedience to the Gospel be more apparent'. He also wanted ministers to ask questions about family worship and encourage their literate parishioners to 'join with it the reading of the Scriptures'. This appeal to church discipline was presumably heartening for the clergy.

Leighton next turned his attention to dignifying worship in his diocese. He wanted to change the normal order of service:

> instead of Lecturing and preaching both at one meeting larger portions of the Holy Scriptures, one whole chapter at least, of each Testament, and Psalms withal be constantly read, and this not as by-work, while they are convening but after the people are well convened.

Sunday worship was to be 'solemnly begun, with confession of sins and prayer, either by the Minister or some person by him appointed'. Leighton also insisted 'that the Lords prayer be restored to more frequent use and likewise the Doxology and the Creed'. The bishop suggested 'that Daily public prayer in churches morning and evening, with reading the Scriptures be used where it can be conveniently'. These instructions were echoed in Aberdeen when Bishop David Mitchell met with his synod, the main addition being that the Aberdeen synod specified the use of 'the liturgy in the old psalm book'.[39] This early phase of reform imagined a return to the pre-1618 practice of the Kirk as the standard for worship. Gordon Donaldson has questioned how effective this was since these sorts of instructions were repeated throughout the 1660s, but the larger point needs to be kept in mind that this was intended as an incremental step. This initial effort at reform showed a sensitivity to the fact that even this small return to set forms of prayer was radical within the context of the early Restoration. Fuller uniformity with England and Ireland would be attempted later.[40] Mitchell's and Leighton's preference for liturgical worship is well known. Mitchell had read the 1637 book publicly and in later 1661 Leighton had told Alexander Brodie that he 'he lykd [the] Liturgie' and when Brodie asked 'him to use his credit that the Ceremonies might not be broght in upon us. He said, he wishd soe; but he hop'd they should be prest on none'.[41] Thus, these early returns to set prayer were pregnant with the possibility of further reform leading to an officially ordered liturgy that resembled the English Prayer Book.

Gordon Donaldson has argued that this admonition did not represent an innovation and thus cannot be seen as a drastic change.[42] Yet the fact that no liturgy was ultimately imposed on Scotland does not mean that all efforts to bring uniformity to public worship can be seen as ineffectual or irrelevant. Speaking historically about the meaning of worship seems essential. The fact that a more traditional diocese like Aberdeen sought to revive daily prayer signals a readiness to embrace set forms once again. Additionally, whilst the *Book of Common Order* was an old text, returning to it signalled that traditional Scottish ways of worship were being revived. For those who had been satisfied with the pre-1637 method of worship, this was likely a welcome change. To an ear that had become attuned to the free-flowing verbosity of extemporaneous prayer, the return to set prayers read by a designated reader must have seemed alien and startling. In addition, we must not forget that the extempore regime had been largely the form preferred by the spiritual avant-garde in Scotland. For these Presbyterians, episcopacy was the most pressing issue. There was little protest about set prayer in the Restoration Kirk because those who would have protested had already removed themselves because of episcopacy. Donaldson, rightly, harpoons the picture of Covenanters being dragged into church to participate in a liturgy according to the *Book of Common Prayer*. What he seems to ignore is the dynamic nature of piety. Returning to the *Book of Common Order* was a compromise intended to provide a form of worship until another could be readied. The fact that a new liturgy was never passed should not dissuade us from looking at the plans of those who desperately wanted one.

III

Whilst the moves toward more ordered worship in some of the early synods signalled that some bishops favoured set prayers, these efforts were neither uniform nor universal. The prevailing wisdom at the Restoration was that bishop and liturgy were inextricably joined, but nothing was done to bring the entire Kirk into uniformity in either worship or canons. Without a stable liturgical identity and the legal procedures to enforce it, the Episcopal Church looked like a less desirable version of the Presbyterian Church it was supposed to replace. The ideal place to enact a liturgy and canons of the Kirk was a national synod. According to Gilbert Burnet, the synod would have allowed the bishops to 'settle a book of common prayer, and a book of canons'.[43] The reasons why a national synod never met are beyond the scope of this work, involving as they do the interface between court politics and the activities of Presbyterian dissenters. The delay caused a younger Gilbert Burnet to complain that episcopal worship was 'extremely flat in all the parts of it' and that 'our Church prayers are long without any order and often very dull. I must say that this Church is the only one in the world which hath no rule for worship.' The lack of a set order was 'heavy and grievous' because it ensured that 'all the prayers of the Church depend upon the extemporary gift of the minister'. The solution to this problem was 'the compiling of a grave liturgy, the prayers whereof shall be short and Scriptural and fitly depending one upon another'. Burnet tried to qualify this need for a liturgy by saying that it should be

> without any ceremonies (which are of no necessity and give great occasion of stumbling) and without imposing of it upon any one person it should certainly at long run turn to our great advantage.[44]

Burnet avoided the most serious consequences for offering his unsolicited advice, but he silenced himself voluntarily.

The irony of Burnet's critique is that the bishops were in the midst of drafting a liturgy. This next and most crucial phase of liturgical reform is a bit mysterious because it is not clear why the king decided in the winter of 1665 to order the Scottish bishops to draft a liturgy. After their winter meeting, the bishops sent a letter to Lauderdale informing him that 'in obedience to his majesty's command . . . we have been considering those set forms of prayer and ecclesiastical constitutions, which we intend to offer to his sacred Majesty's view'.[45] The aim of this meeting had been known for some time. Earlier in September, John Nicoll noted in his diary that several important people in Edinburgh had been arrested by the earl of Rothes because it was alleged 'that their persons were set to oppose the Bishops courses in bringing in the Service book and book of Canons'. In their letter to Lauderdale, seven bishops claimed they were hesitant to cause additional trouble given the war with the Dutch so they did not have a draft of either the liturgy or canons. Yet it is clear that their hesitance also stemmed from significant disagreements about the form of the liturgy.

We know of these because Archbishop Alexander Burnet of Glasgow also reported on the progress of the efforts to Archbishop Gilbert Sheldon of Canterbury. In February 1666, he told Sheldon that 'for our confession it is likely we may approve the articles of the Church of England, but our liturgy doth not please me, and (unless it be rectified) I fear it will not please others'.[46] A month later Burnet reported that 'we have had many debates about our liturgy, and to no great purpose'.[47] To settle this impasse

> another book of common-prayer was produced, which is that our predecessors offered to King Charles the first, and is made up of the ordinary confession, collects, and other prayers used in the Church of England; only the litany and responses are waived; this gave more satisfaction and . . . is to be offered to his Majesty by my lord St. Andrews some time the next month.[48]

This compromise liturgy was apparently based on the third draft of the liturgy approved by the Perth Assembly. It had been shown to Charles I in 1629, but the king rejected this draft, stating his preference for the English Prayer Book.[49] Despite the agreement around this liturgy, Burnet felt that 'those that have suffered in the late troubles and incline to a conformity with the Church of England are under great discouragements and the opposite party very high'.[50] Burnet's comment reveals the factional divisions in the Kirk. He spoke for those who believed that the goal of liturgical reform was to bring Scotland into the closest possible conformity with England. For patronage this group looked to Archbishop Sheldon and the earl of Clarendon. They were opposed by a larger faction that did not mind if Scotland had moderate episcopacy and a minimalist liturgy, but were not in favour of conformity with England. Archbishop Sharp and many of the other bishops fell into this category. Apart from both these factions was the small group that coalesced around Bishop Leighton. This factional division had produced a stalemate in religious policy and had handicapped the efforts of the bishops to deal with nonconforming Presbyterians. Furthermore, it had left the worship of the Kirk in a state of uncertainty that fostered disunity and prevented the creation of a distinctive Episcopalian identity.

At this point Archbishop Sharp moved to assert his independence from Lauderdale by courting the earl of Rothes, who had managed to obtain all of the highest civil offices in Scotland. Sharp also seems to have used the promise of a Scottish liturgy to win Sheldon and Clarendon to his side. In the summer of 1666, Sharp travelled to court to present a draft of the liturgy to the king and to ask for the disbursement of fine money to aid impoverished clients of Rothes in Scotland. What Sharp did not reckon was that Lauderdale was keenly aware of his plan. Sharp believed he and Lauderdale had 'no difference in opinion as to the matter, manner, or time in pressing the set form of prayer your Grace saw at Lesley, though it be given out so to be I hear'.[51] Yet in moment after moment, Lauderdale used his access to privileged information to subvert Sharp. Although Sharp was able to win Sheldon's approval of the liturgy and to show the king a copy of it, Lauderdale prevented him from winning the funds for Rothes's clients. In fact, Lauderdale engineered his communication to Rothes to make it appear that Sharp was responsible for the fines being spent on raising troops to meet an unlikely Dutch invasion. The waning influence of Clarendon meant that Sheldon was able to do little to help Sharp. As soon as he returned to Scotland, Sharp met with the Scottish Privy Council. Archibald Campbell, 9th earl of Argyll, came late to the meeting in August, but asked Sharp if 'the government of the Church was settled by law, why should not the worship and discipline likewise? That would make conventicles and all disorders of that kind more expressly against the letter of the law.' Sharp replied that 'he knew it was his Majesty's mind when he was at London that it was not a fit time'.[52] Almost simultaneously the Pentland Rising shocked the Scottish establishment. The two archbishops were held primarily responsible and the best chance for liturgical reform since 1637 came to nothing.

We can draw several important conclusions from this aborted reform. It helps us to see that there were those within the Kirk who wanted the English Prayer Book to be the standard for Scottish worship. We also see that drafting a liturgy and enacting it are two very different things. The factional divisions within the Kirk meant that finding a genuine compromise on matters of public worship was nearly impossible. Unlike in England, many of those who conformed to Episcopacy (and all of those who did not) shared the same basic convictions about appropriate worship and suspicion about liturgy. As long as factional interests outweighed the settling of worship and canons, no real change was possible. The best that could be hoped for were pockets of like-minded individuals working to create a conscientious religious identity that saw set prayer and liturgical worship as the surest path to a fruitful and peaceful Christian life. Thus, the failure to enact a liturgy that had received royal assent and approval from the archbishop of Canterbury had the unintended consequence of deepening not only the spiritual practice of those who favoured set forms but also the theological reflection that went along with it. It was this theological liberation that would come to mark the final phase of liturgical reform.

IV

Robert Leighton is best remembered for his piety and his efforts to bring moderate Presbyterians back into the Kirk during the early 1670s. As we have already seen, Leighton was one of the few bishops to give explicit directions about worship in 1662. Leighton had enjoyed a good relationship with his diocesan clergy in Dunblane, but grew tired of the efforts to punish dissent through the stringent application of the law. This led him to retire, but the dismissal of the archbishop of Glasgow for overstepping his boundaries brought him back into the episcopate. As archbishop of Glasgow, he was tasked with finding a way to allow peaceful dissenters to preach legally while preserving episcopal government.

Leighton's influence can be seen through the writing of one of his younger protégés, Gilbert Burnet. What Burnet had to say about extemporaneous prayer helped to lay a foundation for the reception of liturgy, and they connect the Restoration to the far more fruitful liturgical efforts of the eighteenth century. In his *A Modest and Free Conference*, Burnet launched a full frontal assault on extemporaneous prayer. He echoed several of Leighton's criticisms, but also critiqued the notion that only the extemporaneous were inspired by the Holy Spirit. This was a negation of the prevailing theology of most Presbyterians regarding the manifestation of the Holy Spirit. Burnet argued that

> extemporary prayer, cannot be called praying by the Spirit, except by spirit you understand the animal or natural spirits: for, if it be by the Spirit, it must be infallible, since all that is dictated by the Spirit of God is so: yet your people do not assert their prayers as such.

Mockingly he challenged dissenters' view of prayer, saying

> let one with a short-hand, follow that man's prayer, who you says prays by the Spirit; then may not the prayer be read and used over again? Or, Is the Spirit in the prayer so volatile, that it evaporates in the saying, and the prayer becomes carnal when it is repeated?

For Burnet there was no question that spontaneous prayer was incompatible with orderly, public worship. It was animated not by God but by raw emotion and thoughtless enthusiasm.

So, what sort of prayer did Burnet and the Leightonians favour? Their answer depended on the context of the prayer. For public worship, they clearly favoured the use of a liturgy, although they insisted that all prayer should flow out of an inner devotion. Burnet argued that extemporaneous prayer was not truly spiritual because it merely excited the mind. In his view of the soul, 'the Will is the supreme power . . . and the fancy is a lower faculty'. True devotion 'must be that which lies in the Will, and not in the Fancy'. Consequently

> the varying of one thing into several shapes, is only a gratifying of Fancy: and all the devotion can be raised by such Chimes, is only sensible, whereas one of a deep and steadfast spirit, is equally affected with a thing, though still in the same dress.

This favoured the use of set prayers for all forms of devotion:

our petition for pardon of sin, is fully comprised in this, have mercy upon me, O God, doth it not show, that the thing, and not the words effect him, who with a newness of affection, can make that prayer, though a hundred times repeated, at every return, new? whereas he must have a lower mind, who needs a new phrase to renew his fervour. And thus you see, it expresses a more spiritual temper, to be able to worship God in simple and constant forms.

The key quality here was the ability of the soul to focus on the divine. Extemporaneous prayer distracted from this aim so set forms of devotion and worship were the only ones that allowed for truly spiritual prayers. Burnet's defence of liturgy and set prayer seem a bit Quixotic given that both he and Leighton would be forced to go to England and the efforts to bring in a service book for the Kirk were fruitless. Yet in an otherwise barren liturgical landscape the Leighton circle stands out. For these sorts of arguments would be taken up throughout the Restoration. Set prayers would come to be seen as more reliable and orthodox. As the spectre of heterodoxy arose in the later Restoration, a whole industry arose to supply lay people with explanations of the Prayer Book, paraphrases of its prayers, and commentaries on its meaning. Initially these were restricted to England, but in the eighteenth century these sorts of works were published in Scotland as well. This also, not coincidentally, was when Episcopalians added books to their bishops.[53] While these Episcopalians borrowed from English authors, precedents and texts, their work had been founded by the Restoration apologists and bishops. It was they who had first suggested a path to the full reform of worship, and it would be later generations who would see this work come into maturity.

V

The Restoration can be vindicated from the charge of being a do-nothing era in the history of Scottish liturgy. There were serious attempts to restore a more orderly form of worship, but the damage done by the Covenanting period was profound. Its remedy would only be found in efforts to rebuild the basic structure of devotion. In the end, this was best done not through royal fiat but through the direct cultivation of arguments in favour of set prayer. These arguments did not convince anything like the majority of Scots, but they convinced those who would form the Scottish Episcopal Church. That church's influence in liturgical practice and theological reflection was global and far beyond what its small size might lead one to believe. This is why the failure of the 1660s needs to be better known. For it was out of the chaos and rancour of the early Restoration, that the first steps were taken towards breaking the monopoly of Calvinism in theology and extemporaneous prayer and preaching in public worship.

Notes

1. J. Durham, *The Dying Man's Testament to the Church of Scotland* (London, 1659), p. 334.
2. J. Stewart and J. Stirling, *Naphtali, Or The Wrestlings of the Church of Scotland for the Kingdom of Christ; Contained in A True and Short Deduction Thereof, from the Beginning of the Reformation of Religion, until the Year 1667* (Holland, 1667); J Buckroyd, *Church and State in Scotland, 1660–1681* (Edinburgh: John Donald, 1980).
3. C. Jackson, *Restoration Scotland, 1660–1690: Royalist Politics, Religion and Ideas* (Woodbridge: The Boydell Press, 2003).
4. M. Todd, *The Culture of Protestantism in Early Modern Scotland* (New Haven, CT: YUP, 2002).
5. A. Raffe, 'Presbyterians and Episcopalians: The Formation of Confessional Cultures in Scotland, 1660–1715', *EHR*, 125 (2010), 573; A. Raffe, *The Culture of Controversy: Religious Arguments in Scotland, 1660–1714* (Woodbridge: The Boydell Press, 2012).
6. R. Baillie, *The Letters and Journals of Robert Baillie*, ed. David Laing, 3 vols (Edinburgh: Bannatyne Club, 1841–2), III, 404–8, 444, 470.
7. G. Donaldson, 'Covenant to Revolution', in Duncan B. Forrester and Douglas M. Murray (eds), *Studies in the History of Worship in Scotland*, 2nd ed. (Edinburgh: T. & T. Clark, 1996), p. 65.
8. Raffe, 'Presbyterians and Episcopalians', p. 593; B. D. Spinks, *Liturgy in the Age of Reason: Worship and Sacraments in England and Scotland, 1662–c. 1800* (Burlington, VT: Ashgate, 2008), p. 22.
9. J. Kirk, 'The "Privy Kirks" and their Antecedents: The Hidden Face of Scottish Protestantism', *Studies in Church History*, 23 (1986), 155–70.
10. Baillie, *Letters and Journals*, I, p. 362.
11. NLS, Wodrow MSS, Quarto XXIX, ff. 52–4.
12. *The Letters and Journals of Robert Baillie*, II, 51.
13. R. Leighton, 'Exposition of the Lord's Prayer', in *The Whole Works of Robert Leighton*, ed. James Aikman (New York: John C. Riker, 1844), p. 596.
14. Ibid., p. 596.
15. Ibid., pp. 596–7.
16. Ibid., p. 597.
17. Ibid., p. 597.
18. *The Diary of Alexander Brodie of Brodie, MDCLII.–MDCLXXX. and of His Son, James Brodie of Brodie, MDCLXXX.–MDCLXXXV*, ed. David Laing (Aberdeen: Spalding Club, 1863), pp. 200, 225.
19. Bodleian Library, Oxford, Clarendon State Papers, Volume 75, ff. 427–42r.
20. Ibid., fo. 42r.
21. Baillie, *Letters and Journals*, III, p. 406.
22. Ibid., III, p. 469.
23. T. Sydserff, *Mercurius Caledonius, Comprising the Affairs Now in Agitation in Scotland: With a Survey of Forraign Intelligence*, 31 December – 8 January, vol. 1, 1661.
24. J. Buckroyd, 'Mercurius Caledonius and Its Immediate Successors, 1661', *SHR*, 541 (1975), 11–21.
25. T. Sydserff, *Mercurius Caledonius*, 8–15 March, vol. 10, 1661. Internal evidence almost certainly shows that this barb was directed at Baillie.

26. R. Baillie, *A Parallel, or Briefe Comparison of the Liturgie with the Masse-Book, the Breviarie, the Ceremoniall, and Other Romish Ritualls* (London, 1641).
27. T. Sydserff, *Mercurius Caledonius*, 25 January – 1 February, vol. 4, 1661.
28. BL, Turner Manuscripts, Add. MS. 23115, f. 59.
29. Sydserff, *Mercurius Caledonius*, vol. 4.
30. T. Sydserff, *Mercurius Caledonius*, 15–22 February, vol. 7, 1661 and 22 February – 1 March, vol. 8, 1661 and 1–8 March, vol. 9, 1661.
31. Osmund Airy (ed.), *The Lauderdale Papers*, 3 vols (London: Camden Society, 1884–5), I, p. 88.
32. T. Sydserff, *Edinburgh's Joy for His Majesty's Coronation in England* (Edinburgh, 1661) and *The Work Goes Bonnely On* (Edinburgh, 1661).
33. Sydserff, *Edinburgh's Joy for His Majesty's Coronation in England*.
34. J. Stuart (ed.), *Selections from the Records of the Kirk Session, Presbytery, and Synod of Aberdeen* (Aberdeen: Spalding Club, 1846), p. 262. Mitchell was one of the few Edinburgh ministers who had supported the reading of the Scottish Prayer Book in 1637 and had been exiled in the aftermath. Whilst it can be argued that this return to the status quo was a minor step, it could alternatively be seen as an initial step towards further reform.
35. Sydserff, *The Work Goes Bonnely On*.
36. NLS, Wodrow MSS, f. XXVI.
37. NLS, Wodrow MSS, f. XXVI.
38. NRS, Records of the Episcopal Church of Scotland: Episcopal Chest, CH12/12/1760.
39. Stuart (ed.) *Records of the Kirk Session*, p. 263.
40. Donaldson, 'Covenant to Revolution', p. 65.
41. *Diary of Brodie of Brodie*, 229.
42. Donaldson, 'Covenant to Revolution', pp. 63–8.
43. Gilbert Burnet, *Bishop Burnet's History of His Own Time*, 2 vols, 2nd edn (Oxford: OUP, 1883), I, p. 381.
44. H. C. Foxcroft (ed.), 'Certain Papers of Robert Burnet, Afterwards Lord Crimond, Gilbert Burnet, Afterwards Bp. of Salisbury, and Robert Leighton, Sometime Archbishop of Glasgow' in *Miscellany of the Scottish History Society Vol. II*, (Edinburgh: SHS, 1904), pp. 354–5.
45. BL, Lauderdale Papers, Add. MS 23122, f. 315.
46. *The Lauderdale Papers, II*, appendix A, p. xxxiii.
47. Ibid.
48. G. W. Sprott (ed.), *Scottish Liturgies of the Reign of James VI* (Edinburgh: Edmonston and Douglas, 1871).
49. G. Donaldson, 'Reformation to Covenant' in Forrester and Murray (eds), *Studies in the History of Worship in Scotland*, pp. 51–3.
50. *The Lauderdale Papers, II* appendix A, p. xxxiii.
51. NLS, Wodrow MSS, Octavo XLV, no. 57, f. 177.
52. Historical Manuscripts Commission, *Report on the Laing Manuscripts Preserved in the University of Edinburgh*, 2 vols (London: Stationery Office, 1914), I, pp. 353–4; BL, Lauderdale Papers, Add. MS 23125, f. 34.
53. P. Barclay, *A Letter to the People of Scotland in order to remove their prejudice to the Book of Common Prayer* (London, 1713).

CHAPTER FIVE

Henry Scougal and the Move Away from Calvinism in the Later Seventeenth Century

Isaac M. Poobalan

Henry Scougal's treatise *The Life of God in the Soul of Man*, published anonymously in 1676, has proved to be a Christian spiritual classic in its quality and substance. Isobel Rivers highlights the significance of a work that has attracted the attention of the likes of 'the latitudinarian Gilbert Burnet, the Scottish Episcopalian Patrick Cockburn, the Scottish moderate Presbyterian William Wishart, the Arminian Methodist John Wesley, the American Episcopalian William Smith, the Baptist Unitarian Joshua Toulmin, and the Church of Ireland bishop John Jebb'.[1] If such was the appeal of the treatise and its reach which transcended religious and philosophical boundaries of the Christian religion, its author remains a mystery and has been acclaimed as widely as possible by Episcopalians, Presbyterians, Evangelicals, the Orthodox and the Jacobites as one of their own. In the latter context, while it is possible to locate non-juring tendencies in the generation of clergy and laity in the later seventeenth century, locating these tendencies in the author of the *Life of God in the Soul of Man* opens up a space hitherto uninhabited.

This chapter places Scougal in the context of the religious and political controversies of post-Restoration Scotland. It aims to reveal why his life and work along with those of his contemporaries in Aberdeen, namely James and George Garden, became the source of transformation in the lives of many Church leaders in succeeding generations. This chapter contends that the position of Scougal and the Gardens is a transcendent space from the Calvinists, the Anglo-Catholics, those of the *via media* and the Latitudinarians. This exploration, however, will focus on Scougal and his work with some reference to George Garden's exegesis of the life of his friend Scougal and James Garden's *Comparative Theology; or The True and Solid Grounds of Pure and Peaceable Theology*.[2]

I

George Garden, regent of the University of Aberdeen, said at his friend's funeral service held in the chapel there in 1678:

Length of life is not to be measured by many revolutions of the heavens, but by the progress we have made in the great design for which we are sent into the world: and in this respect he [Scougal], being sanctified in a little time, hath fulfilled a long time; so that he hath truly lived much in a few years, and died an old man in eight and twenty.[3]

The text for the sermon was from the Epistle of St Paul to the church at Philippi, 'For me to live is Christ, to die is gain'. In this sermon, which lasted at least three hours, Garden explored the life of our Lord, and how St Paul came to see it and how Scougal came to live it.

The sermon has very little out of place and rarely anything repeated. Besides, the systematic development of the theme and the essential meaning and significance of it to the occasion transcend the boundaries of a funeral. Garden was addressing a nation and a period caught up in turmoil. Professor Rivers notes that Scougal's life marked a departure from the Presbyterian order of the Church and to its Calvinistic roots. 'Scougal approved [Gilbert] Burnet's Arminian statement of Christ's function as offering of redemption to all, not only the elect, which blatantly contradicts the theology of the Westminster Confession'.[4] Clare Jackson's similarly careful observations on Restoration Scotland depart from polemical views established by an inherent Presbyterian myth of a bloody, tyrannical Cavalier state committed to the persecution of the Lowland Covenanters.[5] Dr Garden's sermon addresses these issues skilfully and effectively.

Scougal, second son of Margaret or Jean Wemyss and Patrick Scougal, is likely to have been born in June 1650 in Leuchars, Fife, where his father was a minister at the time of his birth. His father, preparing him a career in the Church, took the greatest care of him from his infancy, and had the pleasure to observe such a desire in him to piety and virtue, even in his tender years. As a young child he was allowed by his father to 'stay in the Room, when Clergymen, or Scholars, or others, from whom any Thing might be learn'd were with him', in order to nurture 'an early Disposition of judging right of both Men and Things'.[6] George Garden, in his Funeral Sermon, had this to say:

While the reason for allowing the young boy to 'stay in the Room' appears true and noble, the fact that young Scougal lost his mother at the tender age of nine may have had some relevance. Be that as it may, young Henry very soon lost interest in school playground games and was more interested in books. As the son of a Manse, he seemed to have taken special interest in the Scriptures and enjoyed reading the historical parts of the Old Testament. Sometimes he would be taken up with the thoughts of the law of Moses, wondering how altars and sacrifices, and its other ceremonies, were not now among the exercises of our worship; at other times employing himself in little imitations of the exercises of the holy function, as preaching, and the like.[7]

In 1664 Scougal entered King's College, Aberdeen, where he was subsequently 'made constant president' of the regular meetings held among the student body to discuss philosophical and religious issues. It is claimed that he disliked the philosophy then taught and studied natural philosophy which was gaining popularity in the university faculties. As a result of such intense interest in academia at about eighteen years of age, he wrote the *Reflections* and short *Essays*. Although it was a youthful performance, not designed for the press, and some of them left unfinished, they breathe forth so much devotion. The quality of his writings reflected his grasp of thoughts and ideas as if he received special revelation. After graduating MA on 9 July 1668, Scougal was subsequently appointed a regent, or lecturer, at King's, where his father was by then Chancellor. As a regent, he was remembered for being 'the first in this corner of the land' to structure his philosophy teaching according to Cartesian principles to discourage his students from acquiring 'a disputing humour and vanity in hard words and distinctions', while remaining concerned to 'guard them against the debauched sentiments' to be found in Thomas Hobbes's *Leviathan* (1651).[8]

In the summer of 1673 Scougal was ordained and appointed minister of Auchterless, Aberdeenshire, in which capacity he also served as precentor in the cathedral church, Old Aberdeen. At Auchterless his zeal and fitness in the service of God were eminently displayed. He catechised with great plainness and affection and used the most endearing methods to recommend religion to his bearers. He endeavoured to bring them to close attendance on public worship and joined with them himself at the beginning of it. He insisted on being present during all church services, thus abandoning customary practice whereby the minister joined the congregation just before the sermon and allowed the first part of the service to be conducted by the reader.

> He endeavoured to bring them to a devout and constant attendance on the public worship; where be always went, and joined with them at the beginning of it; thinking it very unfit, that the invocation of Almighty God, the reading of some portions of the Holy Scriptures, making a confession of our Christian faith, and rehearsing the ten commandments, should be looked upon only as a preludium for ushering in the people to the church, and the minister to the pulpit.[9]

In a sermon preached before the synod of Aberdeen, he explored the considerable challenges confronting a rural minister, including, for example, the duty of catechising, which involved telling 'the same things a thousand times to some dull and ignorant people, who perhaps, shall know little when we have done'. On 12 August 1674, however, the synod appointed Scougal professor of Divinity at King's College, following his successful defence of a set of theses entitled *Positiones aliquot theologicae, de objecto cultus religiosi* (Some of the theological positions, the object of religious worship). He was reluctant to take on such responsibility from a modest sense of his unfitness for it, but the choice was unanimous. He developed a curriculum for ministry through pastoral care, systematic theology and church history. He avoided speculative theology because he believed that 'secret things belong to God, and things revealed, to us and our children'.[10]

As professor he continued to dissuade his students from developing 'an itching curiosity about questions and strife of words, which minister to vanity and contention', while spending his summers purchasing books and conversing with clerical colleagues in England and France. His spirituality is best seen in his writings; and the whole of his outward behaviour and conversation was the constant practice of what he preached. In 1677, Scougal consented to the anonymous publication of his manual of personal devotion entitled *The Life of God in the Soul of Man* in which he characterised 'true Religion' as a 'Union of the Soul with God, a real participation of the Divine Nature, the very Image of God drawn upon the Soul'.[11] It is a Christian classic. Its Nine Sermons are the most elegant compositions written in Scotland during the seventeenth century and were graciously received by people of every denomination.

He became increasingly ill with consumption and died, on 13 June 1678, aged twenty-eight. He was buried in King's College Chapel. Following his father's death in 1682, over a thousand volumes from the Scougals' shared collection were bequeathed to King's College Library, together with a sum of 5000 merks to augment the professor of Divinity's salary. A copy of the morning and evening service forms which Scougal devised for the cathedral church was published in 1791. Entrenched antipathy towards liturgical forms within the Scottish kirk ensured that their regular use was, however, quickly abandoned following the re-establishment of Presbyterianism at the Revolution of 1688–9.

II

James Bruce wrote in 1841:

> the works of Henry Scougal consist of his famous treatise, 'The Life of God in the Soul of Man,' which has gone through numerous editions; nine Discourses, which have also been several times republished; some 'occasional Reflections' which we have not seen; and three Latin Tracts, still in manuscript – the first being a short system of ethics, the second, 'A Preservative against the Artifices of the Romish Missionaries,' and an unfinished treatise on the Pastoral Care. All of his productions that have been given to the world are of the highest excellence as works of practical religion. Of the merits of his 'Life of God' it is nearly impossible to speak in terms of too high praise. This work, which was written for the private use of a noble friend, and not intended for the press, was made public in the year 1677 by Dr Burnet,

afterwards the Bishop of Sarum into whose hands the manuscript had fallen, and who has warmly expressed his feeling of the value of the treasure which he was giving to the world.[12]

In his Funeral Sermon, George Garden said of Scougal's *The Life of God in the Soul of Man*:

> whoever considers the importance of the matter of that book, the clear representation of the life and spirit of true religion and its graces, with the great excellency and advantages of it, the proposal of the most effectual means for attaining to it by the grace of God, the piety and seasonableness of the devotions, together with the natural and affectionate eloquence of the style, – cannot but be sensible of its great usefulness to inspire us with the spirit of true religion, to enlighten our minds with a right sense and knowledge of it, to warm our hearts with suitable affections and breathings after it, and to direct our lives to the practice of it. And, indeed, it seems to have been, in a great measure, the transcript of his own life and spirit.[13]

Garden goes on to say:

> He did not act it to serve little designs, and private interests; but he was full of cordial love and affection. So far was he from desiring to engross the love and kindness of his friends, that he made it his business and delight to propagate true friendship, and make them friends to one another: and in this he studied to render it the most useful thing in the world, and to make it serve the great ends of piety and religion. Those in whom he observed the spirit of true piety and goodness, or any appearance and likelihood of the one having influence on, and bettering the other's life and practice, he endeavoured to bring them into acquaintance and familiarity; to endear them to each other, and make their friendship useful for promoting true piety and goodness, both in themselves and others: and this, perhaps, is the most effectual means for recovering something of the ancient Christian spirit in the world.[14]

In *The Life of God in the Soul of Man,* Scougal sets the discourse in acknowledging the unity of purpose between two people who journey towards the life of God. The framework for unity of purpose is friendship. The depth of this friendship is expressed in affection, gratitude and immediacy. He begins by defining the term 'Friend' as a title which is a relationship of meaning and purpose. Jesus chose to reveal his intimate thoughts and feelings to his disciples in a heightened mode of communication and relationship. There is something self-revelatory about Scougal in defining this relationship which is not fully found in human relationships. This unique relationship is in itself an evidence of the life of God in human soul.

The centre of this exploration, Scougal's most famous work, *The Life of God in the Soul of Man*, which has seen generations of publications, had signs of obscure origins. Rivers noted that the first edition, with 1677 on the title page, has an imprimatur of 18 August 1676, and was printed and published in Michaelmas Term 1676. She continues with new evidence that this text has not previously been studied. The small quarto bound book was acquired by the National Library of Scotland in 1956; and sheds new light both on the author and his work. The title page of this edition of the treatise indeed contains an epistle addressed to a personal and a special friend. According to Rivers, 'The title page identifies the original recipient of the work, which the printed edition of 1677 does not'. The title page reads:

> THE / Life of God in the Soul of man / Or / The nature, excellency and advantages of Religion / With the proper methode of attaining thereunto / In a letter / to / The most virtuous Lady and the / most generous friend / My Lady Gilmoir / August 21 / 1676.

Rivers observes that the Lady in question may have been the fourth wife of the Edinburgh judge Sir John Gilmour.[15] Scougal thus gains new colour, a speculation not on the character of the author, who died in 1671, but on his inner motions about God and God's inner nature.

Most of the editions in print have three main sections. In Part 1, Scougal gives the occasion (objective) of this discourse and highlights the errors about religion. He goes on to define what religion is. His use of the word 'religion', which could mean the 'Christian Faith', whose nature is to be seen in its permanency and flexibility, its freedom and unconstraint – a divine principle. It is then compared and contrasted with the Natural Life and the different tendencies thereof. He then demonstrates Christian faith as the divine life which is better understood by actions than words. The divine life is nothing but divine love exemplified in our blessed Saviour, his diligence in performing God's will, his patience in bearing it, his constant devotion, his charity to humanity, his purity and his humility.

In Part 2, Scougal considers the excellency and advantage of the Christian faith as the life of God. He reflects on this life as the divine love revealed and offered in Christ Jesus. He explores the blessings of the gift of God in Jesus Christ as benefits and advantages of divine love. The worth of the object of that love is to be regarded as inestimable and that love requires nothing less than a reciprocal return. This is a framework expounded by the apostles but lost to the church of his time which was drawn back to legalism. He then says that love requires the object to be present and the divine love makes us partake of an infinite happiness. The reciprocal love of God finds sweetness in all his dispensations and the duties of that divine life are delightful. It results in universal charity and love. The life of God in the soul of a person is expressed in purity of life, in humility and in the blessedness taught by our Lord in the Beatitudes.

The final part explores the life of a Christian with its applications. Scougal advocates moderation of life through restraint in many lawful things and to put ourselves out of love with the world, conscientiously performing the outward actions of faith. We must endeavour to form internal acts of devotion, charity, a Christlike life. Consideration, a regular invitation offered by Christ next to repentance, is a great instrument in religion. Scougal says we must consider the excellency of the divine nature to beget divine love in us. We must often meditate on God's goodness and love, to create charity and remember that all people are nearly related to God, that they bear his image. To attain purity, we must consider the dignity of our nature and meditate often on the joys of heaven. Humility arises from the consideration of our failings and the thoughts of God give us a humble sense of ourselves. Prayer is another essential instrument of religion and mental prayer is very profitable. The ultimate meaning and purpose of faith is advanced by the same means with which it began – the frequent use of the Holy Sacrament.

Scougal's *The Life of God in the Soul of Man* quickly attained the status of an enduring religious classic. Clare Jackson claimed that its latitudinarian theology, mystical piety and intense spiritualism bore close affinity to works produced by Cambridge Platonists, such as John Smith and Jeremy Taylor.[16] After Gilbert Burnet published a second edition of the work in 1691, over a dozen subsequent editions appeared in the century following Scougal's death. Whilst John Wesley reprinted the work in 1744, a French translation appeared at The Hague in 1722, followed by a German version in 1755 and a Welsh edition in 1779. In 1756 Benjamin Franklin printed another German version which he distributed among the German-speaking settlers in Pennsylvania where it 'proved most acceptable at this time'.[17] During the eighteenth century there also appeared several editions of Scougal's collected works, which comprised his sermons, together with several *Private Reflexions and Occasional Meditations* composed while he was a student.

Besides *The Life of God in the Soul of Man*, nine short discourses were published posthumously. Each of these discourses has foundational quality and contributes significantly to the Episcopal Church of his time. All have strong links to *The Life of God* and function almost as commentaries. The discourse on the Passion of our Saviour gives us his insight into true human condition and the transforming power of the Passion of our Lord. Of particular interest is the discourse on the Nativity of our Saviour, a meditation on Psalm 2:11. Preached at Christmas in the King's College Chapel, his exploration of joy in Christian life is commendable and indicates a departure from the prevailing Calvinism of his era. He begins by advocating joy, then seasons it with fear and trembling and concludes with a need for moderation. And moderation has its core not in Presbyterian Scotland but in the *via media* of the Caroline divines of the second episcopate.

On the importance of joy, his astute observation of human condition is more than latitudinarian. Scougal concluded his Christmas sermon as follows:

I hope it doth appear that we have great reason to rejoice in the exaltation of the human nature, and the great salvation purchased to us by the incarnation of the Son of God. I shall add, that even this joy admits of holy fear; even on this occasion we must rejoice with trembling. Salvation is come into the world; but woe to them that neglect it. Little cause have obstinate sinners to rejoice on this festival. The time is coming that they shall wish that either Christ had never come into the world, or they had never heard of him: Behold, this child is set for the rise and fall of many. And they that are not the better, shall be the worse for his coming.

He goes on to admonish those that make this solemn anniversary an opportunity of sinning and debauchery:

Indeed a forenoon's sermon will never compensate an afternoon's debauch; nor will your service in the church justify your intemperance at home . . . our behaviour on the solemnity may be such as suits with the infinite holiness of that person whom we profess to honour, that we may serve the Lord with fear, and rejoice with trembling.[18]

III

The President of Princeton Theological Seminary, at the Centenary celebrations of King's College Chapel in 2009, said, 'Here the mystic Henry Scougal is buried'.[19] However, there is little evidence of him having mystical visions and experiences which are a requisite for the mystic. His critical observation of the state of the Church with its divisions does not make him a latitudinarian as claimed by Jackson.[17] His passion for liturgical worship and his high notion of the sacraments exclude him from the strict Puritan and Presbyterian camps. The Episcopalians maintain their silence with his name appearing nowhere in their liturgical calendar. What do we make of this unique character and his invaluable treatise in the life of the Church?

Scougal finds a place in the range of Christian denominations, each having a claim on him. Scholars have placed him in several settings of theological colours. Yet this short-lived life with a singular short treatise on religion seem to have found a place beyond the reach of many in similar situation. There is enough evidence in his life and works to attest his genius and to go beyond speculations.

If the Aberdeen divines can be regarded as the fathers of Episcopalian spirituality, Scougal was their leader and the Garden brothers made up the circle. These are the products of the second episcopate in Scotland and successors to the Aberdeen Doctors, who despite their diverse opinions can still be regarded as Calvinist in their theology.[20] However, the Aberdeen divines were making new discoveries in biblical interpretation and Christian worship. James Garden was looking for biblical evidence to prove that the gospels went beyond the claims of Calvinistic Protestantism. Christian faith was not protesting the idolatry of Roman Catholicism but the source and foundation of the world's salvation. Garden read the words of the Lord in the gospels deeply, and found richness and diversity in understanding. He duly framed his discoveries in *Comparative Theology* (1700), which not only coined the phrase but created a space between the rivalry of Roman Catholicism and Calvinistic Protestantism.

This space had been anticipated by Henry Scougal in *The Life of God* and his teaching on the Sacraments evident from his posthumous discourses which moved the dominant Christian thought of Restoration Scotland beyond Calvinism. Scougal's understanding of the state of Adam before the Fall was a radical departure. His supralapsarian position was radically moderate in that Adam, made in the image of God, still retained the image of God with minimal distortion. His observation of humanity both within the Church and without made him regard that that which was made by God and pronounced good is good. He could not see the force of predestination into God's creation which is essentially good. It is this goodness that finds people without the Church morally better than those within the Church with unchristian morals.

Scougal, who embraced the Cartesian philosophical framework of observed reason, judged religion integral to human life and found ample evidence within the revealed scripture. Implying that the possibility of universal salvation is grounded not on a liberal view of God but on the atoning power of the Cross of Christ, Scougal's meditation on the Passion of Christ points to the efficacy of the cross rather than the speculation over St Paul's reference to election which was at the root of the double destination of Calvin where humanity is predestined for eternal salvation or eternal damnation.

Notes

1. I. Rivers, 'Scougal's *The life of God in the soul of man*: The Fortunes of a Book, 1676–1830' in R. Savage (ed.), *Philosophy and Religion in Enlightenment Britain: New Case Studies*, Oxford Scholarship Online: September 2012, p. 1.
2. J. Garden, *Comparative Theology; or The True and Solid Grounds of Pure and Peaceable Theology* (London, 1700).
3. *The Works of the Rev. Henry Scougal: with his funeral sermon by Dr Gairden and an account of his life and writings* (New York: R. Carter, 1846), p. 219.
4. Rivers, 'Fortunes of a Book', p. 7.
5. C. Jackson, *Restoration Scotland, 1660-1690: Royalist Politics, Religion and Ideas* (Woodbridge and Rochester: Boydell Press, 2003); J. Buckroyd, *The Life of James Sharp, Archbishop of St. Andrews, 1618–1679: A Political Biography* (Edinburgh: J. Donald, 1987), and *Church and State in Scotland, 1660–1681* (Edinburgh: J. Donald, 1980).
6. J. Cockburn, *A specimen of some free and impartial remarks in publick affairs and particular persons, especially relating to Scotland* (London, 1724), p. 29.

7. *The Works of the Rev. Henry Scougal*, p. 235.
8. Ibid., pp. 265, 267. (Scougal was born the year Descartes died.)
9. Ibid., pp. 240, 241.
10. Ibid., p. 231.
11. H. Scougal, *The life of God in the soul of man: or, the nature and excellency of the Christian Religion* (London, 1776), p. 4.
12. James Bruce, *Lives of Eminent men of Aberdeen* (Aberdeen: Aberdeen University Press, 1841), p. 285.
13. *The Works of the Rev. Henry Scougal, The life of God in the soul of man: with nine other discourses on important subjects* (Boston, 1831), p. vi.
14. *The Works of the Rev. Henry Scougal, The life of God in the soul of man* (Glasgow, 1830) p. 346.
15. Rivers, 'Fortunes of a Book, 1676–1830', p. 4.
16. Jackson, *Restoration Scotland*, pp. 176–9
17. Rivers, 'Fortunes of a Book', p. 8.
18. *The Works of the Rev. Henry Scougal, The life of God in the soul of man* (London, 1822). p. 184.
19. I. Torrance, President, Princeton Theological Seminary, 4 October 2009. Sermon available online from the University of Aberdeen website https://www.abdn.ac.uk/news/3359/.
20. G. D. Henderson, *Religious Life in Seventeenth Century Scotland* (Cambridge: CUP, 1937), p. 88.

CHAPTER SIX

Worship and Devotion in Multiconfessional Scotland, 1686–9

Alasdair Raffe

The short reign of the Catholic King James VII is remarkable not only for the revolution that brought its end but also for the seismic religious changes that the king set in train. In his two declarations of indulgence in February and June 1687, James granted freedom of worship for all Scottish Christians, excepting only the United Societies, a small body of radical Presbyterians who had declared war on the king. The first indulgence was principally of benefit to Catholics and Quakers, but the second declaration was the trigger for a sudden resurgence of organised Presbyterianism in southern and central Scotland. Thus the indulgences signalled the start of the eclipse of episcopacy as the country's established Church polity. And yet James's policy should not be seen simply as a step towards the re-establishment of Presbyterianism in 1690. Rather, the king permitted an unprecedented degree of religious competition, in which Episcopalians, Presbyterians and Catholics vied for followers. At the same time, the king's policy was a bold attempt to encourage Scots of different religious persuasions to live side by side. James initiated what we might call a 'multiconfessional experiment'.[1]

This chapter examines worship and devotion among Episcopalians and Catholics during this Revolutionary period in confessional relations. It argues that multiconfessional competition encouraged churchmen to emphasise and defend the beliefs and practices that distinguished their religious group from the others. Presbyterians affirmed their commitment to the Westminster Confession of Faith, and to the process of Presbyterian ordination formalised in the 1640s. They deliberately revived the use in church services of lectures, sermon-like discussions of a short biblical text, given by the minister, in place of the reading of passages of the Bible by the precentor or reader.[2] Catholics, meanwhile, sought to justify to Scots the Latin mass and the authority of the Church and tradition in Christian theology. The circumstances of the Restoration settlement had entailed that Episcopalian worship was in most respects similar to that of the Presbyterians, particularly in the absence of a formal liturgy. But in their sermons, and in the theology underlying their preaching, Episcopalians had developed a different tone, less rigid in doctrinal certainties, more sympathetic to patristic and ancient wisdom, and increasingly open to the strands of English theological writing that emphasised free will and a holy life.[3] By the 1680s, moreover, some Episcopalians aspired to more formality in worship and piety. Thus when the Episcopalian John Sage wrote in 1690 that worship was 'exactly the same both in the Church and the [Presbyterian] Conventicle', he added that 'our Clergy are not so overbold nor fulsome in their extemporary Expressions as the others are, nor use so many vain Repetitions'.[4] By the time of this statement, one influential Episcopalian congregation had begun to use the English *Book of Common Prayer* in public worship.[5] But even if Sage was not yet sympathetic to this development, his words reflected the extent to which the multiconfessional experiment had exposed and deepened the differences between Episcopalians and Presbyterians.

The chapter begins by considering the growing interest in liturgical worship in the Episcopalian Church of the 1680s. Though the English Prayer Book was not used publicly before 1689, there were signs of support for more ceremonial worship. After briefly reviewing textual evidence of Episcopalians' enthusiasm for the liturgy, the chapter examines the decoration of the chapel at Glamis Castle and the construction of the Canongate Kirk. These building projects serve as examples of what could be done, within the constraints of the establishment, to create spaces suitable for formal worship. If the first part of the chapter concerns buildings and forms of worship, the second section turns to the books and pamphlets published to promote one confessional tradition over another. The striking development of James VII's reign was the setting up of a Catholic printing press at Holyroodhouse. Supported by royal funds, the press issued a large number of books, pamphlets and broadsides, including at least twenty-two Catholic works. Meanwhile, the Crown made efforts to suppress anti-Catholic printing, and few writings by Episcopalians and moderate Presbyterians were published.

I

The indulgences of 1687 undermined the established Church. By suspending the penal laws that had compelled reluctant conformists to attend their parish churches, the king collapsed a vital pillar of the Kirk's constitutional fabric. As a result, Episcopalian congregations in parts of southern Scotland shrunk dramatically, as worshippers left for Presbyterian meeting houses. Earlier in the 1680s, by contrast, the cancelling of the indulgences of 1669, 1672 and 1679, under which Presbyterian ministers were licensed to preach in specified parishes, together with the vigorous enforcement of the penal laws, had given leading Episcopalians a new sense of confidence. Among the indications of this mood were several steps to promote liturgical worship in the Church. In February 1680, the Privy Council considered a 'representation' made 'by some of their owne number that diverse persons of quality and others ... were very desireous to have the allowance of the use of the solemne forme of divine worship' authorised by the Church of England. The council agreed to protect families using the Prayer Book in domestic worship.[6] One of the councillors present was James Drummond, earl of Perth – later a convert to Catholicism and James VII's chancellor – who in this period employed the *Book of Common Prayer* in his household.[7] In the summer of 1684, Perth and William Douglas, duke of Queensberry, were among the proponents of the use of the Prayer Book in the royal chapel in Holyroodhouse. This project did not survive the accession of James VII; the new king was determined to introduce the mass in his chapel royal. But Episcopalian supporters of liturgical worship continued to draw succour from the decline of Presbyterian dissent and the weakness of opposition to the Crown. In July 1685, following the defeat of the rebellion of the 9th earl of Argyll, Bishop John Paterson of Edinburgh expressed the wish that the Church should 'have devout forms of worship setled therin, when we have so faire a prospect of halcyon-days and tranquillitie dureing this his Majesties reigne'.[8]

This is the context for the remarkable projects of ecclesiastical construction and adornment that took place in 1688 in Glamis Castle, Angus, where a new chapel was created with extensive figurative decoration. Glamis was the property of Patrick Lyon, earl of Strathmore and Kinghorne, a nobleman of Royalist background, albeit a minor figure in public life. As part of an extensive programme of building at Glamis, Strathmore added a wing containing the new chapel between 1679 and around 1683. In January 1688, he signed a contract for the chapel's decoration with the Dutch artist Jacob de Wet, who had recently worked at Holyroodhouse, where he painted portraits of James VII and his 110 real and legendary predecessors as king of Scots. De Wet was commissioned to paint panels and an altarpiece for the earl's chapel. On the ceiling of the chapel, de Wet was to illustrate the life of Christ in fifteen panels; on the walls, he was to paint the apostles. In each case, the contract required de Wet to reproduce the images in 'a bible here in the house or the Service Book'.[9] The books to which de Wet referred have disappeared from Glamis, but recent scholars have suggested that he drew on early seventeenth-century engravings by, or after, the Dutch artist Boetius à Bolswert and the Frenchman Jacques Callot. It is possible that some of de Wet's portraits, particularly those of the apostles, were based directly on contemporaneous engravings by Frederick Hendrick van Hove. Religious images by van Hove, which imitated the engravings of Bolswert and Callot, appeared in various English bibles and prayer books of the period.[10] Conceivably Glamis had one of the bibles published in Edinburgh in 1633: some of the Edinburgh New Testaments included Bolswert's plates.[11]

The completed chapel was a striking ecclesiastical interior, appropriate for a ritualistic use of the Anglican Prayer Book. As well as the figurative paintings and altarpiece, altar rails were fitted, though it seems that the late seventeenth-century chapel had a communion table placed against the wall, rather than a stone altar.[12] By specifying the source of de Wet's decorative scheme, Strathmore had linked the devotion of his Episcopalian chapel to two overlapping traditions. First, there was the piety of seventeenth-century Jesuitism. Bolswert's engravings of the life of Christ, the models for de Wet's ceiling, had first appeared in the *Vitae, Passionis et Mortis Jesu Christi* (Antwerp, 1622), by the French Jesuit Jean Bourgeois. Among the ceiling panels are several painted with the 'IHS' monogram, often the symbol of the Society of Jesus. Strathmore resisted the pressure to convert to Catholicism felt by many nobles in James VII's reign. But whilst his chapel was intended for Protestant worship, it shared in a culture of Catholic decoration. At the same time, the Bolswert images associated Glamis chapel with Archbishop William Laud of Canterbury and his influence on the liturgical development of Scottish Episcopacy in the 1630s. Laud himself owned Bourgeois's *Vitae, Passionis et Mortis Jesu Christi*; Laud's English critics alleged that the archbishop gave his support to the inclusion of the Bolswert engravings in editions of the Bible.[13] The imagery of de Wet's work, then, associated the chapel at Glamis with a ceremonial aspect of early seventeenth-century Episcopalian culture, in England and Scotland.

Of course, Glamis was a private chapel. There was nothing comparable to its interior in any post-Reformation parish church or cathedral in Scotland. It suggests a path of development that Scottish Episcopalian churches could perhaps have followed, had many of the country's landed elite shared Strathmore's tastes, and had an Episcopalian establishment backed by penal laws been maintained. Alternatively, we might conclude that Glamis illustrated a divergence between the devotional aspirations of an unrepresentative nobleman and the more informal preferences of the Scottish laity at large. Yet the Catholic influences on Glamis are significant, especially if we consider the chapel in the context of contemporary building developments in Holyrood and the Canongate.

In August 1686, six months before his first declaration of indulgence, James VII instructed the Privy Council to protect private Catholic worship and to provide a Catholic chapel in his palace of Holyroodhouse.[14] The chapel, at first located in the former council chamber, was duly furnished before being consecrated on St Andrew's Day (30 November) 1686.[15] In 1686 or 1687, silver objects were produced for the chapel, including a chalice, a paten and a hand-bell by the Edinburgh gold- and silversmith Zacharias Mellinus.[16] By international standards, the quality of worship at Holyrood was probably not high. Richard Hay, an Augustinian canon recently returned to his native Scotland, described the Benedictine who officiated at Christmas 1686 as 'a man not mutch skill'd in singing'.[17] The chapel was quickly seen as too small, and, in June 1687, the king ordered its removal to the nave of Holyrood Abbey, adjacent to the palace, which had been suggested as the home of the chapel in 1672. This in turn evicted the congregation of the Canongate parish, which had worshipped in the Abbey nave, and was now rehoused in Lady Yester's Church in

Edinburgh.[18] The new chapel royal was also to serve as the meeting place of the recently revived Order of the Thistle.[19] To make the chapel suitable for daily worship and the order's ceremonies, decorative work was ordered in December 1687. Carved pieces were prepared in London; an order for payment in the summer of 1688 shows that the court sculptor Grinling Gibbons worked on the chapel's altarpieces.[20]

Unlike in the case of Glamis, where the chapel survives, it is impossible to assess the interior of the chapel royal of 1688. Its furnishings were destroyed in the riot of 10 December that year, and the building later became a ruin.[21] A contemporary picture of the interior shows a throne on a raised dais, in a prominent position at the west end. This plausibly suggests that the fittings glorified monarchy, but offers no information about the character of worship in the chapel.[22] Whatever its appearance, the chapel was the focal point for public Catholic worship in Scotland, being attended by curious Protestants as well as committed Catholics.[23] And as a consequence of its creation, another important development in Episcopalian architecture took place, with the building of a new church nearby in the Canongate.

In his order of June 1687, the king promised that the Canongate congregation's use of Lady Yester's Church would be temporary, and that a new parish church would be constructed, funded by a mid-seventeenth-century bequest for church-building in Edinburgh.[24] Thomas Moodie, a merchant in the burgh and town treasurer in 1642–3, had pledged 20,000 merks for the construction of a new church as long ago as 1649. Though interest earned on the money was used to modify existing churches in the mid-1650s, the mortification remained unspent.[25] In 1681, the town council and Moodie's heir petitioned parliament, arguing that the Grassmarket, then proposed as the location of a new church, was unsuitable for the purpose. Edinburgh's petition called for the money to pay for a bell-tower and peal of bells in the Westport, but parliament instead left the final decision about the bequest's use to the Privy Council.[26] There followed two attempts, resisted by the burgh council, to devote the Covenanter Moodie's mortification to the building of a house for the bishop of Edinburgh.[27] But in March 1688, after offering a new church for the Canongate, James finally ensured that the bequest was applied to its original purpose.[28]

The resulting Canongate Kirk was among the most remarkable buildings of the period. Its architect, James Smith, had grown up in Forres before training for the Jesuit priesthood at the Scots College in Rome in the 1670s. After his return to Scotland, he probably remained a practising Catholic. His religion endeared him to the duke of York; Smith became overseer of the king's works in 1683. Crucially, his aesthetic formation in the Roman centre of Catholic baroque culture led him to construct a church unique in seventeenth-century Scotland.[29] Though aisles flanking the nave had been built at Greyfriars, Edinburgh, in the early part of the century, the Canongate Kirk's Latin-cross plan and bell-shaped façade derived from

Catholic models. The architectural instructions of the Catholic reformer Carlo Borromeo were observed; Smith perhaps had in mind the Gesù, the Jesuits' mother church in Rome, though other Italian churches bear at least as strong a resemblance.[30] A later generation of Protestant burghers bricked up the Canongate's incongruous chancel to form a standard box-shaped Presbyterian church, albeit the acoustics may have remained poor for preaching.[31] It is impossible to know whether the king or his architect imagined that mass would one day be celebrated in the church. But the fact that the major church-building project of the reign should plant a piece of the continental baroque in James's multiconfessional capital is significant. The Canongate Kirk was not completed in time to become a showpiece of the Episcopalian establishment. Yet it was in origin an Episcopalian project, drawing on Catholic influences, and illustrating the potential for new directions in worship and devotion in James's Scotland.

II

We can gain another perspective on the multiconfessional competition over worship in James's reign by examining the output of the Scottish printing press. With the king's support, there was a massive increase in the supply of Catholic books. Fundamental to this temporary reorientation of Scottish publishing was the setting up of a Catholic printer, based in Holyroodhouse. As a result of this press's activity, the 1686–8 period saw the publication of more devotional and polemical writings by Catholics than comparable works by Episcopalians and Presbyterians. Scottish Episcopalians made surprisingly little use of print in James's reign, though their printed output earlier in the Restoration period had also been quite small. The majority of printed Protestant sermons, devotional and controversial works continued to be by Presbyterians. In the years 1687–8, almost all Presbyterian publications in Scotland were works by radical Cameronians.[32] Thus in the output of the book trade, mainstream Protestants were outnumbered by Presbyterian extremists and Catholics. A selection of English tracts against Catholicism was reprinted at Edinburgh in 1687 with the bishop of Edinburgh's imprimatur.[33] In general, however, the government did not welcome such publications. In August 1687, the Privy Council attempted to prevent booksellers from stocking anti-Catholic works imported from England.[34] It is difficult to assess the effectiveness of the government's attempts to suppress anti-Catholic works. But under James, printed literature promoting Catholic worship and devotion was more available than ever before.

The origins of the Holyroodhouse printing press are a little obscure. In 1684 or 1685, the Aberdonian merchant James Watson, a Catholic, bought out Joshua van Solingen and Jan Colmar, indebted Dutch printers who had been active in Edinburgh. Seeking repayment of a debt owed by Charles II, Watson then went to court. Rather than money, he was there offered a gift of the sole right to print almanacs in Scotland, together with the title of printer to James VII's 'family and household'. It is unclear when the latter designation was bestowed, but a royal letter of 21 August 1686 confirmed Watson's monopoly over the printing of 'prognostications'. At the same time, Watson was provided with a workshop in Holyroodhouse at royal expense.[35] He published at least four works in 1686, though some of his early titles are difficult to identify because no publisher or place of publication is given in the imprints.[36] In May 1687, the king ordered that £100 sterling be allocated to support Watson's Catholic printing, to be spent on the advice of the earl of Perth. The press produced nineteen surviving editions in 1687, despite Watson's death that year. He was quickly replaced by the German Peter Bruce (or Breusch), who continued to print until the shop was destroyed in the anti-Catholic riots of December 1688.[37]

In total, the surviving output of the Holyroodhouse printing press numbers at least forty-four titles, and two other works were probably produced there (see Appendix 6.1).[38] In addition, Bruce reprinted four issues of the pro-government London newspapers *The Test-Paper*, *The Weekly TEST-Paper* and *Publick Occurrences Truely Stated*, all dating from May 1688. Indeed, much of the press's output was reprinted from recent London titles. Watson and Bruce issued at least ten official publications produced by the government in England, including royal proclamations and special forms of prayer for use in the Church of England. The press also reprinted several topical and polemical writings that had previously been published in London, most relating to international affairs and the Crown's campaign to repeal the English Test Acts. Aside from almanacs compiled by James Paterson, and the same writer's *Geographical Description of Scotland* (1687), few of the Holyroodhouse books were by Scottish authors. The press issued only two publications directly relating to royal policies in Scotland – significantly both concerned the declarations of indulgence – and most proclamations continued to come from the more longstanding royal printer, the heir of Andrew Anderson.[39]

Twenty-two or twenty-three of the press's titles were devotional, polemical and literary works by Catholics: by Scottish standards, a considerable printed output. Beyond the involvement of the earl of Perth, we know nothing about how the Catholic books were selected for publication, though the prominence of Jesuit works suggests that members of the Society of Jesus such as Robert Widdrington, a spiritual adviser to Perth, had some influence over the press.[40] After the establishment of a Jesuit 'college' in Holyroodhouse in 1688, Bruce explicitly served the Jesuits, styling himself printer to the king, his 'Houshold, Chappel and Colledge'. When the college opened, Bruce issued *The Rules of the Schools of the Royal Colledge at Holy-Rood-House* (1688), based on two London broadsides describing institutions of Jesuit education in the English capital.[41] The Edinburgh edition included a revealing addition: a promise that the Jesuits would teach philosophy (which was not offered in London), thus competing with the Protestant town college in Edinburgh.

Of the Catholic works, only two were original publications, issued for the first time by the Holyroodhouse printer. Both were by Jesuits. Written after the birth of Prince James Francis Edward in June 1688, *A Loyal Anagrame on the Prince and Stewart of Scotland* (1688) was a single sheet with an anagram on the names of the king and queen, 'Made by a *Scots* JESUITE'. *An Answer, to a little Book call'd Protestancy to be Embrac'd* (1686) was an original Scottish contribution to Catholic apologetics. Its author, the Jesuit Alexander Con, was the nephew of George Conn of Auchry, the papal agent at Charles I's court. The work to which Con responded, *Protestancy to be Embrac'd*, was by David Abercromby, a Scottish Jesuit who converted to Protestantism.[42] It was appropriate that the Catholic answer to this book should come from the Holyroodhouse press.

As with the press's non-Catholic publications, however, a majority of the works by Catholics were reprinted from earlier editions published elsewhere, without significant additions or changes. Most of the controversial pamphlets and the two poems by the Catholic convert John Dryden had been first published in London. Apart from the two entirely new works already discussed, up to six of the Catholic works were substantially new editions, or were reprints with new prefaces added.[43] Of these, perhaps the most interesting is the edition by Watson of Thomas à Kempis's *Following of Christ*. This was based on previous translations of the *Imitatio Christi*, but is sufficiently distinctive to be considered a unique edition of the devotional classic. Unlike Protestant versions of the work, Watson's included the fourth book concerning the mass.[44] Though the main function of the Holyroodhouse press was to reprint, the à Kempis shows that independent and scholarly work lay behind the promotion of Catholicism in Scotland.

Several of the Holyroodhouse Catholic books were dedicated to the noble patrons of the Catholic cause in Scotland. A 1687 edition of *An Introduction to a Devout Life* by Francis de Sales, which was almost certainly printed at Holyroodhouse, was dedicated to the earl of Perth.[45] Con's *Answer* was dedicated to Perth and, with wishful thinking, to the Protestant senators of the college of justice. *Sure Characters, distinguishing a Real Christian from a Nominal*, by Cyprien de Gamaches, spiritual adviser to Queen Henrietta Maria (wife of Charles I and mother of James VII), contained a new dedication to the duchess of Gordon, signed by John Reid. Gordon Castle, the duchess's residence, was a centre of Catholic worship and a meeting place for missionaries in northern Scotland during James's reign.[46]

Despite these dedications, most of the publications of Watson and Bruce seem to have been addressed to lay people of modest means. Of the twenty-two or twenty-three Catholic works, nine were in the portable and cheap duodecimo format. Among the eight quartos, six were short pamphlets of under ten pages. The only large-format publications were two or three single-sheet broadsides. The types of books published also indicate that the press aimed its output at ordinary readers. Ten of the Catholic books can be classified as anti-Protestant polemics.[47] Most of these were short, and several focused on Catholic teaching on the mass, clearly an essential subject in which to instruct potential converts. Eight or nine titles were devotional and expository works.[48] Only four do not fit either classification.[49] The number of devotional writings is noteworthy, and suggests that Catholics hoped to win converts not only by defeating their Protestant rivals in argument but also by promoting Catholic piety. Indeed, the dedication of de Sales's *Introduction* argued that, among other proofs that Rome was the true Church, the quality of Catholic devotional writing was forceful evidence.[50] By attempting to demonstrate this, the Holyroodhouse press made an important contribution to the debate over devotion and worship under James VII.

III

By granting freedom of worship to all but a small minority of Scots, King James unleashed the forces of multiconfessionalism. His religious policy was experimental: James departed from the coercive enforcement of uniformity, practised with varying levels of conviction by his royal predecessors. James's indulgences created the conditions in which distinctive practices and doctrines could be asserted and new agendas pursued. At this interval, therefore, the Catholic influences on Episcopalian devotion were explored, and Episcopalian support for a formal liturgy grew. In their different ways, the chapel at Glamis and the Canongate Kirk manifested the desires of some Episcopalians to emulate England in worship and continental Jesuitism in imagery and symbolism. These building projects took place at a time when Scottish readers had unprecedented access to works advocating Catholic worship and piety. Indeed, it was with respect to the book trade that the Crown made its most systematic attempts to intervene in – and place restrictions on – the free market in religious services that the king himself had initiated. In terms of worship and devotion, then, James's reign was a moment of aesthetic innovation and a major promotional campaign using the press. The Revolution of 1688–90 ensured that toleration was short-lived, and that the degree of religious pluralism seen in James's reign was not again present in Scotland for many decades. But the years 1687–9 should be remembered for more than the revival of Presbyterianism and the overthrow of Episcopacy. Fundamental to these processes was the vibrancy of religious competition stimulated by King James's multiconfessional experiment.

Appendix 6.1: Works printed by James Watson or Peter Bruce, Holyroodhouse

This appendix is a supplement to William Cowan's bibliography, listing titles not noted by Cowan, together with all the Holyroodhouse press's surviving Catholic works.[51] Counted as 'Catholic' works are titles known to be written by Catholics, and works explicitly promoting Catholicism. Excluded from the list of Catholic works (2.1 and 2.2) are proclamations and other items directly connected to royal government. Titles 3, 10, 11, 12, 18, 20 and 23 on this list were omitted by Cowan. In volumes where James Watson is specified as the printer, he is described variously as 'Printer to His [most Excellent / Sacred] Majesties Royal Family and Houshold'. Peter Bruce is usually described as 'Mr. P. B. enginier, Printer to the King's Most Excellent Majesty, for His Houshold, Chappel and Colledge'.

1. 'Non-Catholic' publications omitted by Cowan

1.1 Definite
His Majesties gracious Declaration to all His Loving Subjects, for Liberty of Conscience (London, Printed 1687. Edinburgh, Re-printed at Holy-Rood-House, by James Watson, 1687), J189A. The king's English declaration of indulgence of 4 April 1687.

A Form, or Order of Thanksgiving. And Prayer, to be used in London, and Ten Miles round it, on Sunday the 15th of this instant January (Re-printed at Holy-Rood-House, 1688), C4182B. A form of prayer, reprinted from the London editions (C4182, C4182A), for use in Anglican churches on the national thanksgiving for the queen's pregnancy, to be observed on 15 January in and around London, and on 29 January elsewhere in England and Wales. An equivalent thanksgiving was kept in Scotland on 29 January and 19 February, though the form of prayer was not to be used.

R[oger] L'[E]s[trange], *Two Cases Submitted to Consideration 1. Of the Necessity and Exercise of a Dispensing Power. 2. The Nullity of any Act of State that Clashes with the Law of God* (Printed at Holy-Rood-House, 1687), L1320B. Reprinted from the London edition of 1687 (L1320A).

1.2 Possible
Thomas Cartwright, *A Sermon preached upon the Anniversary Solemnity of the Happy Inauguration of our Dread Soveraign Lord King James II. In the Collegiate Church of Ripon, February the 6th. 1685/6* (Printed London and Re-printed at Edinburgh, 1686), C708. This sermon, promoting an absolutist understanding of royal authority, and criticising Anglican opponents of Catholicism, seems to have been reprinted to encourage parliament to repeal the penal laws in 1686.

2. Catholic works

2.1 Definite and probable
(1) Nicolas Caussin, *The Christian Diurnal. of F.N. Caussin, S.J. Reviewed, and Much Augmented. And Translated into English by S. T. H. Third Edition* (Printed, An. Dom. 1686), C1544A; Cowan 22; Clancy 194. The Jesuit Nicolas Caussin

published his *Journée Chrestienne* in or before 1628. The English translation by Sir Thomas Hawkins was first published in 1632 (STC 4871).

(2) [Alexander Con,] *An Answer, to a little Book call'd Protestancy to be Embrac'd or, A New and Infallible Method to reduce Romanists from Popery to Protestancy* (Printed in the Year, 1686), C5682; Cowan 1; Clancy 242. Published by Watson at Holyroodhouse. Though Wing lists an edition of the *Answer* dated 1682 (C5681), C5682's preface to the earl of Perth and College of Justice suggests that the 1686 edition was the first.

(3) [James Dymock,] *The Great Sacrifice of the New Law. Expounded by the Figures of the Old* (Printed 1686), D2974; Clancy 340. A Jesuit work, it was first published in Antwerp in 1676 (D2972).

(4) Paul Bruzeau, *The Faith of the Catholick Church, concerning the Eucharist. Invincibly Proved by the Argument used Against the Protestants, in the Books of the Faith of the Perpetuity, written by Mr. Arnaud* (Printed at Holy-Rood-House, 1687), B5241A; Cowan 11; Clancy 34. The French original (Paris, 1681) contributed to a controversy about whether the Eastern Churches held the real presence in the Eucharist.

(5) John Dryden, *The Hind and the Panther. A Poem. In Three Parts* (Holy-Rood-House: Re-printed by James Watson, 1687), D2282; Cowan 6; Clancy 328. Reprinted from the first edition, published in London 11 April 1687 (D2281).

(6) Thomas à Kempis, *The Following of Christ. Divided into Four Books: Written in Latin, by the Learned and Devout Man Thomas à Kempis Canon-regular of the Order of St. Augustin. Translated into English* (Holy-Rood-House: Printed by James Watson, 1687), T954; Cowan 12; Clancy 952.

(7) James Mumford, *The Catholic-Scripturist: or, The Plea of the Roman Catholics. Shevving the Scriptures to hold the Roman Faith in above Forty of the Chief Controversies now under Debate* (Holy-Rood-House: Printed by James Watson, 1687), M3065; Cowan 7; Clancy 697. An English Jesuit work, first published in Ghent, 1662 (M3063), then in London, 1686 (M3064).

(8) [John Gother,] *A Letter from a Dissenter to the Divines of the Church of England in order to an Union* (Re-printed at Holy-Rood-House, 1687), G1331; Cowan 10; Clancy 452. Reprinted from the London edition of 1687 (G1330). Despite the title, Gother (1654–1704) was a Jesuit. He aimed to make dissenters suspect Anglicans' professions of good will.

(9) N.N., *The Catholick Answer to the Seekers Request in a Letter directed to the Seeker, proving the Real Presence, by the Scripture only* (Re-printed at

Holy-Rood-House, 1687), N31; Cowan 9; Clancy 707. A sequel to, and uniform in format to, (13) below. Reprinted with minor changes from the London edition (1687; N30).

(10) *Protestancy Destitute of Scripture-Proofs* (Printed London 1687. Edinburgh: Re-printed by James Watson, 1687), P3818; Clancy 808.

(11) *Resolutions of a Penitent Soul, desirous of Eternal Salvation. With a Short and Easie Method, directing Worldlings, how they may Spend the Whole Day in Gods Service* (Holy-Rood-House: Printed by James Watson, 1687), R1165; Clancy 831. A reference to Francis de Sales, 'who dyed not forty years since' (p. 30), suggests that the work was written in the 1650s or early 1660s. No other edition appears to have survived.

(12) Francis de Sales, *An Introduction to a Devout Life, of S. Francis de Sales Bishop and Prince of Geneva* (Printed in the year, 1687), ESTC 006170358; Clancy 391.5.

(13) *A Seekers Request to Catholick Priests, and Protestant Ministers, for Satisfying his Conscience in the Truth of what he Ought to Believe of the Lords Supper* (Re-printed at Holy-Rood-House, 1687), S2412; Cowan 8; Clancy 879. Reprinted without textual changes from the London edition (1687; S2411). It was followed by title (9).

(14) Cyprien de Gamaches, *Sure Characters, distinguishing a Real Christian from a Nominal: together with some Certain Directions, how to Render the Baptismal Graces Effectual: which Instructions, if truly Observed, will undoubtedly Guide us to eternal Hapiness. Done originally in French, and faithfully Translated in English* (Re-printed at Holy-Rood-House, 1687), C7716; Cowan 13; Clancy 290.

(15) *An Address presented to the Reverend and Learned Ministers of the Church of England, by One sincerely Desireous of finding out the Truth, in behalf of Himself and Others equally Concern'd, as well for their Own as the general Satisfaction* (Reprinted at Holy-Rood-House, 1688), A560; Cowan 24; Clancy 14. A Catholic pamphlet reprinted without textual changes from the London edition of 1688 (A559).

(16) John Dryden, *Britannia Rediviva: a Poem on the Birth of the Prince* (Holy-Rood-House: Re-printed by Mr. P. B. enginier, 1688), D2252; Cowan 31. Reprinted from the London edition, whose imprimatur is dated 19 June 1688 (D2251).

(17) Richard Hudleston, *A Short and Plain Way to the Faith and Church. Composed many years since by that eminent Divine, Master Richrd Hudleston, of the English Congregation, of the Order of St. Benedict; and now Published for*

the Common Good by his nephew Mr. John Hudleston, of the same Congregation: Chaplain to the Queen Dowager To which is Annexed, His late Majesty King Charles II.'s Papers found in his Closet after his Decease. As also a brief Account of what Occured on his Death bed in Regard to Religion (Holy-Rood-House: Printed by Mr. P. B. enginier, 1688), H3258; Cowan 21; Clancy 522. Reprinted from the London edition 1688 (H3257) without significant changes.

(18) *A Loyal Anagrame on the Prince and Stewart of Scotland, Prince of Wales, Duke of Rothsay and Cornwall, born the 10th. of June 1688* (Holy-Rood-House: Printed by Mr P. B., 1688), L3336B.

(19) *A Manual of Devout Prayers and Devotions, fitted for all Persons and Occasions. With diverse Choice, select Prayers before and after Confession and Communion, and an Examen of Conscience.* (Holy-Rood-House: Printed by Mr. P. B. enginier, 1688), ESTC 006085123; Cowan 20.

(20) *A Manuel of Devout Prayers, fitted for all Persons and Occasions. Last Edition, with Necessary Additions* (Holyroodhouse: Printed by Mr. P. B. Enginneer, 1688), ESTC 006098135; Clancy 637. This edition is different from, and probably subsequent to, (19).

(21) *A Pastoral Letter from the four Catholic Bishops to the Lay-Catholics of England* (Holy-rood-house, Re-printed by Mr P. B. Enginier, 1688), P675A; Cowan 23; Clancy 761. This pamphlet was a reprint of the version published in 1688 at London (P675).

(22) *The Rules of the Schools of the Royal Colledge at Holy-Rood-House* (Holy-Rood-House: printed by Mr. P. B. Enginneer 1688), R2260; Cowan 25; Clancy 842.

2.2 Possible
(23) *Christians Solemn Vow in Baptism Explicated and Renewed* (Edinburgh: reprinted, 1688), T948. It may derive from one of Thomas à Kempis's minor works.

Notes

1. A. Raffe, *Scotland in Revolution, 1685–1690* (Edinburgh: Edinburgh University Press, 2018), chs 2–3. On 'multiconfessionalism', see esp. T. M. Safley, 'Multiconfessionalism: A Brief Introduction' in T. M. Safley (ed.), *A Companion to Multiconfessionalism in the Early Modern World* (Leiden: Brill, 2011), pp. 1–19.
2. Raffe, *Scotland in Revolution*, pp. 46–7, 66–7.
3. A. Raffe, 'Presbyterians and Episcopalians: The Formation of Confessional Cultures in Scotland, 1660–1715', *EHR*, 125 (2010), 570–98, at 580–8.

4. [J. Sage,] *The Case of the Present Afflicted Clergy truly Represented* (London, 1690) sig. [A3]r.
5. [A. Monro,] *Presbyterian Inquisition; as it was lately Practised against the Professors of the Colledge of Edinburgh* (London, 1691), pp. 31–3, 95–6; A. à Wood, *Athenae Oxonienses: an Exact History of all the Writers and Bishops who have had their Education in the most Ancient and Famous University of Oxford*, 2 vols (London, 1691–2), II, cols 632–3.
6. *RPCS*, 3rd ser., ed. P. Hume Brown, H. Paton and E. Balfour-Melville, 16 vols (Edinburgh, 1908–70), VI, p. 388. There were discussions in the 1660s about introducing a liturgy, but the project was aborted by a king wary of provoking unrest (see Chapter 4).
7. *The Memoirs of Sir Robert Sibbald (1641–1722)*, ed. F. Paget Hett (London: OUP, 1932).
8. *A Collection of Letters addressed by Prelates and Individuals of High Rank in Scotland and by Two Bishops of Sodor and Man to Sancroft Archbishop of Canterbury*, ed. W. N. Clarke (Edinburgh: R. Lendrum, 1848), pp. 69, 72, 86.
9. *The Book of Record: A Diary Written by Patrick, First Earl of Strathmore, and other Documents relating to Glamis Castle*, ed. A. H. Millar (Edinburgh: SHS, 1890), 92, 104–6; R. MacInnes, 'Lyon, Patrick, third earl of Strathmore and Kinghorne (1643?–1695)', *ODNB*; H. G. Slade, *Glamis Castle* (London: Society of Antiquaries, 2000), ch. 7; S. Bruce and S. Yearley, 'The Social Construction of Tradition: The Restoration Portraits and the Kings of Scotland' in D. McCrone, S. Kendrick and P. Straw (eds), *The Making of Scotland: Nation, Culture and Social Change* (Edinburgh: British Sociological Association, 1989), pp. 175–88.
10. M. R. Apted and R. L. Snowden, 'The de Wet Paintings in the Chapel at Glamis Castle' in D. J. Breeze (ed.), *Studies in Scottish Antiquity Presented to Stewart Cruden* (Edinburgh: John Donald, 1984), pp. 232–48; R. A. Guilding, 'The de Wet Apostle Paintings in the Chapel at Glamis Castle', *Proceedings of the Society of Antiquaries of Scotland*, 116 (1986), 429–45; D. M. Gauld and H. Howe, *The Chapel at Glamis Castle* (Glamis: privately published, 2013). I am grateful to David Gauld for sending me a copy of this guide book.
11. T. H. Darlow and H. F. Moule, rev. A. S. Herbert, *Historical Catalogue of Printed Editions of the English Bible, 1525–1961* (London: British and Foreign Bible Society, 1968), pp. 167–70.
12. Slade, *Glamis Castle*, p. 50.
13. *Historical Catalogue*, 167–8.
14. NRS, Warrant book of the secretary for Scotland, 9 Apr. 1686 – 25 Feb. 1687, SP4/11, pp. 257–60; printed in R. Wodrow, *The History of the Sufferings of the Church of Scotland from the Restoration to the Revolution*, ed. R. Burns, 4 vols (Glasgow, 1828–30), IV, 389–90; *RPCS*, 3rd ser., XII, 435.
15. John Lauder, *Historical Notices of Scotish Affairs*, ed. D. Laing, 2 vols (Bannatyne Club, 1848), II, 763, 764–5.
16. National Museums of Scotland, IL.2009.16.1, IL.2009.16.2, IL.2009.16.4; R. and J. Dietert, *The Edinburgh Goldsmiths: I: Training, Marks, Output and Demographics* (New York: Cornell University, 2007), p. 29.
17. R. A. Hay, *Genealogie of the Hayes of Tweeddale* (Edinburgh: Stevenson, 1835), p. 55. In May 1687, two payments of £100 sterling were to be made for communion elements and music in the chapel: NRS, Warrant book of the secretary for Scotland, 1 March 1687 – 23 Apr. 1688, SP4/12, pp. 143–5.

18. NRS, SP4/12, pp. 218–20; *Extracts from the Records of the Burgh of Edinburgh, 1681 to 1689*, ed. M. Wood (Edinburgh: Oliver & Boyd, 1954), p. 211; Lauder, *Historical Notices*, II, 808-9; *RPCS*, 3rd ser., III, 593–4.
19. M. Glozier, 'The Earl of Melfort, the Court Catholic Party and the Foundation of the Order of the Thistle, 1687', *SHR*, 79 (2000), 233–8.
20. NRS, SP4/12, pp. 489-91; *RPCS*, 3rd ser., XIII, p. xlviii.
21. R. A. Houston, *Social Change in the Age of Enlightenment: Edinburgh, 1660–1760* (Oxford: Clarendon Press, 1994), 306–9; C. Rogers, *History of the Chapel Royal of Scotland with the Register of the Chapel Royal of Stirling* (Edinburgh: Grampian Club, 1882), app., pp. 102–13.
22. The image is reproduced in A. MacKechnie, 'The Earl of Perth's Chapel of 1688 at Drummond Castle and the Roman Catholic Architecture of James VII', *Architectural Heritage*, 25 (2014), 107–31.
23. Lauder, *Historical Notices*, II, 794; Mark Dilworth, 'The Scottish Mission in 1688–1689', *Innes Review*, 20 (1969), 68–79.
24. NRS, SP4/12, pp. 218–20.
25. *Extracts from the Records of the Burgh of Edinburgh, 1642 to 1655*, ed. Marguerite Wood (Edinburgh, 1938), pp. 223, 391–2; *Extracts from the Records of the Burgh of Edinburgh, 1655 to 1665*, ed. M. Wood (Edinburgh, 1940), p. 181; *Extracts from the Records of the Burgh of Edinburgh, 1665 to 1680*, ed. M. Wood (Edinburgh, 1950), pp. 3, 21, 41.
26. *Extracts from the Records of the Burgh of Edinburgh, 1681 to 1689*, pp. 13–14, *RPS*, ed. K. M. Brown et al.; [http://www.rps.ac.uk/; 1681/7/59].
27. *Edinburgh Extracts, 1681 to 1689*, pp. 79, 151; *RPCS*, 3rd ser., XI, pp. 97–8, 102, 185–6.
28. NRS, SP4/12, pp. 628–30; *RPCS*, 3rd ser., XIII, xlviii; *Edinburgh Extracts, 1681 to 1689*, pp. 238–9. For Smith's overspending and the long process of settling his debts, see: *RPC*, 3rd ser., XIV, 22; RPS, M1690/4/18, 1690/4/50, 1690/4/71, A1693/4/17, M1693/4/15, M1693/4/27; *Extracts from the Records of the Burgh of Edinburgh, 1689 to 1701*, ed. H. Armet (Edinburgh: Oliver & Boyd, 1962), pp. 52, 241; *Extracts from the Records of the Burgh of Edinburgh, 1701 to 1718*, ed. H. Armet (Edinburgh; Oliver & Boyd, 1967), p. 99.
29. C. González-Longo, 'James Smith and Rome', *Architectural Heritage*, 23 (2012), 75–96; A. MacKechnie, 'A King, Catholics, and Canongate Kirk', *History Scotland*, 7:6 (2007), 22–8; A. Roberts, 'James Smith and James Gibbs: Seminarians and Architects', *Architectural Heritage*, 2 (1991), 41–55.
30. González-Longo, 'James Smith and Rome', 87; J. Gifford, C. McWilliam and D. Walker, *Edinburgh* (New Haven, CT: YUP, 2003), 149; MacKechnie, 'The Earl of Perth's Chapel'. I am grateful to Ian Campbell for advice on this point.
31. M. Glendinning, R. MacInnes and A. MacKechnie, *A History of Scottish Architecture: From the Renaissance to the Present Day* (Edinburgh: EUP, 1996), p. 143. The chancel was unblocked in the church's 1946–54 restoration (R. S. Wright, *The Kirk in the Canongate: A Short History from 1128 to the Present Day*, 2nd edn (Edinburgh: Oliver & Boyd, 1958), p. 141.
32. A. Raffe, 'The Restoration, the Revolution and the Failure of Episcopacy in Scotland', in *The Final Crisis of the Stuart Monarchy: The Revolutions of 1688–91 in their British, Atlantic and European Contexts*, ed. Tim Harris and Stephen Taylor (Woodbridge: Boydell, 2013), pp. 87–108, at pp. 103–7; H. G. Aldis, *A List of Books Printed in Scotland before 1700, including Those Printed Furth of the Realm*

for Scottish Booksellers, rev. edn (Edinburgh: NLS, 1970); ESTC [http://estc.bl.uk/F/?func=file&file_name=login-bl-estc].

33. *A Collection of Discourses lately Written by some Divines of the Church of England against the Errours and Corruptions of the Church of Rome* (Edinburgh, 1687).
34. Lauder, *Historical Notices*, II, 816.
35. J. Watson, 'The publisher's preface to the printers in Scotland', in [J. de la Caille,] *The History of the Art of Printing* (Edinburgh, 1713), pp. 15–16; A. J. Mann, *The Scottish Book Trade, 1500–1720: Print Commerce and Print Control in Early Modern Scotland* (East Linton: Tuckwell Press, 2000), pp. 119, 127–8; W. Cowan, 'The Holyrood Press, 1686–1688', *Publications of the Edinburgh Bibliographical Society*, 6 (1901–4), 83–100; NRS, SP4/11, pp. 276–8; *RPCS*, 3rd ser., XII, 455.
36. Lauder, *Historical Notices*, II, 784. Moreover, a fire broke out near Watson's shop in February 1687.
37. NRS, SP4/12, pp. 142–3, 522, 541–3; Watson, 'Publisher's preface', 16, 17.
38. A partial bibliography is contained in Cowan, 'Holyrood Press', 92–100. Additions to Cowan's bibliography, together with all the press's Catholic works, are listed in Appendix 6.1.
39. On the monopoly held by Anderson and his widow Agnes Campbell, see Mann, *Scottish Book Trade*, pp. 120–1, 130–2.
40. H. Foley, *Records of the English Province of the Society of Jesus*, 7 vols (London: n.p., 1875–83), VII, p. 842.
41. *The Rules of the Schools at the Savoy* (London, 1687); *The Rules of the Schools at the Jesuits in Fanchurch Street* (London, n.d.).
42. M. V. Hay, *The Blairs Papers (1603–1660)* (London and Edinburgh: Sands & Co., 1929), p. 98, n. 2; P. Tomassi, 'Abercromby, David (*d.* 1701?)', *ODNB*.
43. Titles 6, 12, 14, 22 and perhaps 4 and 11.
44. D. Crane, 'English Translations of the *Imitatio Christi* in the Sixteenth and Seventeenth Centuries', *Recusant History*, 13 (1975–6), 79–100. On earlier translations, see also Maximilian von Habsburg, *Catholic and Protestant Translations of the* Imitatio Christi, *1425–1650: From Late Medieval Classic to Early Modern Bestseller* (Farnham: Ashgate, 2011).
45. I am grateful to Mary Hardy for alerting me to this work and for several suggestions relating to this part of the chapter.
46. SCA, Alexander Winster and others to William Leslie, Gordon Castle, 6 Apr. 1688, BL/1/109/28.
47. Titles 2, 4, 7–10, 13, 15, 17, 21.
48. Titles 1, 3, 6, 11–12, 14, 19, 20 and 23, if the last is a Catholic work.
49. Titles 5, 16, 18, 22.
50. F. de Sales, *An Introduction to a Devout Life* (n.p., 1687) sig. [*8]v.
51. As well as references to Cowan's list (in 'Holyrood Press', 92–100), entries refer to T. H. Clancy, SJ, *English Catholic Books, 1641–1700: A Bibliography*, new edn (Aldershot: Scolar Press, 1996), and give Wing numbers and information derived from ESTC.

CHAPTER SEVEN

The Episcopalian Community in Aberdeen in the Jacobite Period

Kieran German

In October 1711, Patrick Dunbreck delivered the inaugural sermon at a newly formed Episcopalian meeting house in Aberdeen. In it he said:

> The prayer for the whole state of Christ's Church Militant here on earth ... is more full and particular in our Scots Liturgy published in K.Ch[arles]: the Martyr's time than is to be met with in any of our Modern Liturgies, and in this particular it breaths nothing but primitive devotion.[1]

That salute to the Scottish liturgy was exceptional under the circumstances. The new meeting house had riled the town magistrates because it sought to capitalise on the confusion caused by the case of James Greenshields being considered by the House of Lords. Greenshields had challenged the magistrates of Edinburgh on their legal competence to prohibit use of the Anglican *Book of Common Prayer* and Dunbreck and his congregation were doing the same in Aberdeen.[2] Such cases led directly to the Toleration Act of 1712 which explicitly permitted the use of the English liturgy in Episcopalian services in Scotland. There followed a major uptake of the Anglican Prayer Book across the north-east of Scotland as congregations which had rejected Presbyterian governance of the Church of Scotland since 1689 were able to worship in accordance with Episcopalian manners.[3] Yet the specific legal situation of Dunbreck's congregation was at odds with Dunbreck's professed belief in the superiority of the Scottish liturgy. This short example shows that as early as 1711 the Episcopalians of Aberdeen were drawn between satisfying legal requirements, thereby benefiting from legislated provisions for Episcopalian worship; and practising ceremonial worship in a fashion which met their interpretation of scripture, liturgy and tradition. As time went on, the former was increasingly used as a foil for the latter.

The confessional behaviour of Episcopalians was further complicated by attitudes towards the royal dynasty. Christopher Whatley has claimed there existed 'glue-like bonds ... between episcopalianism in Scotland and the Stuarts'.[4] Jeffrey Stephen has written, 'the bulk of Episcopalians happened to be Jacobites'.[5] Whilst Whatley and Stephen qualify their assertions – and Alasdair Raffe has also done detailed research linking

Episcopacy with Jacobitism[6] – the generalisation persists. The inherent question of what it was that made a person a Jacobite is difficult to answer, and their religion often provides only clues rather than evidence or proof. Whilst acts of explicit support for the Jacobite cause can be assigned to many Episcopalians during the Jacobite risings, can a minister who prayed for King James in 1715 be judged retrospectively to have been a Jacobite in 1713 at a time when he was qualified to Queen Anne? Episcopalian conduct between Jacobite risings may tell us something of their attitudes towards Stuart legitimacy, but it can also tell us much about how they sustained their church through a period of disestablishment, disendowment and a series of legal obstacles. This chapter will explore the Episcopalian community in Aberdeen with a focus on their legally established meeting-houses and chapels. It will show how Episcopalians would flit between qualified and non-juring congregations in the Jacobite period and in so doing it will investigate the organisation of the Episcopalian community, the nature of their worship and what this can tell us about the relationship between juring Episcopalians and Jacobitism.[7]

I

Prior to the accession of Queen Anne in 1702, the Episcopalians of Aberdeen were growing disparate and destitute. The Church Act (1695) prevailed as the legal framework defining the status of Episcopalian ministers and their ability to administer divine service and fill vacant churches. Incumbent ministers were permitted to remain in their churches without subscribing to Presbyterian church government and the Westminster Confession, but they were required to have given allegiance to the civil government. Nominally, these were jurors. Incumbent ministers who declined to give allegiance were automatically deprived by this legislation, and they became, officially, 'intruders'. These were non-jurors. The rest of the Episcopalian clergy had been similarly deprived, either rabbled or deposed. However, they cannot be uniformly categorised as juring or non-juring, since their deposition may have been before 1695 and on account of their unwillingness to conform to Presbyterian church government, rather than to civil government. No deprived minister willing to conform after 1695 was entitled to be restored to his former benefice. These ministers were debarred from presiding at marriages and baptisms. Furthermore, the settlement of 1689 had deprived Episcopalians of the ability to ordain new ministers with a view to the eventual diminution of the Episcopal clergy legally established in Scottish churches by natural attrition.

However, the deaths of James VII in 1701 and William of Orange in 1702 presented the Episcopalians, and particularly the non-jurors, with the opportunity to make a shift of conscience. It enabled them to view William's successor, Anne, James's younger daughter, not necessarily as a *de jure* queen but at least with a legitimacy that William and Queen Mary,

James's eldest daughter, had been unable to claim while James VII was living. Furthermore, Anne held a personal sympathy for Scots Episcopacy on account of its affinity to Anglicanism. Despite a failure to achieve a toleration settlement in 1703, the queen had privately instructed her Privy Council to relax persecution of Scots Episcopalians and she also arranged for a pension to be paid to the primus, Bishop Alexander Rose of Edinburgh. As a consequence, many ministers who had not taken the requisite oaths in 1695 were willing to qualify after Anne's accession.[8] In 1710, there were thirty-two Episcopalian ministers in the diocese of Aberdeen, of whom only two were identified as non-jurors. This compares with seventy-six ministers across Scotland, six of whom were not qualified. Despite this relatively low number of non-jurors, it was claimed that there were many more who preached in meeting houses and explicitly prayed for King James.[9] Two years later, following the Act of Toleration, the number of ministers in the diocese of Aberdeen had risen to thirty-eight and use of the Anglican liturgy was being actively encouraged.[10]

The response across Aberdeen to the parliamentary debate on a proposed toleration of Episcopacy in Scotland illustrates the positions in the city. The Episcopalians became more bullish. Following the death of the Presbyterian incumbent, James Osborn, in 1711, Andrew Burnet and his congregation lobbied the town magistrates (unsuccessfully) for Burnet to be restored to St Nicholas's Church. Burnet (who prior to the Revolution had been a candidate for bishop of Aberdeen) was established at a meeting house in Trinity Chapel, having been deprived in 1695 for failing to qualify to civil authority. However, as he had qualified to Queen Anne in 1702, his congregation argued that, as the pulpit was now vacant, he should be restored. The magistrates braced themselves for a mob and boarded the church doors shut. The mob did not come, but legal proceedings were initiated which suspended the appointment of a Presbyterian minister. Robert Wodrow feared an appeal to the House of Lords could prove more damaging to the Presbyterian endeavour than Greenshields.[11] The Earl Marischal's chaplain likewise presided over an Episcopalian meeting house in the town. In fact, Patrick Dunbreck (formerly chaplain to the earl of Erroll) read the English liturgy in the Earl Marischal's town house. He was referred to the magistrates by the presbytery, and his right to minister in the burgh was contested on several grounds. However, the council was advised that it lacked the jurisdiction to prosecute Dunbreck as chaplain to the Earl Marischal. Nevertheless, they remained committed to forcing his deprivation. The provost, John Ross of Arnage, began by formally protesting to Marischal and Episcopalian nobility in Aberdeenshire; failing that, the council attempted to raise the problem with the central government, even seeking a royal dispensation to prosecute Dunbreck.[12] The town's senior Presbyterian minister, Thomas Blackwell, recognised this measure as somewhat excessive and, given the queen's sympathies, unrealistic and potentially damaging.[13] Meanwhile, the eminent Aberdeen Episcopalian

James Garden launched legal proceedings to be restored to his position as professor of Divinity at King's College. He was intent on taking his case to the House of Lords and for a period enjoyed the support of staff at King's and members of the Aberdeenshire nobility including John Erskine, the earl of Mar, and James Ogilvy, the earl of Findlater and Seafield. Garden was eventually convinced by his supporters to withdraw his appeal as it was deemed incendiary in the context of the toleration debates.[14]

Throughout the reign of Queen Anne, the town council of Aberdeen routinely demonstrated its Presbyterian credentials. The magistrates provided the synod with property, at the town's expense, so that it could meet regularly in comfort.[15] John Allardes, a former provost and the town's most experienced councillor, began collections to support the Scottish Society for the Propagation of Christian Knowledge.[16] In March 1705, punitive fines had been introduced against burials in the kirkyard and those who burned incense at funerals.[17] In January 1715, fines were similarly imposed against the Episcopalians for burying their deceased at Trinity Church, not the parish Kirk of St Nicholas. It seems that the council felt that if it found itself unable to eradicate the Episcopalian community it should at least profit by its continued existence. The council asserted its civic authority by offering a begrudged toleration of Episcopalian practices.[18] The council also revelled in its relationship with Thomas Blackwell, an energetic Presbyterian minister initially appointed to St Nicholas Kirk in 1700. By 1711, Blackwell had been promoted to professor of Theology at Marischal College and the pulpit at Greyfriars; both were council nominations. There was reciprocal respect. In 1710, Blackwell published a theological tome, *Ratio Sacra*, which he dedicated to the town magistrates.[19] Blackwell also represented the General Assembly as it lobbied the government against Episcopal toleration between 1710 and 1711, an effort which was funded to a great extent by Aberdonian burgesses, most notably Provost Ross.[20] This coincided with a period when the Episcopalian presence on the council was in terminal decline (although infrequent exceptions did occur only in particular circumstances when the economic leverage of some Episcopalian merchants was irresistible).[21]

In Old Aberdeen, the Episcopalian community was sustained by support from a broad section of society. For example, when Robert Calder, 'ane abdicat Episcopall incumbent', set up an Episcopalian meeting house in Old Aberdeen in April 1702 the magistrates ignored the presbytery's exhortations to act. They argued that, as a burgh of regality, they did not have the authority. In 1704, when the presbytery called a minister to the chapel at King's College, the magistrates, trades council, heritors and college professors all protested. The council's reticence is given a less legalistic and more confessional hue when one considers that, within two years, two of the town's baillies requested from the kirk session the communion cup, explicitly for use in Episcopal services in King's College Chapel. They were refused.[22] Calder was a non-juror, but the presbytery also opposed jurors in their district. Thus, in 1709 David Hedderwick was charged under the Act against irregular baptism and marriage (1695), as well as for intrusion, drunkenness and encouraging non-jurors.[23] From 1704, King's College Chapel was occupied by Hedderwick, a juring Episcopalian. However, Hedderwick was not in complete accordance with the law. Officially, he was perceived as an 'intruder' into King's chapel. Accordingly, as a deprived minister he was subject to the 1695 Act discharging irregular marriages and baptisms; in spite of his legal position, he officiated at such ceremonies. The Presbytery of Aberdeen also alleged that Hedderwick permitted non-juring Episcopal clergy to minister in the chapel.[24] Hedderwick was still in possession of the chapel in 1712.[25] 'Gate-keeping' of the nature alleged against Hedderwick was not an unusual practice in the north-east. For example, James Gordon routinely administered divine service by these means. Indeed, his father, the conciliatory James Gordon of Banchory-Devenick, amongst many others, permitted him to minister in his church.[26]

Following the Act of Toleration, Hedderwick was considered to be a legally qualified minister. Hedderwick used the Anglian liturgy and, in 1713, he and George Middleton (the Principal of King's College) were instrumental in importing five hundred Common Prayer books from London.[27] In 1714, Episcopalian citizens, including William Gordon – the pro-Episcopalian pamphleteer and sometime baillie – and the masters of King's College staged a takeover of St Machar Cathedral. The Presbyterian incumbent having died, nomination to the altar fell to the university regents (patronages having been restored in 1712), who nominated Dr John Sharp. Sharp was described as having intruded 'in a most tumultuous manner', 'the mob having broken open the Church door on Saturday night in order to [force] his entry'. Sharp and Hedderwick took turns to officiate in English services. They also removed the pulpit cloth, bibles and other utensils (possibly the communion chalice the town magistrates had requested several years before). Gordon and four others were imprisoned in Aberdeen Tolbooth for four weeks and ordered to pay 100 merks. Among them, William Black, sub-principal at King's College, was held in custody for six months and died of ill-health in prison. Sharp was prosecuted in Edinburgh for his 'intrusion' and suspended from the ministry for seven years. Hence he went to England where he served the useful purpose of distributing appeals of the Scots clergy to sympathetic hearers south of the border.[28] The occupation of St Machar Cathedral was hardly successful in the medium term, and demonstrates Episcopalian confidence more than it does a serious challenge to the Presbyterians established in the burghs.

II

After the 1715 rising, the government army targeted Episcopalian meeting houses during its campaign in Scotland. Ministers such as Alexander Robertson of Longside and Alexander Hepburn of St Fergus were threatened with prison, compelling them to flee, and their flight was consequently used against them as an insinuation of culpability for Jacobite offences.[29] King George I's proclamations deliberately conflated episcopacy and Jacobitism to permit civil actions against the clergy in addition to the ecclesiastical measures which were being brought against them.[30] Although only three ministers out of approximately thirty-eight in the diocese of Aberdeen could prove they were not involved in the rising, the allegations made against many of the Episcopalian clergy were likewise unproven.[31] Thus, when William Swan, minister at Pitsligo, wrote privately to a co-accused that he had not prayed for King James, had not excited rebellion in his parish and had not supplied arms to the Jacobites, he was probably being truthful.[32] Of course, as minister to Alexander Forbes, 4th Lord Pitsligo, who was significantly involved in the Fifteen, it is also wholly conceivable that Swan was active for the Jacobites. Pitsligo was himself a deeply spiritual, juring Episcopalian, an important Jacobite in both 1715 and 1745, and a philosopher who battled with the dichotomy of Jacobite and Hanoverian loyalties.[33]

The 1719 penal laws sought to round-up the Episcopalian ministers who had evaded prosecution for Jacobitism in 1715–16. These laws prevented Scots Episcopalian ministers from ministering at meeting houses and restricted congregations in private family chapels to no more than five communicants. The laws were introduced against a backdrop of Episcopalian nonchalance in Aberdeen, where six ministers who had all been indicted for Jacobitism in the Fifteen continued to openly operate in the burgh.[34] The magistrates had previously complained that informal meeting houses did not keep a registry of baptisms; now they had the legal powers to address Episcopalian activity in their domain.[35] The laws immediately tempered the Episcopal clergy, who went from brazenly holding services to moving through the town only under the cover of darkness for fear of prosecution and imprisonment.[36] All of which presented something of an ecclesiastical vacuum in the town. The Episcopalian gentry of the locality became concerned that the multitude of the Episcopalian congregation within the town would be drawn 'astray' to the Presbyterian Kirk for the simple fact that there was not a sufficient alternative. As a consequence, the congregation of St Paul's was established 'according to law' in 1720. The congregation sought the nomination of a 'pious, grave preacher' from the bishop of London, and Joseph Robertson duly became the minister at St Paul's, where he would read the English liturgy and pray for King George by name.[37]

The congregation of St Paul's can be traced back to the Trinity Chapel congregation of Aberdeen. This congregation had something of a Jacobite background. Its minister had been Andrew Burnet, formerly of the East Kirk of St Nicholas before being deposed in 1695 on account of his refusal to qualify to King William. Burnet later qualified to Queen Anne and when the pulpit as St Nicholas became vacant in 1711, as discussed above,

Burnet's congregation lobbied the city council, albeit unsuccessfully, to have Burnet restored.[38] During the Fifteen, when Aberdeen was administrated by a Jacobite council, Burnet was returned to St Nicholas where he prayed for King James by name. He went on to deliver an address to James in person on behalf of the Episcopal clergy of the diocese while the king was in Aberdeenshire. Upon the establishment of the juring congregation after the rising had failed, the congregation applied to the town council for use of the Greyfriars church next to Marischal College. They were refused. So they sought to lease the Trinity Kirk from the Incorporated Trades of the burgh. Again, they were refused, partly on account of inventive gerrymandering of the Trades' executive by the council. When the congregation, including Trades Guild members among them, appealed that the church was not in use, Thomas Blackwell, minister at Greyfriars and now principal of Marischal College, commenced weekly services on Wednesdays in the chapel. At that point the congregation removed the 'decent desks and lofts' with which they had furnished Trinity at 'considerable expense' and other property from the chapel, suggesting that they owned the furniture and thus had indeed been Andrew Burnet's congregation, the previous tenants, and they began the process of building their own chapel.[39]

The building of St Paul's was an endeavour supported by the Episcopalian community in the burgh, and in the rural hinterland of the town. The foundation charter of St Paul's suggests that Episcopalian members of Aberdeen's burgess community led the campaign to establish a juring Episcopalian church, provide suitable accommodation for such and secure the services of the minister. A significant proportion of the burgesses who took this leading role had served on Aberdeen's Jacobite town council of 1715, including its provost, Patrick Bannerman, and the Jacobite baillies John Burnet and William Simson. To be specific, ten of the nineteen men who formed that Jacobite council were subscribers to the foundation document of St Paul's Episcopal Chapel. Of the twenty-four men who founded St Paul's, ten had sat on the Jacobite council of Aberdeen just seven years earlier.[40]

Interestingly, the genesis of the foundation of St Paul's actually lay with the non-juring landed gentry of Aberdeenshire. John Arbuthnott, 5th Viscount of Arbuthnott, promoted the idea to Alexander Cumming of Culter, MP for Aberdeenshire, and encouraged him to raise the possibility of establishing a legally qualified meeting house with James Catanach and the 'trading men in the Episcopal communion' in the town. Arbuthnott vouched that the local community (presumably landed gentry such as himself) would provide tacit financial support for a legally established minister. Commenting on his involvement with the Chapel of St Paul, Arbuthnott stated that he 'would not countenance his publick worship' himself. Arbuthnott was so in favour of high church Scots Episcopacy that he was in regular correspondence with non-juring bishops in London including Archibald Campbell and Jeremy Collier, and he hosted the bishop of Aberdeen, James Gadderar, at Arbuthnott for a prolonged period during Gadderar's contested appointment as diocesan bishop. With Gadderar, Campbell and Collier, Arbuthnott made a significant contribution to the non-juring liturgical and usages projects of the 1720s.[41] Such was Arbuthnott's religious positioning, he even asked Cumming not to identify him with the project of establishing a qualified minister in Aberdeen. Cumming was no stranger to the delicacies of confessional politics (as will be discussed below) and he certainly honoured and followed Arbuthnott's advice. The foundation of St Paul's Episcopal congregation came six months after Arbuthnott first raised the idea with Cumming. While this reveals that there was in fact a wide spectrum of Episcopalian beliefs, there was also a common ground and sense of community between non-jurors and jurors. The wider significance of the foundation of St Paul's was that wealthier segments of the community did not want to see the Episcopalian congregation being drawn to the Presbyterian Kirk for want of an alternative.[42]

The burgess leadership of Bannerman, Catanach, and Simpson began fundraising efforts to solicit donations and loans from the local landed Episcopalian sympathisers.[43] 'Those of the Episcopall perswasion in Aberdeen' did not stop there in their efforts. They also appealed to the archbishops, bishops, clergy and laity in England to contribute financially towards the building of the new chapel.[44] Meanwhile, landed Episcopalians were making efforts of their own. Alexander Cumming of Culter, John Middleton of Seaton and Alexander Abercromby of Glashaugh choreographed a fundraising effort for the building and maintenance of the chapel.[45]

The services at the chapel of St Paul's were emphatic in collecting juring credentials – a qualified minister, the Anglican liturgy – and they even installed an organ and sang the service in the fashion of the English. Nevertheless, the extent of the affection for Hanover was limited. An English visitor to the chapel wrote:

> When the Minister came to that Part of the Litany, where the King is prayed for by Name, the People all rose up as one, in Contempt of it, and Men and Women set themselves about some trivial Action, as taking Snuff, &c., to show their Dislike ... and when the Responsal should have been pronounced, though they had been loud in all that preceded, to our Amazement there was not one single Voice to be heard but our own.[46]

The unwillingness of the congregation to pray audibly for King George was in spite of two publications made by Patrick Cockburn, during his time as minister at St Paul's between 1726 and 1739, which advocated praying for the king. There is considerable paradox to Cockburn's appointment to St Paul's. Considering that the cultural and ecclesiastical environment of Aberdeen was conservative, particularly in terms of kinship and Episcopal patronage, it is striking that Cockburn should be the nephew of James and

George Garden and second-cousin of Henry Scougal. His father-in-law was Alexander Garden, another leading Aberdonian cleric. At the Revolution, Cockburn's father qualified. Cockburn himself forfeited a pulpit in London in 1714 for refusing to abjure the Stuarts.[47] Nevertheless, St Paul's gave the outward impression of loyalty and allegiance to the established government, making it an adequate foil for non-jurors and crypto-Jacobites. William Harper, a minister who assisted at St Paul's between 1740 and 1744, was nevertheless involved with the development of the non-juring church and recognised the bishops. Harper was also conspiring Jacobitism with Lord Pitsligo in the 1730s and was 'very active' in the Forty-five.[48] William Urquhart of Meldrum frequented St Paul's and non-juring chapels alike. Urquhart's son, Keith, was baptised by Bishop James Gadderar at Old Aberdeen. Nevertheless, Urquhart would be installed as Sheriff-depute of Aberdeen after the Forty-Five.[49] This was in line with concerns being raised, among Hanoverians in Aberdeen, that from the 1720s non-jurors were pragmatically taking oaths for the sake of preferment.[50]

III

The truth is that there was a degree of fluidity to ecclesiastical approaches from all segments of society. Bona-fide Presbyterians, such as David Verner, a Glaswegian Presbyterian inducted to Marischal College after the purge of Jacobite staff in 1717, appear as witnesses to baptisms in St Paul's. Councillors and burgesses did the same. Indeed, Alexander Aberdein, provost of the burgh in 1744, baptised his daughter at St Paul's in 1730, all of which reflects the level of legitimacy that the chapel did have.[51] This is surely confirmed by its being left standing in 1746 after Cumberland's army had proceeded through the north-east burning Episcopalian meeting houses to ashes with little discrimination. One observer wrote that in Aberdeen 'All the Episcopal meetings are pulled down. The alters, pulpits, and seats were imploy'd to heat the ovens'.[52] The level of suspicion of Episcopalians as Jacobites after 1745 was intense. Colonel Joseph Yorke wrote to his brother, Philip Yorke, earl of Hardwicke, the lord chancellor, that he believed many of the non-jurors were 'Popish' and that their meeting houses were seminaries of Jacobitism. Jacobites, he wrote, should be 'reduced to reason on the points of our bayonets'. The indiscriminate nature of Cumberland's reprisals against the non-juring Episcopalians, and the repeated insinuation that non-jurors were active Jacobites, meant that even the innocent felt threatened. Upon hearing that Cumberland was 'to take up such as frequented nonjuring Meeting Houses', Robert Nairn, a fisherman, left Aberdeen for Pitfodels and Culter. Nairn's caution, and his deliberate avoidance of Jacobites, nevertheless gave the outward impression of guilt and he was summoned to explain himself to the authorities.[53]

The case of Thomas Mercer offers one illustration of the type of worshipper at St Paul's. In 1720 Mercer was an emerging merchant in Aberdeen, dealing primarily in Dee salmon. He had business links to established burgesses such as the Jacobite Episcopalian James Catanach and the Presbyterian Hanoverian former provost James Allardyce, also his uncle. Mercer was also related to Viscount Arbuthnott. There is little reason to doubt that Mercer was a Jacobite. He sourced portraits of James and Clementina from the continent, and he commemorated Jacobite occasions such as the birthday of James VIII and the Restoration of Charles II. Mercer, and his son (Hugh, who would go on to distinguish himself alongside George Washington in the American Revolutionary War) were both 'out' in 1745, with the senior acting as aide-de-camp to Lord Pitsligo. Mercer was probably a discreet non-juror too. He was a subscriber to Thomas Rattray's *Liturgy of St James* and while in Rotterdam in 1719 he met with George Garden and attended his sermons there and facilitated the transfer of money between Garden and his family in Scotland.[54] Mercer was also an inventive smuggler, but that's another matter.

Meanwhile, Alexander Cumming of Culter, who supported initial fundraising initiatives for the chapel, presents another example of the confessional sensitivities of the region after the Fifteen. As heritor of Culter he had the right of patronage of Maryculter parish church, which had been vacated in 1716 following the deprivation of George White on account of Jacobitism. The presbytery contested Cumming's patronage and, although they were not certain of winning their case, they hoped to delay Cumming's nomination of a minister, allowing the statutory six months to pass before the nomination would fall to the presbytery. Here's where it gets interesting: Cumming, in spite of the work he was simultaneously doing to assist juring Episcopalians in the burgh of Aberdeen, nominated a thoroughly Presbyterian candidate, John Willison of Dundee.[55] Yet this appointment was rejected by the presbytery, who encouraged the parishioners to agitate for an alternative candidate, their nominee, Andrew Honyman. Eventually Cumming acquiesced to the presbytery's choice but pointedly nominated Honyman as an expression of his right of patronage, not theirs.[56] Nevertheless, the ousted George White continued to serve the parish as an intruding minister for another two years, presumably with the connivance of Cumming.[57]

Cumming nominated Willison following a drawn-out and ultimately unsuccessful campaign to retain George White as the Episcopal minister of the parish church. And although Willison had little truck for Episcopalian intruders – having suffered at the hands of one in Brechin – he was nevertheless the moderate choice.[58] Honyman was the presbytery's candidate, thoroughly at odds with Episcopalian sentiment. He became moderator of the presbytery of Fordoun and would go on to initiate legal proceedings against James Gadderar, bishop of Aberdeen, for a series of alleged offences including trafficking Jesuit priests; Gadderar would, in turn, seek advice from Cumming.[59] Honyman had the support of the presbytery and some parishioners before his nomination and was much preferable to a candidate who owed his nomination to Cumming. Cumming, however, had a constituency to consider, and, although he was evidently willing to lend tacit support to the Episcopalian clergy, he was not to become an ambassador for their cause.

IV

It would be futile to argue that there was not a correspondence between Episcopacy and Jacobitism. What this chapter shows is that Episcopalian communities were engaged in the process of rejuvenating, organising and sustaining their churches. The determination to retain Episcopalian services in the churches of Aberdeenshire required support from the landed elite in collaboration with the local burgess community. Their success depended on a flexibility of confessional principles and preferences but scarcely anything which amounted to public indications of Jacobite allegiance. To that extent, the juring churches served a very significant purpose, which was to confer legitimacy on the Episcopalian congregation which held in public, despite whatever private political or confessional sensibilities the churchgoer held. Which returns us to the original point – that Episcopalians and Jacobites have been seen as two sides of the same coin. It raises the question, how far did one have to go before one was a Jacobite? Did being an Episcopalian make you one? Did not explicitly praying for King George make you one? Or did you have to stand in arms? The various approaches of Scottish Episcopalians in the Jacobite period form a spectrum of confessional commitment, not a binary distinction of political dissidence.

Notes

1. AUL, Diocese of Aberdeen and Orkney, MS 3320/6/5.
2. J. Stephen, 'English Liturgy and Scottish Identity: The Case of James Greenshields' in A. I. Macinnes and D. U. Hamilton (eds), *Jacobitism, Enlightenment and Empire, 1680–1820* (London: Pickering & Chatto, 2014), pp. 59–74.
3. T. Clarke, '"Nurseries of Sedition"?: The Episcopal Congregations after the Revolution of 1689' in J. Porter (ed.), *After Columba, After Calvin: Religious Community in North-East Scotland* (Aberdeen: Elphinstone Institute, 1999), p. 65.
4. C. A. Whatley, *The Scots and the Union* (Edinburgh: EUP, 2006), p. 40.
5. J. Stephen, 'Defending the Revolution: The Church of Scotland and the Scottish Parliament, 1689–95', *SHR*, 89 (2010), 19–53.
6. A. Raffe, 'Religious Controversy and Scottish Society, 1679–1714' (Ph.D. Thesis, University of Edinburgh, 2007), pp. 14, 122–6.
7. For an analysis of Episcopalians in active Jacobite rebellion see K. German, 'Jacobite Politics in Aberdeen and the '15' in P. K. Mond, M. G. H. Pittock and D. Szechi (eds), *Loyalty and Identity: Jacobites at Home and Abroad* (Basingstoke: Palgrave Macmillan, 2010), pp. 82–97.
8. R. Wodrow, *Analecta or Materials for a History of Remarkable Providences Mostly*

Relating to Scotch Ministers and Christians, ed. M. Leishman, 4 vols (Edinburgh: Maitland Club, 1842), I, p. 330; 'Register of S. Paul's Episcopal Church, Aberdeen, 1720–1793', ed. A. E. Smith, in *Miscellancy of the New Spalding Club* (Aberdeen, 1908), II. p. 83; W. G. Rowntree Bodie, 'St Paul's Chapel, Aberdeen: Its History and Architecture', *Proceedings of the Society of Antiquaries of Scotland*, 108 (1976–7), 327.

9. *The case of Mr. Greenshields, as it was printed in London, with remarks upon the same; and copies of the original papers relating to that affair, as also a list of the late Episcopal ministers, who enjoy churches or legal benefices in Scotland* (Edinburgh, 1710), p. 4.
10. NRS CH12/12/6A.
11. Wodrow, *Analecta*, I, pp. 329–30.
12. NRS, Papers of the Erskine Family, earls of Mar and Kellie, GD124/9/73; ACA, Miscellaneous bundles, Press 18, 8/32-34.
13. 'Letters from Professor Blackwell, and Others, to John Ross of Arnage, Provost of Aberdeen, 1711–12' in *The Miscellany of the Spalding Club*, ed. J. Stuart (Aberdeen, 1841), p. 201.
14. G. D. Henderson (ed.), *Mystics of the North-East* (Aberdeen: Third Spalding Club, 1934), pp. 61–5.
15. ACA, Aberdeen Council Letters (1700–1719), IIX, f. 118.
16. ACA, Aberdeen Council Letters (1700–1719), IIX, f. 149.
17. *Extracts from the Council Register of the burgh of Aberdeen, 1643–1747*, ed. J. Stuart (Edinburgh: Scottish Burgh Record Society, 1872), p. 333.
18. ACA, Aberdeen Council Register (1705–1721), LVIII, f. 384.
19. T. Blackwell, *Ratio Sacra, or an appeal unto the rational world, about the reasonableness of revealed religion*, (Edinburgh, 1710) p. vii; ACA, Aberdeen Council Register (1705–1722), LVIII, f. 190.
20. 'Letters from Professor Blackwell', p. 223.
21. German, 'Jacobite Politics'.
22. *Records of Old Aberdeen*, ed. Alexander M. Munro, 2 vols (Aberdeen: New Spalding Club, 1900–9), I, p. 171, II, p. 115.
23. NRS CH12/12/4.
24. NAS CH12/12/4.
25. NRS CH12/12/6A.
26. *James Gordon's Diary, 1692–1710*, ed. G. D. Henderson and H. H. Porter (Aberdeen: Third Spalding Club, 1949), pp. 1, 14, 20; Clarke, 'Scottish Episcopalians', pp. 49, 70.
27. NRS, CH12/12/8: approximately twenty thousand copies of the *Book of Common Prayer* were delivered to Scotland between 1712 and 1714 (Clarke, '"Nurseries of Sedition"?', p. 65).
28. AUL, MS 3320/1/51; ACA, Aberdeen Council Letters (1705–1719), IIX, f. 196; *Records of Old Aberdeen*, II, p. 127; NRS, CH12/12/401–402; R. L. Emerson, *Professors, Patronage and Politics: The Aberdeen Universities in the Eighteenth Century* (Aberdeen: Aberdeen University Press, 1992), p. 26.
29. *A Representation of the State of the Church in North-Britain as to liturgy; and of the sufferings of the Orthodox and Regular Clergy, From the Enemies to Both. But more especially of the Episcopal Churches within the Diocese and Shire of Aberdeen* (London, 1718).
30. AUL, Papers of Duff House/earls of Fife, MS 3175/2048/(3).
31. *The Correspondence of the Rev. Robert Wodrow*, ed. T. M'Crie, 3 vols (Edinburgh: Wodrow Society, 1842–3), II, p. 227; NAS, CH12/126A.

32. AUL MS 3175/2048/(3) and (35).
33. M. G. H. Pittock, 'The Political Thought of Lord Forbes of Pitsligo', *Northern Scotland*, 16 (1996), pp. 73–86; AUL, Papers of Ogilvie-Forbes of Boyndlie, MS 2740/4/18/1/14.
34. ACA, Aberdeen Council Letters, VIII, f. 252.
35. Ibid., VIII, ff. 227–8.
36. AUL, MS 3175/F51/4/1 and MS 3175/z/172/2.
37. 'Register of St Paul's' II, pp. 86–7; AUL, MS 3175/2048/(16) and MS3175/z/172/2.
38. Wodrow, *Analecta*, I, pp. 329–30.
39. AUL, MS 3175/2048/(15); MS 3175/2048/(16) and MS 3175/z/172/2.
40. 'Register of St Paul's' II, pp. 86–7; ACA, Council Register, LVIII, f. 49. The other Jacobite councillors were Alexander Strachan, Thomas Shand, Patrick Gray, James Catanach, James Gordon, Robert Pittendreich and Dr John Gordon.
41. K. German, 'Non-Jurors, Liturgy, and Jacobite Commitment, 1718–1746', *RSCHS*, 47 (2018), 74–99.
42. AUL, MS 3175/F51/4/1. Cumming was also an associate of the non-juring bishops James Gadderar and Archibald Campbell in London.
43. 'Register of St Paul's' II, pp. 86–7.
44. AUL MS 3175/2048/(15).
45. AUL MS 3175/2048/(49).
46. E. Burt, *Letters from the North of Scotland; with Facsimiles of the Original Engravings*, 2 vols (London, 1754; repr. Edinburgh, 1876), I, pp. 223–4.
47. P. Cockburn, *On the Duty and Benefit of Praying for our Governors* (Edinburgh, 1728) and *The Lawfulness and Duty of Praying for our Present King and Governor* (Edinburgh, 1735); R. Strong, 'Cockburn, Patrick (1678–1749)', O*DNB* [http://www.oxforddnb.com/view/article/5775]. Cockburn's father served Anglican congregations in the Netherlands at the time of the Revolution.
48. D. M. Bertie, *Scottish Episcopal Clergy, 1689–2000* (Edinburgh: T. & T. Clark, 2000), pp. 60, 145; AUL, MS 3320/6/75/15.
49. 'Register of St Paul's' II, pp. 155, 188, 196, 207, 221: AUL, Records of the Scottish Episcopal Church, Diocese of Aberdeen and Orkney, MS 3499/11/1; TNA, SP 54/36/55.
50. W. Duff, *An amazing and extraordinary instance of frauds and oppression in a country govern'd by laws, and an affront upon the equity and justice of Ab—n* (London, 1743), p. 6.
51. 'Register of St Paul's' II, pp. 50, 62, 74, 78, 85, 97, 126.
52. *The Lyon in Mourning*, ed. H. Paton, 3 vols (Edinburgh: SHS, 1895–6), III, p. 172; A. and H. Tayler, *Jacobites of Aberdeenshire and Banffshire in the Forty-Five* (Aberdeen: Milne & Hutchison, 1928), pp. 65, 90; J. Ray, *A compleat history of the rebellion* (London, 1759), pp. 298, 315; Sir J. Sinclair (ed.), *The Statistical Account of Scotland Drawn up from the Communications of the Ministers of the Different Parishes*, 21 vols (Edinburgh, 1791–9), XVII, p. 399; W. Donaldson, *The Jacobite Song: Political Myth and National Identity* (Aberdeen: Aberdeen University Press, 1988), p. 78; Bertie, *Scottish Episcopal Clergy*, p. 73.
53. ACA, Jacobite Papers, Parcel L/I/20.
54. NRS, Papers of the Hamilton-Dalrymple Family of North Berwick, GD 110/1156; AUL, Thomas Mercer, merchant, Aberdeen: copy letterbook and ledger, MS 2947.

55. AUL, MS 3175/2048/(31) and MS 3175/2048/(33).
56. AUL, MS 3175/2048/(32).
57. AUL, MS 2041: Extracts from the Kirk Session Records of Maryculter, 1719–1812.
58. M. Jinkins, 'Willison, John (1680–1750)', O*DNB*.
59. AUL MS 3175/2048/(14).

CHAPTER EIGHT

Jurors and Qualified Clergy: Adopting the Liturgy at Home and Abroad

Tristram Clarke

The Toleration Act of 1712 is usually seen as the start of the split between the juring and non-juring Episcopal traditions, whose terminal point can be located in the period that followed the repeal of the penal laws in 1792, when the clergy who were qualified in terms of the 1712 act submitted to the Scottish bishops, and several congregations united. The focus of this study is on the post-Revolution period and the growing importance of the liturgy for Episcopalians in Scotland as well as those who sought livelihoods elsewhere. This chapter considers the evidence for the adoption of the Anglican *Book of Common Prayer* of 1662 by Episcopalians, and its importance in shaping their identity. It is not concerned with the controversies surrounding this process, or with the development of a specifically Scottish liturgy by the non-jurors, which have been examined elsewhere.[1]

I

Toleration in 1712 was an important turning point in the development of the juring and non-juring traditions, and has been described as an official recognition of the bifurcation of Scottish Protestantism.[2] However, the notion of a distinct ecclesiastical group protected under law had its roots in the Episcopalians' predicament during the preceding two decades. The bishops' and clergy's responses to the Revolution initiated the split between the Jacobite majority and a Williamite minority who were willing to comply with the changes in the state. A few of this minority were even ready to accommodate themselves to the restored Presbyterian church government. Attempts to include the Episcopalians within the national church effectively ended in 1695. The Act concerning the Church that year not only spelled the end of church comprehension, but enacted a *de facto* toleration for the benefit of some 116 Episcopal clergy still in possession of parish churches. The ministers' political loyalty to William was guaranteed by the obligation to swear the Oath of Allegiance and sign the Assurance. These Episcopal ministers were able to baptise and marry legally, unlike deprived ministers who were banned from doing so by a separate act of 1695 concerning irregular baptisms and marriages. Provided these incumbent ministers behaved themselves 'worthily in doctrine, life and conversation', they did not have to accept the Kirk's authority, which had been a stumbling block in the attempt to persuade Episcopal ministers to comply in 1693. In these respects the 1695 act foreshadowed 1712.[3]

The change from a church which on the eve of the Revolution of 1689 did not adhere uniformly to a liturgy, and whose liturgical practices were not systematically distinct from Presbyterian worship, to a communion distinguished in part by its devotion to Prayer Book worship was never easy. For Episcopal clergy schooled in Restoration liturgical practice, with its emphasis on preaching, extemporary prayer and occasional communion, adopting liturgical practices could be uncomfortable and difficult, both for the clergy and for the laity. This was compounded by the political tensions between juring and non-juring ministers during the 1690s and 1700s.

Other elements of Episcopalian identity, particularly the necessity for Episcopal ordination and authority, began to assume greater importance for the clergy and laity who adhered to the Episcopal system. This was an inevitable process for co-religionists who were trying to distinguish themselves from the established church. The Scottish Episcopalians' adoption of the *Book of Common Prayer* in the early eighteenth century was another profoundly important development in formulating their denominational identity. It opened the way, as it turned out, to the later adoption of a distinctive Scottish liturgy by the non-jurors, which evolved through complex interactions between the English and Scottish non-jurors during the second decade of the eighteenth century. By about 1730 the Scottish non-jurors had consolidated the liturgy at the core of their being. As a recent historian has expressed it, 'Liturgy was the sacramental soul of Jacobitism'.[4] This has sometimes been viewed as the Church's historic destiny, but it was not an inevitable outcome. Although the promotion and acceptance of liturgical practice using Anglican rites was associated with those who accommodated themselves to Queen Anne's government, it is important not to assume a neat distinction between jurors and non-jurors when examining the crucial period of liturgical development during her reign.

After the Revolution a few clergy continued to use the *Book of Common Prayer* privately, but also began to use it in semi-public services during the 1690s.[5] When William Nicolson, archdeacon of Carlisle, visited Edinburgh in 1699, he observed that

> the late Change of Ecclesiastical Discipline in Scotland has brought our Common-prayer book into greater Request in that Kingdome, than (in all probability) we should ever have seen it without such a Revolution.

He was impressed with what he witnessed:

> Both Minister and People bore their parts with the strictest Gravity and Devotion imagineable. The meanest Servant had his book in his

hand, and his responsals as ready as those of the best Fashion and Education.[6]

Nicolson records a moment in the transition towards a much wider acceptance of set forms by Episcopalians of different classes. Although the identity of the officiating minister is not known, he was probably either a deprived minister or one ordained since the Revolution. In either instance the legality of his ministering was doubtful even if he outwardly acknowledged the civil power by oaths or prayers. Such clergy at this period were subject to sanctions if the Privy Council or magistrates wished to suppress their services or stop them baptising or marrying.[7]

Archdeacon Nicolson witnessed a growing liturgical appetite among Episcopalians. His visit also marks the growing realisation that the adoption of the Anglican service impressed English sympathisers. In its supporters' eyes its use therefore became expedient as well as being a good in itself. During Anne's reign this awareness became a marked feature of cross-border contacts and the output of controversial literature. English sympathy paid dividends when English bishops lent political support to the Scottish Episcopalians' struggles with the ascendant Presbyterians. Their sympathy also helped the Scots clergy to find preferment and obtain financial support in England and the American colonies.

By 1705, three congregations in Edinburgh and many more in the north were using the *Book of Common Prayer*. When the Privy Council reacted by prohibiting unauthorised ministers in 1706, the Episcopalians complained that many of the affected clergy had taken the oaths of loyalty, and that in some places the English liturgy was being used. Among the first places to adopt it after 1701 was Elgin, where the parish congregation had even tried to call an Episcopal minister in 1703. The growth in liturgical practice continued, with some English support in the novel form of the donation of prayer books, devotional literature and the money to buy more, much of it being channelled through the non-juring Bishop Alexander Rose of Edinburgh.[8]

It is evident that liturgical worship was being adopted not only by clergy prepared to take the oaths to Queen Anne but also by non-juring clergy. In 1709, complaints against the many non-juring ministers using the prayer book in Edinburgh prompted the General Assembly to pass an Act against Innovations in the Worship of God in order to suppress its use. The ensuing Greenshields case involved a minister who claimed to be a loyal subject of the queen but whose freedom to use the liturgy was being suppressed by the Kirk. The decision in the House of Lords in favour of James Greenshields led in 1712 to the passage of the Toleration Act. During the two years while the case was in progress and before the Act was passed, the Episcopalians took advantage of the Kirk being pushed on to the back foot.[9]

During 1711, the use of the *Book of Common Prayer* increased in the north, and was reported to have been set up at Perth and along the east coast at

Dundee, Montrose, Brechin and New Aberdeen.[10] Fortunately we have a contemporary account by an Episcopal minister of how this came about at Brechin. In 1711, the earl and countess of Panmure, the earl of Southesk and other leading laity 'thought it would be very happy if we could get the liturgie introduced entirely' in the meeting house. As there were more than twelve hundred communicants at Easter that year, this was no mean undertaking. Gideon Guthrie, the newly installed minister, recorded in his memoir:

> I undertook to be at all the pains I could, and took the most effectual methods to recommend it to them both by public sermons & private discourses I could and was still introducing it piece meal ... which at last by Gods blessing had the wished effect, notwithstanding that the two Presbyterian Preachers were daily disclaiming and inveighing against it from their pulpits, and using all the Interest they could privately among the people, who brought all their Objections to me ... and it pleased God so to assist me as that both in public and private I convinced them of the unreasonableness of them, in so much as upon the Eighteenth of October, St Lukes day, 1711, we read the liturgie publicly in our meeting house with the general approbation and good liking of all the people.[11]

The propitious first service that Guthrie records was held on a Sunday, and, apart from its favourable reception, its striking feature is his observance of St Luke the Evangelist's day as prescribed in the 1662 Prayer Book. The calendar of prayers and readings would be unfamiliar to a congregation of this period. Set forms of prayer were not a complete novelty, because Episcopalian worship in many parishes had already included the saying of the Lord's Prayer, the doxology and the creed at baptisms, which made it distinct from Presbyterian worship.[12] However, adopting Anglican forms involved more frequent communion and scripture reading in services. For this to work, all literate members of the congregation needed prayer books, a disadvantage not experienced by the Presbyterians in their public worship, with its emphasis on preaching the word and singing psalms. The challenge posed at Brechin by the large and indeed growing number of hearers was met during the next two years by the acquisition of some 640 prayer books. These were mainly gifted by the bishop of Edinburgh, and some were purchased. Gideon Guthrie noted that this 'hath supplied all who can use them' in his congregation.[13]

Brechin's acquisition of prayer books occurred just before a much grander programme that, in response to growing demand, distributed large numbers of liturgies and devotional books throughout Scotland between 1712 and 1714. A London committee raised funds in England, while Scottish trustees, assisted by James Greenshields and others in London, managed the distribution. Poorer members of about a hundred parishes and meeting houses in Perthshire, Angus and Mearns, Aberdeenshire,

Moray, Banffshire, Inverness-shire and Ross-shire were the beneficiaries.[14] It is hard to gauge the Prayer Book's reception, but reports of the book's popularity suggest that a remarkable shift in religious worship was occurring. It was observed of the country parishes: 'it takes mightily with the Commons, who think they never had before any real worship . . . it is true the old Episcopal way of worship was too much akin to the rhapsodical presbyterian gargon'.[15]

At Contin in Ross-shire Aeneas Morrison not only used the liturgy on Sundays and litany days but went so far as to install an altar in the parish church he still occupied, a reversal of the widespread replacement of altars by communion tables in Reformed worship.[16] A few other Ross-shire parishes witnessed the introduction of the liturgy, including Avoch, where Morrison also ministered, and in the burgh of Cromarty. However, this picture of renewed strength was deceptive, for in some landward parishes the remaining Episcopal clergy struggled to retain their congregations. The Cromarty meeting house gave up in 1713 'for want of maintenance', despite the reported zeal of the laity for the liturgy.[17] Of thirty-nine clergy listed in Aberdeen diocese in 1712, fifteen were users of the liturgy, and most of them were non-jurors. However, time was against the Episcopal incumbents clinging to their pre-Revolution charges, and their declining numbers help explain the unravelling of the gains of this period, even before the effects of the Rising of 1715 were felt.

The qualified congregations as generally understood came into existence in order to benefit from the Toleration Act of 1712, by which Episcopal clergy could legally minister using the *Book of Common Prayer*, provided they qualified by taking oaths and registered their letters of orders. These congregations generally flourished in the east-coast burghs, partly because they attracted English exchequer and customs officials, who had come to Scotland after the Union as part of the new public administration, sometimes bringing with them or raising their families in Scotland. This is evident in 1711 in Edinburgh, where James Greenshields, who was then in England, learned of his successor Robert Blair: 'Mr Blair has sett up in your place and prays for the Queen, and is like to have a very topping Congregation by the English who were your Hearers frequenting him.'[18]

A meeting house formed in Glasgow in 1712 provides a case of a qualified congregation whose social composition, political allegiances and liturgical preferences were by no means neatly aligned. The meeting house was established by William Cockburn, a minister ordained after the Revolution and now qualified in terms of the Toleration Act. He enjoyed some success in introducing the Episcopalian laity to Prayer-Book worship. However, it was reported that 'the most substantial of the old Episcopal way refuse to join C[ockburn] because of the Liturgy, and others stumble at him for his qualifying'.[19] Conflicting political views and liturgical preferences are highlighted by a report that more laity might be persuaded to join the congregation if John Fullarton, a non-juror at Paisley, would minister alongside

Cockburn. Significantly, Fullarton had begun to use the *Book of Common Prayer*. In the event another non-juring minister, Alexander Duncan, joined the congregation and seems to have assisted Cockburn. As Roger Edwards has argued, having a qualified minister provided the respectable, legal front for this congregation, which included Jacobite-inclined laity.[20] This pattern was to be repeated after the Fifteen, when the penal laws increased the pressure on the Episcopalian laity to employ qualified ministers.

In 1712, Cockburn broke a sort of taboo when he conducted a public burial service for a soldier in the High Churchyard. Prudently Cockburn only put on his clerical gown at the entry to the churchyard 'and ventured not up the street with it'. Robert Wodrow reported that, despite the many spectators, there was 'no rabble or opposition'.[21] This might have been due to the presence of soldiers among the mourners. Burial services at the grave using the Prayer Book were a novelty that offended Presbyterian sensibilities, and caused friction in various places in Perthshire, Angus and Mearns at this period. Such a service could provoke a violent reaction, as at Auchterarder in 1712, when the use of the *Book of Common Prayer* at a burial caused a small riot. Mourners and hostile onlookers struggled over the coffin, which was tumbled 'heels o're head in the Grave'.[22] Cockburn's ministry in Glasgow stored up resentment among local Presbyterians that found expression immediately after the death of Queen Anne and the accession of George I in August 1714. A mob attacked and smashed up Cockburn's meeting house, forcing him to leave Glasgow and withdraw to Dundee, where he ministered in another qualified meeting house for a period.

A striking feature of the growth of liturgical worship during Anne's reign is that both juring and non-juring clergy began to adopt set forms. This made it a vital ingredient in the increasingly separate Episcopalian identity, transcending the divisions which largely stemmed from political allegiances. However, the liturgy was not uniformly or consistently adopted by Episcopalians.[23] As has been shown in the case of the Glasgow meeting house, the conduct of services varied according to the preferences of the leading laity as well as of the clergy themselves. Evidence adduced in the criminal trials of Episcopalians for offences such as intruding into parishes around the time of the Fifteen throws further light on the mixed services conducted by some clergy.

At Forfar in autumn 1716, a member of Mr James Small's congregation witnessed that he conducted his services partly according to set forms, and partly by traditional extempore praying. The witness saw him 'performe Religious Worship in his own house at Forfar, and heard him read Homilies Conforme to the manner of the Church of England, Say ex tempore prayers, sing Psalms and read some Chapters out of the Bible'.[24] Scripture readings were prescribed by the Westminster Directory, but not practised by most Presbyterians at this period.[25] Elsewhere in Angus, in the parish of Lethnot, witnesses stated that Robert Thomson read the prayers of the Church of England 'and likewise read a Sermon out of a printed book'. Another witness said that Thomson

> read prayers, & read a Sermon out of a printed book, and sing Psalms in the Manse of Lethnot, which was the panels dwelling house, And did at these times hear him read according to the prayer book, the Chapters which were the Lessons of the day.[26]

In 1710, at Longforgan near Dundee, William Elphinstone had set up a meeting house, where it was reported that he preached, baptised and married and exercised all parts of the ministerial function without a legal call or admission to the parish, 'and he useth the form of the Church of England in his public worship'.[27] It was clergy such as these, who exposed themselves by support for the Old Pretender during the Fifteen, who were punished and deprived by the civil and church authorities. In the aftermath of the Rising the narrower opportunities for Episcopal clergy to minister without retribution probably encouraged more Episcopalians to follow a well-worn path south to England.

II

The Episcopalian diaspora is a less-studied part of post-Revolution history, but it also helps reveal liturgical developments in the emergent denomination. The upheavals of the Revolution in 1688–90 had initiated a pattern of migration by a minority of ministers seeking parishes or positions in the Church of England. Archbishop John Sharp of York and other sympathetic prelates offered parishes in their dioceses, but Bishop Henry Compton of London was the Episcopalians' outstanding patron. He not only found places for migrant Scots clergy but ordained many more laymen as deacons and priests, men who were effectively lost to the Scottish Church. Of the 488 deacons whom he ordained between 1699 and 1709, about 75 (15 per cent) were Scottish graduates.[28] Compton's patronage was unique because he also controlled appointments to naval chaplaincies and to parishes in the American and Caribbean colonies. During the decade in question the Scottish deacons were evenly divided between naval chaplaincies, the colonial ministry and church places in England.[29]

All these men were obliged to accept the Thirty-Nine Articles and take the oaths to William and Mary, and later to Anne, as well as to adapt to the Anglican practice of liturgical worship. Williamite clergy such as Dr James Fall and Dr James Canaries, and ministers such as Dr John McQueen and Dr John Cockburn who overcame their Jacobite loyalties in order to obtain parish positions, all faced similar challenges in abandoning the forms of worship in which they had been trained and had long practised.[30] Generally it appears that the barriers of unfamiliarity with the liturgy, and differences of language and accent, could be overcome. This probably owed something to the fact that almost all Scots were graduates, and therefore on a more or less equal footing with the products of Oxford and Cambridge. Despite the patronage of English bishops in helping migrant Scots to adapt to their new condition, the process did not occur without friction. This can be observed in the diocese of Carlisle where Bishop William Nicolson employed Scots clergy when he could, partly on account of their often superior education to the English clergy. In 1706, Dr Hugh Todd, vicar of Penrith in Cumberland, who begrudged his bishop's policy, complained that the Scots clergy in the diocese could not or did not practise 'any Exact Conformity to Rubrick or Canon'.[31] It was hardly surprising that such deficiencies in conducting services were noticed by other Anglican clergy, or indeed any alert lay people, but they seem not to have caused serious problems.

Scots who were already settled in English parishes and other posts could help newcomers with instruction in unfamiliar ways of worship. Formal patronage played its part. James Blair, Bishop Compton's Commissary for Virginia, was criticised for favouritism in placing fellow Scots in colonial parishes.[32] Informal networks of influence and patronage also sprang up among the Scottish diaspora, exploiting where possible existing connections of churchmen, merchants, professional men and politicians. In 1701, when it was being discussed where two Scots could be placed once ordained by the bishop of London, it was pointed out that, as most of the clergy in Somerset and Dorset counties in Maryland were Scottish, the men could be sent there.[33]

As at home, the experience of Scots migrants in search of church posts outside Scotland also shows up the pattern of unfamiliarity with set liturgical forms gradually giving way to fluency as clergymen grew more familiar with unaccustomed forms of worship. In July 1702, while on a visit to London to seek an English parish, the Episcopal minister James Gordon was persuaded to take a Sunday afternoon service in a city church. He recorded his reaction in his diary:

> It being my first publick appearance in England, I found myself more Concerned with that exercise than with both preaching & praying in Scotland without book.[34]

Gordon's comparative difficulty in reading unfamiliar prayers from the *Book of Common Prayer* is a telling measure of how set forms could be a challenging novelty to the Episcopal clergy in the early 1700s. We know from his diary that, like his contemporaries, he was able to preach at great length, but that he had only limited experience of the liturgy. He seems not to have used it in his earlier ministry as an intruder in the parish of Foveran in Aberdeenshire, nor later in a meeting house in Montrose. However, in 1703 after his return from England he does seem to have read the English service when assisting his father at Banchory.[35]

Not only was it difficult for men like Gordon to adjust to prayer book worship, it could also be hard for their congregation beyond Scotland. A minister's pronunciation sometimes meant that he had to alter how he spoke in church or meeting house. Writing in 1694, Dr James Fall, who had become precentor of York Minster after being removed as principal of Glasgow University, told a friend of the benefit he derived from attending public prayers twice daily, and a weekly communion. In adapting to Anglican practices as part of his duties, his preaching had also been going 'happilly enough . . . my northern accent is now over with me, they say, I speak good enough English, that is, they understand me well enough'.[36]

Familiarity with English and the style of Anglican worship and preaching were an advantage, if not a prerequisite, for success in church posts beyond Scotland. In 1714, William Johnstone, a Scots clergyman who had been serving a comfortably supported parish in Jamaica for a decade, wanted a curate appointed in order that he could revisit Scotland the next year. He wrote to the Episcopalian agent in London setting out terms and conditions. He remarked:

> If he chance to be one of our country men, I wish he may be at some pains to study the English language, so as to pray and preach with a due pronunciation. It is a concern to me, to find some of our young ministry come over here, tho'roly unacquainted with the prayers of the Church of England, and so full of their own whine and cant. The people here, that are of any religion, are tho'roly in the interest of the Church and love no other sort of clergy, but what are so.[37]

His observation points to the fact that young Scots clergy were still being appointed who were essentially unschooled in Anglican worship. Nevertheless his view also supports a general conclusion that there is little evidence that differences of language and accent prevented ordained ministers from being accepted into parishes, or candidates from being ordained by English bishops with a view to obtaining one.

The testimonials in the ordination papers of the bishop of London provide further evidence of the attitudes that migrant Scottish Episcopalians carried with them in their search for preferment beyond Scotland. In addition to the usual formulations about a candidate's qualities and abilities, they often contain useful insights into the preparations they undertook. The evidence concerns those Episcopalians who moved to England for work such as teaching, or with a view to entering the church. The liturgy is occasionally mentioned in connection with their preparations. In 1709, Robert Riche, an English parish clergyman, recommended his nephew, a young Aberdeen graduate named David Mustard. He reported that, since he had lived with him in the south of England, 'he has applied himself to understand our constitution by reading of Rubrick Articles homilies and canons of the Church'.[38] It was stated on behalf of another candidate in 1709, William Stevenson, that while living at Edinburgh he

> always attended morning and Evening Prayers, I mean the Liturgie of the Church of England, and did communicate not only the high

Festivals, but also every first Sunday of the month; for which he was nott much encouraged by his Friends being, most of them Presbyterian.[39]

His determined dedication to liturgical worship was well calculated to appeal to those reading the letter of recommendation.

As he stated in his address to the Bishop of London, David Duncombe was raised and educated as a Presbyterian in Scotland, but found himself unable to subscribe to the Westminster Confession of Faith. He moved to London, where he taught in the dissenting community, and preached occasionally. Around 1713 he was inclining towards Episcopacy. Heading his list of conclusions was the statement 'That the Common Prayer is absolutely necessary for the form of a Constituted Church'. Next on the list were Episcopal ordination as the only apostolic form, which might be expected to be the chief distinguishing point of the Episcopal system, and third the doctrine of absolute reprobation being contradictory to the covenant of grace.[40]

In a further illustration of the common cause of liturgical worship among Scottish Episcopalian expatriates, instruction in the basics of set forms might also be carried out by Scottish non-jurors. It was James Gadderar in London who in 1711 instructed John Donaldson, a young Presbyterian convert, in the necessity of Episcopacy as divinely instituted, and catholic practice, and satisfied him as to the 'Government, Doctrine and worship of the Church of England'.[41] Gadderar was not the only Scottish non-juror to support a candidate by recommending him to the bishop of London for confirmation, deacon's orders and a naval chaplaincy. Among the ordination papers there are several examples of Bishop Rose of Edinburgh and other Scottish clergy recommending candidates to the bishop of London.

III

Not surprisingly, in the recommendations of candidates for ordination their commitment to liturgical practice vied with claims of their orthodoxy, theological knowledge and moral character. Also evident were claims to participation in the confessional struggle against the Presbyterians, expressed in language that reflected contemporary controversial literature. In 1711, letters testimonial in favour of James Strachan, an Edinburgh graduate who resisted career opportunities in Scotland, stated that 'he has stedfastly adhered to the Persecuted Truth, still frequenting the worship of God according to the Excellent form of the Church of England'.[42]

This recommendation is phrased in the language of confessional suffering that was typical of the Episcopalians' representations and pamphlet literature, and it contains the key message that the Anglican liturgy was now an essential expression of the Episcopalians' orthodoxy and worship. The alteration in their worship that had occurred since 1689 was such that by 1714 the Episcopalians' religious practices, among both the jurors and the non-jurors, had been set on a firmly liturgical basis. Although the use of the English Prayer Book seems gradually to have become the preserve of the juring clergy who were qualified in terms of the Toleration Act of 1712, the Episcopalians' liturgical habit stuck. Even if the Scottish non-jurors' worship was already diverging from the norms of the Anglican liturgy and developing a distinctive Scottish character, it could not have developed without the shift in worship that had occurred with the adoption of the *Book of Common Prayer*.

Notes

1. A. Raffe, *The Culture of Controversy: Religious Arguments in Scotland, 1660–1714* (Woodbridge: Boydell Press, 2012); J. Dowden, *An Historical Account of the Scottish Communion Office* (Edinburgh: R Grant, 1884).
2. Raffe, *Culture of Controversy*, p. 51.
3. T. Clarke, 'The Williamite Episcopalians and the Glorious Revolution in Scotland', *RSCHS*, 24:1 (1990), 33–51; *Acts of the Parliaments of Scotland*, ed. T. Thomson and C. Innes, 12 vols (Edinburgh, 1814–72), IX, pp. 387, 449–50.
4. A. E. Nimmo, 'Liturgy: The Sacramental Soul of Jacobitism' in A. I. Macinnes, K. German and L. Graham (eds), *Living with Jacobitism, 1690–1788: The Three Kingdoms and Beyond* (London: Pickering and Chatto, 2014); p. 39; K. German, 'Non-jurors, Liturgy and Jacobite Commitment, 1718–1746', *RSCHS*, 47 (2018), 74–99.
5. T. Clarke, 'Politics and Prayer Books: The Book of Common Prayer in Scotland, c1705–1714', *Edinburgh Bibliographical Society Transactions*, 6:2 (1993), 58; A. Raffe, 'Presbyterians and Episcopalians: The Formation of Confessional Culture in Scotland, 1660–1715', *EHR*, 125 (2010), 594.
6. EUL, Special Collections, Laing MSS, MS.La.II.644, f. 7.
7. Raffe, *Culture of Controversy*, pp. 194–5.
8. Clarke, 'Politics and Prayer Books', p. 59.
9. Ibid., 58–60; Raffe, *The Culture of Controversy*, p. 51.
10. Clarke, 'Politics and Prayer Books', p. 60.
11. *Gideon Guthrie: A Monograph Written 1712 to 1730*, ed. C. E. Guthrie Wright (Edinburgh: Blackwood, 1900), pp. 72–3.
12. Raffe, *Culture of Controversy*, pp. 144–5; Raffe, 'Presbyterians and Episcopalians', 592-3; G. Donaldson, 'Covenant to Revolution' in D. Forrester and D. Murray (eds), *Studies in the History of Worship in Scotland* (Edinburgh: T. & T. Clark, 1984), pp. 61–2.
13. *Gideon Guthrie*, pp. 73–4.
14. Clarke, 'Politics and Prayer Books', pp. 61–8, quoting Bodleian Library, MS Ballard 36, f. 151.
15. Clarke, 'Politics and Prayer Books', p. 67.
16. Clarke, 'Scottish Episcopalians', p. 352.
17. Ibid., pp. 351–2 and note 214, quoting Bodleian Library, MS Ballard 36, ff. 120–1.
18. Clarke, 'Politics and Prayer Books', p. 60.
19. R. Edwards, 'Terror and Intrigue: The Secret Life of Glasgow's Episcopalians,

1689–1733', *RSCHS*, 40 (2010), 54, citing letter of Robert Wodrow, 31 Dec. 1712.
20. Ibid., pp. 54–5, 60–1.
21. Ibid., p. 55.
22. T. Clarke, 'The Scottish Episcopalians, 1688–1720' (Ph.D. thesis, University of Edinburgh, 1987), p. 355; Raffe, *Culture of Controversy*, p. 145.
23. G. White, *The Scottish Episcopal Church: A New History* (Edinburgh: General Synod of the Scottish Episcopal Church, 1998), pp. 25–6.
24. NRS, High Court of Justiciary, Book of Adjournal, 31 January 1718, JC3/8, p. 418.
25. Raffe, *Culture of Controversy*, p. 145.
26. NRS JC3/8, pp. 411, 412.
27. NRS, Justiciary Court North Circuit dittay rolls, March 1710, JC17/2, p. 29.
28. M. Harris, 'Naval Chaplains in the Late Seventeenth and Early Eighteenth Century', *Mariner's Mirror*, 1:2 (1995), 207–10; estimate of Scots derived from Bishop of London's Ordination Papers, Guildhall Library, London, MS 10,326/28–40.
29. Harris, 'Naval Chaplains', p. 208.
30. T. Clarke, 'James Canaries', 'James Fall' and 'John Cockburn', *ODNB* (2004); for John McQueen see D. Bertie, *Scottish Episcopal Clergy, 1689–2000* (Edinburgh: T. & T. Clark, 2000), p. 91.
31. Clarke, 'Scottish Episcopalians', p. 182.
32. W. Brock, *Scotus Americanus* (Edinburgh: EUP, 1982), pp. 31, 87–8.
33. Guildhall Library, Bishop of London's Ordination Papers, MS 10,326/31.
34. *James Gordon's Diary, 1692–1710*, ed. G. D. Henderson and H. H. Porter (Aberdeen: Third Spalding Club, 1949), p. 112.
35. Ibid., p. 39.
36. NLS Wodrow MS Folio xxvi, ff. 332–3.
37. *Scotland and the Americas, c.1650 – c.1939: A Documentary Source Book*, ed. A. I. Macinnes, M. D. Harper and L. G. Fryer (Edinburgh: SHS, 2000), pp. 257–8.
38. Guildhall Library MS 10,326/39.
39. Ibid.
40. Guildhall Library MS 10,326/45.
41. Guildhall Library MS 10,326/41.
42. Ibid.

CHAPTER NINE

Devoted Episcopalians, Reluctant Jacobites? George and James Garden and their Spiritual Environment

Marie-Luise Ehrenschwendtner

In 1715, Dr James Garden, formerly professor of Divinity at King's College in Aberdeen, supposedly drafted a sermon which was directed at his fellow Episcopalians. He bewails the removal of

> our (then) king . . ., against all divine and human law, deposed by a prevailing faction of his own seditious and unnatural subjects, with the help of a forraign prince, and forc'd into exile with his Royal Consort of the Crown, and the Heir, (our present King) in his cradle: the fundamental laws of the Kingdom subverted: the Hereditary right of succession to the Imperial Crown of this Realm diverted from the right line.

After dwelling on all the misfortunes which had since affected Scotland, the sermon appeals to the audience that they should implore God

> that he wou'd avert his judgements, under which the nation groaneth, and the yet more dreadful plagues that are in view: That he would in his great goodness restore our King, our ancient Constitution, privileges and liberties: That he would deliver our Church from persecution, and establish her on righteous and solid foundations.[1]

This sermon mirrors an address which was presented to James VIII by the Episcopal clergy of Aberdeen at Fetteresso Castle in December 1715,[2] where among other Episcopal clergymen James and his brother George Garden were present. Because of their presence at the event and the content of the address both brothers are often considered as convinced Jacobites who were loyal to the Stuart monarchs since the dynasty had been deposed in 1689. However, under closer consideration, the picture is less clear: they appear determinedly averse to the shape the Kirk of Scotland took after the Revolution, not so much for dynastic reasons but because their religious views and practice were not accepted by the Presbyterian establishment. In 1715, the brothers certainly were part of an articulate group whose 'Episcopalian bitterness and insecurity' had sharpened their Episcopalian Jacobitism.[3] Despite this characterisation of their later state of mind, though, during the 1690s and then under the reign of Queen Anne, the brothers were focused less on politics than on their religious and spiritual interests, trying to keep their reputations and livelihoods.[4]

This chapter will explore the spirituality and religious environment of the brothers James and George Garden as theologians from Aberdeen. Although the labels 'mystics' or 'mysticism' are attached too easily to any kind of introspective spirituality,[5] this chapter will attempt to unravel whether their religious convictions tie in with their political persuasions and whether the religious or the political components decided their actions and loyalties. They are often used as examples for this type of quietist Jacobitism since both had manifold links to Jacobite circles with interests in mystical literature, and the younger brother, George, was openly spreading the ideas of the Flemish mystic Antoinette Bourignon. However, as Kieran German remarks, 'Episcopalianism did not automatically equate to Jacobitism'.[6]

I

James and George Garden both grew up in Forgue, Aberdeenshire, where their father was the minister.[7] The family was well connected, '[o]ne uncle was Principal of King's College, and another was the first Earl of Middleton, prominent in Scottish politics in the reign of Charles II'.[8] The Gardens were also part of the network of Scottish theologians 'bound by numerous ties of blood, doctrine and emotion',[9] interrelated to or closely affiliated with other families of the same background. Both brothers were educated at King's College, Aberdeen. James graduated in 1662 and was a minister in several parishes in eastern Scotland. In 1680 he was appointed professor of Divinity at his old university. James succeeded Henry Scougal, whose father, Bishop Patrick Scougal, admitted him into office.[10] George, having started his studies in 1662, graduated as MA in 1666.[11] We have no records where he spent the following years. G. D. Henderson supposes that he studied Divinity, perhaps in Aberdeen or possibly abroad. In his later years, George Garden had close connections with the continent, he was well acquainted with the continental book production, knew the Amsterdam printer Wetstein and was fluent in French.[12]

While studying at King's College, George formed a close friendship with Henry Scougal. When Henry became professor of Divinity, George Garden returned to his college and succeeded him as Regent, 1673–74. 'This meant that he was responsible for giving dictates and guiding disputations on all subjects of the Arts curriculum'.[13] The following years saw him as a successful minister in the Restoration Kirk. On 22 November 1683, George Garden, by now Doctor of Divinity, was installed as a minister of St Nicholas's Church. Both brothers were now married, had children and belonged to the city's ecclesiastical and academic establishment.[14] They also had contacts to members of the Royal Society: James Garden corresponded with John Aubrey about Scottish antiquities and Highland beliefs, namely concerning stone circles, druids and the second sight.[15] George Garden was interested in medical topics; he actually was approved as fellow of the Royal Society in 1695 but never formally elected.[16] However, both brothers were to lose office, status and security after the Revolution of 1688–90 when Mary and William of Orange ascended to the throne and Episcopacy was disestablished.[17]

Pre-Revolution Aberdeen and the surrounding countryside are often described as 'religiously conservative', indicating a homogenous religious environment, but if one takes a closer look this claim of 'conservatism' has to be modified.[18] There was considerable support for the Presbyterians and their brand of radical Protestantism. Roman Catholicism also survived, and some families were fiercely loyal to the old Church.[19] The third group which was – despite its numbers and influence – also dependent, for its welfare, on the political situation, was the Episcopalians.

In terms of Church politics, the Restoration era belonged to the Episcopalians since they were the establishment in the Kirk. The Presbyterians lost out; their leading ministers and preachers either switched their loyalties, or they lost their influence.[20] This was the situation in which both Garden brothers started and pursued their early careers. Theologically, there were manifold options if you did not stray too far from the mainstream. Deeply rooted in Reformed theology, Presbyterians and Episcopalians shared many theological beliefs but over the decades Restoration Episcopalians 'gradually diverged from the presbyterians, became critical of predestination and began to stress the role of the christian's free will in his or her salvation'.[21] The Gardens were part of this development. Additionally, their theological convictions were linked to political loyalties. At the time of its re-establishment in 1662, Episcopacy was – as Alasdair Raffe argues – 'less an assertion of Episcopalianism than of Erastian principles'[22] or, as the Act for the restitution and re-establishment of the antient Government of the Church proclaims: 'the ordering and disposal of the externall Government & Policie of the Church, Doth propperlie belong unto his Maiestie as ane inherent right of the Croun'.[23] The close relations of the Gardens with the bishop's family and the ecclesiastical establishment of their time and area illustrate quite clearly that they readily accepted the Episcopal government of the Church. It was not a matter of political decision-making, though: in a pamphlet of 1703, *The Case of the Episcopal Clergy*, George Garden claims that Christ instituted manifold offices in the Church and that 'Christ directs to one, that had the chief Care of every Church' – for him, the bishop, whose office is biblically authorised and divinely instituted, is the one to lead and to have ultimate responsibility for the Church.[24] For George Garden the issue of Episcopacy is a matter of being faithful to the gospel.

Before 1690, however, questions of church government were not George or James Garden's main spiritual or theological concerns. Their piety had been shaped by influences they encountered at King's College. George Garden's earliest published work was the funeral sermon for his intimate friend, Henry Scougal, who died in 1678 from consumption, at not yet twenty-eight years of age.[25] Scougal was a decisive theological influence on George and also James Garden who shared his hostility to theological controversy and sympathy to continental mysticism.[26] In 1677 Scougal had consented to the anonymous publication of his manual of personal devotion entitled *The Life of God in the Soul of Man.* In it, he characterised 'true Religion' as a 'Union of the Soul with God, a real participation of the Divine Nature, the very Image of God drawn upon the Soul, or in the Apostle's phrase, *it is Christ formed within us*'.[27]

George Garden, in his Funeral Sermon, exalts Scougal's deeply felt piety, and likens him to St Paul as the archetypical follower of Christ. He describes Scougal as of 'plain life, of justice and charity, meekness and humility, patience and contentedness, and ... readiness to do good to all man', in short, 'a life that is imitable by all'.[28] His undogmatic approach to the faith made him reject the 'disputing humour' of his colleagues, 'their vanity in hard words and distinctions',[29] and especially one aspect of contemporary discussions he shied away from: 'There was no debates he was more cautious to meddle with, than those about the decrees of God ... secret things belonging to the Lord'.[30] Thus, George Garden concludes, 'religion was the matter of his serious and impartial choice and not merely the prejudice of custom and education'.[31] In detail he describes Scougal's service to the Church as preacher and his concern for liturgy, his personal piety and experience-centred spirituality, and his ascetic lifestyle which culminated in his approach to food and his celibacy.[32] In Henry Scougal, George Garden found his ideal of the Christian life personified, and the Funeral Sermon is a mixture of a saint's life and a *Consolatio* - he desperately tries to understand why God called his friend so early despite his exemplary life. The topics which George addresses in his friend's Funeral Sermon were to accompany him for the decades to come, and these topics are also those which were central in his promotion of Antoinette Bourignon's concept of a Christian life; as we will see, like the late friend, she personified true Christian life and virtue to him.[33]

An important aspect of this is George Garden's concept of divine grace: God's love to us culminated in the coming of Jesus Christ 'into the world, full of grace and truth to renew the spirit of our minds'.[34] The divine grace offering us salvation requires human beings to return God's love by the adequate response: we have to follow Jesus Christ, living as he did; shaping our daily lives according to the 'transcript of his own life and spirit', i.e. the gospels. If we do so, 'Christ be formed in us'.[35] Or as his brother James expresses it in his *Theses Theologicae de Gratiae Efficacia*, his theological theses about the 'Efficiency of Grace' which earned him the professorship of Divinity: '[God's] efficient grace does not destroy our will and does not remove our freedom ... it is not God who wants, loves, hopes etc. in the believer but the believer himself'.[36] Both brothers promote the role of free will offered in response to the divine offer of salvation. If we try to summarise the Gardens' idea of Christianity which already emerges before the theological turbulences of the 1690s we can refer to James Garden's bestseller, the *Theologia comparativa* or *Comparative Theology*:[37]

> [T]he generality of Christians either do not know, or will not consider how much *repentance, self-denial, mortifying of the flesh, charity, humility* &c. are of more weight than *orthodoxy* or a *sound belief*, and *sin* and *vice* more hateful than *error*.[38]

II

The religious power structures in Scotland changed with the change in government: in 1689, under the new monarchs William of Orange and his wife Mary, all laws in favour of the Episcopal Church were reversed. A year later, the Westminster Confession became obligatory and Presbyterian ministers who had lost their offices under the old regime returned to their parishes. For Episcopalians who were not prepared to take the Oath of Allegiance and subscribe to the Westminster Confession it got uncomfortable – the new masters took measures to remove them from their parishes.[39] The situation was difficult and confused, especially in the north-east of Scotland where many ministers (and their flocks) tried to remain loyal to the Episcopal Church and the House of Stuart.[40]

In Aberdeen, both Garden brothers got into trouble. Both were passionate and unwavering Episcopalians. Their religious convictions were not compatible with the Westminster Confession since both brothers professed a largely undogmatic and latitudinarian form of Christianity; George Garden reveals a strong predilection for the theology and spirituality of a Flemish mystic, Antoinette Bourignon, who had provoked lots of controversy during her lifetime (1616–80). And it is not only George – some of Bourignon's ideas are also mirrored in James's *Comparative Theology*.

Before we look more closely into the issue of their spirituality we should try to unravel the issue of the Gardens' Jacobitism after the 'Glorious Revolution'. In 1690, James Garden and two other ministers from Aberdeenshire addressed a petition to the king, offering 'their sincere affection, submission & obedience to the persons and government of King William and Queen Mary'.[41] As Kieran German remarks, 'in consequence there was a species of what was effectively dual allegiance within the ranks of the non-jurors ... which manifested itself in recognition of William and Mary's *de facto* authority alongside the *de jure* authority of James'.[42] So whatever James Garden's attitude toward the Stuart dynasty's hereditary rights, there is a very pragmatic ring to this petition: James Garden, and with him the members of the Synod of Aberdeen, tried to remain in their parishes and churches: they 'implore yor Ma^{ts} Protection for themselves and others their Brethren of the Episcopall Clergy in the Church of Scotland'.[43] Nevertheless, in October the same year he tried to wriggle out of the request to 'subscrive the confession of faith, and swear the oath of alledgeance to ther majesties king William and queen Mary, and subscrive the certificate and assurance'. He did not outright reject the demand but asked 'to be excused for not giving his opinion'.[44] Even if he had been able to acknowledge the new political constellation he would not have accepted the Presbyterian settlement within the Church since his theological views differed widely from what is documented in the Westminster Confession.

James Garden lost his professorship in January 1697; this was the consequence of a discussion which had taken place some months earlier when he had been asked whether he 'was willing to qualifie himself by taking the oathes'. His answer is significant: as to the Oath of Allegiance and Assurance he answers that he 'was not as yet clear to take the oathes' – indicating that his political loyalties were at that point not decidedly Stuart or he was trying to dissemble his true colours – the latter appears more probable given that this happened seven years after the Revolution. Asked about his willingness to sign the Westminster Confession as required by the Act of Parliament, however, he is unambiguous:

> he had not nor was not willing to signe the said confession in the terms of the act of parliament, but that at his entry to his employment he had given testimony, and ever since, of his soundness in principalls.[45]

The divisive issue was the Westminster Confession; he is vague as to his Stuart loyalty. His insistence on his proven orthodoxy, however, did not help him and he was deposed by an act of parliament.[46] James Garden himself refers to this event in his last letter to John Aubrey from May 1697, and here he indicates that he did not take any of the required oaths:

> I was deprived of my office and my living, for not obeying an act of Parliament, that requests all Masters of Schools and Colledges to take the oaths of alleagaunce & assurance, to subscribe the Westminster Confession of Faith, & to declare there submission to the present church government.[47]

His fight for his professorship, however, does not end there. In 1703, after the Act of Indemnity, Garden tried to regain his post when the (Presbyterian) Synod of Aberdeen appointed a commission in order to fill the vacant position:[48] James Garden was not the candidate of choice, however, since 'the commission do charge the said Dr Garden with the errors of Arminius and Ant[oinette] B[ourignon] and cites a book published by him where these errors are to be found'. He is rejected because his theology is not compatible with the Presbyterian mainstream – as the commission says, Garden cannot refute heresies like Arminianism and Bourignonism because he himself is their advocate.[49] At this point, politics do no longer come into the equation. His successor George Anderson held the chair until 1709, and Garden made further attempts to regain it only after his retirement.[50]

After having been chosen as one of the city's representatives to address 'the Prince of Orange' in 1689,[51] George Garden's career came to an end in 1693. He lost his office in St Nicholas's Kirk in March when he was deprived of his ministry 'by ane act of the majies. privie counsell'.[52] The city council records testify to

> depryving Doctor George Garden on of the minsters of the brugh of his benefice at the kirk of Aberdeen and declareing the same kirk vacant and dischargeing him from preacheing and exercising any part of the ministeriall functione within this kingdom untill sich he qualifie himself according to the law.[53]

Unfortunately, we do not hear in which respect he did not qualify himself according to the law. From what we have heard so far about his religious convictions we may safely assume that he would not easily have accepted the Westminster Confession. His political convictions, however, are not wholly obvious. Already in January 1692, he was accused of 'not praying for ther Majesties King William and Queen Mary, and also . . . not observeing the fasts and thanksgiving dayes', an objection he himself rigorously dismissed:

> some of the present counsellers, and particularlie those who prest the said representatione to be made, hade not heard him for some yeirs bygone, and that he himselfe was of the opinione that he prayed materialy for ther Majesties King William and Queen Mary, and for the preservatioun of ther forces both by sea and land, and that he hade actualie preached upon feast dayes, and that those who never heard him could not give ther judgement so justlie as thos that wer his ordi-narie hearers.[54]

As a fervent Episcopalian he certainly had enemies who used his religious convictions and political vagueness to get rid of him.[55]

He became less ambiguous when Queen Anne ascended to the throne. In 1702, he took part in a literary campaign[56] justifying the Episcopalians' ecclesiology and asking the queen for toleration of their ways: he admits that Episcopalians had not always been very co-operative and prepared to give 'Active Obedience to some Laws then enacted' but overall he blames their Presbyterian counterparts whom he accuses of imposing their form of church government and their form of confession on the Episcopalian ministers;[57] for George Garden, the hierarchically ordained Church is a 'Divine and Apostolical Institution'.[58] Another indicator that he tries to curry favour with the queen is that in 1703 he dedicates his edition of works of John Forbes of Corse to her.[59] After the passing of the Toleration Act of 1712 both brothers seem to have been optimistic as to their prospects. On 10 April 1714, they presented an address to Queen Anne, acting as representatives of the Episcopal clergy of the diocese of Aberdeen;[60]

introduced by the earl of Mar, they thanked the queen for the freedom they now enjoyed with respect to their pastoral care for their flocks and to the use of the liturgy of the Church of England. They complained about the past sufferings of the Episcopal clergy – and there is also a note of self-interest in this address if one considers the situation of James Garden's lost professorship. The queen is reminded 'how much loss the Church sustains through the want of divinity professors of the Episcopal persuasion, for training up youth in orthodox and loyal principles'.[61] All changes, however, after the queen's death when they get involved in the 1715 Rising and again the Gardens address royalty as representatives of the Episcopal clergy of the diocese of Aberdeen – this time it is James VIII during his stay in Fetteresso Castle in December 1715. Again, they are introduced by the earl of Mar.

At the core of the Gardens' opposition to the new ecclesiastical situation lay, as it seems now, not primarily political reasons. Their militant Jacobite inclinations can be confirmed only after 1714 when Queen Anne's death started a new period of insecurity for the Episcopal Church. They may have come as an ultimate result of their frustration with all that had happened to them after 1690. According to Frank McLynn, they were Jacobites 'for reasons of self-interest' who 'attached themselves to the cause of the house of Stuart for a sustained period of time'.[62] Their once successful careers had been uprooted by the rise of Presbyterianism, its close links to politics and its firm grip on power. All efforts to get back on track had turned out to be unsuccessful – James Garden never got back his chair in Divinity; George Garden, briefly considered for the office of Episcopalian bishop of Aberdeen after 1720, was not acceptable to the College of Bishops because of his promotion of Bourignonism.[63]

III

Both Gardens were no politicians; their lives were guided by an introspective spirituality and an undogmatic approach to Christianity, centred on the person of Jesus Christ and the gospels. Their spirituality determined their allegiances and loyalties, not political convictions.

In the book which finally ended George Garden's career as minister in the Kirk of Scotland, *An Apology for M. Antonia Bourignon*,[64] anonymously published in London 1699, he explains how he perceived contemporary Presbyterian spirituality: 'There's a certain Driness and Deadness in most of Writings and Sermons nowadays about Divine Things, that they do not at all touch the heart'.[65] He complains about theologians and ministers who are 'more zealous for their particular Forms and Confessions, than for the Gospel and Laws of Jesus Christ'[66] – and it is obvious that remarks like this target his Presbyterian opponents. The 'essence of Christianity'[67] is not at all touched by the discussion of speculative subtleties; quite the opposite:

there is no way to salvation but by Mortification of our corrupt Nature and Self-love, and by the Imitation of Jesus Christ, dying with him to all the Eases, Honours, Riches, and Pleasures of this World.[68]

The way to do so is what he calls the 'Gospel-Law'.[69]

His spirituality and theology were deeply influenced by the views of his late friend Henry Scougal; the Scougals, father and son, were great collectors of books; their large collection, in 1684 bequeathed to King's College, did not only contain contemporary spiritual writings but also Thomas à Kempis's *Imitatio Christi*, the *Theologia Germanica* and St Teresa's *Life*.[70] Likewise we have in George (and James) Garden's writings references to ideas derived from 'S. Augustine and S. Bernard, Tauler and S. Teresa, Monsieur de Renty and Pascal, de Molinos and John of the Cross, Francis de Sales and Thomas à Kempis'.[71] George Garden – as his Presbyterian opponent Andrew Honyman admitted in the controversy over his Bourignonism – 'is supposed to be a known Pattern of *Piety* and *Temperance*, and deserves so well of the *Learn'd World*'.[72] From his convictions and writings, however, Honyman draws the conclusion: 'The Dr. can no longer put on a *Protestant Face*'.[73] Small wonder that Honyman saw it this way. The Gardens referred back to medieval mystic traditions as well as contemporary Roman Catholic literature, deeply influenced by asceticism and monastic spirituality. George Garden's interest in mystical literature clearly predates his promotion of the teachings of Bourignon. He had already come across these ideas through Scougal; in his later life he was acquainted with other men of similar learning and similar interests. Some members of the Scottish gentry and nobility who shared the Gardens' interest, had, like them, close connections to the continent and collected devotional and mystical literature.[74] The Gardens were also in contact with Pierre Poiret,[75] a disciple of Madame Bourignon.[76] Poiret did not only collect and edit her texts; he also published a collection of mystical works, the *Bibliotheca mysticorum selecta*, published 1708 by the Amsterdam publisher Wetstein. The first item in this collection significantly is James Garden's *Theologia comparativa*[77] followed by a broad selection of medieval and early modern mystical and devotional writers – including John Tauler, Hendrik Herp, Catherine of Genoa, Angela of Foligno, Hildegard of Bingen, Teresa of Avila, John of the Cross and – of course – Antoinette Bourignon.

At the time, Bourignon's mystical writings had spread all over Europe.[78] She was a Catholic who fell out with her Church when she increasingly came to emphasise the Holy Spirit or 'Inward Light' and to reject outward sacraments and the church with its hierarchy; she founded a religious community (which failed); and she was a theologian and prolific writer with some very controversial ideas. She has been labelled a mystic, a quietist and a pietist.[79]

From 1696 until 1708, George translated in quick succession several of her works, authored in French, into English.[80] Although he published them anonymously it soon became widely known who was behind the translations and the *Apology*; the latter put him directly into the spotlight and cost him ultimately his ministry within the Church of Scotland. In 1701, the book was condemned by the General Assembly and its author deposed 'from the office of the ministry, prohibiting and discharging him from exercising the same, or any part thereof in all time coming, under pain of the highest censures of the Church'.[81]

It did not help that for a short time George Garden was quite successful in his mission. In 1710, the Synod of Aberdeen stated 'the great increase of Bourignonism in this province, especially by means of Dr Garden' who 'keeps up a settled society of unmarried men and women living together into the house of Rosehearty for propagating the principles of A[ntoinette] B[ourignon]'.[82] An enemy called the retreat 'a mixt *Mungrel-Monasterial-Nunery*'.[83] Here the by now widowed George Garden[84] followed his ascetic inclinations with like-minded followers. The same year the General Assembly released the 'Act for suppressing Bourignonism' detailing that 'societies of Bourignonists' and their ideas should be suppressed.[85] By 1711, future ministers had to 'disown all ... Bourignon ... doctrines, tenets, and opinions whatsoever'.[86] The Kirk again felt persecuted; some of its members even suspected links between Quakers, Bourignonists and Jesuits.[87]

Why was George Garden (and to a lesser extent his brother James) so interested in the Flemish mystic? George Garden's promotion of Bourignon's spirituality started only after the new developments post-Revolution in Scotland gradually took hold and began to look irreversible. It is probable that he had come across her writings earlier[88] but only now does he seem to have arrived at the conclusion that she provided the answers he was looking for.

The *Apology* makes it abundantly clear that in her writings Garden found some issues which had already been occupying his mind since the Funeral Sermon for Henry Scougal. As the centre of Bourignon's spirituality, George Garden sees the 'love of God' – the love which God showed to humanity by redeeming us through his son Jesus Christ and the love with which we reciprocate the divine love by 'imitating' Christ (*imitatio Christi*) – 'in the Love of God consists all Good and all Happiness'.[89] Human beings acquire fruitful knowledge only in following Jesus's example, and this is the prerequisite that 'God communicates himself to the Soul, and brings along with him his Love, and Light, and Joy, and Peace'.[90] As a consequence of his rejection of denominational narrowness Garden promoted Bourignon's distinction between essentials and accidents within Christian teaching in general – a rule which he applied to Bourignon's own teachings as well.[91] As essential in her life, teaching and conduct George Garden highlights her exemplary life, her constant prayer and meditation, continuously mortifying her 'corrupt nature', her asceticism and voluntary poverty and her charity towards others.[92] He accepts that some of her ideas may be seen as unconventional; consequently he classifies them as accessories and contents himself with proving that they are possible interpretations of the Holy Scriptures. These accessories, however, need 'divert none from laying to Heart those great and necessary truths'.[93] The central truth he finds in Bourignon's writings is that she says,

> Tho' Christ has satisfied all for us on his part, yet that the merits of his Satisfaction will not be applied to us, unless we our selves do satisfie the Justice of God for our sins, and in order to our Purification.[94]

Accordingly, Garden postulates free will.[95] In Bourignon's writings Garden did also find an outspoken rejection of the doctrine of Predestination and Reprobation which she calls 'most blasphemous and dangerous'.[96]

This short summary helps explain why the writings of Madame Bourignon were so attractive to George and – to a lesser degree – James Garden in whose book *Comparative Theology* we also discover some of Bourignon's central ideas.[97] George Garden accepted that Bourignon was divinely inspired; she encapsulated what he had understood to be the essence of Christian belief and practice ever since he had encountered the spiritual influence of Henry Scougal. And – confirming his own views – Bourignon rebuked the denominational divisions and theological subtleties with which he seems to have struggled before 1690.

There are several ways to read mystical literature, and the Gardens used it as others had done before them: they studied these texts as practical guides to the fulfilling spirituality they longed for. Their ascetic inclinations, their quest for a life of prayer and contemplation, and their predilection for liturgical forms were incompatible with the Kirk of their time. In Madame Bourignon's works George (and less obviously James) Garden found a focus for their devotional pursuits. Their difficulties with the Presbyterian Kirk were less the result of their political persuasions than of their uncompromising rejection of the Westminster Confession and of Presbyterian teaching and Church government, which in their view lacked the spiritual depth they had been yearning for since their time as students at King's College. Only when it transpired that the political situation after the death of Queen Anne would make it impossible for them to regain their lost position in society or even to keep what they had achieved after the Revolution of 1689–90, they finally became outspoken supporters of the Stuart dynasty's claim to the throne.

Notes

1. NLS, MS 1012 (transcript). This sermon was never published in print. The preface names James Garden as authority behind the argument.
2. M. K. and C. Ritchie (eds), 'An Apology for the Aberdeen Evictions' in *Miscellany of the Third Spalding Club*, vol. III (Aberdeen, 1960), pp. 61–95; see also A. and H. Tayler, *1715: The Story of the Rising* (London: Nelson, 1936), pp. 129–31.

3. B. Lenman, *The Jacobite Risings in Britain 1689–1746* (London: Eyre Methuen 1980), p. 284.
4. K. German, 'Aberdeen, Aberdeenshire and Jacobitism in the North-East of Scotland 1688–1750' (Ph.D. Thesis, University of Aberdeen, 2010), pp. 33, 44.
5. M. B. Riordan, 'Mysticism and Prophecy in Scotland in the Long Eighteenth Century' (Ph.D. thesis, University of Cambridge, 2015), assesses the wider context of the 'mystics of the North-East' but does not question their Jacobite convictions. He also scrutinises their use of the term 'mysticism' and their reason for doing so, pp. 87–95.
6. German, 'Aberdeen, Aberdeenshire and Jacobitism', p. 53; see also: K. German, 'Jacobite Politics in Aberdeen and the '15' in P. Monod, M. G. H. Pittock and D. Szechi (eds), *Loyalty and Identity: Jacobites at Home and Abroad* (Basingstoke: Palgrave Macmillan, 2010), pp. 82–97.
7. A. and H. Tayler, *Jacobites of Aberdeenshire and Banffshire in the Rising of 1715* (Edinburgh: Oliver & Boyd, 1934), pp. 226–7, and D. M. Bertie, *Scottish Episcopal Clergy 1689–2000* (Edinburgh: T. & T. Clark, 2000), p. 48.
8. G. D. Henderson, *The Burning Bush: Studies in Scottish Church History* (Edinburgh: The Saint Andrew Press, 1957), p. 117.
9. D. G. Mullan, *Scottish Puritanism 1590–1638* (Oxford: OUP, 2000), p. 13, observes this for early seventeenth-century Presbyterian theologians in Scotland but it is still true for their Episcopalian counterparts during the Restoration period.
10. *Selections from the Records of the Kirk Session, Presbytery and Synod of Aberdeen*, ed. J. Stuart (Aberdeen: Spalding Club, 1846), pp. 334–7. The disputation of James Garden's thesis was held in King's College Chapel on 2 February 1681: the *Theses theologicae de gratiae efficacia: A.P.D.O.M. secundo die Febr. 1681, in Collegio Reg. Aberdonensi, publico examini subjiciendae, Propugnante Iacobo Garden Presbytero, & designato S.S. Theologiae Professore* were printed by the university printer John Forbes in the same year.
11. *Fasti Aberdonenses: Selections from the Records of the University and King's College of Aberdeen, 1494–1854*, ed. C. Innes (Aberdeen: Spalding Club, 1854), p. 478.
12. G. D. Henderson (ed.), *Mystics of the North-East* (Aberdeen: Spalding Club, 1934), pp. 33–4; on the connections of the Wetstein publishing house and north-east Scotland see Riordan, 'Mysticism and Prophecy', pp. 127–30.
13. *Fasti Aberdonenses*, p. 493; *Mystics of the North-East*, p. 33.
14. Bertie, *Episcopal Clergy*, p. 48.
15. Riordan, 'Mysticism and Prophecy', pp. 107–9; M. Hunter, *The Occult Laboratory: Magic, Science and Second Sight in Late 17th-Century Scotland* (Woodbridge: The Boydell Press, 2001), p. 22; an edition of James Garden's letters is provided, pp. 118–59.
16. S. Handley, 'Garden, George', *ODNB*.
17. F. Goldie, *A Short History of the Episcopal Church in Scotland from the Restoration to the Present Time*, 2nd edn (Edinburgh: The Saint Andrew Press, 1976), p. 29.
18. G. Donaldson, 'Scotland's Conservative North in the Sixteenth and Seventeenth Centuries', *Transactions of the Royal Historical Society*, 5th series 16 (1966), 65–79; B. Lenman, 'The Scottish Episcopal Clergy and the Ideology of Jacobitism' in E. Cruickshanks (ed.), *Ideology and Conspiracy: Aspects of Jacobitism, 1689–1759* (Edinburgh: John Donald, 1982), pp. 36–48.
19. G. DesBrisay, 'Catholics, Quakers and the Religious Persecution in Restoration

Aberdeen', *IR*, 47 (1996), 136–68; A. I. Macinnes, 'Catholic Recusancy and the Penal Laws, 1603–1707', *RSCHS*, 23 (1987), 27–63.

20. DesBrisay very reasonably doubts 'Restoration Aberdeen's reputation for quiescent Episcopacy and enlightened toleration' and states: 'Aberdeen's was a persecuting society': DesBrisay, 'Catholics, Quakers', pp. 143, 147–51; G. W. Sprott [rev. R. P. Wells], 'Menzies, John', *ODNB*.
21. A. Raffe, 'Presbyterians and Episcopalians: The Formation of Confessional Culture in Scotland, 1660–1715', *EHR*, 125 (2010), pp. 570–98 on p. 571.
22. Raffe, 'Presbyterians and Episcopalians', p. 571.
23. *The Acts of the Parliament of Scotland*, VII, p. 372.
24. G. Garden, *The Case of the Episcopal Clergy and of those of the Episcopal Perswasion* (Edinburgh, 1703), pp. 6–7.
25. G. Garden, 'A Sermon preached at the funeral of the Revd. Henry Scougal, A.M., 1678' in *The Works of Mr. Henry Scougal*, 2 vols (Aberdeen, 1759), II, pp. 369–458.
26. I. Rivers, 'Scougal's *The life of God in the soul of man*: The Fortunes of a Book, 1676–1830' in R. Savage (ed.), *Philosophy and Religion in Enlightenment Britain: New Case Studies* (Oxford: OUP, 2012), pp. 29–55, p. 40.
27. H. Scougal, *The life of God in the Soul of Man: or, the Nature and excellency of the Christian Religion; With the Method of attaining the Happiness it proposes. And An Account of the Beginnings and Advances of a Spiritual life* (London, 1677), p. 5.
28. G. Garden, 'A Sermon', p. 378.
29. Ibid., p. 397.
30. Ibid., p. 411.
31. Ibid., p. 395.
32. Ibid., p. 428.
33. On Antoinette Bourignon see M. de Baar, *'Ik moet spreken': Het spiritueel leiderschap van Antoinette Bourignon (1616–1680)* (Zutphen: Walburg Pers, 2004).
34. G. Garden, 'A Sermon', p. 382.
35. Ibid., p. 378.
36. J. Garden, *Theses theologicae de gratiae efficacia*, p. 10: 'Gratia efficax non destruit voluntatem, nec libertatem tollit, ... neque Deus est qui vult, credit, amat, sperat &c. in fideli, sed ipse fidelis'.
37. [J. Garden], *Comparative Theology; or The true and solid grounds of pure and peaceable THEOLOGY* (3rd edn, Edinburgh, 1735), p. xii. For the publishing history of this book see Henderson, *The Burning Bush*, pp. 112–13.
38. J. Garden, *Comparative Theology*, p. 7.
39. G. Grub, *An Ecclesiastical History of Scotland, from the Introduction of Christianity to the Present Time* (Edinburgh: Edmonston and Douglas, 1861), III, pp. 303–15, gives an exhaustive overview over the events; see also Goldie, *Short History*, pp. 27–30, and more recently German, 'Aberdeen, Aberdeenshire and Jacobitism', pp. 18–25.
40. Goldie, *Short History*, p. 33; in the diocese of Aberdeen nearly all parishes kept their Episcopal ministers until 1694 (E. Butterworth, 'Episcopalians in Scotland, 1689–1745: with Special Reference to the North East and the Diocese of Aberdeen' (M.Th. Thesis, University of Aberdeen, 1978), p. 3); see also J. Archibald, *A Ten Years' Conflict and Subsequent Persecutions: Or, A Struggle for Religious Liberty* (Dumfries: R. G. Mann, 1907), pp. 2–3.
41. NRS, Leven and Melville Papers, GD 26/10/33.

42. German, 'Aberdeen, Aberdeenshire and Jacobitism', p. 19.
43. NAS, GD 26/10/33.
44. *Fasti Aberdonenses*, p. 365.
45. Ibid., p. 379.
46. Ibid., pp. 379–80.
47. K. J. Williams, 'The Network of James Garden of Aberdeen and North-Eastern Scottish Culture in the Seventeenth Century', *Northern Studies*, 47 (2015), 102–30, p. 125.
48. See German, 'Aberdeen, Aberdeenshire and Jacobitism', pp. 44–50, who also considers the wider political context.
49. NAS, Papers of the General Assembly of the Church of Scotland, CH 1/2/4/1.
50. G. D. Henderson, 'A Professorship Goes A-Begging', *The Aberdeen University Review*, 20 (1932-3), 25–33. Henderson speculates that Anderson was Garden's brother-in-law.
51. *Extracts from the Council Register of the Burgh of Aberdeen, 1643–1747*, ed. J. Stuart (Edinburgh: Scottish Burgh Records Society, 1872), p. 310.
52. ACA, St Nicholas Kirk Session Minute Books, CH 2/448/21, p. 196.
53. ACA, Council Register, vol. 57, CA/1/1/57, p. 404.
54. *Extracts from the Council Register of the Burgh of Aberdeen*, p. 312.
55. The situation of Episcopalian ministers increasingly deteriorated since often accusations of immorality were introduced to get rid of the incumbents (Butterworth, *Episcopalians in Scotland*, p. 13).
56. G. Garden, *A letter to the Episcopal clergy in Scotland, being the sincere and humble advice of an unknown friend* (Edinburgh, 1703); G. Garden, *Primitive church government, in the practice of the Reformed in Bohemia* (1703). See also Raffe, 'Presbyterians and Episcopalians', p. 577.
57. G. Garden, *Episcopal Clergy*, pp. 12, pp. 14–15.
58. Ibid., p. 13.
59. [J. Forbes of Corse], *Revendi viri Johannis Forbesii à Corse, Presbyteri & SS. Theologiae Doctoris, ejusdemque Professoris in Academia Aberdonensi opera omnia, inter quae plurima posthuma, reliqua ab ipso auctore interpolata, emendata atque aucta*, ed. G. Garden (Amsterdam, 1703).
60. *The London Gazette* from Saturday April 10. to Tuesday April 13. 1714; Goldie, *Short History*, p. 41; Bertie, *Scottish Episcopal Clergy*, p. 48.
61. J. Skinner, *Annals of Scottish Episcopacy from the year 1788 to the year 1816, inclusive* (Edinburgh, 1818), pp. 298–330 (note), p. 299; E. Gregg, 'Was Queen Anne a Jacobite?', *History*, 57 (1972), 358–75.
62. F. McLynn, *The Jacobites* (London: Routledge & Kegan Paul, 1985), pp. 79–80.
63. Goldie, *Short History*, p. 47; about the fates of the Garden brothers after 1715 see German, 'Aberdeen, Aberdeenshire and Jacobitism', pp. 70–115.
64. Riordan, 'Mysticism and Prophecy', p. 111, about the history of the *Apology* which was originally written in Latin.
65. G. Garden, *An Apology for M. Antonia Bourignon* (London, 1699), p. 31.
66. Garden, *An Apology*, p. 16.
67. Ibid., p. 23.
68. Ibid., p. 25.
69. Ibid., p. 17.
70. Henderson, *Religious Life*, p. 136. A copy of Teresa of Avila's *The life of the holy mother S. Teresa, foundress of the reformation of the Discalced Carmelites, according to*

the primitive rule. Divided into two parts (London, 1671), nowadays in Aberdeen University Library, bears the inscription Hen. Scougall.
71. *Mystics of the North-East*, p. 35.
72. A. Honyman, *Bourignonism displayed in a discovery and brief refutation of sundry gross errors mantain'd* [sic] *by Antonia Bourignon and the author of the preface to the English reader* (Aberdeen, 1710), p. xxi.
73. Honyman, *Bourignonism displayed*, p. xvi.
74. For Alexander Forbes, 4th Lord Pitsligo, who was a Jacobite and interested in mystic spirituality. Riordan scrutinises these connections, *Mysticism and Prophecy*, pp. 91–136.
75. de Baar, *'Ik moet spreken': Het Spiritueel leiderschap van Antoinette Bourignon*, p. 528 (with note 74); the correspondence between Poiret and the Gardens is lost.
76. Henderson, *Religious Life*, pp. 221–31; *Mystics of the North-East*, passim.
77. [Poiret, Pierre], *Petri Poiret Bibliotheca mysticorum selecta, 1. Theol. Mysticæ idea generaliori, 2. Auctorum mystic. characteribus præcipuis, 3. Eorumdem catalogo, ac de plerisque judicio* (Amsterdam, 1708), pp. 5–95.
78. A. R. MacEwen, *Antoinette Bourignon: Quietist* (London. 1910), provides a very good overview over her life and theology.
79. J. Irwin, 'Anna Maria van Schurman and Antoinette Bourignon: Contrasting Examples of Seventeenth-century Pietism', *Church History*, 60 (1991), 301–15, p. 303.
80. For a list of Antoinette Bourignon's works and their translations see Marthe van der Does, *Antoinette Bourignon 1616–1680: La vie et l'œuvre d'une mystique Chrétienne précédée d'une bibliographie analytique des éditions des ses ouvrages et traductions et accompagnée de notes, d'une liste des ouvrages cites et d'un index* (Amsterdam, 1974), pp. 6–41; for George Garden's translations see pp. 8, 14, 19, 26, 29, 40. On the whole issue see also Baar, *'Ik moet spreken': Het Spiritueel leiderschap van Antoinette Bourignon*, pp. 525–8.
81. *Acts of the General Assembly of the Church of Scotland M.DC.XXXVIII.–M.DCCC.XLII* (Edinburgh, 1843), pp. 306–8.
82. *Mystics of the North-East*, p. 35; on the Rosehearty community see D. E. Shuttleton, 'Jacobitism and Millennial Enlightenment: Alexander, Lord Forbes of Pitsligo's "Remarks" on the Mystics', *Enlightenment and Dissent*, 15 (1996), pp. 33–56.
83. Honyman, *Bourignonism displayed*, p. xxii.
84. Bertie, *Scottish Episcopal Clergy*, p. 48.
85. *Acts of the General Assembly*, pp. 443–4.
86. Ibid., p. 455.
87. *The Correspondence of the Rev. Robert Wodrow*, ed. T. M'Crie, 3 vols (Edinburgh: Wodrow Society, 1842–3) I, pp. 169–70.
88. *Mystics of the North-East*, p. 37; Riordan, 'Mysticism and Prophecy', pp. 107–11.
89. Garden, *An Apology*, p. 20.
90. Ibid., p. 27.
91. *Mystics of the North-East*, p. 38, insists perhaps a bit too firmly that 'Garden found his own thoughts so admirably echoed by Madame Bourignon that he became instantly blind to the crudities and absurdities of her teaching'.
92. Garden, *An Apology*, p. 42.
93. Ibid., p. 243.
94. Ibid., p. 94.
95. Ibid., pp. 115–17.

96. Ibid., p. 108.
97. See for instance the distinction 'between the accessories of religion and the principals' (J. Garden, *Comparative Theology*, p. 4) or his assumption of free will (see above). Both brothers' attraction to her ideas was also noted by de Baar, *'Ik moet spreken'*, p. 527.

CHAPTER TEN

The Liturgical Tradition of the English Non-jurors

Richard Sharp

For the first generation after their deprivation in 1690, liturgical innovation was not a priority for English non-jurors. Although assembling in their own chapels and oratories, and avoiding use of distinct names in prayers for the King and royal family,[1] they continued to worship in accordance with the *Book of Common Prayer*. However, absence of innovation did not reflect lack of interest in liturgical matters. Together with their High Church contemporaries who contrived to accommodate conscience to the new orders in Church and State, non-jurors persevered in a common scholarly enterprise to raise awareness of the faith and practice of the primitive Church of the first four centuries. Eamon Duffy has observed that 'more and more the appeal to antiquity became the criterion of orthodoxy, and in that antiquity Anglicanism found ... increasingly, a mirror image of itself'.[2] High Churchmen at this time in England were not only aware of the recorded archaeological and liturgical remains of the ancient Churches of the East but also familiar with recent advances in continental scholarship, particularly the French editions of records of the early Church Fathers and councils.

I

Beset by fresh challenges from anti-clerical authors encouraged by the lapse of the Licensing Act in 1695, post-Revolution High Churchmen drew heavily upon such records of the 'Primitive Church'. When Matthew Tindal, a self-styled 'Christian Deist', published *The Rights of the Christian Church asserted against the Romish, and all other Priests who claim an Independent Power over it* (1706), the work was immediately recognised by High Churchmen as designed

> to root out of men's minds all notion of a Church, as a society instituted by Christ, with peculiar powers and privileges, and proper officers to administer the word and sacraments; and so to blend and confound the spiritual society with the temporal as to make everything in religion ... dependent on the will of the civil magistrate.[3]

Tindal's book provoked more than twenty responses, the most important being *Two Treatises* by the non-juring bishop George Hickes, in which he urged 'diligent reading of the apostolic fathers [and] provincial councils to the first Council of Nice, and the ecclesiastical histories of Eusebius, Socrates and Sozomen'. If 'students of Divinity' were to 'take this method in their studies, the Church would not suffer so many latitudinarians among her divines, nor should we have so many strange and dangerous assertions preached and printed'.[4] Invoking primitive precedent against the charge of 'priestcraft', High Churchmen like Hickes insisted that the Church was bound to claim independent jurisdiction in matters spiritual, since the privileges of priesthood derived, through apostolic succession, from the institution of Christ himself. Just as duly commissioned clergy alone could administer valid baptism and pronounce absolution from sin,[5] so the definitive priestly act was offering the Eucharist,[6] not as a merely symbolic memorial but as a proper sacrifice, foreshadowed by the typical sacrifices of the Old Testament. The application of ancient authorities for the doctrines of Eucharistical oblation and sacrifice to contemporary practice was exemplified within the interconnecting circle of Robert Nelson, an eminent non-juring layman. Biographer of George Bull, bishop of St David's and an authority on the ante-Nicene Fathers,[7] Nelson was also a close friend and literary executor to John Ernest Grabe, a German scholar resident in Oxford, 'the most outstanding patristic and biblical scholar of late seventeenth century England'.[8] Grabe corresponded on liturgical matters with Bishop George Hickes, primus of the English non-jurors, described by Nelson as 'my very learned and worthy friend, that great master of ecclesiastical antiquity, and the most considerable reviver of primitive theology that hath appeared in our times'.[9] Other scholars associated with Nelson were John Johnson, vicar of Cranbrook in Kent, and William Reeves,[10] rector of Cranford in Middlesex. Reeves was best known as the translator of a widely circulated collection of patristic texts supporting High Church doctrine and practice, comprising the Apologies of Justin Martyr, Tertullian and Minutius Felix, and the Commonitory of Vincent of Lerins. In his *Two Treatises,* Hickes discussed the primitive manner of administering the Eucharist, emphasising the 'testimonies of the ancient liturgies, which suppose the Eucharist to be a sacrifice, in which the bread and wine were solemnly offered in a proper literal sense by prayer and thanksgiving to God', and giving particular consideration to Book VIII of the Apostolic Constitutions, with its description of early forms of oblation and invocation.[11] Reeves, similarly, in his commentary upon Justin Martyr's First Apology, emphasised the significance of this early evidence for mixture, oblation of the elements and the completion of consecration by means of a solemn Invocation of the Holy Spirit,[12] distinguishing such Eucharistic doctrine from that of the Church of Rome:

> the Ancient Fathers, Justin Martyr and Irenaeus in particular, do teach, that in the Eucharist the Bread and Wine are by or upon Consecration made the Body and Blood of Christ, but then they

explain themselves in such a manner as makes not the least for the Doctrine of Transubstantiation; their Notion in short was this . . . upon the Sacerdotal Benediction the Spirit of Christ or a Divine Virtue descends upon the Elements, and accompanies them to all worthy Communicants, and therefore are said to be the Body and Blood of Christ . . . likewise the Bread and Wine in the Sacrament . . . was in Commemoration of the Body and Blood; and . . . was generally styl'd by the Ancients . . . an unbloody Sacrifice.[13]

Hickes acknowledged a particular debt to Joseph Mede, whose *Christian Sacrifice* (1648) had taught, first, 'that the holy eucharist is an oblation'; secondly, 'that it is an oblation of thanksgiving and prayer'; thirdly, 'that it is an oblation through Jesus Christ, commemorated in the creatures of bread and wine'; fourthly, 'that the commemoration of Christ, according to the style of the ancient Church, is also a sacrifice'; fifthly, 'that the body and blood of Christ in this mystical service was made of bread and wine, which had been first offered to God to acknowledge him the Lord of the creature', and sixthly, 'that this sacrifice was placed in commemoration only of Christ's sacrifice upon the cross, and not in a real offering of his body and blood anew'.[14]

Despite demonstrably deriving from a long-established school of opinion within the Church of England, Hickes's *Two Treatises* were promptly denounced by Whig Low Churchmen. In 1709, Bishop Charles Trimnell of Norwich criticised three 'opinions . . . revived of late with some zeal . . . The independence of the Church upon the State; the power of offering sacrifices, properly so called; and the power of forgiving sins'. These teachings, along with 'the invalidity of baptism, administered by persons not episcopally ordained', were again attacked in 1712 by Bishop William Talbot of Oxford.[15] In the ensuing controversy, several conforming High Churchmen identified publicly with Hickes, whose third edition of the *Two Treatises* (1711) was enlarged to include a Preface, summarising exchanges since the original publication of that work. Hickes's most notable supporter was John Johnson, vicar of Cranbrook in Kent, whose reflections on Eucharistic oblation had also been censured by Trimnell.[16] Johnson first endorsed Hickes's teaching on Eucharistic sacrifice in an anonymously-published treatise: *The Propitiatory Oblation in the Holy Eucharist* (1710). When Trimnell returned to the attack, he was answered again, with heavy irony, in Johnson's most substantial work, *The Unbloody Sacrifice and Altar, Unvailed and Supported, in which the Nature of the Eucharist is explained according to the Sentiments of the Christian Church in the Four First Centuries* (Part I, 1714; Part II 1718). Republished in 1724, The *Unbloody Sacrifice* influenced many conforming High Churchmen, including Charles Wheatly, the foremost liturgical commentator of the age,[17] whilst, for non-jurors, Johnson's influence was to be a significant spur to practical reform.[18]

II

Dissatisfaction with the Prayer Book liturgy was nothing new. Although few High Churchmen in the seventeenth century ventured as far as Bishop Andrewes, who had reintroduced several liturgical usages into the ceremonial of his private chapel,[19] several, like Peter Heylyn in *Ecclesia Restaurata* (1661), anticipated the eighteenth-century commentators who deplored the second Edwardian liturgy of 1552 for being imposed without the authority of Convocation, under the alien influence of foreign Reformers like Peter Martyr and Martin Bucer.[20] By contrast, the liturgy of 1549 was held in high esteem.[21] Dr John Sharp, archbishop of York from 1691 to 1714, 'admired the communion office, as it now stands, yet, in his own private judgment, he preferred that in King Edward's first service book'.[22] In 1714, the text of the 1549 liturgy was appended to the massive two-volume folio Ecclesiastical History compiled by the non-juring bishop Jeremy Collier, together with guidance as to relevant ceremonial uses.[23]

Growing familiarity with historical liturgies, and desire to bring forms of Common Prayer closer to ancient and universal practice, obliged High Churchmen to confront a dilemma first acknowledged by Henry Hammond, as he contemplated the impending overthrow of episcopacy by triumphant sectarianism in 1645: 'What if the particular Church wherein I was baptized shall ... set up that which ... is ... contrary to the Doctrine or Practice of the Universal Church?' The answer was unequivocal: 'If ... I am actually convinced that the particular Church wherein I live is departed from the Catholick Apostolick Church, then ... my Obedience and Submission [is due] ... to the Catholick and Apostolick Church, and not to this novel, corrupt, not Catholick Doctrine'.[24] For non-jurors, liberated by the fact of deprivation from Erastian constraint, the application to their own situation was clear: 'The best service we can do the Church of England, is to recover the main of her first Reformation: to retrieve what she has suffered by interested views, by foreign direction, and Calvinistical alloy.'[25]

Such convictions demanded liturgical expression, above all in the manner of Eucharistic celebration. Collier related how Hickes had told him about the pioneering example of John Ernest Grabe, whose antiquarian researches led him

> to deliver his mind very freely in defence of the Ancient Catholick usages of all churches ... the oblation of Bread and Wine and the prayer of Invocation to God the Father, to send down the Holy Spirit upon the consecrated elements, to make them the Body and Blood of his Son Jesus Christ to the communicants, not in Substance, but in Grace and Vertue. Dr Grabe likewise declared frankly for Chrism in Confirmation, for anointing the Sick with Oil, for confession and judicial absolution, for prayer for the souls of the deceased who die in the faith and fear of God ... And for this reason he lamented the

alterations made in the Communion office, when the first Reformed English Common-prayer book was brought under a review.[26]

For Grabe, and others, such practices were of no mere antiquarian significance, for he

> made choice of ... Bishop George Hickes for his Confessor, from whose Hands he received the Holy Eucharist, the last time of his Life, as he had done several times before, according to the first Liturgy of King Edward the VIth ... he did not care to Communicate by the present Liturgy, as believing it Defective in several parts of that Office, and looking upon the other as approaching nearer to the Primitive Forms.[27]

Growing familiarity with primitive Christian liturgies brought realisation that even the 1549 liturgy was capable of improvement. As Thomas Brett observed:

> We have now much better means of enquiring into the true doctrine and practice of the Ancient Church ... than either the Council of Trent or the first Reformers had ... And therefore I conceive it may be a shame to us, if having the means of following this rule more perfectly, we shall yet forbear to do it.[28]

Particular regard was had for the so-called 'Clementine liturgy' contained in the collection known as the Apostolical Constitutions.[29] Remarking on its close resemblance to such early sources as Justin Martyr's First Apology and Dialogue with Trypho, Hickes concluded that the Eucharistic order set forth in the Apostolical Constitutions was 'most conformable to the primitive and apostolical form'.[30] John Johnson, likewise, had 'an especial Eye and regard to the Clementine Liturgy', declaring that 'if we had the very Words in which S. Peter and S. Paul consecrated the Eucharist, it would not differ in Substance from what is contained in this most ancient Liturgy'.[31] Accordingly, Johnson set forth 'The True Method of administering the Eucharist':

> by virtue of those words spoken to the Apostles, and, in them, to all Christian Priests, 'Do', or offer, 'this in remembrance of Me': and, further, by the repeating of this history, the Bread and Wine separated for this use are particularly declared to be the symbols, image, or representation of His Body and Blood. Then they are to be offered to God in memory of that great Sacrifice once offered by Him. After which, the Priest and Congregation are to pray to God, that He would render the Bread and Wine offered to him, not only mere figures and images of Christ's Body and Blood (for that they were before) but such figures and images as may be in power and effect, though not in substance, the Very Body and Blood of our Redeemer.[32]

His translation of those essential features from the Clementine Liturgy was to be incorporated, almost verbatim, into the non-jurors' New Communion Office of 1718, yet Johnson himself remained within the conforming Church of England. Johnson's public practice never deviated from the prescribed forms of the *Book of Common Prayer*. George Hickes originally considered the Prayer Book forms sufficient, declaring 'this oblation is made in substance, and according to the intention of the Church in the prayer of consecration',[33] but later came to different conclusions which, unlike Johnson, he put into practice. Hickes 'always mix't the Cup ... offered it mixed and received it mixed ... he always said the Prayer of Oblation immediately after the Words of Institution',[34] and advised Thomas Brett to practise open mixture and to pronounce aloud the Clementine form of invocation and oblation.[35]

Denying that private intention could remedy defects in the liturgy, commentators such as Hickes and Brett were unable to understand those who continued to adhere to Prayer Book forms. In his *Dissertation on Liturgies* (1720), Brett recorded how his own practice had evolved:

> I left out the Words Militant here in Earth, and said only Let us pray for the whole State of Christ's Church: Conceiving that if those Words were omitted, the Petition, That we with them may be Partakers of thy Heavenly Kingdom, might fairly be interpreted as a Prayer for the Saints departed ... And immediately after the Words of Institution, before I administered or received the Elements, I privately said the Prayer of Oblation and Invocation very near as it is in the Clementine liturgy ... When I had quitted the publick Communion, and joined myself to the Communion of Bishop Hickes ... I conceived I might very reasonably ... do those Things which he had so much recommended in his publick Writings. I from that time ... always mixed Water with the Wine; I left out the Words Militant in Earth, and I said the Prayer of Oblation and Invocation aloud.[36]

In 1718, Brett insisted upon the four 'Uses': the mixed chalice; oblation 'as a proper sacrifice of the Representative Body and Blood of Christ'; Invocation of 'the Holy Ghost on the Elements so offered, to make them Christ's Body and Blood in Power and Effect' and prayer for the dead; besides anointing the sick and the use of chrism in confirmation.[37] Even among those sympathetic to revision, opinion varied as to what changes were essential. Consequent variation in practice soon indicated that the unity of the non-juring body could not be maintained without agreed liturgical standards. Accordingly, on 23 July 1716, guidelines were issued, providing for the use of a form of invocation and omission of the words 'Militant here on Earth' in the communion office and allowing anointing for such sick persons as might desire it.[38] However, most clergy had little desire for even such moderate change and doubted the wisdom of introducing 'primitive' practices without knowing where such experimentation would end. On 20 December 1717, Bishops Collier and Brett issued further directions for alterations in the communion office: omitting the Ten Commandments; openly mixing the chalice; providing a form of explicit prayer for the Dead and stipulating that 'after the words of Institution there shall always be said the prayer of Oblation and Invocation from the Clementine Liturgy'.[39] Energetic efforts to justify these proposed liturgical changes were made, to no avail.[40] Schism ensued.[41]

III

The group known subsequently as 'usagers' remained convinced that liturgical revision was an essential precondition for recovering the unity of Christendom. As Brett insisted:

> The only means to remove ... disunion, is by every church's returning to a closer union with the Primitive Church in doctrine, discipline and worship ... The Church never was united but upon the principles and usages, which obtained at the time of the Nicene Council ... That Church, then, which shall first restore all those principles and usages, may justly be said to lead the way to Catholick Union.[42]

Capitulation to Protestant sensibility, as with the proposed comprehension scheme of 1689, was unacceptable, since it could 'not be more for the Honour of the Church of England ... to bring a few Protestant Dissenters into her Communion, than to bring the Apostolical and Primitive Catholick Church into it'.[43] Injunctions issued by Bishops Collier and Brett in December 1717 provided for immediate 'Alterations in the Communion Service', to be observed 'until a fuller and better Form can be fram'd'. A summary of the law replaced recitation of the Ten Commandments; mixture was to be made openly; prayer for the dead was to be included with the prayer for the Church, and petitions of oblation and invocation, from the Clementine liturgy, were added to the prayer of consecration.[44] Brett commended the Greek and Eastern Churches for their teaching 'that the Bread and Cup are sanctified by the Descent of the Holy Ghost upon them according to their Prayer, and are therefore made the very Body and Blood of Christ, not by Transubstantiation, but spiritually and virtually'.[45] This doctrine had been expressed in the first English reformed liturgy of 1549.

A Communion Office, taken partly from the Primitive Liturgies and partly from the first English Reformed Common Prayer Book together with the Offices for Confirmation and the Visitation of the Sick was published in 1718. Jeremy Collier, Thomas Brett and the young Thomas Deacon are thought to have collaborated in its production[46] and the publisher, James Bettenham, was himself a non-juror.[47] A short preface restated the familiar principle that 'the safest way is to be governed by the Practice of the Ancient Church' and outlined the structure of the Eucharistic service:

at the placing of the Elements on the Altar, there is a Prayer for Acceptance, abridg'd out of S. Basil's Liturgy. The most signal Instances of the Divine Providence and Bounty are likewise briefly recounted, as introductive to the Words of Institution. This recital is paraphrastically taken from S. James's Liturgy. After the Words of Institution, the Prayer of Oblation and Invocation is subjoin'd from the Apostolical Constitutions . . . compleating the Sacrifice and giving it the highest degree of Consecration. The Prayer for the whole state of Christ's Church is much the same with that in the First Reform'd English Liturgy. But the Order is chang'd, by putting it after the Prayer for Consecration.[48]

Brett later explained that 'we have followed the first Liturgy of King Edward VI excepting where we found it not so agreeable as we could wish to the ancient liturgies'.[49] Accordingly, whereas the 1549 order had followed the Roman canon by placing the prayer of invocation before the words of Institution, the 1718 'New Office' returned it to the end of the anaphora. Rubrics directed that only known members of the Church were to be admitted to communion and that 'two persons at the least' were to communicate with the Priest. Celebrations were enjoined, 'every Sunday and Holy-day', and 'the Altar at the Communion time having a fair white linen cloth upon it, shall stand at the East end of the Church or Chapel'. The bread was to be 'such as is usual to be eaten', received in the hand.[50] Provision was made for reservation of the sacrament, but only for those who are to receive at home: the consecrated elements were otherwise to be consumed in Church directly after service.

A revised order of confirmation restored the use of chrism, directing that 'sweet Oil of Olives, and precious Balsam commonly called Balm of Gilead' was to be consecrated by the officiating bishop, and every candidate was to be anointed with the sign of the cross upon their forehead. The order for the visitation of the sick directed that confession was now mandatory, with anointing and absolution if the sick person should 'humbly and heartily desire it'. Communion was given to the sick from the reserved sacrament, 'if the same day there be a Celebration of the Holy Communion in the Church', but otherwise the priest was to celebrate in the sick person's house.

Some of those who rejected the 'usages' did so because they regarded scripture, not tradition, as authoritative;[51] others, while allowing them to be primitive, considered this insufficient justification for separation, especially without due synodical process.[52] Attempting to contain such objections, 'usager' contributions to the ensuing controversy were numerous and mostly conciliatory. In pastoral situations, this approach could work, as it did in Newcastle, where the fragile unity of a large congregation was preserved by the tactful restraint of its priest, Abraham Yapp, who, rather than insisting upon use of the entire 'New Office', continued to officiate until his death in 1728 in accordance with the injunctions of December 1717.[53]

Attempts to end the separation continued throughout the 1720s, with apparent agreement eventually being reached through a final 'Instrument of Union' in 1732, in which 'the Usagers really abandoned their whole position'.[54] Having protested against preparations for this settlement,[55] several of Brett's former colleagues, including Archibald Campbell, Thomas Deacon, John Griffin and Roger Laurence, formed a separate communion, after Deacon and Laurence had been consecrated to the episcopate by Campbell, acting alone, in 1733. By now, only tenuous allegiance to the liturgy of the Church of England remained. In *The Doctrines of a Middle State* (1721), Campbell had declared that the Church should use not even the New Order of 1718 but, rather, 'the most Ancient Liturgies of all, such as the Clementine, That of St Chrysostome, of St Mark, and of St James ... interchangeably, or at the different Seasons of the Year, or upon different Occasions'.[56] Roger Laurence, similarly, insisted that the Usages were of 'the Primitive and Universal Church and of our little Church now in Union and Communion with her':

> We are ready ... to communicate with all Orthodox Christians who use any sound Liturgy ... be it the Clementine, St James's, St Basil's, St Chrysostom's, K. Edward the VIth first Liturgy, nay the present English Liturgy, when brought up to the PRIMITIVE STANDARD.[57]

IV

Such ideals achieved practical expression in a remarkable volume: *A Compleat Collection of Devotions, Both Publick and Private: Taken from the Apostolical Constitutions, the Ancient Liturgies, and the Common Prayer Book of the Church of England.*[58] Compiled by Thomas Deacon and first published in 1734, it did not supersede the New Office of 1718 until 1748.[59] In a Preface to the Reader, Deacon explained:

> The following Collection of Devotions is founded upon these two principles. 1st. That the best method for all churches and christians to follow, is to lay aside all modern hypotheses, customs, and private opinions, and submit to all the doctrines, practices, worship, and discipline, not of any Particular, but of the Ancient and Universal Church of Christ, from the beginning to the end of the Fourth century ... 2ndly. That the Liturgy in the Apostolical Constitutions is the most Ancient Christian Liturgy extant ... If these two principles were once put into practice, all the Ecclesiastical distractions which subsist at present would cease; and a truly Catholick union would be restored among all christian churches.

An 'Appendix, in Justification of the foregoing Undertaking' comprised seventy-eight pages of 'Extracts and Observations, taken from the Writings of very Eminent and Learned Divines of different Communions'. The first part of the *Compleat Collection of Devotions*[60] began with General Rubricks. One required that 'such ornaments of the Church and of the Clergy ... shall be retained ... as were in the Church of England in the second year of the reign of King Edward the Sixth' while another directed that 'men and women are to sit separate in the publick assemblies'. A second part provided 'a Primitive Method of Daily Private Prayer ... All taken from the Apostolical Constitutions and the Ancient Liturgies, with some Additions', and recommended 'pious Christians of Every communion' to reserve a fixed place for regular prayer in the home.[61] Prayer was directed towards the East 'being the situation of Paradise ... whither we hope to be restored'.[62]

The order for public baptism of infants[63] provided for exorcism, anointing on forehead, breast and palms; trine immersion; the use of a passive formula, and the giving of a white garment, milk and honey.[64] Weak infants might be baptised at home by a priest or, in case of necessity, by a deacon, but baptism by the 'usurped administration' of laymen was considered both invalid and sacrilegious.[65] Visitation of the sick provided for anointing with holy oil and a form of consecrating the oil.[66] Communion of the sick employed elements reserved 'at the publick Communion' (no longer necessarily on the same day) and there was also an office 'for the use of those, who, by reason that the Holy Eucharist is not publickly celebrated in the Church, communicate Daily in Private of the Consecrated Eucharistick Elements, which were reserved at the Publick Communion'.[67] The office for the burial of the dead included a clear expression of the doctrine of a middle state, 'the region, in which there is no sorrow, grief or trouble, but which is a calm and quiet place of peace to the godly, and an haven of rest to the just, who therein behold the glory of thy Christ'.[68] As in the New Office of 1718, the Eucharistic doctrine of the 1734 liturgy reflected the teaching of Johnson's *Unbloody Sacrifice*. Thomas Deacon's commentary (1747) explained that Christ

> entered upon his Priestly office in the Eucharist; there he began the one oblation, there he offered himself in a spiritual mystical manner, as he afterwards did corporally upon the cross ... These two parts of the one oblation were but one continued solemnity.[69]

The sacrifice was real, yet spiritual,[70] and the Eucharistic elements were 'consecrated by the secret influence of the Holy Spirit' (to become) 'the very Body of Christ in power and energy ... and so far as it was possible for one thing to be made another without change of substance'.[71] Rubrics directed that 'none but the Faithful are to be present at this Office';[72] that 'the Eucharist shall be celebrated on every festival at least for which proper lessons are appointed, and that the bread 'may either be unleavened or such as is usual to be eaten'.[73] With the words 'Holy Things for Holy Persons', the priest invited the people to communion.[74] A concluding rubric directed that 'the priest shall always consecrate more than is necessary for the communicants; and the remainder of the consecrated elements he shall carefully reserve for the use of the sick, or other persons who for any urgent cause desire to communicate at their house'.[75]

Various occasional liturgical and devotional works were subsequently produced by Deacon and his followers in what they now styled the 'Orthodox British Church'. A collection published in 1746[76] included prayers upon the death of the members of the church, 'to be said, by a Clergyman, if to be had, but if not, by Any One of the Faithful' – a provision acknowledging the dwindling condition of the non-juring cause.

The liturgical practice of the non-jurors in the regular line of succession, who followed Thomas Brett in accepting the 1732 'Instrument of Union', is less well documented. However, as with practice immediately prior to 1718, a measure of improvisation by individual clergy seems to have occurred.

V

It remains necessary to consider the significance of the non-juring liturgical experiment for the Church of England at large. The indebtedness of the later Anglican Communion to its inheritance, via Bishop Samuel Seabury, from the Scottish Episcopal liturgical tradition and thereby, indirectly, from the English non-jurors' 'New Office' of 1718, has long been generally acknowledged.[77] English non-jurors and Scottish Episcopalians collaborated from the outset,[78] Bishop Archibald Campbell resided full-time in London, and both he and a colleague, James Gadderar, participated in English consecrations. Awareness of deficiencies in the Prayer Book rite, particularly regarding Eucharistic oblation and invocation, led some clergy in Scotland, as in England, to strive for liturgical reform.[79] The most distinguished member of that party, Thomas Rattray,[80] claimed he had been aware of defects in the communion office 'long before the starting of this controversy in England or that I had seen the excellent performance of the learned Mr Johnson on the Christian Sacrifice'.[81] His posthumously-published *The Ancient Liturgy of the Church of Jerusalem* (1744)[82] acknowledged debts, not only to Johnson's *Unbloody Sacrifice* but also to Hickes's *Christian Priesthood*, Grabe, and George Bingham's multi-volume *Origines Ecclesiasticae* (1710), for esteeming the Clementine Liturgy 'the Standard and Test by which all the others are to be tried'.[83] Bishop Robert Forbes regarded Deacon's *Comprehensive View* and *Catechisms* as an 'incomparable performance . . . the best system of divinity which has ever yet appeared',[84] while in 1829 Bishop Jolly was still using Deacon's catechism at Aberdeen.[85]

The extent to which the doctrines of usager non-jurors were shared, though not always liturgically expressed, within the main body of the eighteenth-century Church of England has been less generally recognised. It is significant that the most explicit visual depictions of the Eucharistic doctrine taught in *The Unbloody Sacrifice* and expressed in the liturgies of 1718 and 1734 were two engraved frontispieces, illustrating successive editions of *The Church of England Man's Companion; or A Rational Illustration of the Book of Common Prayer*, by the conforming High Churchman, Charles Wheatly.[86] These represent a priest celebrating the Eucharistic sacrifice, standing at the north end of the holy table, vested in surplice and hood. A kneeling congregation is gathered in the chancel, while Christ, the eternal High Priest, attended by clouds of angels, is shown above, offering his parallel sacrifice at the heavenly altar.

These images were more than idealised representations. Recent research on Hawksmoor's 'Basilica after the Primitive Christians' has 'established a direct connection between the patristic scholarship of Bingham and [William] Beveridge, the theological influence of George Hickes, and the principles laid down by the Commission for the design of the fifty churches'.[87] Demonstrating that such principles were extensively followed, and noting how altar furnishings of the period frequently incorporated emblems of oblation, material sacrifice and invocation of the Holy Ghost,[88] Peter Doll has questioned whether views regarding Eucharistic sacrifice as symbolic and commemorative rather than material[89] were normative for the eighteenth-century Church. Such doubts are corroborated by consideration of written material, including such definitive texts as Charles Wheatly's *Rational Illustration of the Book of Common Prayer*, the standard commentary on the English liturgy for over 150 years.[90] Wheatly admired the 1718 liturgy[91] and, later, expressed interest in Deacon's *Compleat Devotions*,[92] although, like the moderate non-usager non-jurors, he did not consider that the new practices were sufficiently essential to justify breach of communion.

Comparison between the second (1714) and third (1720) editions of the *Rational Illustration* reveals extensive revision, reflecting Wheatly's developing belief that the Prayer Book liturgy could be considered compatible with the doctrine of the *Unbloody Sacrifice*.[93] Accordingly, despite originally commending the mixed chalice as 'most eligible, as being more primitive and significant', this statement was subsequently qualified: 'since there is no Reason to suppose it essential . . . it must be an Argument sure of a very indiscreet and over-hasty Zeal to urge the Omission of it, as a Ground for Separation'.[94] The section on prayer for the dead was entirely reworked in 1720, claiming this need was already implicitly supplied in the existing Prayer Book order.[95] Regarding Invocation, Wheatly added observations on an explicit epiclesis to his 1720 edition. He allowed that 'there was always inserted in the Primitive Forms a particular Petition for the descent of the Holy Ghost upon the Sacramental Elements' and regretted its omission in 1552.[96] A similar compromise was made regarding oblation: 'Great Part of this Prayer indeed we have still in our Liturgy, tho' thrown I think into an improper Place . . . after the People have communicated. Whereas it was always the Practice of the Primitive Christians to use it as soon as the Elements were consecrated.'[97]

The doctrine of material sacrifice in the Eucharist was further maintained in two enormously influential works by Robert Nelson. The first, *A Companion to the Festivals and Fasts of the Church of England* (1704), was advertised by Wheatly 'to all sincere members of the Church of England' as 'a Book which, next to the Bible and Common-Prayer, I would heartily recommend',[98] and was claimed by Dr Johnson to have 'the greatest sale of any book ever printed in England, except the Bible'.[99] Following Mede, Nelson presented the Eucharist as

> the Christian Sacrifice, wherein Bread and Wine are offered to God, to acknowledge him Lord of the Creatures; and accordingly in the ancient Church they were laid on the Table by the Priest ... which by Consecration being made the Symbols of the Body and Blood of Christ, we thereby represent to God the Father the Passion of His Son ... as Christ intercedes continually for us in heaven, by presenting His death and satisfaction to His Father, so the Church on Earth, in like manner, may approach the throne of grace, by representing Christ unto His Father in these holy Mysteries of His death and Passion.[100]

The Eucharistic elements were consecrated not merely by the words of institution but by explicit invocation:

> a Prayer of Consecration to God, beseeching him, that he would send down his Holy Spirit upon the Bread and Wine presented to him on the Altar, and that he would so sanctifie them, that they might become the Body and Blood of his Son Jesus Christ; not according to the gross Compages or Substance, but as to the spiritual Energy and Virtue of his holy Flesh and Blood, communicated to the blessed Elements by the Power and Operation of the Holy Ghost descending upon them.[101]

Nelson's second work, *The Great Duty of Frequenting the Christian Sacrifice*, was also frequently reprinted,[102] teaching an identical doctrine: that the Eucharist was 'a sacred rite to supplicate God the Father by the merits of our Saviour's passion, representing to Him the images of His Body and Blood ... as has been evidently proved by the learned, judicious and pious Mr Mede'.[103] Similarly, Bishop Thomas Wilson's *Short and Plain Instruction for the better understanding of the Lord's Supper* (1736) included prayers at the presentation of the elements (oblation); a secret form of invocation and commendation of Johnson's *Unbloody Sacrifice*.[104] Finally, as a leading scholar of the Tractarian movement has noted, 'High demand for non-juring eucharistic literature continued in the early years of the nineteenth century'.[105]

Notes

1. J. H. Overton, *The Nonjurors* (London: Smith, Elder & Co., 1902), pp. 286–7.
2. E. Duffy, 'Primitive Christianity Revived: Religious Renewal in Augustan England', *Studies in Church History*, 14 (1977), 287–8.

3. [F. Atterbury], 'A Representation of the Present State of Religion' (1711), cited in George Every, *The High Church Party, 1688–1718* (London: 1956), p. 136. See also G. V. Bennett, *The Tory Crisis in Church and State 1688–1730: The Career of Francis Atterbury, Bishop of Rochester* (Oxford: Clarendon Press, 1975), p. 137, on the Representation as 'a classic expression of Tory ecclesiastical doctrine'.
4. G. Hickes, *Two Treatises, On the Christian Priesthood, and on the Dignity of the Episcopal Order: with a Prefatory Discourse in Answer to a Book entitled, The Rights of the Christian Church, &c . . . (1707)*, 2 vols, 4th edn (Oxford, 1847–8), I, p. 326.
5. R. Laurence, *Lay Baptism Invalid* (1709), prefaced by a substantial Letter to the Author by George Hickes; T. Brett, *A Sermon on Remission of Sins* (1710, 2nd ed. 1712).
6. For early statements of this doctrine, see G. Hickes, 'The Christian Priesthood Asserted' in G. Hickes, *Two Treatises*; John Johnson, *Propitiatory Oblation in the Holy Eucharist* (1710); and *The Unbloody Sacrifice*, 2 vols (1714–18); also, in abbreviated form for popular readership, Robert Nelson, *A Companion for the Festivals and Fasts of the Church of England* (1703) and *The Great Duty of Frequenting the Christian Sacrifice* (1706).
7. For Nelson see C. F. Secretan, *Memoirs of the Life and Times of the Pious Robert Nelson* (London: John Murray, 1860), and A. Cook 'Nelson, Robert (1656–1715), Philanthropist and Religious Writer', *ODNB*. For Bull see R. D. Cornwall, 'Bull, George (1634–1710), Bishop of St David's', *ODNB*.
8. G. Thomann, 'Grabe, John Ernest (1666–1711), Patristic and Biblical Scholar', *ODNB*, and 'John Ernest Grabe (1666–1711): Lutheran Syncretist and Anglican Patristic Scholar', *Journal of Ecclesiastical History*, 43 (1992), 414–27.
9. R. Nelson, *The Life of Dr. George Bull: Late Lord Bishop of St David's* (London, 1713), pp. 514-15.
10. R. D. Cornwall, 'Reeves, William (1667–1726), Church of England Clergyman', *ODNB*.
11. G. Hickes, 'The Christian Priesthood Asserted', ch. II sect. x, in *Two Treatises*, II. pp. 122–6.
12. 'First Apology' in *The apologies of Justin Martyr, Tertullian, and Minutius Felix, in defence of the Christian religion*, ed. William Reeves (London, 1709), pp. 114–20.
13. Ibid., p. 121n.
14. Hickes, 'The Christian Priesthood Asserted', ch. II sect. ix, in *Two Treatises*, II, pp. 90–1.
15. C. Trimnell, *A charge deliver'd to the clergy of the Diocess of Norwich* (1709); W. Talbot, *The Bishop of Oxford's Charge to the clergy of his diocese* (1712).
16. For Johnson's Eucharistic doctrine see W. J. Grisbrooke, *Anglican Liturgies of the Seventeenth and Eighteenth Centuries* (London: Alcuin Club Collections, 1958), pp. 71–88.
17. In *A Rational Illustration of the Book of Common Prayer*, 3rd edn (1720), Wheatly deplored the failure of later revisers to restore forms removed by the revisers of the second Edwardian Prayer Book in 1552.
18. Grisbrooke, *Anglican Liturgies*, p. 71.
19. Such as the mixture of water with wine in the Eucharistic cup, and the return of the prayer of oblation to its ancient place before the distribution of the consecrated elements.

20. The Scottish non-juring bishop Archibald Campbell was characteristically vehement against 'Zealots [whose] Aversion to Popery . . . threw away . . . the Real Presence in the Holy Eucharist, and its being a Sacrifice or Oblation'. A. Campbell, *Some Primitive Doctrines Reviv'd* (1713), preface.
21. Sir J. Hawkins, *The Life of Samuel Johnson, LL.D.*, 2nd edn (1787) p. 270: 'Johnson once told me, he had heard his father say, that when he was young in trade, King Edward the Sixth's first liturgy was much enquired for, and fetched a great price.'
22. T. Sharp, *The Life of John Sharp, D.D., Lord Archbishop of York*, 2 vols (London, 1825), I, p. 355.
23. J. Collier, *An Ecclesiastical History of Great Britain*, 2 vols (London, 1708-14), II, pp. 255–60 and appendix pp. 64-70.
24. H. Hammond, *A Practical Catechism*, 15th edn (London, 1715), Book II, section 1. This passage was repeatedly quoted by non-jurors.
25. J. Collier, *A Defence of the Reasons for Restoring some prayers and directions*, (1722), p. 122. See also A. Campbell, *The Doctrines of a Middle State between death and the resurrection* (1721), p. 252.
26. J. Collier, 'Great Historical Dictionary', vol. IV, reprinted in the appendix to [Thomas Deacon,] *A Compleat Collection of Devotions, both publick and private* (London, 1734), p. 67.
27. Campbell, *Doctrines*, p. 79.
28. T. Brett, *An Essay to Procure Catholick Communion upon Catholick Principles* in [Deacon,] *A Compleat Collection of Devotions* (1734), Appendix, pp 100–19, at p. 117.
29. These are now dated to the late fourth century but in Brett's time were believed to be substantially earlier. Thomas Wagstaffe was one of several who ventured to date the collection as early as AD 180. T. Wagstaffe, *The Necessity of an Alteration* (London, 1718), p. 56.
30. Hickes, 'The Christian Priesthood Asserted', ch. II, sect. x, in *Two Treatises*, II, p. 127. Compare T. Brett, *A collection of the principal liturgies, used by the Christian Church in the celebration of the Holy Eucharist: . . . Translated into English by several hands. With a dissertation upon them* (London, 1720), p. 431.
31. Johnson, *The Unbloody Sacrifice*, I, p. xliii; II, p. 148.
32. Johnson, 'Unbloody Sacrifice' (pt II, 1718) in Johnson, *Theological Works* (Oxford, 1847) II, p. 280.
33. Hickes, 'The Christian Priesthood Asserted', ch. II sect. ix, in *Two Treatises*, II, p. 121.
34. Grisbrooke, *Anglican Liturgies*, p. 88; see also R. Laurence, *The Indispensable Obligation of Ministering Expressly and Manifestly the Great Necessaries of Publick Worship* (London, 1732), p. 210.
35. H. Broxap, *Later Non-jurors* (Cambridge, 1924), p. 43.
36. Brett, *Dissertation*, p. 359.
37. Thomas Brett, *Tradition Necessary to explain and interpret the Holy Scriptures* (London, 1718), p. 105.
38. See Brett, *Dissertation*, p. 360; Broxap, *Later Non-jurors*, p. 45; Grisbrooke, *Anglican Liturgies*, p. 90.
39. Broxap, *Later Non-jurors*, pp. 61–2.
40. J. D. Smith, *The Eucharistic Doctrine of the Later Nonjurors: A Revisionist View of the Eighteenth-century Usages Controversy* (Cambridge: Grove Books, 2000);

R. D. Cornwall, 'The Later Nonjurors and the Theological Basis of the Usages Controversy', *Anglican Theological Review*, 75 (1993), 166–86.
41. Grisbrooke, *Anglican Liturgies*, p. 112.
42. T. Brett, *The Independency of the Church upon the state, as to its pure spiritual powers* (London, 1717), introduction.
43. Brett, *Dissertation*, p. 363.
44. Grisbroke, *Anglican Liturgies*, pp. 94–5.
45. T. Brett, *A Discourse concerning the Necessity of discerning the Lord's Body in the Holy Communion* (London, 1720), pp. xiv–xv, 27.
46. Grisbrooke, *Anglican Liturgies*, pp. 71–112, 273–96.
47. H. R. Plomer, *A Dictionary of the Printers and Booksellers who were at work in England, Scotland and Ireland from 1668 to 1725* (London: Bibliographic Society, 1968), pp. 33–4.
48. *A Communion Office* (1718), preface.
49. Brett, *Dissertation*, p. 382.
50. Ibid., p. 217.
51. Cf. N. Spinckes, *No sufficient reasons for restoring the prayers and directions of King Edward VI's first Liturgy* (London, 1718); [W. Snatt,] *Mr Collier's Desertion Discuss'd* (London, 1719); C. Leslie, *A Letter from Mr Charles Leslie Concerning the New Separation* (London, 1719).
52. Cf. [W. Scott,] *No Necessity to Alter the Common Prayer* (London, 1718) on the epiclesis: 'The question is not, whether the prayer be good, but whether it be essentially necessary. For if it be not necessary, your separation has been no tolerable pretence', p. 40.
53. Broxap, *Later Non-jurors*, pp. 135–7.
54. Ibid., p. 172. The reunion negotiations are surveyed in detail, pp. 107–89.
55. Ibid., pp. 147–8 and *passim*.
56. Campbell, *Doctrines*, p. vi.
57. Laurence, *Indispensable Obligation*, p. 96.
58. Deacon's 1734 liturgy is discussed in Grisbrooke, *Anglican Liturgies*, pp. 113–35, 297–316.
59. H. Broxap, *Biography of Thomas Deacon, the Manchester Non-Juror* (Manchester, 1911); Broxap, *Later Non-jurors*, pp. 202–3. Deacon's compilation was then used in association with an exhaustive commentary: [T. Deacon,] *A Full, True, and Comprehensive View of Christianity* (London, 1747).
60. Contents summarised in Thomas Lathbury, *A History of the Book of Common Prayer and other books of authority* (Oxford, 1858), pp. 496–501; Grisbrook, *Anglican Liturgies*, pp. 118–23.
61. [T. Deacon,] *Compleat Collection*, p. 249.
62. [Deacon,] *Full, True*, p. 176.
63. [Deacon,] *Compleat Collection*, p. 249.
64. Ibid., pp. 130–40.
65. [Deacon,] *Full, True*, p. 234.
66. [Deacon,] *Compleat Collection*, pp. 166–7; 172–3.
67. Ibid., pp. 174–85; 327–37.
68. Ibid., p. 195.
69. [Deacon,] *Full, True*, p. 259. Compare Johnson, *The Unbloody Sacrifice*, I, pp. 60–96.
70. [Deacon,] *Full, True*, p. 281.

71. Johnson, *The Unbloody Sacrifice*, I, p. 193.
72. [Deacon,] *Compleat Collection*, p. 74.
73. Ibid., p. 100.
74. Ibid., p. 100; *Longer Catechism*, pp. 343–93.
75. Cf. 'An Office for those, who ... communicate daily in Private of the Consecrated Eucharistick Elements' in [Deacon,] *Compleat Collection of Devotions* (1734), pp. 327-37.
76. [Deacon,] *Devotions, To be Used by Primitive Catholicks, At Church and At Home. In Two Parts* (Liverpool, 1747).
77. See Grisbrooke, *Anglican Liturgies*, p. 112, on the 1718 liturgy as the 'primary source of all the Anglican rites descended from the Scottish Liturgy of 1764'. See also G. J. Cuming, *A History of Anglican Liturgy* (London: Macmillan, 1969), pp. 143–6.
78. E.g. [Laurence,] *A Supplement to The Indispensable Obligation &c.* (1733), pp. 110–13.
79. Grisbrooke, *Anglican Liturgies*, pp. 150–9; 335–48. See also John Dowden, *The Scottish Communion Office 1764* (Oxford, 1922).
80. Of Craighall, Perthshire, Primus 1739–43.
81. Dowden, *Scottish Communion Office*, p. 48.
82. Grisbrooke, *Anglican Liturgies*, pp. 136–49; 317–32): '[Rattray's] eucharistic doctrine ... in no wise departed from that common among his Nonjuring brethren in England' (Dowden, *Scottish Communion Office*, p. 145).
83. Rattray, *Ancient Liturgy*, pp. v–vii, xi–xii.
84. Quoted in Broxap, *Later Non-jurors*, p. 252.
85. Broxap, *Life of Thomas Deacon*, p. 181.
86. 2nd edition, octavo (1714); 3rd edition, folio (1720).
87. P. Doll, *After the Primitive Christians* (Alcuin Club/GROW Joint Liturgical Studies 37; Cambridge: Grove Books, 1997), pp. 37–8. See also P. de la Ruffiniere du Prey, *Hawksmoor's London Churches: Architecture and Theology* (Chicago: University of Chicago Press, 2000), and Christopher Moody: '"The Basilica after the Primitive Christians": Liturgy, Architecture and Anglican Identity in the Building of the Fifty New Churches', *Journal of Anglican Studies*, 15:1 (2017), pp. 37–57.
88. Doll, *After the Primitive Christians*, pp. 32–3. See also J. W. Legg, *English Church Life from the Restoration to the Tractarian Movement* (London, 1914), pp. 126–34.
89. C. W. Dugmore, *Eucharistic Doctrine in England from Hooker to Waterland* (London: SPCK, 1942).
90. 1st edition 1710; 8th edition 1759; another 1794; at least 15 further editions 1802–90.
91. Broxap, *Later Non-jurors*, p. 70.
92. Ibid., p. 199.
93. Notably in ch. VI, 'Of the Communion Office'; also 'Additions and Emendations' (3rd edn (1720), pp. 540-2).
94. Wheatly, *Rational Illustration* (1714), p. 206; (1720), p. 280.
95. Ch. VI, sect. 11.2, p. 280.
96. Ch. VI, sect. 22.2, pp. 289–90.
97. Ch. VI, sect. 22.3, p. 291 and n.
98. Wheatly, *Rational Illustration*, 3rd edn, 1720, p. 252.

99. G. B. Hill and L. F. Powell (eds), *Boswell's Life of Johnson* . . . (Oxford, 1934), II, p. 458.
100. Nelson, *Companion*, 13th edn (1726), p. 579, citing Joseph Mede, *Christian Sacrifice*.
101. Ibid., p. 580.
102. Nelson, *The Great Duty of Frequenting the Christian Sacrifice*, 1st edn, 1706; 15th edn, 1779.
103. Ibid., cited in *Tracts for the Times by Members of the University of Oxford* (new edn 1839), iv, p. 303.
104. Ibid., pp. 361–9). Wilson's *Parochialia* and *Sacra Privata* also considered Invocation and oblation.
105. P. B. Nockles, *The Oxford Movement in Context* (Cambridge: CUP, 1994), p. 237.

CHAPTER ELEVEN

Archibald Campbell: A Pivotal Figure in Episcopalian Liturgical Transition

A. Emsley Nimmo

The support by non-juring Scottish Episcopalianism of Jacobitism was a physical, political, temporal and ecclesiastical disaster. Yet as far as theology, ecclesiology and liturgy were concerned, the opposite obtained. It was as if the non-jurors on account of earthly disappointment, concentrated on things necessary for spiritual well-being and eternal salvation. The Revolution Settlement of 1689–90 gave them a freedom from Erastianism which created an opportunity that pushed the Scottish Episcopal Church towards the cutting edge of liturgy and placed it at the forefront of liturgical development in the Western Church.[1] It gave it a unique and distinguished liturgy that had influence beyond Scotland, most notably in the American Episcopal Church after the consecration of Samuel Seabury by three Aberdeenshire bishops, Robert Kilgour, Arthur Petrie and John Skinner, as first Bishop *apud Americanos* at St Andrew's Chapel in the Longacre Aberdeen on 14 November 1784.[2]

Early in the eighteenth century the Episcopalians in Scotland had become divided over the subject of the usages in the liturgy, namely admixture, epiclesis, oblation, prayers for the departed, also chrism for confirmation and the sick, and immersion in baptism. Subsequent to the death of Bishop George Hickes in 1715 the division between usagers and non-usagers began in England. The English non-jurors Jeremy Collier, Thomas Brett and Thomas Deacon were in close contact with Archibald Campbell, James Gadderar and Thomas Rattray, Scots who were all in London at that time. In a letter to James VIII on 25 April 1720, George Lockhart of Carnwath, then leading Jacobite agent in Scotland, wrote scathingly of Campbell:

(who 'tho adorn'd with none of these qualifications requisite in a bishop, and remarkable for some things inconsistant with the character of a gentleman, was most imprudently consecrated some years agoe) is coming here from London, with a view of forming a party and propagating those doctrines which were at least unseasonably broached some few years agoe in England. Both clergy and laytie have a great regard for Bishop Fullerton [John Fullerton, bishop of Edinburgh and primus, 1720–7][3] and contempt of the other, it is probable he will make few proselytes; however it is still fitt to provyde against the worst, and leave nothing undone to prevent a breach which would be attended with bad consequences with respect to both Crown and Mitre.[4]

On 7 December 1722, he again made reference to the usages and the usagers:

> You have heard no doubt of some contests of late years amongst the nonjuring English clergy, concerning some alterations that some of the number desired in the Liturgy and forms of worship, which were driven so far as to occasion a great breach amongst them, to the no small prejudice and discredit of the whole party. Of those who sett up for alterations, two of our Scots Bishops, Campbell and Gatherer made a considerable figure at London where they have resided these many years; and Falconar [John Falconar, College Bishop 1709–23, who took part in Gadderar's consecration at London in 1712][5] favoured them in Scotland, in the northern parts wherof some of the layity began lately to think after the same manner; and as the clergy, of all mankind, are most zealous to propagate and establish their own schemes, Gatherer on ane invitation from some people of notte, is lately come to Edinburgh in order to his going north and heading that party.[6]

How wrong Carnwath was. The Scottish Prayer Book of 1637 had previously set liturgical precedent for some of the usages. The die was now cast, Scotland was fertile ground and, despite opposition in some quarters, the usages from thereon would slowly gain in wider currency amongst the Episcopal clergy in Scotland. Pamphlets expressed the diversity of liturgical opinion. On the one hand, George Smith argued that there was neither authority nor reason for laying the English office aside. One of the societal arguments was the recent political Union with England, the argument being that it would encourage greater unity between the two countries.[7] But on the other hand, the case was made with clear conviction, for the superiority and advantage of the Scots Rite.[8] Pivotal in this process was Archibald Campbell, bishop of Aberdeen from 1721 to 1724, an irascible character, perhaps due to frequent attacks of gout and with many years of financial and legal difficulties stemming from misappropriation by John Campbell, earl of Breadalbane, of heritable land in Argyll.[9] He was an absentee from his diocese and residing in London and was one of the greatest minds produced by the Scottish Church. This chapter will focus on one aspect of the usages: the reasons for and the importance of why Episcopalians pray for the dead as part of their core belief.

I

In 1718, the envoy of the English non-jurors to the Scots bishops, one Mr Peck, wrote to Bishop Falconar and suggested that, as the Scottish Prayer Book of 1637 was scarce and costly, the communion office (ten thousand copies) should be printed by itself with two changes: first, in the rubric where the presbyter is directed to offer up and place etc., after the word 'wine' should come a parenthesis (i.e. mixed with a little pure water) and, second, that the whole or at least the latter part of the title of the prayer 'for the whole state' should be omitted. Peck was the first to suggest the disingenuous trick of still calling the book *The Liturgy of the Church of Scotland*. Using this title he suggested 'will go down best with the people'.[10]

Twenty-five years later in 1743, the year before Campbell died, Mr James Dundass, in support of the Reverend David Fyffe in his revolt against Bishop James Raitt in the usages controversy at the Seagate Chapel in Dundee, published *An Impartial Enquiry into the Rise and Progress of the Ancient Usage of Prayers for the Dead*.[11] This publication provides a very neat and succinct précis of what the jurors believed about those in the non-juring tradition. As far as Dundass was concerned, it was evident that the petitions in the later liturgies, for the dead and their peace, rest, refreshment and light were to be considered none other than superstitious corruptions of the ancient forms, according to the groundless conceits, and unwarrantable opinions of those who had the chief hand in compiling them. For Dundass, all the unscriptural innovations were evident from the new communion office (the Scots Communion Office of 1637 reprinted) for the introduction of which the usagers brought from England over five hundred copies and dispersed them throughout Scotland.[12]

Dundass went on to list the following deprivations:

> 1) Whereas the genuine *Scots* Communion Office has the whole Rubrick *Let us pray for the whole state of Christ's Church militant here on Earth*; the spurious one hath it curtailed thus, *Let us pray for the whole state of Christ's Church* This is done to make that Prayer comprehend a Prayer for the Dead.
>
> 2) And, which is a Thing very remarkable, The place of prayer is materially altered; Whereas in the genuine Office, it immediately follows the Offertory; in the spurious one it is postponed to the Prayers of Consecration and this is called *its natural Order*, on the Title page: to wit, that the dead, as well as the living, may be interceded for in the Virtue of their Eucharistick Sacrifice.
>
> 3) Whereas the genuine Office, in the Prayer of Oblation, hath only these Words, *viz. We thy humble Servants do celebrate and make here before thy divine Majesty, with these thy holy Gifts, the Memorial which thy Son hath willed us to make;* the spurious one hath these, *viz We thy humble Servants do celebrate and make here before thy divine Majesty, with these thy holy Gifts,*

which we now offer unto thee, *the Memorial thy Son hath willed us to make.* This is not only to make the holy Sacrament a *Memorial*, but a true and real Sacrifice of the Body and blood of our Lord.[13]

To understand why the non-jurors were so convinced of their theological and liturgical tradition we have to go back to the pre-Revolution Kirk.

By the reign of Charles I, knowledge of Greek liturgies was gaining wider currency in the West. The renowned John Forbes of Corse, professor of Divinity at King's College, Aberdeen, leader of the Aberdeen doctors and one of the greatest patristic scholars and theologians that Scotland has ever produced, was reading Greek liturgy.[14] He in many ways initiated a process which encouraged Episcopalian divines in the Church of Scotland to look to the East. This legacy was received and developed by the non-jurors in the post-Revolution Church, not only with their devotion to primitive rites but also with their particular fascination with what became known as the usages. Douglas Kornahrens has argued that John Forbes underlined the Early Fathers' belief in a separate state for souls in his *Instructiones Historico-Theologicae de Doctrina Christiana* (1645). However, Forbes was not prepared to suggest that the living might influence the state of the dead, declaring that it is 'not safe for us to imitate the ancients' by praying for departed souls. However Kornahrens would assert that Scottish Episcopalians would generally accept praying for the dead thereafter.[15] In the liturgy of St Mark which was read by John Forbes of Corse there is definite reference to praying for the dead, as there is in the liturgies of St Chrysostom and St Basil. These are all expertly laid out in the style of a synopsis by Bishop Thomas Rattray in his *The Ancient Liturgy of the Church of Jerusalem being the Liturgy of St James*, published posthumously in 1744.[16]

Margaret Barker gives insights on the 'mysteries' which have been handed down. She makes reference to St Basil the Great who was Bishop of Caesarea in Cappadocia, now central Turkey, in the fourth century.

> He was a towering figure in the history of the Church, and one of the great liturgies, still used ten times a year by the Orthodox Churches, is ascribed to him. Basil, together with his brother Gregory of Nyssa and his friend from student days Gregory of Nazianzus, are known as the Cappadocian Fathers, three men who were a formative influence in developing the understanding of the Trinity . . . Since he helped to form Christian thinking about their fundamental Trinitarian doctrine and shaped the worship of countless eastern and oriental churches, *it is very significant indeed that he claimed to know of authentic Christian traditions not recorded in the Bible.*[17]

With reference to the Holy Spirit, Basil spoke of two ways in which Christian teaching had been handed down: 'Of the dogma and kerygma which are preserved in the Church, we have some from teachings in writing, and the others we have received from the tradition of the apostles, handed down in a mystery'. He said that they were of equal importance, and that rejecting the unwritten customs reduced the gospel. He gave many examples: signing with the cross (at baptism), blessing the oil for anointing, anointing itself, facing east to pray, and the words of epiclesis at the Eucharist. He stated that 'The apostles and fathers who prescribed from the beginning the matters that concerned the Church, guarded in secret and unspoken, the holy things of the mysteries'. Basil distinguished between doctrine and proclamation, between the deepest theology and what was given as public teaching, believing that one form of this silence was the obscurity of some passages of scripture, which held the theology, but not obviously. There were meanings in scripture apart from what was obvious. Basil gave some examples; where the proclaimed public practice was to pray facing east, the theology underlying this, but less widely known, was that Christians were looking towards their old home, Paradise, the garden of the east. Unwritten mysteries, Margaret Barker argued, 'meant aspects of the faith that were not fully open to human language and logic. They were beyond words.'[18]

Concurrent with John Forbes at King's College, William Forbes became the principal of Marischal College in Aberdeen in 1620. Like his namesake, he had travelled widely in Europe and was a noted theologian. His defence of Episcopacy made him a target for those contemporaries committed to the Presbyterian polity. In 1633 he was appointed the first Bishop of Edinburgh, but died before the furore over the Scottish Prayer Book of 1637. The intercessions in that Eucharistic rite are introduced by the phrase 'Let us pray for the whole state of Christ's Church militant here in earth': an invitation to prayer which later had the word 'militant' deleted by the non-jurors in the 1735 Rite, as it conflicted with their beliefs. The 1637 Rite, following the style of the English 1549 Rite, clearly prays for the departed in the words 'And we also blesse thy Holy name for all those servants, who having finished their course in faith, do now rest from their labours'. In the revision of the English Rite in 1552, the Church of England had ceased praying for the departed.[19]

William Forbes had paved the way with prayers for the dead:

> let not the custom of praying and offering for the dead, which is most ancient, and thoroughly received in the universal Church of Christ almost from the very times of the Apostles, be any longer rejected by Protestants as being unlawful or at least useless.[20]

For Forbes, the Christian commonwealth stands by holy antiquity. In a sense Forbes paved the way for Campbell. The influence of the Aberdeen doctors on the theology of the non-jurors should not be underestimated.[21] However, it should be noted that Campbell, unlike the Doctors, certainly did not stand in the irenic tradition.

II

The title page of Campbell's prolific *work Doctrine of the Middle State* first published in 1713 then in 1721 contains the following from the Vincentian Canon: '*Quod ubique, quod semper, quod ab omnibus creditum est*' (what has been believed everywhere, always and by all). It was Campbell's clarion call and his appeal was to ancient Catholic orthodoxy and doctrine. Campbell himself was so convinced and so determined in his resolve that he could write 'I pray God to restore Primitive Doctrine, Discipline, Worship and Government, Primitive Lives and conversation, Primitive Love, Peace Unity and Concord' and added:

> Publick Considerations . . . I think ought to be laid totally aside when Truth and Primitive Doctrine, Discipline and Worship are the subjects under consideration for I think we ought to do what is right and leave events to God.[22]

On 27 May 1720, Campbell wrote to Bishop Falconar in quite melancholy terms expressing his sadness about being seemingly ignored by his colleagues in Scotland. He mentions that he was not even consulted in regard to recent consecrations of bishops in Scotland before going on to advertise his preference for the usages:

> If yr people would use themselves to the Scotch Liturgy two of the 4 things upon wch we insist are here already and the Mixture could be easily introduced almost unperceivably and the omitting of the words *Militant here on earth* would make all well, thus all we insist upon were safely engrafted upon the Scotch Liturgy and if your people were right in these things our old friends here would the more easily come to terms with us, for their great strength lys in yr peoples being on their side. This Engraftment on the Scotch Liturgy is what I laboured hard with the Bishop [Rose] of Edinburgh for as I did not find him so averse to it in his own inclinations as afraid of the unrulyness of some of his old priests. If this can now be done I shall be very glad.[23]

Several months later he further writes to Falconar from London on 7 November 1720 correcting defects in the 'Scotch Liturgy':

> It is perfectly easy, unobserveably to leave out these words [Militant here on Earth]. It is also easy to mix a little water with the wine and then there will be no objection, and indeed without these our English friends, to say nothing of our selves, here will think the Administration imperfect but if these be done they will think all who do so of one entire Communion with themselves, and further I see no such probable way of ending all our differences here as officiating in this manner there, for then the weight of Majority would be great on our side. These are

but hints yet from them you may conceive that even Polliticks as well as Religion makes them proper to be Considered.[24]

For the English non-jurors it was all about the need to defend the Church as a spiritual society independent of the state. The non-jurors had a strong sense of the sacred and that the Church was a distinct society: the practice of the usages was very much the litmus test of being the church. John Kettlewell, the English non-juror, believed that religion ought not to stand on scattered individuals but to be born up by communions, or pastors and people or by regular societies. Religion for him denoted a kind of sociality: membership in a distinct society.[25] The non-jurors possessed a high doctrine of priesthood, 'an increasingly robust sacerdotalism, which stressed the indispensability of the priesthood and the priestly, sacramental function to Christianity'.[26] This was the very sinews of communion. Campbell was a leading light in English non-juring circles. For him a cross border communion was about building up this distinct ecclesial society a true 'Catholick remnant of the Britannick Church'[27]. In one of his prayers he heartily commends to God's merciful hands 'all the Orthodox and Loyall Bishops of the Christian Church and particularly those of this island ... give them an opportunity, each of them, who are now debarred from the publick exercise of their function by a raging Schism and a successful, Rebellion and Usurpation'.[28]

On 20 June 1721, Campbell has sent a copy of his *Middle State* to Falconar:

> When you have read it I shall be glad to know yr opinion of it wch I do assure you, always weighs much with me. If there is anything unsound or that is not orthodox contained in it I disclaim it beforehand. Meantime I am fully satisfied that I am in the right and cannot think otherwise, than I do, unless I be so moved to alter by the force of Reason and Authority both wch I think at present are on my side.[29]

However, Campbell was still waiting impatiently for Falconar's response on 11 November 1721.[30] Falconar was not having an easy time. Although there may have been increasing support for liturgical innovation both amongst the clergy and the laity, 'no external influence had been exerted in their favour. Against them was arrayed the whole weight of popular prejudice, the force of habit, the aversion to ritual which since the Reformation had almost become part of the Scottish character.'[31] Within the Episcopal College, it seemed that Falconar was on his own.

By 12 April 1722, relationships between Campbell and the Episcopal College in Scotland had become extremely fraught. Campbell had been elected bishop of Aberdeen by the Diocesan electors the previous May. The choice was not satisfactory to the majority in the College of Bishops, perhaps mainly due to the division that had been caused amongst English non-jurors on account of the usages. Notwithstanding their grievance at being by-passed, the College would have ratified the election if Campbell would promise not to maintain any doctrines or usages which were without sanction from the canons of the Church. But he refused to comply and the bishops therefore intimated to the diocese that their choice was not approved of. Campbell held himself to be canonically elected.[32] He dispatched James Gadderar to Aberdeen to serve as his vicar, suffragan or commendator. In 1725, Campbell resigned the see to Gadderar by a formal deed and Gadderar was duly elected by the diocesan clergy.

Campbell not only castigated Bishop John Fullarton of Edinburgh as primus of the College as 'your Pope' but also admonished Fullarton's two leading associates, Bishops Miller and William Irivine, whom he deemed the 'Triumverate', for their 'very wicked stupid and impudent' treatment: 'for if they do not speedily make me sufficient amends, I shall make them the Jest and Contempt of the island and infamous to posterity, in the most publick manner'. Determined to vindicate his honour with his pen, Campbell affirmed, 'I never joined in Presbyterian worship as your Pope did', and further disparaged the Scottish bishops:

> I find that they have lost their reputation in the North for their treatment of me. I have been fighting their battles here, while they were demolishing me there: so I sit between two stools. If they are Angry at my book, I thank God, much better scholars and much better judges than they are do like it.

Notwithstanding his differences with Fullarton, Miller and Irvine, 'his holiness & and his two cardinals', Campbell was thankful to God for showing him:

> that if my repentance be genuine here: and duly prosecuted with diligence, till death, I may hope through the merits of Christ to be maid so much purer and more holy afterwards, as to be qualified first for the joys of paradise, and after my resurrection for the Beatific Vision for wch I thank God the Triumvirate cannot debar me.[33]

The Triumvirate were not as intemperate. Fullerton, Millar and Irvine sought mediation through Bishop Falconar to heal divisions with Campbell, who had no intention of leaving London to take up residence in Aberdeen.[34] Campbell duly wrote a more conciliatory letter to Falconar on 3 May 1722. He still maintained that Fullarton, Miller and Irvine 'do not acknowledge me a member of yr College: until they think fitt to admit me and upon their own terms' and claimed that 'the primus expressly calls me a heretick, a schismatic, an incendiary, (and tells me wch is very false) that I am the principall person who divided the Non-Jurors here'. Yet he discounted if not excused his past excesses of language:

> And I wrote in such a severe stile merely as being that wch would move them, most probably, to Recollection, as I had certainly would first in a much softer stile but that I reckon you had tried all wch good sense

and meekness could do, in my favour, and therfore it fell to my share to try the rough, yet I shall be glad how much of yr soft water you will pleased to throw upon my Fire; to prevent a rupture, and therefore I shall be glad if you interpose yr mediation. But would not have them know this I would rather they believe me to be a very angry, and difficult to be appeased. And they with the help of God, I hope to stand to viz, never to renounce these primitive usages wch has so disgruntled these gentlemen.

Campbell remained adamant that he would not make unconditional concessions.[35] But at the instigation of Bishop Irvine, on 12 February 1723, a remonstrance and injunction to which Bishop Campbell was not party, in the name of the plurality of the College of Bishops, to the Episcopal Church of Scotland, as well as clergy as laity was published, whereby they censured all the clergy in the kingdom to practise any of the usages and exhorting them all:

> to shun these fatal rocks, whereon others have been shipwrecked before: and requiring the clergy in particular, to forbear the *mixture* and other obsolete usages, and avoid the being accessory to the breaking of the peace of the church, and the incurring our just and necessary censure.[36]

At that point, the usager clergy were most numerous in Campbell's Diocese of Aberdeen and must have taken exception to this, especially since it was most likely that the admixture had continued there since the Reformation.[37] Thomas Rattray reported that 'the admixture was "almost universal throughout the north" ever since the Reformation'. Kieran German also argues that since Gadderar was invited to oversee the diocese of Moray in 1725 it would suggest that there was a broader body of support for the usager position opposite to the College.[38]

Bishop Falconar had felt uneasy with this action of the plurality of the bishops. In a letter of 6 March 1723 to Robert Keith, an Edinburgh presbyter who later was consecrated as a bishop, he wrote:

> the clearest view we can have of these things is in the pure primitive church: and I am apt to think that God has his rod on the back of this church to bring about such a blissful reform; and I despair of the removal of this rod till this be brought about, if not to ripeness; yet at least in wish and endeavour.[39]

Falconar died on 6 July 1723 and in a letter to Bishop Irvine shortly afterwards Bishop Campbell wrote:

> I hope this stroke will make those that remain, strive to cultivate peace more industriously than ever, rather than take occasions, from the death of so good a man to be more severe upon tender consciences.[40]

It would seem that Campbell's admonition was taken to heart, and in 1724 Bishop Fullerton wrote, in the name of his brethren, to Bishop Gadderar, inviting him 'to a close free and, and amicable conference, for bringing things to that happy crisis, as we may harmoniously concur together in advancing what doth most tend to the interest of true religion'.[41] The result of this colloquy was that despite Gadderar being an enthusiastic proponent of the usages, in the interests of unity in a bond of peace, Gadderar assented that he would receive the 'unmixed cup' from his brethren and that he would not mix publicly in his ministrations to congregations and that he would encourage others to follow his lead. Use of the Scottish liturgy had been granted by the College to clergy who wished to use it provided the introduction of further usages was not pursued. Gadderar, within his own district, would not encourage usages, unless it was with the sanction of the Primus and his brethren that they could operate differently, and as a result of lawful convocation. The College of Bishops were fighting a losing battle. By the terms of the Concordat of 1731, all Episcopalian clergy were permitted to use either the Scottish or the English Prayer Book, implicitly sanctioning the prayers of invocation and oblation.[42] The 1735 edition of the Prayer Book included the line 'Let us pray for the whole state of Christ's Church' without the addendum 'militant here on earth'. The same pattern was followed in the 1764 liturgy, which was adopted as the *textus receptus*.

III

In addition to Campbell's contribution to the inspirational non-juring liturgy of 1718, his extensive liturgical writings in his *Book of Prayers and Several Holy Offices* include the first hymn extant written by an Episcopalian.[43] Campbell's *magnum opus*, his largest published work, was his *Doctrine of the Middle State* published in 1721, which he had been working on for many years. In the introduction he summarises the purpose of the work:

> I endeavour to prove from *Holy Writ*, from the *Fathers* of the First Centuries, and from several learned, Pious, and Great Men of our own and others since the *Reformation.*
>
> That there is an intermediate, middle state for the Departed Souls to Abide in, between Death and Resurrection, far different from what they are afterward to be in when our Blessed LORD JESUS CHRIST shall appear at his Second Coming.
>
> That there is no Immediate Judgement after Death-
>
> That to Pray and Offer for, and to Commemorate, our Deceased Brethren, is not only Lawful and Wilful, but also our Bounden Duty.
>
> That the Intermediate State between Death and the Resurrection, is a State of Purification in its Lower, as well as of Fixed Joy and Enjoyment in its Higher Mansions.[44]

Was Campbell's *Doctrine of the Middle State* actually a form of Protestant purgatory? This intriguing question was the subject of an enquiry by Martha McGill, who has argued that 'Archibald Campbell, Thomas Rattray and George Innes produced tracts in support of the intermediate state. By the end of the century it had become a standard element of doctrine among the episcopalians, reflecting the formation of a more distinctive theological and liturgical identity, based on the teachings of the early church fathers.'[45] For Campbell the latter end of the sixth and beginning of the seventh centuries saw the rise of corruptions to these scriptural and primitive doctrines. The doctrine of Purgatory as it now stands in the Latin Church, and the invocation of the saints departed that grew out of them was all error and heresy. What was solid and primitive truth has become a perversion. But this had not been rectified at the Reformation. He attacks its instigators in Scotland:

> these *fiery Zealots*, from their Aversion to *Popery*, and their Hatred of the whole *Constitution* of the *Western Church*, with which they were best acquainted, and with the Ambitious desire of having the *Reins of Government* in their own hands, threw away *Episcopacy*, and all *Superiority* of *Church Officers* over *Presbyters*, and all *Regular Ordination*, as *Popish*.
>
> Thus the *Real Presence* in the *Holy Eucharist*, and its being a proper *Sacrifice Propitiatory* came first to be *Disputed* and at last *Denyed*.
>
> Thus *Prayers* and *Offering* for, and *Commemoration* of, the *Faithful Departed* came to be abolished as *Popish* and *Sinful*.
>
> Thus were the *Ancient* and *Primitive Rites* and *Usages* overthrown, and the Remains of the *Ancient Discipline*, together with the *Primitive Worship, Disused, Rejected, Exclaimed against*, and at last almost *forgot* and *lost*.[46]

In his Preface, Campbell questions whether his painstaking description of the state and circumstances of departed souls will make people live better or believe 'that there is an Intermediate or *Middle State* between *Death* and the *Resurrection*'. He goes on to provide a three-part answer:

> First, The HOLY GHOST has thought fit to shew us these things, which I am endeavouring to *Revive*, by the *Inspired Writers* of the *Holy Scriptures*, and this I think, I have by GOD's help, fully and plainly proved in the subsequent *Treatise* . . .
>
> *Secondly*, THE *Fathers*, during the *Aera* of the *Charismata*, believed these *Truths*, and this, I think, I have also fully proved, and if so, I have both the *Holy Scriptures*, and the best *Interpreters* of them on my side, and therefore am in no manner of Concern for what can be said against me.[47]

He would also, thirdly, re-establish the ancient truths which he states had been perverted by the Church of Rome but preserved by the Greek Church.

It was Campbell's view that the deceased brethren go from strength to strength and that God would grant them light, rest and refreshment. He cites a plethora of scriptural texts to support his argument; likewise, quotations from the Fathers and even Reformation divines like John Calvin.[48]

In much of Campbell's correspondence, there is constant reference to prayer and also praying for the dead when he is at the altar. In the 1718 non-juring English Rite, the intercessions came immediately after the prayer of consecration. This also became the pattern in the 1735, 1755 and 1764 Scots Rites. Therefore since Christ was truly present in the consecrated elements on the altar, the prayers would have more effect:

> it is not to be doubted that we who are that part of CHRIST's *Body* and *Family* which resides upon *Earth*, under *Mortality*, do *receive*, many *Great* and *Spiritual Advantages*, and *Reap* much *Benefit* from the *Prayers* of the *Righteous Departed*.[49]

Dr George Hickes, the celebrated English non-juror, was Campbell's great friend in London. The following extract from a prayer for the dead is an example of his devotion and belief and is typical of the non-juring style. It was discovered recently in an old handwritten book most probably of the provenance of Bishop Arthur Petrie from the now defunct library at St George's Folla Rule, Aberdeenshire. This prayer was given by Bishop Hickes to a friend to be said for him after his death. Bishop Rattray received it from this friend at London 1717:

> Do thou O Lord, now look upon this thy servant, whom thou hast chosen and taken from thus unto the other state.
>
> O thou lover of men, forgive him all his offences, which he hath committed willingly or unwillingly against thee; and send thy benevolent Holy Angels to him, to conduct him unto the bosom of the Patriarchs, Prophets and Apostles and all thy righteous Servants, who have pleased Thee from the beginning of the world into that region of Light, where there is no Sorrow, no Grief, no Lamentation, but a calm and quiet place of bliss and blessed spirits, and a Haven of rest, free from the storms and tempests of this world, and where the souls of the just converse together in a joyful expectation of their future reward and behold the glory of thy Christ.[50]

Bishop Campbell's prayers are in many ways a précis of his spirituality and his belief:

> And we humbly pray Thee, O Mercifull Father, to Grant Light, Rest and Refreshment and Joy in the Holy Ghost, to all those our fellow members of Christ's Body, who have dyed with the sign of Faith [particularly to our relations and friends] [here name such of them as you think fit] Do Thou O Lord, Accept of their sincere repentance whether they were called, and began to turn to Thee, in the Morning of their lives, at noon or in the afternoon of them, or even at the

eleventh hour, whether by an early repentance and conversion, they had time in this life to grasp up, and to root out, all or most of their evil habits. Or that by a later repentance and though sincere and in good earnest, and although they laboured hard to purify their souls, yet being prevented by Death, they did not obtain a compleat victory over all their unruly passions and corruptions and so do stand in need of further purification even after their own demise, before they can be fitt to be fully possessed of immutable Permanent Light, Rest, Refreshment, and Joy, without ceasing in paradise. Give them grace O Lord, to make a daily progress in what was begun here: the love of God, resignation to his holy will, humility, virtue, purity and holiness, untill, in Thy due time Thou vouchsafe them admittance into the joys of Paradise.[51]

To sum up, what Campbell was advocating in the *Middle State* was:

to break a *Custom* and *Habit* of *Thinking* and *Believing* wrong about things which seem plain to me, from the *Holy Scriptures*, and form the *Testimonies* of the *Early Fathers* of the *first* and *Illuminated Ages*, and which have been very much Perverted by some, and totally *laid aside* by others . . . Thus it hath fared with several very Primitive Principles, and Usages, which I heartily wish were *Restored*.[52]

IV

Campbell anticipated his own castigation:

I doubt not but I shall be blamed for what I have said . . . concerning *Prayer* for the *Dead*, whom die with the *Sign* of *Faith*, in the *Communion* of the *Church*. And also for what I say concerning *Purification* after *Death*. And concerning the *Probatory, Purifying, Fire* after the Resurrection: But if all these Doctrines be as *Primitive*, and were once Universally believed, and be really as *Useful* and Charitable to the *Living* and the *Dead*, as I believe them, and think I have proved them to be, I must think it our duty still to *Believe* them, and to *Practice* accordingly.[53]

The Middle State Campbell subdivided into the following: First, Hades is in his understanding the general state of the dead, where all go upon their demise and remain until the resurrection, either to the beatific vision or to damnation after the judgement. Hades is the general place of custody appointed for the departed souls until the resurrection and reunion of their souls and bodies. Second, Hades is divided into two sides, right hand and left hand: Those on the right, after being reunited with their bodies at the resurrection and after judgement are to be admitted ultimately into the beatific vision. Those on the left are to be cast into Gehenna or the proper Hell of Torment. The two sides of Hades are impenetrably divided. The right side of Hades is Abraham's bosom full of different mansions.

Progress from mansion to mansion was possible. Though the gulf between the mansions of paradise and the lower mansions could not be entered until the soul had been purified and purged by the fires of divine love.[54] To complete the process for Campbell there had to be a true contrition, an inward sorrow for sins committed. Good resolutions had to be made, and promises too, to forsake all sin. There had to be a mortification and extirpation, an *annihilation* (to use Campbell's language)[55] of all sin and evil habits. There must be an introduction of all virtues, graces and habits, opposite to sin and evil habits. Our repentance was embryonic; it was to be a thread of faith which determined the soul to the right side of Hades. Further purity was then required to take the soul into the higher mansions; the proper paradise or Abraham's bosom:

> The *Doctrine* of *Purification* after *Death*, when there has been a good *Foundation* laid of True *Repentance* in *this Life*, we may go from *Strength* to *Strength*, and *Rise* from *Lower* to *Higher Mansions* until at last we Shoot the *Gulf* which is between the *Proper Paradise* and the *Lower Mansions* and arrive at the *Haven* of *fixed Light, Rest, Refreshment* and *Joy*, which is called the *Sinus Abrahae, Abraham's Bosom* there to await with *Pleasure* for the *finishing* the *Work* (not the *Act*) of our *Redemption* at the *Resurrection*. Thus the *Patriarchs* and *Prophets* and other *Saints* of the Old World waited without the *Gate* of the *Proper Paradise*, until CHRIST opened it to them when HE DESCENDED INTO HADES, and introduced them and the *Penitent Thief*, into that *Joyful State* and *Place* of *Light* and *Divine Contemplation*, for none could enter there before Him who purchased Admission for us.[56]

The presence of the Spirit of God was a particular thread running through Campbell's and the non-jurors' theology. A trust in the power of the Holy Spirit to renew, to reinvigorate, gave them a spiritual conviction. They might have lost everything in a material sense but their belief in baptismal regeneration, the epiclesis and the sanctification by the Holy Spirit of the elements in the Eucharist with Christ's real presence, and in death the Spirit drawing the soul forward towards the beatific vision gave them a spiritual confidence which surmounted all the trials and tribulations of life. It was a concise and schematic theology. It was a theology of hope and a religion of a gentler persuasion.

In Campbell's *Book of Prayer and Several Holy Offices* there is a prayer of delightful aspiration entitled 'One way of recommending a Departing Soul to God':

> Acknowledge, we humbly beseech Thee, A work of Thine own Hands, A Sheep of Thine own Fold, a Sinner of Thine own Redeeming, receive [him] into the Blessed Arms of Thy Unspeakable Mercy, into the Sacred Rest of Everlasting Peace and Joy; into the Bosom of Abraham, Isaac and Jacob.[57]

Campbell was not expecting his work to be well received. He predicted that the book would be roundly condemned as part of an over-zealous reaction against anything reminiscent of popery.[58] Nevertheless, he endeavoured to engage a broad audience. Naturally he discussed the attitudes and beliefs of the Church of England, but also addressed the Scottish Presbyterians and included Calvin 'for the sake of those who are fond of his Authority'.[59] As one would expect, his book received a more favourable response in the north of Scotland[60] and particularly in the diocese of Aberdeen, that bedrock of Episcopalian tradition and doctrine.[61] Prayers for the dead were part of the medieval doctrine of purgatory. Campbell attempted to legitimate them as part of primitive Christianity. He was right to do so as Christians appear to have prayed for the dead from inscriptions in the time of the catacombs in Rome and also as evidenced in early liturgies and in the writings of early Church Fathers. St Augustine took up the issue of praying for the dead. He believed that prayer could do nothing for the damned but he suggested that prayers were of help to those persons who were neither particularly good nor particularly evil. Archibald Campbell stood in the Augustinian tradition.[62]

For Campbell, God was all loving and all merciful. He suggested the ultimate restoration of all through the understanding of God's justice as essentially reformative.[63] His reassertion of prayers for the departed 'at least allowed the living a hope for and a charity towards those who, not paragons of virtue on this side of the grave were presumed to be progressing through the labyrinthine mansions of the middle state towards the Beatific Vision after the day of Judgement'.[64]

Of all the proponents of the usages, it was Campbell's devotion to and his vehement defence of them, that guaranteed they would eventually become the accepted norm and the received tradition within the Scottish Rite.

That legacy and burning conviction still fires spiritual belief and aspiration today.

Notes

1. K. German, 'Non-jurors, Liturgy, and Jacobite Commitment, 1718–1746', *RSCHS*, 47 (2018), 74–99.
2. AUL, Scottish Episcopal Church Papers, MS 2180/2. In a letter from Alexander Jolly to Arthur Petrie, dated 11 January 1785, we read that a 'Collection of Tracts presented to Bp Seabury when in Ab'd is the best Summary View of the Arguments for the Ancient Doctrines and Practices about the Blessed Eucharist which we have'.
3. D. Bertie, *Scottish Episcopal Clergy, 1689–2000* (Edinburgh: T. & T. Clark, 2000), p. 46.
4. D. Szechi (ed.), *Letters of George Lockhart of Carnwath* (Edinburgh: SHS, 1989), pp. 146–7.
5. Bertie, *Episcopal Clergy*, p. 40.
6. *Letters of George Lockhart*, p. 182.

7. G. Smith, *A defence of the communion-office of the Church of England, proving there is neither reason nor authority for laying it aside* (Edinburgh, 1744).
8. [Anon.,] *An enquiry into the decent and beautiful order of the administration of the Lord's supper* (London, 1723).
9. NRS, Papers of the Campbell Family, earls of Breadalbane (Breadalbane Muniments), GD112/9/1/31–8; GD112/39/222/14; GD112/2/9/34. Archibald Campbell eventually resigned his heritable rights on Nether Lorn on 29 March 1734.
10. J. Dowden, *The Annotated Scottish Communion Office* (Edinburgh: R. Grant & Son, 1884), p. 78.
11. J. Dundass, *An impartial enquiry into the rise and progress of the ancient usage of prayers for the dead, and also a query answered, viz. Whether it be safe or sufferable to alter liturgy established either by authority or long custom?* (1743).
12. AUL, pi 26404 Dun: *An Impartial Enquiry into the Rise and Progress of the Ancient Usage of Prayers for the Dead* (Edinburgh: James Cochran and Co., 1748) (reference to the introduction of English five hundred printed copies of the Scots Liturgy some years before 1743 is written in pencil inside the back cover).
13. NRS, Records of the Episcopal Church of Scotland, the Episcopal Chest, CH12/12/150.
14. B. D. Spinks, *Sacraments, Ceremonies and the Stuart Divines: Sacramental Theology and Liturgy in England and Scotland 1603–1662* (Aldershot: Ashgate, 2002), p. 90.
15. W. D. Kornahrens, cited by M. McGill, 'A Protestant Purgatory? Visions of an Intermediate State in Eighteenth-century Scotland', *SHR*, 97 (2018), pp. 159–60.
16. T. Rattray, *The Ancient Liturgy of the Church of Jerusalem being the Liturgy of St James Freed from All Later Additions and Interpolations of Whatever Kind, and so Restored to its Original Purity: By Compromising it with the Account Given of that Liturgy by St Cyril in his Fifth Mystagogical Catechism, And with the Clementine Liturgy* (London, 1744).
17. M. Barker, *Temple Themes in Christian Worship* (London: T. & T. Clark, 2007), p. 1.
18. Ibid., pp. 1–2.
19. G. Donaldson, *The Making of the Scottish Prayer Book 1637* (Edinburgh: EUP, 1954), p. 67. Thanksgiving for the faithful departed was certainly not contrary to the views of the Scottish reformers.
20. W. Forbes, *Considerationes modestae et pacificae controversiorum de justificatione, purgatorio, invocatione sanctorum, Christo mediatore, et Eucharista*, 2 vols (Oxford: J. H. Parker, 1850–6), I, p. 139.
21. A. E. Nimmo, 'Liturgy: The Sacramental Soul of Jacobitism', in A. I. Macinnes, K. German and L. Graham (eds), *Living with Jacobitism, 1690–1788: The Three Kingdoms and Beyond* (London: Pickering and Chatto, 2014), pp. 39–53.
22. LPL, Thomas Brett Papers, MS 2179.
23. AUL, MS 2180/1, f. 4.
24. AUL MS 2180/1, f. 6.
25. B. Sirota, *The Christian Monitors. The Church of England and the Age of Benevolence, 1680–1730* (New Haven: YUP, 2014), p. 140.
26. Ibid., p. 152.
27. NRS, CH12/12/269.

28. AUL, Archibald Campbell, Bishop of Aberdeen: 'A Book of Prayers and several Holy Offices', MS 2418.
29. AUL, MS 2180/7.
30. AUL, MS 2180/7.
31. G. Grub, *An ecclesiastical history of Scotland from the introduction of Christianity to the present time*, 4 vols (Edinburgh, 1861), III, p. 387.
32. Ibid., III, p. 386.
33. AUL MS 2180/9.
34. AUL MS 2180/11.
35. AUL MS 2180/12.
36. J. Skinner, *An ecclesiastical history of Scotland, from the first appearance of Christianity in that kingdom, to the present time*, 2 vols (London, 1788), II, p. 631.
37. Eeles, *Traditional Ceremonial*, p. 36.
38. German, 'Non-jurors', pp. 82–5.
39. Skinner, *Ecclesiastical history*, II, p. 632.
40. Ibid., p. 632.
41. Ibid., p. 632.
42. Dowden, *Scottish Communion Office*, p. 162.
43. A. E. Nimmo, 'Archibald Campbell: Aberdeen's Absentee Bishop?', *RSCHS*, 47, 2018, 100–27.
44. A. Campbell, *The doctrines of a middle state between death and the resurrection* (London, 1721), p. ii.
45. McGill, 'Protestant Purgatory', p. 153.
46. Campbell, *Doctrines*, p. iii.
47. Ibid., pp. xv–xvi.
48. Ibid, pp. 157ff.
49. Ibid, pp. xvii–xviii.
50. A. Petrie, Unpublished MSS (which also contains two prayers by Campbell to be said before Divine Service). Private Collection: Chancellor of the Diocese of Aberdeen and Orkney.
51. AUL, MS 2418, ff. 92.
52. Campbell, *Doctrines*, p. i.
53. Ibid., p. xvii.
54. Ibid., p. xx.
55. AUL, MS 2418. p. 76 ('We humbly beseech Thee to Anihilate in us all the inclinations wch separate us from Thee').
56. Campbell, *Doctrines*, p. xxi.
57. AUL, MS 2418, f. 61.
58. Campbell, *Doctrines*, pp. i–ii.
59. Ibid., p. 157.
60. McGill, 'Protestant Purgatory', p. 165.
61. A. E. Nimmo, 'Bishop John Skinner and the Resurgence of Scots Episcopacy' (Ph.D. thesis, University of Aberdeen, 1996), pp. 16–17.
62. P. C. Almond, *Heaven and Hell in Enlightenment England* (Cambridge: CUP, 1994), pp. 77–9.
63. Ibid., p. 153.
64. Ibid., p. 79.

CHAPTER TWELVE

Clerics Behaving Badly: Ecclesiastical Commitment in the Jacobite Rising of 1745–6

Darren S. Layne

A central point of contention during the civil war occasioned by the final Jacobite rising in 1745–6 was that of confessional commitment, though by no means was it the only significant factor.[1] As demonstrated by a broad cadre of competent scholars, moral, doctrinal and liturgical disputation ran hotly between the established Presbyterian Church and those of dissenting Scottish Episcopalian, non-juring Anglican and Roman Catholic congregations throughout the three kingdoms of Britain and Ireland.[2] Whilst the Church of Scotland staunchly allied itself with the Hanoverian government during the conflict, the dissenting churches had institutionally similar interests in supporting a Stuart restoration and were therefore most often – officially or unofficially – sympathetic to the rebellion. That this division was a fundamental component of the Jacobite struggle is not in question, but it bears examining just how demonstrably influential were the zealous ministers who spoke in favour of Jacobite aims immediately within the rising itself. This chapter seeks to take a closer look at empirical evidence of martial and logistical assistance implemented by a select quantity of ministers involved in the Forty-Five, and whether their practical commitment was indeed as energetic as their ideological enthusiasm.

I

Much like the variable outcomes for the fortunes of the Union of 1707, the question of eighteenth-century religious freedoms must be considered in the context of regal authority and what tolerances would be established by the reigning monarch. The concept of a Stuart-imposed divine right of kings appealed to Roman Catholics, as well as the fact that the traditional faith of that dynasty happened to match their own, and Stuart proclamations explicitly tempted Catholic toleration from as early as 1717, reviving the policies of James VII & II from the 1680s.[3] Whereas Irish Jacobitism was able to be sustained between the major risings by the broad base of Catholic clergy on an island consisting of a 75 per cent Catholic majority, English and Lowland Scottish Catholicism was primarily maintained by the landed gentry and was relatively sparse. Evidence of accurate, widespread plebeian Catholic presence outwith Ireland is difficult to come by, and its waning constituency was a feature across class divides after the failure of the Fifteen, partially due to the imposition of anti-Catholic taxes and penal laws.[4]

Despite a mythological belief that the Scottish Highland clans were primarily Roman Catholic, only a quarter of the clans held more than a divided adherence to that church; many of them bifurcated even further by 1745.[5] Regardless of its lack of breadth, however, the devotion of the Roman Catholic minority in mainland Britain to the exiled House of Stuart was formidable and long-lived. The exceptional feature of this Catholic dedication to Jacobite efforts in Scotland was in fact its endurance, made possible partly by the geographical remoteness of its Highland constituents.[6] Meanwhile, Presbyterian polemics equated all agents of 'popery' as Jacobite who supported successive rebellions with their efforts to subvert the government using 'Zeal, Concurrence & private Encouragement from the whole Popish Party'. In response, the establishment sought to curtail such activities through imposing the registration of Catholic estates (regarded as 'known Asylums of Priests') and the prevention of gatherings at inns and taverns by denying public licences.[7] To the Church of Scotland, the Catholic threat was obstreperous and explicitly promoted the cyclical financing of sustained rebellion between Highland clergy and the exiled monarchy. As successful as Jacobite recruitment was in traditionally Roman Catholic areas, however, the ability of that faith alone to stoke action was questionable. Yet Catholic support of the Jacobite cause, as Bruce Lenman calls out, was taken for granted by nearly everyone.[8]

Scottish Episcopalians likewise saw their church structure enfeebled and replaced at the Revolution, and they were subsequently barraged for decades by the Williamite and Hanoverian governments with the full support of the Presbyterian establishment.[9] England alone witnessed over forty dissenting (likely non-juring Anglican) meeting houses destroyed in 1715 and this would be a common occurrence across Britain through the century, and especially in Scotland in the months after Culloden.[10] Scottish universities were nonetheless seeded with Episcopal sympathies after the Restoration and were responsible for churning out educated clergy who spread the belief that the established Church post-1689 was 'as illegitimate as the new political regime'.[11] This went some way towards ensuring that non-juring doctrine gave Jacobitism perhaps its most constant tenets throughout the decades of political jockeying and dynastic upheaval, and it naturally became a confessional citadel in which the disaffected could shelter. To be a non-juror was to denounce the authority of the illegitimate Orange or Hanoverian monarch in favour of the rightful Stuart one who could restore core moral values upon the kingdoms of Britain.[12] As such, Scottish Episcopalian and Anglican non-jurors were viewed with unmitigated suspicion and their congregations were considered to be 'nurseries of Jacobitism'.[13] In December 1746, Lord Justice Clerk Andrew Fletcher of Saltoun sent a list of seventeen non-juring ministers in Edinburgh to Thomas Pelham-Holles, 1st duke of Newcastle and secretary of state to George II. Its purpose was to inform the government about where their perceived enemies were operating, and Fletcher promised to stay vigilant in case any had 'attempted to preach or teach and educate children'.[14] Predictably, the 'qualified' Episcopal clergy who had taken oaths of allegiance and abjuration in favour of the Hanoverian regime were expected to uphold the *de facto* sovereign's legitimacy, sounding 'the Trumpet against Popery and the Pretender'.[15]

Confessional interests are inextricably tied to Jacobite motivation and were closely aligned with Stuart objectives through the entire life of the movement. The issue, however, is a complex one with no clearly defined boundaries. Richard Findlay asserts that religion was at the very centre of Scottish national identity during the eighteenth century, and that the conflict between the established Presbyterian and displaced Episcopalian Churches was a 'national project'.[16] The non-jurors of north-east Scotland and Lowland Perthshire who made up a significant percentage of Jacobite support during the Forty-Five were duty-bound to re-establish their religious freedoms and felt that the restoration of the Stuarts was the most efficacious way to see it happen.[17] But in the Highlands, defence or assertion of faith was rarely, if ever, the primary call to action for either chief or clan. The importance of this dichotomy in the context of later Jacobitism is that shared religious beliefs provided a bond of common sentiment only so far as to organise action within a much larger opposition movement.[18] Though the Jacobite constituency reflected numerous faiths, a feature which easily debunks the old maxim of the Forty-Five representing a struggle between Catholics and Protestants, it is extremely relevant that they were only moderately united under a common actionable cause. Donald Cameron of Lochiel brought three chaplains into his regiment to attend to the mixed faiths of his men, each one of a different denomination: Episcopalian, Catholic and Presbyterian.[19] In May 1746, twelve rebel tenants in the parish of Lochlee in Angus were willing to put confessional doctrine aside to make peace with the government. Promising 'out of Gratitude and to Shew a just Sense of our Sin and Folly' after being released on the king's mercy, they admitted to 'having imbibed wrong principles' by attending a non-juring meeting house, and signed a declaration that they and their families would from now on attend 'the established Church where his Majesty and the Royall Family are duely preyed for'.[20] Whilst faith played a prominent role in the motivations of Jacobites in 1745–6, the evidence shows that loyalties were not cleanly divided down denominational lines.[21]

II

At least fifty-three Roman Catholic and non-juring Episcopal ministers, four bishops and one precentor of a non-juring congregation were somehow involved in the final rising.[22] As expected, many of these men were from the north-east of Scotland, with significant representation also in Inverness-shire and Edinburgh. Included are some recognisable names, such as the devoted bishop Robert Forbes, who painstakingly collected for posterity heaps of documents and Jacobite ephemera during and after the campaign. The Anglican minister Thomas Coppock became the chaplain for the Manchester regiment and was executed as a traitor in October 1746, as was the Scottish Episcopal minister Robert Lyon for marching with Lord Ogilvy's regiment and officiating dissenting public services in Perth.[23] The Reverend James Taylor, a non-juring minister in Thurso, was taken prisoner after Culloden for allegedly collecting arms for the Jacobite army in his meeting house. After nearly dying in captivity, he was eventually released upon the favourable recommendations of no fewer than five Justices of the Peace.[24] The effects of the enduring link between the non-jurors and Jacobitism is exemplified by Taylor's capture, and government ire was squarely levelled at dissenting congregations after Culloden. Non-juring assemblages were sought out and sundered, with twenty-seven meeting houses destroyed in the counties of Angus, Aberdeen, and Moray alone. Many more throughout the country were chained and padlocked so they could not be used as houses of worship, and the government spared no expense to ensure this was regulated.[25] Significantly, Episcopal ministers were treated with a greater degree of harshness than their Roman Catholic counterparts, and this is borne out by the lack of any recorded executions of the latter in prison and trial records.[26]

Upon closer examination of the demographic evidence left mostly within government records, a clearer picture of the 'active' Jacobite clergy is revealed.[27] Of the identifiable ministers involved in the Rising, the clear majority (60 per cent) were noted as being either non-juring Episcopal or Anglican, while 28 per cent were Roman Catholic, 9 per cent were labelled as Jesuits and only two had no denominational information associated with them. Though specific parish and congregational associations were generally not static and often changed through a minister's career, 28 per cent can be linked to the north-east of Scotland, including Aberdeenshire, Banffshire, Morayshire and Angus. Nearly half operated in other Lowland counties, with most of these residing in the environs of Edinburgh.[28] Only around 18 per cent were definitively from Highland parishes, notwithstanding oral traditions to the contrary. Three ministers were from England and one came from France; the remaining 5 per cent offer no record of ecclesiastical territory. Putting aside the statistical aberration from the Edinburgh reports, this pattern of confessional adherence does not deviate too far from recent estimates of the Jacobite constituency by region where the north-east and Lowland counties combine to form a distinct primacy of plebeian Jacobite support.[29] As regards the physical maturity of these clerics, just five of their ages are recorded during 1745 or 1746, collectively averaging out to just under forty years old, which is nearly a decade older than the average Jacobite prisoner.

Not all of the clergy noted here were engaged in direct military activity with the army under Charles Edward Stuart, but many did indeed risk their lives in the field. Government evidence leveraged against these 'warrior-priests' varies from actively carrying arms with the rebels on the battlefield to marching along with the troops as chaplains at the regimental level.[30] David Brodie, chaplain to Margaret, Lady Blantyre, in Lanarkshire, for example, was thought to have been present in arms at the Battle of Prestonpans in September 1745. Brodie was listed in early reports by the Commissioners of Excise which were used to establish initial evidence against alleged Jacobites, but he was never captured.[31] Thomas Syme, a non-juring minister from the parish of Errol in Perthshire, was accused of having 'carried arms and went north with the rebels'. Syme eventually returned home and likewise was never brought up on formal charges. The Roman Catholic priest Allan Macdonald, probably from South Uist, was a kinsman of Macdonald of Clanranald and was therefore disposed to march with that particularly loyal Jacobite clan through the entire eight months of the campaign. He was present for all three major battles of the Forty-Five and was seen riding up and down the rebel lines at Falkirk, giving blessings to those about to engage in combat. Serving as the Prince's personal confessor, Macdonald was apprehended during Charles Edward's flight and examined by the duke of Newcastle himself, eventually being released upon promise of never returning to Britain.[32] The aforementioned Thomas Coppock was appointed chaplain of the Manchester regiment and was taken with the rest of the unit in Carlisle during the winter of 1745-6. Upon the gibbet he openly admitted his actions, which he described as 'taking up arms to restore the royal and illustrious house of Stewart, and to banish from a free, but inslaved people a foreigner, a tyrant, and an usurper'.[33] Coppock's own words comprise one of the few formal admissions that specifically demonstrates adherence to the Jacobite cause for the defence of a united Britain.

Numerous other clergymen marched with the army despite never admitting to picking up arms against King George – a condition that may have lessened the severity of their punishment according to government judicial policy.[34] John Gordon, a Roman Catholic priest from Enzie in Banffshire, was accused of meeting the Jacobites at Perth with a number of recruits to aid the cause. After Culloden, British army soldiers intent on retribution destroyed his library at Presholme, whereupon they publicly burnt hundreds of books – many of which, ironically, were liturgical works of Protestantism. In the end, however, Gordon was released under bail in March 1747.[35] Glenlivet's John Tyrie, also a Catholic, was 'universally known' to have recruited extensively for the rebels under John Gordon of Glenbucket and was wounded in the head at Culloden while administering the last rites to those who lay dying on the moor. Tyrie was never captured and remained in hiding until 1750–1, finally returning to his birthplace of

Dunnideer in Aberdeenshire.[36] The Jesuit Colin Campbell, Tyrie's close friend and fellow pilgrim with whom he travelled to Rome in 1735, was also at Culloden but is assumed not to have survived the battle.[37] Other Catholic clergymen offered their confessional services to Jacobite soldiers while on campaign, like George Law from Aberdeen who joined James Moir of Stoneywood's unit and was ultimately captured at Culloden. Law was seen by numerous witnesses preaching to a rebel congregation when the army was at Glasgow, but no one could verify that he actually spoke in favour of the Pretender, and he was therefore acquitted in February 1747 after a long trial.[38] Alexander Gordon of Aboyne served as a chaplain to troops in the French service under Lord John Drummond and was also captured at the final battle of the Forty-Five, dying after three weeks in captivity within the foetid gaol at Inverness.[39] Little is known about James Gordon, a Catholic priest who was captured at Carlisle with the garrison of Jacobites left behind as the army retreated back into Scotland, other than the fact that he was acquitted in August 1746 after his trial at Southwark. Considering the fate of many laymen who were also taken at Carlisle, Gordon was fortunate to be released.[40] Others set out with the intention of undertaking military service, but were intercepted before they could meet the main body of the Jacobite force. Robert Forbes, the extraordinary bishop of Ross and Caithness who assembled the collection of Jacobite ephemera known as *The Lyon in Mourning*, was captured in early September on his way to join the army along with two other Episcopal clergymen, Thomas Drummond and John Willox. None of the three ever made it to battle, instead spending the next nine months in prison until their collective release at the end of May 1746.[41]

III

Though the military expression of the Jacobite movement was arguably its most vital component, one should not underestimate the power of civilian logistical support and clandestine behaviour to transmit dissenting ideologies and coalesce regional dissatisfaction with both the Hanoverian government and the established Church.[42] Through their congregational networks and ministerial charisma, Jacobite-minded clergy were able to keep the seed of dissension alive from the pulpit without leaving their respective parishes.[43] It is reasonable to surmise that many sympathetic churchmen were never revealed to the watchful eyes of government loyalists, but several were indeed turned in or otherwise sought out for spreading treasonous words through their sermons. George Robertson, a non-juring minister from Edradynate, was brought before officials in Perthshire for 'praying publicly in his meeting house for the Pretender', and he was committed to the tolbooth there until released for lack of evidence against him.[44] The Episcopal William Seaton was likewise apprehended in Forfar and taken to prison in Montrose after 'preaching a Sermon to excite His

Majesties Subjects to Rebellion', finally being discharged in late August 1746.[45] Numerous others were accused of assisting the rebels in some manner, whether it be recruiting in the localities or offering logistical support by taking on the responsibilities of factoring for Jacobite officials. John Maitland, an Episcopal minister originally from the parish of Forgue in Aberdeenshire, undertook the duties of collecting rent on the Jacobite-held estates in Angus during the winter of 1745–6. A series of letters from the rebel sheriff of that county, James Carnegy Arbuthnott of Balnamoon, gives an account of the depth of his task:

> to levy all the Rents Victual & money, of the forfeited Estates of Panmure & South Esk ... & I do here by Require all the Tennants to answer to Courts appointed by you, at any Place you shall judge convenient, & all the Ground Officers to do their duty according to your directions All this I order & require every Person to give all due obedience to under the highest Pains & as they shall answer to us on their Peril.[46]

Maitland also served as a chaplain in both Lord Ogilvy's and Lady Mackintosh's regiments and was present at Falkirk and Culloden, at the latter of which he famously administered the Holy Communion with whisky and oatcakes to a mortally wounded Lord Strathallan.[47]

William Harper of Stirlingshire was turned in by a slater and his sons at Falkirk who witnessed the Episcopal cleric attending to Charles Edward when the army was in the area. Though Harper is present in the excise lists which were tallied in May 1746, it appears he was never actually apprehended, as the Lord Justice Clerk's surveillance in Edinburgh at the end of the year had him presiding over a meeting house on the east side of Carubber's Close in the capital.[48] William Grant, a Catholic priest operating in Morayshire, was recorded by officials in Elgin as having 'directed the Rebels' by evidence of his being 'noture in the country', but his whereabouts after the rising are unknown.[49] Joseph Robertson, convener of a nonjuring congregation in Haddington, was responsible for guiding a number of people to join the Prince's army in the autumn of 1745, including his own nephew.[50] Neither prison records nor evidence of trials for Grant or Robertson can be found, implying they were never seized for their allegedly treasonable practices.

Conversely, numerous ministers were apprehended and held regardless of any substantive proof of evidence against them. Taking advantage of the suspension of habeas corpus in October 1745, Fletcher and Newcastle were able to 'imprison for Treason or Suspition of Treason' with relative impunity, and over three hundred persons were committed to British gaols with no formal evidence tied to their cases.[51] Twenty-four of the 227 prisoners held at York Castle were incarcerated on suspicion alone, and one-quarter of these were reputed to be 'Popish Priests' who had refused to take the oaths.[52] Declining the oaths did not necessarily equate with being actively

Jacobite, but their swift imprisonment demonstrates the danger that these clergymen represented to the government, regardless of their actual commitment. At Lancaster Castle, Nicholas Skelton was kept without evidence amongst seven others and made himself quite a nuisance to another 'well-affected' prisoner held there on suspicion, Dr Henry Bracken. Though the Crown had arranged to pay subsistence for all inmates at around 3d per day, this was not always disbursed in a timely manner, creating a backlog of debt for government-appointed solicitors who struggled to collect it on behalf of the prisons.[53] In mid-March 1746, Bracken wrote to Newcastle's office that the 'Romish Priest' Skelton had been distributing personal funds amidst the other Jacobite prisoners, amounting to 'five or seven pounds a week in Cloaths money &c', which Bracken cannily forecast would not likely do much to dissuade the 'reformation of principles as to their late attempt while he goes so much amongst them'.[54]

Two brothers from Strathglass who were ordained ('bred') Roman Catholic ministers at Douai, John and Charles Farquharson (or Ferguson), were apprehended by John Campbell, 4th earl of Loudoun in July 1746 and taken to Inverness. Both gave statements that 'absolutely declared' they were innocent of aiding or assisting the rebels in any manner, and no official charges were brought against them.[55] William Reid, a priest in Mortlach, was likewise taken prisoner after the Battle of Culloden, brought to Aberdeen and sent to Edinburgh before eventually being released. As his chapel and residence were never destroyed by government troops, presumably he returned there to continue his ministry.[56] Fr George Duncan of Glenlivet also shows up on the lists of prisoners apprehended during the sweep of recalcitrant Scottish communities after Culloden. Following a short imprisonment during which no damning evidence was levied, he was dispatched to Carlisle by Bishop Alexander Smith where he 'offered spiritual assistance' to Macdonald of Kinlochmoidart and Macdonell of Tiendrish, both of whom were being held there under sentences of death.[57] Peter Gordon, a priest in Braemar since 1736, was seized during the rising and sent to Aberdeen before being bailed by Menzies of Pitfodels. Gordon thereafter returned directly home to continue his ecclesiastical work, where he remained until 1763.[58] Other names related to Jacobite activity during the suppression of the Forty-Five appear in government intelligence reports. Three 'Irish priests' in the Barisdale area, for example, listed as Mcafee, McLachlan and Harrison, were observed by a government agent attempting to 'spirit up the People & persuade them that there will be a Landing against Spring & that they will have all Redress for their Losses'.[59] No action was evidently taken against them, though the six-week intelligence-gathering mission organised by William Anne von Keppel, 2nd earl of Albemarle and commander of the British forces in Scotland after the rising, was designed primarily to get a read on the disposition of the Western Highlands rather than to bring more dissidents into an already beleaguered penal system.[60]

When analysing the known fates of the clergy connected with Jacobitism in 1745–6, the common result trends towards leniency. While government officials were fixated on capturing these 'treasonous' figures who could serve as mouthpieces for organised dissent, the sentences actually carried out upon them were generally no worse than that of the common rebel soldier. By a wide margin, most of the alleged Jacobite ministers (36 per cent) were eventually released either through acquittal, discharge, pardon or bail. A further two (4 per cent) were allowed to leave Britain under the promise of never returning. Only two clerics were executed and two others died in captivity. A further 11 per cent were either known to be hiding near their homes or allowed to return there after initial capture. The remaining 42 per cent of all tracked clergy share ultimate fates that are currently unknown. Comparing this with numbers of general Jacobite prisoners who were captured on suspicion alone, we see that 47 per cent were either released or discharged, with fewer than 1 per cent being executed.[61] Analysis of all current records of captured Jacobites across rank and station (both military and civilian) demonstrates that 37.1 per cent were pardoned while 36.8 per cent were sentenced, the great majority of the latter being transported (70 per cent).[62] Despite the despicable campaign of 'exemplary civilising' tendered by government troops through many areas of Scotland after Culloden, the end result was that most prisoners were released without punishment, usually due to lack of evidence against them.[63] For some of the clerics amongst these numbers, it meant they could and would continue their ministrations in new locales or in seclusion, as many of their former meeting houses were no longer standing or usable.

Bishop Hugh Macdonald of Morar lost his Catholic seminary of Eilean Bàn during the depredations and fled to France with Charles Edward. The bishop returned to Scotland three years later and was eventually captured in 1755 before being confined in Duns until his death in 1773. Though Macdonald was technically sentenced to be banished, it was never enforced – a common result for 'processed' clergy.[64] The 'Romish' Robert Gordon of Kirkhill, accused of being a spy early in the rising, voluntarily appealed to be sent to 'any Catholic country' and was dispatched to Holland at the end of February 1746. He never returned to Scotland, instead taking up residency in Würzburg and Rome as well as a stint at the Scots College in Paris during the mid-1750s.[65] The aforementioned Farquharson brothers, John and Charles, were released after their short imprisonment and remained in Scotland, tending to respective congregations in Strathglass and Glengairn until their retirement and natural deaths in the late eighteenth century.[66] Alexander Forrester, a priest from Benbecula, was captured at Sleat by Allan Macdonald of Knock and was released in May 1747 only on the condition that he would leave the kingdom permanently and never return, though where he went is not charted.[67]

IV

What we learn from an initial survey of clergy associated with Jacobitism during the Forty-Five is that they were collectively a moderate, if not overtly effective, grounding element that helped to convey the ideologies of pro-Stuart schemes. They also intermittently aided the martial effort in the field and supplemented logistical aims in the localities. Due to the cross-denominational nature of their constituency and the fact that both Roman Catholic and non-juring Episcopal congregations were essentially illegal in the government's eyes, Jacobite commanders were never able to employ the systemic communication or cohesive mission-plan enacted by Church of Scotland ministers in combating pockets of rebellion on the other side of the conflict. Whilst the Presbyterian clergy were tasked with directly and institutionally assisting the anti-Jacobite effort through a series of government mandates, ecclesiastics who were sympathetic to the rebel causes had a much steeper hill to climb and much less traction with which to do it.[68] As well, dissenting ministers did not commit in great enough numbers to fashion an effective mechanism that could vitally contribute to the Jacobite military effort. The piecemeal commitment demonstrated by the clergy in 1745–6 appears to have mirrored the popular draw of Jacobitism itself at that late stage of its potency: the decision to engage in rebellion was an intensely personal one that often straddled the lines of ideology and practicality. The great risk that came with the open demonstration of treasonable words and actions also influenced such decisions. Popular support for the final effort was broad but ultimately thin, and the personal depth of commitment to Jacobite ideals was inconstant, changing shape and resilience along with the fortunes of the cause and, more crucially, with those of the individual.[69] There is more surviving evidence of accused rather than of convicted clergy, which reflects the government's inability to come up with sufficient proof of treasonous actions. This also speaks to the inadequacies of the Hanoverian penal system to effectually accommodate and process the vast flood of suspected rebels that overwhelmed courts and prisons during and shortly after the rising.[70] In the case studies above, numerous examples of seemingly 'innocent' clergy are described as having been swiftly captured and slowly released. Few overt actions of treason were proved against them, however critical of the Hanoverian succession their doctrinal beliefs might have been. Nevertheless, there are still likely more churchmen yet to be discovered whose recorded acts and motivations can help illustrate the ecclesiastical contribution to the last Jacobite military effort. This chapter is but a starting point.[71]

Notes

1. Concise typologies of late Jacobite motivation can be found in F. McLynn, 'Issues and Motives in the Jacobite Rising of 1745', *The Eighteenth Century*, 23:2

(1982), 97–133; D. S. Layne, 'Spines of the Thistle: The Popular Constituency of the Jacobite Rising in 1745–6' (Ph.D. thesis, University of St Andrews, 2016), pp. 34–75.
2. Cf. B. Lenman, 'The Scottish Episcopal Clergy and the Ideology of Jacobitism' in E. Cruickshanks (ed.), *Ideology and Conspiracy: Aspects of Jacobitism 1689–1759* (Edinburgh: John Donald, 1982), pp. 36–48; D. H. Whiteford, 'Jacobitism as a Factor in Presbyterian–Episcopalian Relationships in Scotland I & II', *RSCHS*, 16 (1967), 129–49, 185–201; D. Szechi, *The Jacobites: Britain and Europe 1688–1788* (New Haven: YUP, 1994), pp. 17–38; D. Napthine and W. A. Speck, 'Clergymen and Conflict 1660–1763' in *The Church and War, Studies in Church History*, 20 (1983), 231–51; A. Raffe, *The Culture of Controversy: Religious Arguments in Scotland, 1660–1714* (Woodbridge: Boydell Press, 2012), *passim*; P. Monod, *Jacobitism and the English People, 1688–1788* (Cambridge: CUP, 1989), pp. 126–58; C. Brown, *The Social History of Religion in Scotland Since 1730* (London and New York: Methuen, 1987), pp. 1–129.
3. Szechi, *The Jacobites*, pp. 18, 32; A. I. Macinnes, 'Jacobitism in Scotland: Episodic Cause or National Movement?', *SHR*, 86 (2007), 234.
4. Monod, *Jacobitism and the English People*, pp. 126–7, 132–8; Szechi, *The Jacobites*, pp. 18–19; C. I. McGrath, 'Securing the Hanoverian Succession in Ireland: Jacobites, Money and Men, 1714–1716', *Parliamentary History*, 33:1 (2014), 155. See also A. I. Macinnes, *Clanship, Commerce and the House of Stuart, 1603–1788* (East Linton: Tuckwell Press, 1996), pp. 173–7, and 'Catholic Recusancy and the Penal Laws, 1603–1707', *RSCHS*, 23 (1987), 27–63; M. Sankey, *Jacobite Prisoners of the 1715 Rebellion: Preventing and Punishing Insurrection in Early Hanoverian Britain* (Aldershot: Ashgate, 2005), p. 40; R. Blackey, 'A War of Words: The Significance of the Propaganda Conflict between English Catholics and Protestants, 1715–1745', *CHR*, 58:4 (1973), pp. 534–55. Jean McCann calculates that between 4300 and 5300 Catholic troops were raised out of a total Scots Catholic population of 19,000. This represents a rough total of 30 per cent of maximum estimated Jacobite army numbers but only 22–7 per cent of the total Catholic population in Scotland, 'The Organisation of the Jacobite Army in 1745–46' (Ph.D. Thesis, University of Edinburgh, 1963), pp. 123–4.
5. Macinnes estimates that only twelve of the fifty primary Highland clans were Catholic (24 per cent), and half of those were divided or mixed, *Clanship*, pp. 248–9. See also Lenman, 'Scottish Episcopal Clergy', p. 37; M. Sankey and D. Szechi, 'Elite Culture and the Decline of Scottish Jacobitism 1716–1745', *Past & Present*, 173 (2001), 97, McCann, 'Organisation', pp. 115–22.
6. B. Lenman, *The Jacobite Risings in Britain 1689–1746* (Aberdeen: Scottish Cultural Press, 1995), pp. 228–9; A. Roberts, 'Roman Catholicism in the Highlands' in James Kirk (ed.), *The Church in the Highlands* (Edinburgh: Scottish Church History Society, 1998), pp. 63, 83. For Presbyterian presence, see W. Ferguson, 'The Problems of the Established Church in the West Highlands and Islands in the Eighteenth Century', *RSCHS*, 17 (1972), 15–31.
7. TNA, Secretary of State: State Papers Scotland, SP 54/28/47f; N. M. Wilby, 'The "Encrease of Popery" in the Highlands 1714–1747', *IR*, 17:2 (1966), 91–115; C. Prunier, 'Representations of the "State of Popery" in Scotland in the 1720s and 1730s', *IR*, 64:2 (2013), 120–226.
8. Lenman, *Jacobite Risings*, pp. 229, 254; Macinnes, 'Jacobitism in Scotland', pp. 234–5; and *Clanship*, pp. 173–7; D. Szechi, 'Defending the True Faith:

Kirk, State, and Catholic Missioners in Scotland, 1653–1755', *CHR*, 82:3 (1996), p. 400; M. McHugh, 'The Religious Condition of the Highlands and Islands in the Mid-Eighteenth Century', *IR*, 35:1 (1984), pp. 13–14; McCann, 'Organisation', pp. 109–36. See also T. McInally, 'Missionaries or Soldiers for the Jacobite Cause? The Conflict of Loyalties for Scottish Catholic Clergy' in A. I. Macinnes and D. Hamilton (eds), *Jacobitism, Enlightenment and Empire, 1680–1720* (London: Pickering & Chatto, 2014), pp. 43–58. R. Findlay, 'Keeping the Covenant: Scottish National Identity' in T. M. Devine and J. R. Young (eds), *Eighteenth Century Scotland: New Perspectives* (East Linton: Tuckwell, 1999), p. 122; L. Colley, *Britons: Forging the Nation 1707–1837* (New Haven and London: YUP, 1992), pp. 5, 74. For the marginalisation of anti-Catholic sentiment, see S. Pincus, 'The European Catholic Context of the Revolution of 1688–89: Gallicanism, Innocent XI, and Catholic Opposition' in A. I. Macinnes and A. H. Williamson (eds), *Shaping the Stuart World, 1603–1714: The Atlantic Connection* (Leiden: Brill, 2006), pp. 109–11.
9. A. I. Macinnes, *Union and Empire: The Making of the United Kingdom in 1707* (Cambridge: CUP, 2007), p. 245; and 'Jacobitism in Scotland', pp. 234–6; J. P. Lawson, *History of the Scottish Episcopal Church: From the Revolution to the Present Time* (Edinburgh, 1843), *passim*; C. D. A. Leighton, 'Scottish Jacobitism, Episcopacy, and Counter-Enlightenment', *History of European Ideas*, 35 (2009), 1–10.
10. N. Rogers, 'Riot and Popular Jacobitism in Early Hanoverian England' in Cruickshanks (ed.), *Ideology and Conspiracy*, pp. 70–88; NLS, Misc. Papers, MS.3044, f. 123; TNA, SP 54/30/32 and SP 54/32/17.
11. Lenman, 'Scottish Episcopal Clergy', pp. 38–9; M. Goldie, 'The Nonjurors, Episcopacy, and the Origins of the Convocation Controversy' in Cruickshanks, *Ideology and Conspiracy*, pp. 15–35; K. German, 'Aberdeen, Aberdeenshire and Jacobitism in the North-East of Scotland, 1688–1750' (Ph.D. Thesis, University of Aberdeen, 2010), pp. 26, 32–3, 47–8, 54–5, 108–9; and 'The Scots Episcopalians after Disestablishment, 1689–1723' in A. Gémes, F. Peyrou, and I. Xydopoulos (eds), *Institutional Change and Stability: Conflicts, Transitions and Social Values* (Pisa: Pisa University Press, 2009), pp. 49–62.
12. Monod, *Jacobitism and the English People*, pp. 42–3.
13. W. Crookshank, *Popish cruelty represented. In a Sermon Occasioned by the present Rebellion in Scotland* (London, 1745); Anon., *A Letter from a Gentleman at Newcastle, to the Burgesses of Edinburgh* (Edinburgh, 1745).
14. TNA, SP 54/34/39a and SP 54/34/53a–b.
15. R. Garnett, 'Correspondence of Archbishop Herring and Lord Hardwicke during the Rebellion of 1745', *EHR*, 39 (1909), 532; F. Deconinck-Brossard, 'The Churches in the '45' in *The Church and War, Studies in Church History*, 20 (1983), 255; P. Jones, 'The Qualified Episcopal Chapels of the North-east of Scotland 1689–1898', *Northern Scotland*, 20 (2000), 47–69.
16. Findlay, 'Keeping the Covenant', p. 123.
17. R. Mitchison comments that 'because the north-east wanted an episcopal church and was denied it under the new regime, it was jacobite', 'The Government and the Highlands, 1707–1745' in N. T. Phillipson and R. Mitchison (eds), *Scotland in the Age of Improvement* (Edinburgh; EUP, 1970), p. 25; A. and H. Tayler, *Jacobites of Aberdeenshire and Banffshire in the Forty-Five* (Aberdeen: Milne & Hutchison, 1928), p. 9. J. Stephen argues that Episcopalian presence in the north-east

had largely waned by 1745, being replaced by a clear majority of Presbyterian churchgoers, 'Hymns to Hanover: Presbyterians, the Pretender and the Failure of the '45', *RSCHS*, 40 (2010), 69–72.

18. Sankey and Szechi, 'Elite Culture', pp. 95–7; McCann, 'Organisation', p. 52.
19. Roberts, 'Roman Catholicism in the Highlands', p. 83.
20. NLS, Papers and Correspondence of the 2nd earl of Albemarle, MS.3730, ff. 10–11.
21. See Layne, 'Spines of the Thistle', pp. 101–3 and appendix VI for examples of self-stated Presbyterian rebel involvement. Stephen, while conceding that some Presbyterian support was inevitable, maintains that it was ephemeral and disingenuous, 'Hymns to Hanover', pp. 112–13.
22. Jacobite Database of 1745 (hereafter JDB1745) search results. Compare this with ten Episcopal and fifteen Roman Catholic clerics identified within B. G. Seton and J. G. Arnot, *The Prisoners of the '45*, 3 vols (Edinburgh: SHS, 1928), I, pp. 221–4. F. Goldie estimates that there were no more than 150 Episcopal clerics present in Scotland in 1745, *A Short History of the Episcopal Church in Scotland from the Restoration to the Present Time* (London: n.p., 1951), p. 56; McCann claims that a total of forty-two Catholic priests were ministering in Scotland in 1745, 'Organisation', p. 114. See also F. Forbes and W. J. Anderson, 'Clergy Lists of the Highland District, 1732–1828', *IR*, 17:2 (1966), 129–84; and Stephen, 'Hymns to Hanover', p. 72.
23. Forbes's collection was published as the three-volume anthology *The Lyon in Mourning*, ed. H. Paton, 3 vols (Edinburgh: SHS, 1895). For Coppock and Lyon, see Monod, *Jacobitism and the English People*, pp. 333–6, and A. Mackintosh, *The Muster Roll of the Forfarshire or Lord Ogilvy's Regiment* (Inverness: Northern Counties, 1914), pp. 115–16, respectively.
24. TNA, Secretary of State: State Papers Domestic, SP 36/88/191 and SP 54/33/33.
25. E. Luscombe, *Steps to Freedom: Laurencekirk, 1804* (Edinburgh: Scottish Episcopal Church, 2004), pp. 28–9; Memorandum Concerning the Act Anent the Nonjurant Meeting Houses, 1746, NLS, Fletcher of Saltoun Papers, MS.17527, f. 123; TNA, SP 54/32/17; NLS MS.3044, f. 123; German, 'Jacobitism in the North-East', pp. 180–2; Jones, 'The Qualified Episcopal Chapels', pp. 50–1; HL, Loudoun Scottish Collection, Box 35/LO 12056.
26. See Seton and Arnot, *The Prisoners of the '45*, I, p. 224.
27. The demographic and prosopographical analysis that follows is taken from queries of JDB1745.
28. This percentage is heavily skewed due to Fletcher's list of seventeen ministers there, TNA, SP 54/34/53b. There is little damning evidence associated with the names on this list.
29. The Highland Jacobite constituency is estimated at around 30 per cent, with a margin of flexibility due to the liminal nature of the Gàidhealtachd in Perthshire, etc., Layne, 'Spines of the Thistle', pp. 96–8 and appendix III; McCann, 'Organisation', pp. ix–xvii; M. Pittock, *The Myth of the Jacobite Clans* (2nd edn, Edinburgh: EUP, 2009), pp. 110–39.
30. At least five Roman Catholic or non-juring Episcopal clergy were officially given the title of chaplain for distinct regiments or battalions, including Ogilvy's, Clanranald's and Moir of Stoneywood's.
31. *A List of Persons Concerned in the Rebellion, Transmitted to the Commissioners of Excise by the Several Supervisors in Scotland*, ed. Scottish History Society, (Edinburgh:

SHS, 1890), pp. 134–5; Seton and Arnot, *The Prisoners of the '45*, I, p. 63; NLS, Fletcher of Saltoun Papers, MS.17522, ff. 1–65 and MS 17524, *passim*; NLS, Papers of the Society of Antiquaries of Scotland, MS 1918.

32. Macdonald was one of the few clergymen given a captain's commission in the Jacobite army, J. A. Stewart, 'The Clan Ranald and Catholic Missionary Successes, 1715–1745', *IR*, 45:1 (1994), p. 40; Seton and Arnot, *The Prisoners of the '45*, III, pp. 42–3; 'Neil Maceachan's Narrative', in W. B. Blaikie (ed.), *Origins of the 'Forty-Five and Other Papers Relating to that Rising* (Edinburgh: SHS, 1916), p. 228; TNA, SP 54/32/51.

33. Forbes, *The Lyon in Mourning*, I, pp. 60–4; Monod, *Jacobitism and the English People*, pp. 333–5.

34. Monod suggests that the act of taking up arms was as serious as any other symbolic seditious activity, but the government was specifically after those seen in arms and was more inclined to punish rebel combatants rather than those taken for speaking treasonous words, ibid., p. 308. See also Layne, 'Spines of the Thistle', pp. 107, 200; TNA, SP 54/32/40 and SP 54/32/46.

35. Forbes, *The Lyon in Mourning*, III, p. 164; Seton and Arnot, *The Prisoners of the '45*, II, pp. 240–1; *A List of Persons*, pp. 28–9; McCann, 'Organisation', p. 114; C. Johnson, 'Secular Clergy of the Lowland District 1732–1789', *IR*, 34:2 (1983), 72.

36. *A List of Persons*, pp. 130–1; Roberts, 'Roman Catholicism in the Highlands', p. 86; McCann, 'Organisation', pp. 152–55; F. O. Blundell, *The Catholic Highlands of Scotland*, 2 vols (Edinburgh and London: Sands & Co., 1909–17), I, p. 41; J. F. McMillan, 'Jansenists and Anti-Jansenists in Eighteenth Century Scotland: The Unigenitus Quarrels on the Scottish Catholic Mission 1732–1746', *IR*, 39:1 (1998), 12–45.

37. Ibid., pp. 12–15; A. Roberts, 'Gregor McGregor (1681–1740) and the Highland Problem in the Scottish Catholic Mission', *IR*, 39:2 (1988), 81–108.

38. J. Allardyce (ed.), *Historical Papers Relating to the Jacobite Period, 1699–1750*, 2 vols (Aberdeen: New Spalding Club, 1895–6), II, pp. 404–6; Seton and Arnot, *The Prisoners of the '45*, II, pp. 332–3; NLS, Jacobite Relics, MS.2960, ff. 121–2; TNA, SP 54/30/21d.

39. Blundell, *The Catholic Highlands*, II, p. 79; Seton and Arnot, *The Prisoners of the '45*, II, pp. 232–3; *Gordons under Arms: A Biographical Muster Roll of Officers in the Navies and Armies of Britain, Europe, America and in the Jacobite Risings*, ed. C. O. Skelton and J. M. Bulloch, 3 vols (Aberdeen: New Spalding Club, 1903–12), III, pp. 510–11.

40. *Gordons under Arms*, p. 518; Seton and Arnot, *The Prisoners of the '45*, II, pp. 236–7; Layne, 'Spines of the Thistle', appendix XIX.

41. Forbes, *The Lyon in Mourning*, I, pp. xi–xx.

42. D. Szechi, 'Jamie the Soldier and the Jacobite Military Threat, 1706–27' in Macinnes and Hamilton (eds), *Jacobitism, Enlightenment and Empire*, pp. 13–14; M. Pittock, *Material Culture and Sedition, 1688–1760* (Basingstoke: Palgrave Macmillan, 2013), pp. 19–20; Monod, *Jacobitism and the English People*, p. 95; Layne, 'Spines of the Thistle', pp. 80–4.

43. For more on non-juring liturgical context on the eve of the Forty-Five, for example, see German, 'Jacobitism in the North-east', pp. 110–15.

44. Perth & Kinross Council Archives, Documents Relating to Jacobites, B59 30/72/1; Seton and Arnot, *The Prisoners of the '45*, III, pp. 278–9.

45. TNA, SP 54/35/5; *A List of Persons*, pp. 234–5. Seton and Arnot, *The Prisoners of the '45*, III, pp. 306–7.
46. TNA, SP.54/26/123a; *A List of Prisoners*, pp. 180–1.
47. Mackintosh, *Muster Roll of Forfarshire*, pp. 7, 118.
48. *A List of Persons*, pp. 56–7, 316–17; TNA, SP 54/34/53b.
49. *A List of Persons*, pp. 110–11. 'Noture' from the Latin for notorious.
50. Ibid., pp. 132–3, 136–7.
51. TNA, SP 54/29/18. Though most were dismissed or pardoned, at least two dozen prisoners committed on suspicion were transported to the colonies, three were executed and another three died in prison while awaiting trial. See Layne, 'Spines of the Thistle', appendix XVI.
52. TNA, SP 36/81/78–81 and SP 36/93/125. By the end of 1746, most are noted as having been discharged due to insufficient prosecution.
53. NLS, Fletcher of Saltoun Papers, MS 17530, ff. 112, 126, 140–1, 146–7; MS 17529, f. 94. Details are described in Layne, 'Spines of the Thistle', pp. 176–83.
54. TNA, SP 36/81/1/73–75 and Treasury Solicitor and HM Procurator General Papers, TS 11/1080/5533 and TS 11/1081/5608.
55. TNA, SP 54/32/49d.
56. Blundell, *The Catholic Highlands*, I, p. 13; ACA, Jacobite Papers, Parcel L/H/3; Allardyce, *Historical Papers*, I, p. 258.
57. Blundell, *The Catholic Highlands*, I, pp. 41–2; ACA, Parcel L/H/3; Seton and Arnot, *The Prisoners of the '45*, II, pp. 170–1.
58. Blundell, *The Catholic Highlands*, I, pp. 110–11; Seton and Arnot, *The Prisoners of the '45*, II, pp. 240–1.
59. TNA, SP 54/34/42c. The mention of Harrison likely refers to William, who had sworn allegiance to the Hanoverian government so he could continue serving the Catholic Church, R. Black, *The Campbells of the Ark: Men of Argyll in 1745*, 2 vols (Edinburgh: John Donald, 2017), I, p. 60. McLachlan is surely John Maclachlan of Kilchoan.
60. TNA, SP 54/34/43a.
61. From a total sample size of 317, Layne, 'Spines of the Thistle', appendix XVI, fig. 2.
62. Arraignment sample size of 3471 and indictment sample size of 1284 from Seton and Arnot's incomplete *The Prisoners of the '45* alone, ibid., appendix XXI, figs 1–2.
63. Macinnes, *Clanship*, pp. 217–21.
64. Blaikie, *Origins*, p. 82; Stewart, 'Clan Ranald', pp. 33–6; R. Macdonald, 'The Catholic Gaidhealtachd', *IR*, 29:1 (1978), 59–60.
65. Seton and Arnot, *The Prisoners of the '45*, II, pp. 240–1; F. McDonnell, *Jacobites of 1715 and 1745: North-East Scotland* (Baltimore: Clearfield, 1997), p. 23; Johnson, 'Secular Clergy', p. 73.
66. Blundell, *The Catholic Highlands*, I, pp. 79–80, 115–16; Forbes and Anderson, 'Clergy Lists', p. 152, *passim.*
67. TNA, SP 36/88/60 and TS 20/94/5; Forbes, *The Lyon in Mourning*, I, p. 178.
68. Stephen, 'Hymns to Hanover', *passim*; Layne, 'Spines of the Thistle', pp. 183–91. Presbyterian Jacobites notwithstanding, not all Presbyterian clergy were firmly loyal to the government, and some even showed considerable sympathy to suspected rebels despite their responsibility to function as informants, ibid., pp. 190–1. Compare the effectiveness of the Jacobite clergy with the role of

Presbyterian ministers a century earlier during the Covenanting wars, E. M. Furgol, 'Scotland Turned Sweden: The Scottish Covenanters and the Military Revolution, 1638–1651' in J. Morrill (ed.), *The Scottish National Covenant in Its British Context* (Edinburgh: EUP, 1990), pp. 138–41.
69. D. Szechi, *1715: The Great Jacobite Rebellion* (New Haven: YUP, 2006), p. 57.
70. Layne, 'Spines of the Thistle', pp. 179–83.
71. As a supplement to this chapter, an annotated table of the included clergy may be accessed at https://jdb1745.net/data/clergylist.

CHAPTER THIRTEEN

Bishop Thomas Rattray: His Eucharistic Doctrine, *The Ancient Liturgy of the Church of Jerusalem* and its Influence on the Scottish Liturgy of 1764

W. Douglas Kornahrens

Thomas Rattray, born in 1684, was the only son of James Rattray of Rattray, laird of Craighall. In infancy he succeeded his father to the lairdship. He is alleged by his descendants to have studied at the University of Leyden in Holland. It was he, an outstanding classicist, who with the learned non-juring Bishop Nathaniel Spinkes, translated the letters of the non-jurors to the Orthodox Patriarchs into the requisite patristic-style formal Greek. His date of ordination to the Presbyterate is not known. In 1727, he was elected by the Episcopalian presbyters of Angus and the Mearns to be their bishop. In 1739, he was elected bishop of Edinburgh and primus, but his election was contested by the vestige of the remaining 'College Bishops'. He did not move to Edinburgh until a few months before his death at the age of fifty-nine on Ascension Day, 12 May 1743.

Rattray was the most significant figure in the Scottish Episcopal Church of the eighteenth century. It was his scholarly analysis of the liturgy of St James, *The Ancient Liturgy of the Church of Jerusalem*, published in 1744 which laid the foundation for the Scottish liturgy of 1764. His Eucharistic doctrine represents the continuation of the doctrinal tradition of Scottish Episcopacy that began in the 1620s principally in Aberdeen.[1] Rattray's Eucharistic doctrine is contained in a short work entitled *Some Particular Instructions Concerning the Christian Covenant*, published as a pamphlet in London in 1748, five years after his death. George Hay Forbes published it again in his 1854 edition of Bishop Rattray's principal works. This chapter examines Bishop Rattray's Eucharistic doctrine, *The Ancient Liturgy* and the connection between *The Ancient Liturgy* and the Scottish liturgy of 1764.

I

Scottish Episcopacy has been in possession of a definable and consistent tradition of Eucharistic doctrine first articulated by the Aberdeen doctors in the early seventeenth century. In a footnote in his monograph *The Scottish Communion Office of 1764* Bishop John Dowden wrote, 'the feeling in favour of the eucharistic doctrine afterward expressed in the Scottish Liturgy . . . reached Scotland from the South'.[2] Bishop Dowden's statement makes no connection between the Eucharistic doctrine of those who were loyal to Scottish Episcopacy in the Scottish Church before disestablishment, and the writings of post-disestablishment Episcopalians. Bishop Dowden is wrong in his judgement. Ten writers can be identified (between the 1620s and the 1870s), all articulating the same Eucharistic doctrine and all drawing from the same well of patristic writing and thought. Bishop Rattray demonstrates the continuation of that doctrine from the seventeenth into the eighteenth and nineteenth centuries. That he consciously stood in that tradition was, of course, crucial to the continuing of what George Hay Forbes called 'our native traditional theology'.[3]

It must also be said that none of the writers in the Scottish tradition looked to their theological forebears for the vindication of their opinions. They looked directly to the writings of the Fathers themselves. George Hay Forbes wrote of them:

> our Scottish Doctors . . . were deeply imbued with the spirit of Primitive Christianity. It was not a mere book knowledge that they had of the Fathers. They made them the witnesses of Apostolic teaching, fearlessly endeavouring to conform their own faith and their own practice to them, in spite of the opposition of the prudence of this world; and on this account they must carry an all-but conclusive weight with us their children and disciples.[4]

The controlling feature of the theological tradition of Scottish Episcopacy is its adherence to the witness of the Church Fathers alone for the interpretation of holy scripture and for the establishment of doctrine. All of the writers of our tradition attest to this, but Bishop Rattray is explicit:

> Now the authority of the Fathers chiefly depending on their being competent witnesses of apostolical tradition, as we may safely conclude that those things wherein the Catholick Church have been agreed from the beginning, and are attested by the early Fathers of the second and third centuries, are undoubtedly derived from the apostles and ought to be firmly adhered to as such.[5]

William Forbes, briefly bishop of Edinburgh in the 1630s, had made a similar comment in his *Considerationes Modestae et Pacificae*.[6]

II

Rattray wrote *Some Particular Instructions Concerning the Christian Covenant* probably in the 1730s, for an unnamed layperson. It has four sections: the Preface (in which Rattray gives a theological overview of humanity's state before the Fall and the Christian sacraments' function in the restoration of divine grace to the Christian person), baptism, the Eucharist, and confirmation. It contains some sixty pages, of which only seven occupy Rattray's discussion of the Eucharist; those few pages will be discussed here. Bishop Rattray possessed that most valuable of abilities in a writer: the ability to say a great deal clearly in few words; while brief, his discussion is theologically dense. Rattray breaks this discussion of the Eucharist into five sections.

Firstly, at the Last Supper: Jesus offers himself as the sacrifice for the sins of the world. Jesus, as our High Priest of the Order of Melchizedek, at liberty before his arrest and trial, offered himself as the free, voluntary and sufficient sacrifice to his Father for the sins of the whole world, 'under the symbols of bread, representing his body, and wine, representing his blood'. Rattray says that '[Jesus] having thus . . . eucharistized or blessed them', the words 'eucharistized' and 'blessed' are used transitively, 'so that the action signified by them passes upon the Bread and the Cup'.[7] Jesus 'gave thanks to God over them and praised him firstly as the creator and Governor of the world the author of all the fruits of the earth'; secondly for his providence towards the Jewish nation in particular and towards all humanity in general; and thirdly, for their redemption by his own death. Rattray adds the note:

> That the Catholick Church, as instructed by the Apostles, did believe that our Lord's eucharistizing or blessing the Bread and the Cup was to be understood in all three of these senses, plainly appears in her doctrines and practices from the beginning.[8]

He continues,

> he likewise offered them up to God as the symbols of his body and blood . . . and invocated the Divine power of the Holy Spirit to descend upon them . . . and gave them to his disciples as his Body broken and his Blood shed . . . for the remission of sins.[9]

It is very important to understand that 'symbol' is not used by Rattray, or by any writer in the whole of the Scottish Episcopal tradition, to mean one thing that represents another thing which is absent. Fr Alexander Schmemann's discussion of the use of the term 'symbol', in the sense that Rattray (and others) used it, is clear:

> the symbol presupposes faith [because] it is the manifestation, the presence, the operation of one reality within the other . . . One reality *manifests* and *communicates* the other . . . but only to the degree which the symbol itself is a participant in the spiritual reality and is able or called upon to embody it.[10]

The symbols of bread and wine are not empty substitutes for Christ's body and blood; they both manifest and communicate that reality. Louis-Marie Chauvet, a contemporary French Roman Catholic scholar, is also eager to re-establish this ancient use of the term. Chauvet's fundamental aim is to move the question of 'what happens to the bread and wine in the Eucharist' from the frame of Aristotelian categories to the area of the 'symbolic' in precisely the same way as defined by Schmemann. It is the 'terrain of the symbolic' which Chauvet enters to define the change in the Eucharistic bread not as a change of substance, in that it is no longer bread, but that 'this bread is the body of Christ'.[11]

Secondly, it is immediately after the Last Supper that Jesus as the sacrifice was slain on the cross. In a footnote Rattray refers to Leviticus 16 which describes how, on the Day of Atonement, the sacrificial animals were presented to the priest alive before being slain, and then their blood was taken into the Holy of Holies to be sprinkled before the Mercy Seat; Rattray also correlates this to Hebrews 9:12, 'neither by the blood of goats and calves, but by his own blood he entered in once into the holy place, having obtained eternal redemption for us'.[12] The Last Supper was directly introductory to his crucifixion and the shedding of his blood, and after he was raised from the dead he ascended to the right hand of the Father, entering into the true Holy of Holies, there to present his sacrifice to the Father, and 'by virtue of it', to make intercession for his Church.

Thirdly, the requirements of Jesus for Christian sacrifice: 'That He commanded the Apostles and their successors, as Priests of the Christian Church to do [i.e. to offer] this (bread and cup)'.[13] These words from I Corinthians 11:24, 'do this in remembrance of me' or as 'my memorial' and verse 25, 'do this, as often as you drink it in remembrance of me', are the focal point of the idea of the Church's offering of the memorial sacrifice. Rattray's footnote on the verse says[14] this offering is

> done in commemoration of him or as the memorial of his one sacrifice of Himself once offered for the sins of the world and thereby we plead the merits of it before His Father, here on earth as he doth continually in heaven; and [he] appointed it to be the only sacrifice of prayer and praise in the Christian Church, instead of the manifold sacrifices, whether bloody or unbloody, under the Law.[15]

Rattray is not the first Scottish writer to emphasise the verb 'do' as described above. Henry Scougal, in his Preparation Sermon, published in 1677, says,

> in this ordinance Jesus Christ is evidently set forth as crucified before our eyes. We may read and hear of it at other times, but this [Eucharist] is a more clear and solemn representation of it, our dying Lord commanded us *to do it in remembrance of Him.*[16]

Scougal here also makes the connection between the Last Supper and the Cross. He says that while the 'outside of this ordinance is very poor and mean ... a little bread and wine' that in truth it is 'the Lord of glory hanging between two thieves; for in this ordinance Jesus Christ is evidently set forth as crucified before our eyes'.[17] This critical point of the Eucharistic doctrine of Scottish Episcopacy from Rattray onwards receives specific emphasis.

In another note on the phrase 'in commemoration of me', Rattray writes,

> See LXX. Lev. xxiv. 7 (compared with ii. 2, 9, 16.) It is from this text that the Fathers and the ancient Liturgies take the word προκείμενα, 'set or lying in open view before the Lord,'[18] so frequently used by them concerning the ... gifts ... the eucharistical bread and cup.[19]

Here we come to internal evidence that Rattray stands in the tradition of Eucharistic doctrine articulated by the Aberdeen Doctors in the 1620s and 1630s, because this idea of Christ being set forth in his death is specifically mentioned by John Forbes of Corse:

> thus setting forth the Passion of his Son [in the Eucharistic bread and cup] ... can be said in a manner to offer to God Christ immolated in his Passion, or his very obedience and his bloody immolation. And this we offer to God, not sacrificing Christ, or immolating him anew, but commemorating that unique immolation of Christ made once in his Passion suppliantly praying God, that looking on it, he will be propitious to us sinners: not on account of this our commemoration, but on account of that [i.e., his sacrifice].[20]

Thus in the Eucharist, by presenting and offering to God the bread and cup as the memorials of the body and blood of Christ in death and by the recitation of the words of institution, the death of Christ is offered to the Father in representation, that is the cup and bread are the instituted representatives and symbols of his death; and they are offered in thanksgiving for the benefits accrued to humanity by his death, and that the Father 'looking on it will be propitious to us sinners', not on account of our commemoration but on account of what it represents and commemorates.

The idea Rattray presents is that the Church, by the presbyter or priest, offers bread and wine to God the Father, in obedience to the command of his Son, 'do this in remembrance of me' [i.e. in commemoration of Jesus Christ's death on the cross]. As the priest prays over the offered bread and wine, he blesses or 'eucharistizes'[21] them. As the sacrifice commemorative of the cross, the bread and wine become the designated symbols and types of the broken body and the shed blood of Christ for us now, just as Jesus at the Last Supper

> offered to God the bread and cup as His Body and Blood, i.e., He must by these symbols have given or offered to God His Body and Blood as a sacrifice to be slain on the cross for the sins of the world.[22]

The Eucharistic bread and wine are by type and symbol his crucified person in his body broken and blood shed, lying in open view before the Lord and before the communicants.

Rattray makes the point that Jesus Christ made himself the sacrifice for the sins of the world once for all; he sits at the right hand of the Father where he now pleads his sacrifice for the benefit of his church and the salvation of the world. We now on earth make the memorial of that sacrifice, which memorial has been 'appointed ... to be the only sacrifice of prayer and praise in the Christian church instead of the manifold sacrifices whether bloody or unbloody under the Law'.[23]

Fourthly, the celebration of the Eucharist is the propitiatory and expiatory memorial. Rattray's discussion is a description of the Eucharistic action in the church. The description is of an unnamed Eucharistic liturgy which is clearly not from any of the post-Reformation Prayer Books nor of the Western Latin rite. He describes the presentation of the gifts of bread and wine by the people and their being in turn offered to God the Father by the priest. The Eucharistic prayer follows from the opening dialogue between the priest and the people, to the priest giving

> thanks to God for the creation of the world and all things therein, visible and invisible; [then ... the people join with the priest in repeating the seraphic hymn 'Holy, holy, holy'] the priest gives thanks ... for all his benefits and his Providence towards mankind; for preparing them for the coming of Christ ... by the Law and the Prophets, and in the fullness of time sending [Christ] to take our nature upon him and redeem us by his death.

A description follows of the recitation of the words of institution, and a description of the prayer of oblation in which the priest offers up to God the Father the bread and cup as the symbols of the sacrifice of the body and blood of Christ, commemorating his sacrifice with thanksgiving. Next the 'epiclesis' asks the Father to send down his Spirit upon them. Then Rattray says,

> the priest maketh intercession, in virtue of the sacrifice thus offered, for the whole Catholick Church, and pleadeth the merits of this one Sacrifice on behalf of all estates and conditions of men in it ... not for the living only, but for the dead also.[24]

The intercessory character of the Eucharist is demonstrated by the intercessory petitions following the 'epiclesis' in the Eucharistic Prayer, and is of fundamental importance in Rattray's conception of the Eucharist. This entire description is taken from the liturgy of St James, later fully explored in Rattray's edited and annotated text as *The Ancient Liturgy of the Church of Jerusalem.*

Fifthly, Bishop Rattray describes the benefits of receiving Holy Communion as

> being entertained by God in what has been offered up to him; and feasting together at his table [the communicants] renew [their] covenant with him and one another ... are in a state of favour with him and of peace and friendship with one another; and by partaking of the sacrifice of Christ, and [they] have a title to all the benefits purchased by it ... a glorious resurrection ... being quickened by his Spirit.[25]

Thus he concludes, 'we have union and communion with the Father and the Son and the Holy Spirit, ... with one another, and all our fellow members of ... Christ's holy Catholick Church'.[26] It is clear that for Rattray the Eucharist, both in its celebration and its effect, is a dynamic, saving interaction between God the Holy Trinity and the faithful gathered to worship him.

III

The Ancient Liturgy of the Church of Jerusalem[27] is Bishop Rattray's posthumously published analysis of the 'proper Anaphora or Eucharistical service' of the Greek liturgy of St James as it was included by J. A. Fabricius in his *Codex Apocryphus Novi Testamenti* (Hamburg, 1703). Bishop Rattray chose the liturgy of St James for his extensive analysis because it

> is unquestionably one the most ancient and valuable now anywhere extant in the Christian Church. That it ... was used in the Church of Jerusalem will appear to any who candidly compare it to St Cyril's 5th Mystagogical Catechesis.[28]

He chose to study only the 'proper Anaphora' because 'all that part ... which precedes the Anaphora is a latter addition to the service of the church appears from the Account given by Justin Martyr in his first Apology' and other early sources.[29] His analysis begins with the Eucharistic prayer, 'Lift up your hearts', and continues to the dismissal, 'Depart in Peace'.[30]

Rattray's interest in liturgical worship and in the liturgy of St James in particular, springs from his dismay at the confusion in public worship.[31] He described the general chaos of church worship, principally among Episcopalians, from the time of the Revolution in 1688 to about 1710. His pastoral desire was for Scottish Episcopalians to possess a solemn and dignified liturgy of their own, with the provenance of antiquity.

Rattray's *Ancient Liturgy of the Church of Jerusalem*, published by his friend Robert Lyon, an Episcopalian presbyter in Fife,[32] is a masterly work of original scholarship. In it Rattray undertakes a double analysis, grammatical and comparative. He exhibits his analysis in five columns across facing folio pages. On the left-hand page, are two columns, the first is Fabricius's Greek text. That which he determined to be later interpolation he distinguishes by a smaller font. The second column is the Greek text that in Rattray's judgement is the original text of the ancient Jerusalem rite. The comparative analysis, in three columns, on the right-hand page, is the relevant corresponding parts of the Mystagogical Catechesis of Cyril of Jerusalem; the Clementine liturgy; and the relevant parts of the liturgies of Mark, Basil and John Chrysostom.[33] The layout of his analytical approach, fully annotated, makes his findings clear. Every other pair of pages is in English. Whether or not Rattray's analytical approach was unique, it was certainly a hundred years or more before such thorough and painstaking liturgical research analysis became the norm. Rattray was neither ignorant of nor naive about the antiquity of the Greek text. Two letters from Thomas Brett the younger, son of the noted non-juring bishop and liturgical scholar, make clear that Rattray knew that there were no written liturgical texts before the end of the fourth century.[34]

The English liturgical text that Rattray produced, *The ORDER for Celebrating the Sacrifice of the Holy Eucharist*,[35] included as the last item in 'The Appendix' of *The Ancient Liturgy*, is the translation into English of the Greek text that he identified by his analysis as the 'original', with the addition of 'such rubrics as appeared suitable, together with a few marginal notes for illustrating some particulars'.[36] He presents his reader with a Greek liturgy in English clearly intended for use. Bishop Rattray's *ORDER* would itself never find acceptance as a vehicle of Eucharistic worship: Rattray's successors knew that, however much they admired his *ORDER*, 'It was too far removed in character from the service with which priests and people were familiar'.[37]

Rattray's English *ORDER* begins with an interpolated Offertory, original to him but with reference to the Scottish Prayer Book of 1637,[38] and expanded with elements from other early texts[39] including the priest's publicly washing his hands and the deacon's acclamations preceding the 'Kiss of Peace', or 'Holy Kiss' as Rattray terms it. This latter inclusion is astonishingly prescient since it predates the modern custom by about 250 years. Then begins the offertory proper with the sentence, 'Let us present our Offerings to the Lord with Reverence and Godly fear'. Fourteen sentences are then provided to be read or sung.[40] Then comes the deacon's mixture (that is, pouring some water into the wine) of the cup on the 'Prothesis'[41] (a side table) and presenting it to the priest. Rattray daringly introduces the celebrant's making the sign of the cross upon his brow, which he supports with a number of Patristic citations in a footnote.[42]

Thereafter follows Rattray's English text. The anaphora of the liturgy of St James is similar to the major ancient Greek liturgies, but with the two notable exceptions: the use of the manual acts at the words of institution, and the extended number of intercessory petitions following the 'epiclesis'. In Rattray's *ORDER* he inserts the manual acts exactly as they are used in the 1662 *ORDER* for Holy Communion. This is not a liberty; the liturgy of St James uses 'manual acts', similar in character to the 1662 manual acts, and which are not to be found in any of the other Greek liturgies Rattray used in his comparative analysis. Even though he deems these to be a later addition to the text, he none the less inserts the parallel English manual acts. The breaking of the bread is not part of the Greek manual acts, but the fraction in the liturgy of St James Rattray judged to be a later interpolation,[43] leaving his text with no moment identified for the breaking of the bread. The breaking of the bread at the words of institution as in the 1662 manual acts, however, coincides with Rattray's doctrine of the Eucharist as the memorial offering of Christ's death.

The extensiveness of the intercessory petitions in the liturgy of St James is its chief characteristic. In his *ORDER* there are eighteen petitions. Bishop Rattray focuses on this characteristic in the last section of his *Christian Covenant* regarding the Eucharist as the chief locus of Christian intercession. The penultimate petition is a lengthy prayer for departed Christians. This will be the first instance of prayer for the departed being put forward in an English liturgical text proposed for actual use since the order for Holy Communion in the English Prayer Book of 1549.

Rattray's Greek text and *ORDER* specifically include all of the Greater Usages: the mixed cup,[44] the use of the 'epiclesis' and prayer of oblation, and prayer for the departed.[45] Scots Episcopalians (as opposed to the qualified chapels) largely followed the Aberdeen tradition in which the greater usages were accepted.[46]

It is fair to say that Bishop Rattray's theology, insights, scholarship and judgement[47] have made a massive contribution towards forging the essential character of Scottish Episcopacy into the nineteenth century, with his influence identifiable today, and that Rattray's *The Ancient Liturgy* was the precipitating agent in the movement towards organised liturgical worship in the Episcopal Church in the last half of the eighteenth century. It was not only the defining influence on the Scottish liturgy of 1764, but was also both the doctrinal and liturgical foundation of it.

IV

The history and development of the *Liturgy of 1764* has authoritatively been discussed by Bishop John Dowden for whom the posthumous publication of the *Ancient Liturgy of the Church of Jerusalem* 'was of deep moment in the history of the Scottish Office'.[48] The 1764 liturgy is the work of Bishop Robert Forbes with the then primus, William Falconar, and, as Bishop Dowden shows, the text for the 1764 liturgy was closely based on Falconar's text of 1755, which Dowden sees as 'distinctly traceable to Rattray's work'.[49]

Comparison of the 1764 liturgy with Rattray's *ORDER* will demonstrate that the sequence of the various parts of the 1764 liturgy derives directly from Bishop Rattray's *ORDER* of 1744, as its principal and significant source, and that the 1764 liturgy is purposefully faithful in doctrine to the idea of the Eucharist as the 'Commemorative or Memorial Sacrifice' outlined above. Jardine Grisbrooke observes, 'the doctrines held by its compilers ... are doctrines which the rite was intended to express, and does express very effectively'.[50]

The work of Falconer and Forbes was effectively to align the words and prayers of the English Prayer Books of 1549 and 1662 with Bishop Rattray's doctrinal ideas, and the liturgical pattern of *The Ancient Liturgy of the Church of Jerusalem*, to produce the Scottish liturgy of 1764. There are fifteen specific points of identity: five in the offertory, six in the prayer of consecration and four after the prayer of consecration.

The five in the offertory are as follows. Firstly, it is striking that both the original text of the 1764 liturgy, like Rattray's *ORDER*, begins with the offertory, without any synaxis or 'first part'. Those parts of the 1764 liturgy that come before the exhortation after the sermon in Bishop Dowden's text of the liturgy are a reconstruction.[51] Secondly, in both texts the offertory begins with the sentence, 'Let us present our offerings to the Lord with reverence and with godly fear'. Thirdly, the offertory sentences of 1764 are identical with those of the *ORDER*, but with the addition of one extra sentence, Heb. 13:16. Fourthly, the rubric at the end of the 'Offertory Sentences' of 1764 compares with the rubric of the *ORDER* on two points: the deacon receives 'devotions of the people'; and the money collected is referred to as 'oblations'. Fifthly, the 'Offertory Doxology' of 1764 is identical with that in the *ORDER* with the exception of the addition of I Chron. 29:12a, 'Both riches and honour come from Thee', which has been prefixed to verse 14b. 'All things come from Thee ...'.

The six points of identity in the Prayer of Consecration are as follows. Firstly, the change of the word 'one' to the word 'own' in the relative clause of the opening sentence, 'who by his own oblation of himself, once offered'. In the Scottish Book of 1637, and in all of the English Books, the clause reads, 'who by his one oblation of himself, once offered'. The significance of the word 'own' lies in the importance laid upon Christ's voluntary self-oblation.[52] The *ORDER* contains the following sentence which is introductory to the words of institution:

> And when the Hour was come, that he who had no sin, was to suffer a voluntary and life-giving Death upon the Cross for us Sinners, in the same night that he was betrayed, or rather offered up himself for the Life and Salvation of the World.

Bishop Rattray also discusses this point in *The Christian Covenant*. In his chapter entitled 'Notes', Dowden acknowledges the influence of Rattray via Bishop William Falconar's 1755 edition of the liturgy.[53]

Secondly, the substitution of the word 'once' for 'there' in the phrase found in the Scottish 1637 and all of the English Books, '(who by his own oblation of himself *once* offered)'. Having noted that the word 'there' was first omitted in the edition of 1755 and then in the edition of 1764, Dowden writes:

> There can be little doubt that the reason of the omission was the belief of the Non-Jurors that Christ offered Himself to the Father at the institution of the Eucharist, although the oblation was not consummated till the death upon the Cross.[54]

This is Rattray's second point in his *Christian Covenant*.

Thirdly, Robert Forbes's use of the 'Manual Acts' as in the 1662 *Book of Common Prayer*. These 'Acts' are part of Rattray's *ORDER*, and accompany the recitation of the words of institution, as in the 1662 Book. Many revisers of that Prayer Book were of the school of thought that saw the Eucharist in the same terms as their Scottish counterparts. The breaking of the bread at the words 'and when He had given thanks, he brake it' fits precisely with the idea that in the recitation of the words of institution the bread and the wine are made the symbols or antitypes of the crucified body and shed blood of Christ in death.[55] Any sort of 'Manual Acts' are a Scottish idea, first appearing in the Scottish Book of 1637, but fully developed in the 1662 Book. That Rattray uses them at the words of institution in his *ORDER* is testimony to their fitness to express the theological ideas exemplified by Rattray. Bishop Falconar does not use them in his edition of 1755.

The Greek text of the liturgy of St James also contains 'manual acts', that is, at the Words of Institution specific directions for the celebrant to take the bread, and then the cup, into his hands before his replacing them on the altar. Rattray judges the somewhat complicated directions concerning the breaking of the bread, which follow the Lord's Prayer in the Greek text of the liturgy of St James, to be a later interpolation and omits them. Bread is broken at the words of institution.

Fourthly, the use of capitals to emphasise the word 'DO' in the sentence, 'DO this in remembrance of me'. Rattray does not resort to so crude a device, but the emphasis does reflect the idea expressed in *The Christian Covenant* that the Eucharist is the memorial, commemoration and representation of Christ's death on the cross. This idea expresses that the word 'DO' in the Lord's command meant the making of the 'Christian Sacrifice' of the Eucharist, that is offering of bread and wine as the memorial of his death on the cross.

Fifthly, the sequence of the constituent parts of the Prayer of Consecration is certainly the direct influence of Rattray's *ORDER*, which is the first Scottish liturgical text to use the Greek order. He is followed by Bishop Falconar's liturgy of 1755, and by the 1764 liturgy. Dowden acknowledges that 'the influence of Bishop Rattray's work at last secured in 1764 the authorised establishment of this sequence'.[56] The Scottish attachment to the idea of an invocation of the Holy Spirit, as George Sprott makes clear, is not to be underestimated.[57] While Rattray had no regard for contemporary Reformed worship, he would have been keenly aware of John Forbes of Corse's emphasis on the 'epiclesis' in his copy of Forbes's *Instructiones*.[58] It is important to note, however, that the words of the 'epiclesis' in the 1764 liturgy do not follow Rattray's 'epiclesis', 'send down Thy Holy Spirit upon us and upon these gifts'.[59] The words of the 'epiclesis' in the 1764 liturgy follow those in the Scottish book of 1637, 'bless and sanctify . . . with thy . . . Holy Spirit . . . these thy gifts and creatures of bread and wine'.[60] Dowden criticises Forbes's and Falconar's scholarship in this;[61] Dowden's critique led to Rattray's formula being used in the 1929 Scottish liturgy.

Sixthly, the words 'WHICH WE NOW OFFER UNTO THEE' which appear in 1764 first appeared in an unauthorised 'commercial' edition of the office in 1735.[62] Their origin is suggested as being the work of Bishop William

Dunbar of Aberdeen.[63] Even though they cannot be said to have their origin in Rattray's ORDER, they strongly resonate with the clause 'we sinners offer unto Thee, O Lord, this tremendous and unbloody Sacrifice' in the prayer of oblation in the consecration prayer. That the clause was printed in small capitals to emphasise it, suggests the influence of the similar clause from Rattray's ORDER. The theological point in both Rattray's ORDER and 1764 is that the Eucharist is the solemn offering of bread and wine as the instituted representatives of the body and blood of Christ to God the Father in obedience to Christ's command.

The four points which follow the prayer of consecration are as follows. Firstly, the position of the 'Prayer for the whole state of Christ's Church' in the Scottish liturgy of 1764, falling as it does between the prayer of consecration and the Lord's Prayer, is one of the Scottish liturgy's most striking characteristics, and is unique to Scottish Episcopalian liturgical practice. It is also striking that Bishop Dowden makes no comment about this placing. Comparing Bishop Rattray's ORDER and his *Christian Covenant* with the 1764 liturgy, the reason Bishops Falconar and Forbes placed the prayer for the whole state of Christ's Church after the prayer of consecration becomes obvious. The lengthy sequence of petitions which follows the 'epiclesis' in the liturgy of St James is the model. Such petitions follow in other ancient Greek liturgies, but they are not so extensive in scope as in the Jerusalem liturgy.

In the *Christian Covenant* Bishop Rattray carefully outlines the theology of such a practice after the institution, oblation and invocation:

> the priest maketh intercession, in virtue of this Sacrifice thus offered up in commemoration of, and in union with the one great personal Sacrifice of Christ, for the whole Catholick Church, and pleadeth the merits of this one Sacrifice in behalf of all estates and conditions of men in it, offering this memorial thereof, not only for the living, but for the dead also, in commemoration of the Patriarchs, Prophets, Apostles, Martyrs, and all of the saints who have pleased God in their several generations.[64]

Secondly, Bishop William Falconar in his 1755 liturgy and Bishop Robert Forbes in the 1764 liturgy clearly intended to follow both the theology and practice espoused by Bishop Rattray by including a petition for the faithful departed in the Prayer for the whole state of Christ's Church. Hence the deletion of the phrase 'militant here in earth' from the title. It must be noted that the Scottish liturgy was the first, and for many years the only, liturgy in English in common use which included prayer for the faithful departed.

Thirdly, Bishop Dowden observes that the invitation to thanksgiving after having received Holy Communion first appears in 1764. 'It is a modification of the bidding of the Deacon in the Clementine liturgy, which had suggested a form similar to Rattray.'[65] The influence of Bishop Rattray's

ORDER is present in this instance. In the *ORDER*, after everyone has received Holy Communion, the deacon, 'being turned to the people', says, 'Let us now give thanks to God that he hath vouchsafed to make us partakers of the Body and Blood of Christ . . .'. Why Bishop Forbes chose to use the deacon's exhortation from the Clementine liturgy as opposed to the one from Bishop Rattray's *ORDER* is not known, but a guess can be made by comparing the form in Rattray's *ORDER* with the form used in the 1764 liturgy. The deacon's 'exhortation' in 1764 is more explicit in what is required of the communicant, 'and let us beg of him grace to perform our vows, and to persevere in our good resolutions; and that being made holy, we may obtain everlasting life . . .'.[66] In Rattray's *ORDER*, the Deacon's exhortation asks the communicant simply to pray 'that he would keep us unblameable'.[67]

Fourthly is the inclusion of Bishop Rattray's translation of 'Glory to God in the highest', in 'The Appendix'. It is the only item in *The Ancient Liturgy* which Rattray translates and edits not from the liturgy of St James; this Greek version of the hymn is from the *Codex Alexandrinus*, where it is entitled 'The Morning Hymn', which title Rattray retains. The English Prayer Book version, 'Glory be to God on high', was used in the order for Holy Communion in the 1637 Prayer Book.[68] The version of 'Glory be to God in the Highest' in the 1764 liturgy is virtually identical to Rattray's translation, but there are two differences: prefacing the phrase 'and to thee O God' to the ascriptions 'the only begotten Son Jesu Christ' and to 'the Holy Spirit'; and the inclusion of the clause 'O Lord, the only begotten Son Jesu Christ' at the beginning of the second paragraph. Further evidence comes from John Skinner's commentary on the 1764 liturgy. Although Skinner does not mention Rattray, it is obvious that he is drawing on Rattray, by calling the hymn the *Morning Hymn*, and by drawing a distinction between the two texts which Rattray gives, one an orthodox text, from the *Codex Alexandrinus*, and the other, 'altered by the Arian Party' from the *Apostolic Constitutions*.[69] Bishop Dowden acknowledges Skinner's assertion, saying, 'if there were any *tradition* on the subject when he wrote, he certainly would have been as likely as any to have known it'.[70]

V

Drawing together the three elements of this chapter, Rattray's Eucharistic doctrine, his liturgical text and the Scottish liturgy of 1764, it is clear that his impact upon the Scottish Episcopalians of the latter eighteenth century was indeed profound from both a doctrinal and a liturgical standpoint. Notwithstanding the fact that both Rattray's theological and liturgical connection with the Scottish liturgy is largely forgotten, they have had profound impact on the Scottish liturgy and through it on other churches.[71]

The most well-known and undoubtedly the most significant instance the liturgy of 1764 having a direct impact on Eucharistic texts beyond Scotland is, of course, its influence on the American order for Holy Communion of 1789. A brief comparison of the two texts will delineate precisely what is to most a generalised idea. There are three items in the American 1789 text that can be identified as coming directly from the Scottish 1764 liturgy.

First is the summary of the law, which originated with the non-jurors' liturgy of 1718, to replace the recitation of the Decalogue. It was included in the Scottish liturgy of 1764, and could be said as an alternative to the recitation of the Decalogue. The framers of the American 1789 Holy Communion added the summary of the law, but only as a possible addition to the recitation of the Decalogue, not instead of it.

The second and third items are consecutive sections of the prayer of consecration and are by far the most noted and important points of Scottish influence on the 1789 American liturgy. This influence was not, however, a wholesale importation of the 1764 Prayer of Consecration. The American 1789 text follows the text of the 1662 Holy Communion for the prayer of consecration down to the end of the words of institution 'Do this as oft as ye shall drink it, in remembrance of me'. It is at the prayer of oblation, 'Wherefore O Lord and heavenly Father', that the American text then follows the 1764 text onwards to the '*Amen.*' at the end of the prayer of consecration.[72]

The second item is the inclusion of the prayer of oblation following the words of institution, a radical break with the consecration prayer of 1662, and the inclusion of the 'epiclesis', absent from the 1662 consecration prayer. In the 1789 text, the prayer of oblation, from the first edition of 1790 until 1793 used the same typographical device of putting the words 'WHICH WE NOW OFFER UNTO THEE' in small capitals which originated in the early editions of the 1764 liturgy.[73]

The third item is the inclusion of the 'epiclesis' or Prayer of Invocation to follow on the prayer of oblation, which is clearly Scottish influence, and is also a radical divergence from the 1662 liturgy; its wording is a different story. The texts of the prayer of invocation in the liturgies of 1549, 1637 and 1764 are very similar, with only slight rewordings. The principal changes concern the result of the action of the Holy Spirit. The 1549 'epiclesis' asks that the offered bread and wine, 'maie be unto us' the body and blood of Christ; the 1637 'epiclesis' asks exactly the same. The 1764 liturgy asks more objectively that the offered bread and wine 'may become' the body and blood of Christ. The American prayer of invocation in the 1789 rite, however, is far more cautious in its petition. It asks, at some length, that 'we, receiving them according to thy Son our Saviour Jesus Christ's holy institution, in remembrance of his death and passion, may be partakers of his most blessed Body and Blood'. The Scottish influence to have the 'epiclesis' following the oblation is obvious, but, Scottish influence in the wording of the 'epiclesis' is absent in the American text's more cautious wording. The use of the collect of thanksgiving after the reception of communion is consequential, however, because the prayer of oblation and the collect of thanksgiving are alternative to each other after communion in the 1662 *Book of Common Prayer*.

There are three important points where the American 1789 rite consciously did not follow the 1764 liturgy. First is its treatment of the prayer for the 'whole state of Christ's Church'. The American 1789 text follows the 1662 prayer, both in its title 'the whole state of Christ's Church militant' (omitting 'here in earth'), and in locating it immediately after the offertory. The importance that the Scots placed on the prayer following the consecration is not recognised here. Second is the Lord's Prayer being recited after the receiving of communion. Here the 1789 text followed the 1662 Prayer Book usage, not the Scottish usage. The Lord's Prayer's following the prayer of consecration in Scottish usage was established in the Prayer Book of 1637, and is its place in Bishop Rattray's *Ancient Liturgy*, and in the liturgy of 1764. Third, the 1789 rite did not follow the 1764 liturgy with the Communicant's saying 'Amen' in responses to the 'Words of Administration'. In English-language liturgy it is a Scottish practice established in the 1637 liturgy, found in Bishop Rattray's *ORDER*, and continued in the 1764 liturgy and its subsequent revisions.

It is clear that whilst the Scottish liturgy of 1764 has had significant, even profound influence in shaping the Eucharistic worship in the nascent American Episcopal Church, its influence was mitigated by the dominant adherence to the English 1662 Book. None the less, one can say with confidence that Bishop Rattray's learned and scholarly work has found in the American 1789 'Order for the Administration of . . . Holy Communion' a lasting legacy.

It is a sad irony for so great a scholar and bishop that the remembrance of his work and the recognition of his influence has largely passed from the consciousness of history. George Hay Forbes, foreseeing the future, wrote in the 'Preface' to his volume of Bishop Rattray's principal works,

> in these days of development and change, when our native traditional theology seems in no small danger of being quite forgotten, the calm deep learning of these admirable works may be the means of recalling earnest minds to the landmarks which our fathers set up.[74]

The testimony of the Scottish liturgy in the 1929 Scottish Prayer Book, and Scottish influence on the American Episcopalian Eucharistic worship, which so clearly reflects Bishop Rattray's work, however, stand witness to the enduring quality of his scholarship and judgement.

Notes

1. W.D. Kornahrens, 'Eucharistic Doctrine in Scottish Episcopacy, 1620–1875' (Ph.D. thesis, University of St Andrews, 2008), *passim*.
2. J. Dowden, *The Scottish Communion Office, 1764* (Oxford: Clarendon Press, 1922), p. 48.

3. G. H. Forbes, 'Preface', in G. H. Forbes (ed.), *The Works of Thomas Rattray*, 8 vols (Burntisland: Pitsligo Press, 1854), I, p. ii.
4. G. H. Forbes, 'Eucharistical Adoration', *The Panoply*, 2 vols (c.1860), p. 263.
5. T. Rattray, 'The Christian Covenant' in G. H. Forbes (ed.), *The Works of Thomas Rattray*, I, p. 42.
6. W. Forbes, *Considerationes Modestae et Pacificae*, ed., trans. G. H. Forbes, 2 vols (Oxford: J. H. Parker, 1850), II, p. 141.
7. Rattray, 'Christian Covenant', I, p. 15.
8. Ibid.
9. Ibid., p. 16.
10. A. Schmemann, *The Eucharist* (New York: St Valdimir's Seminary Press, 1988), p. 39.
11. L. Chauvet, *Symbol and Sacrament* (Collegeville, MN: Liturgical Press, 1995), p. 400.
12. Citation is from the Authorised Version.
13. Rattray, 'Christian Covenant', I, p. 16.
14. Ibid., n. q. The term 'sacrifice' is not to be understood in the Tridentine sense, but rather as the church's offering of bread and the mixed cup as the memorial of Christ's once for all sacrificial death.
15. Ibid.
16. H. Scougal, *The Life of God in the Soul of Man with Nine Discourses on Important Subjects* (London, 1735), p. 233.
17. Ibid., p. 233.
18. H. G. Liddell and R. Scott, *A Greek–English Lexicon*, abridged (Oxford: The Clarendon Press, 1998), p. 5. Definition III, is 'To lie exposed or to lie dead'.
19. Rattray, 'Christian Covenant', I, p. 16, footnote r. The citation in LXX makes explicit Rattray's point.
20. W. L. Low, *The True Catholic Doctrine of the Holy Eucharist* (Edinburgh: Scottish Chronicle Press, 1923), p. 150.
21. Rattary, 'Christian Covenant', I, p. 15, n. h, p.
22. Ibid., pp. 15-16, n. m., p.
23. Ibid., p. 17
24. Ibid., p. 19.
25. Ibid., p. 20.
26. Ibid., p. 21.
27. T. Ratttray, *The Ancient Liturgy of the Church of Jerusalem* (London, 1744).
28. Ibid., p. iii.
29. Ibid.
30. Ibid., pp. 2–101.
31. Dowden, *Scottish Communion Office*, pp. 35-48.
32. A. Jolly, *The Christian Sacrifice in the Eucharist*, 2nd edn (Aberdeen, 1847), pp. 191–2.
33. Rattray, *Ancient Liturgy*, pp. 3–101.
34. Ibid., p. xvi.
35. Ibid., p. 113.
36. Ibid., p. 110.
37. Dowden, *Scottish Communion*, p. 74.
38. Rattray, *Ancient Liturgy*, p. 114. The offertory sentences are virtually identical with those of 1637.

39. Ibid., pp. 4-5.
40. Ibid., p. 114.
41. Ibid., p. 113.
42. Ibid., pp. 30, 115,
43. Ibid., p. 82.
44. Rattray, 'Christian Covenant', I, pp. 21-2, and *Ancient Liturgy*, p. 30; starred note p. 117.
45. Rattray, *Ancient Liturgy*, pp. 19, 119.
46. Kornahrens, 'Eucharistic Doctrine', pp. 197-8, and 'Praying for the Departed', *Theology in Scotland*, 18:2 (2011), 47-79.
47. W. J. Grisbrooke, *Anglican Liturgies of the* Seventeenth *and Eighteenth Centuries* (London: SPCK, 1958), p. 136; Dowden, *Scottish Communion*, p. 11.
48. Grisbrooke, *Anglican Liturgies*, p. 156; Dowden, *Scottish Communion*, pp. 71, 73.
49. Dowden, *Scottish Communion*, pp. 77-8.
50. Grisbrooke, *Anglican Liturgies*, p. 159.
51. Dowden, *Scottish Communion*, p. 121.
52. Grisbrooke, *Anglican Liturgies*, p. 157.
53. Dowden, *Scottish Communion*, p. 160.
54. Ibid., p. 160
55. C. Wheatly, *A Rational Illustration of the Book of Common Prayer of the Church of England* (London: Henry G. Bohn, 1848), p. 297.
56. Dowden, *Scottish Communion*, p. 155.
57. G. W. Sprott, *Worship and Offices in the Church of Scotland* (Edinburgh: Wm Blackwood and Sons, 1881), pp. 119-20.
58. T. F. Torrance, *Scottish Theology* (Edinburgh: T. & T. Clark, 1996), p. 89.
59. Rattray, *Ancient Liturgy*, pp. 44, 117.
60. Dowden, *Scottish Communion*, p. 198.
61. Ibid., pp. 11-12.
62. Ibid., p. 65.
63. Ibid.
64. Rattray, 'Christian Covenant', I, p. 19.
65. Dowden, *Scottish Communion*, p. 170.
66. Ibid., p. 131.
67. Rattray, *Ancient Liturgy*, p. 121.
68. Gordon, Donaldson, *The Making of the Scottish Prayer Book of 1637* (Edinburgh: EUP, 1954), pp. 201-2.
69. J. Skinner, *The Office for the Sacrament of the Lord's Supper* (Aberdeen, 1807), p. 169.
70. Dowden, *Scottish Communion*, p. 172.
71. Ibid., p. 74.
72. Justice.anglican.org/resources/bcp/1789/1790.pdf
73. Ibid.; also Dowden, *Scottish Communion*, pp. 161-5.
74. Forbes (ed.), *Works*, I, p. ii.

Index

À Kempis, Thomas, 103, 108, 146
Abercorn, Countess, 40–1, 42
Abercromby, Robert, SJ, 38–42, 49, 50n, 54–6
Aberdeen, 7, 8, 10, 11, 12, 14, 19, 21, 22, 30, 39, 49, 55, 60, 75, 76, 78, 86, 88, 93, 112–25, 130, 134, 138–53, 164, 172–88, 192, 194–6, 205, 209, 213, 216
Aberdeen Breviary (1507), 19, 24, 28–30
Aberdeenshire, 11–12, 43, 46, 88, 114–15, 118, 122, 129, 133, 139, 142, 172, 183, 192, 194, 195
Acquaviva, Claudio, SJ, 42, 54–6
Act of Toleration (1712), 11, 114–16, 126, 128, 130, 136, 144
America, 4, 11, 14, 121, 128, 132–3, 172, 218–19
Anna of Denmark, 3, 41, 56
Anne, Queen, 10, 113–15, 117, 128, 131, 139, 144, 148
Anglican 5, 9, 126–37, 164, 192
Anglicanism, 1, 8–12, 15 17, 12, 14, 114, 119, 154
Angus, 55, 98, 129, 131, 191, 192, 195, 205
Antrim, 61, 66, 69
Arbuthnott, John, 118–19, 121
Augustinians, 25–7, 29, 99, 186

Baillie, Robert, 10, 71–3, 77–8, 80–3, 84n
Banffshire, 43, 46, 130, 192–3
Basil, of Caesarea, 175–6, 211
Beaton, James, 3, 38
Benedictines, 24–5, 99
Blackwell, Thomas, 114–15, 118
Book of Common Order (1562), 6, 9, 30, 72, 78–9
Book of Common Prayer (1549), 5, 7–9, 75–6
Book of Common Prayer (1552), 30, 78
Book of Common Prayer (1662), 11, 12, 79–80, 97–8, 112, 126–8, 130–3, 136, 154, 159, 165, 214, 219
Borders, 1, 6, 20
Bourignon, Antoinette, 139, 141–2, 145–8, 152n
Bourignonism, 143, 145–7
Brady, Patrick, OFM, 59–60, 64, 66
Brechin, 13, 121, 129
Brett, Thomas, 158–9, 160–1, 164, 172, 212
Brodie, Alexander, of Brodie, 74, 78
Bruce, Peter, 102, 104–5
Burnet, Andrew, 114, 117–18
Burnet, Gilbert, 79, 82, 86–7, 89, 92

Calvin, John, 94, 183, 186
Calvinism, 1–2, 10, 12, 83, 86–7, 92, 94
Camerons of Lochaber, 14, 191
Campbell, Archibald, 12–13, 81, 118, 124n, 162, 164, 168n, 172–88
  Doctrine of the Middle State, 13, 162, 177, 178, 181–2, 184
Carlisle, 133, 193, 194, 196
Carswell, John, 6
Catanach, James, 118–19, 121, 124n
Charles I, 7–6, 14, 71, 80, 103, 175
Charles II, 8–9, 14, 71, 74, 76, 101, 121, 139
Christie, William, SJ, 42, 47
Cistercians, 25–9
Cockburn, Patrick, 86, 119–20
Cockburn, William, 130–1
Collier, Jeremy, 118–19, 157, 160, 172
Coppock, Thomas, 192–3
Counter-Reformation, 2, 40, 44, 49, 55–6, 58
Covenanting Movement, 8–9, 13, 71–3, 75–6, 78, 83, 87
Culloden, Battle of, 13–14, 190, 192–17
Cumming, Alexander, MP, 118–19, 121–2, 124n

De Gouda, Nicholas, SJ, 37–8
De Sales, Francis, 103–4, 107, 146

Deacon, Thomas, 160, 162, 164–5, 172
Dominicans, 4, 25, 45, 55, 57, 67
Dowden, John, 205–6, 213–17
Dunbreck, Patrick, 112, 114
Dundee, 11, 25, 30, 121, 129, 131, 132, 174

Edinburgh, 1–3, 7–8, 10–11, 13, 21–2, 39, 45, 56, 75–6, 79, 91, 98, 99–102, 112, 114, 116, 127–30, 134, 135, 173, 177, 180, 191, 192, 195, 196, 205–6
Elgin, 23–4, 128, 195
Episcopalianism, 1, 8–10, 12, 112, 139–40, 172
Episcopalians, 1, 5, 8–11, 15, 70–1, 77, 83, 86, 93, 96–8, 101, 104, 112–15, 119–22, 125–8, 131–2, 134–6, 138, 140–2, 144, 164, 172–3, 175, 182, 190, 206, 211, 213, 217
Erastianism, 140, 157, 172

Falconer, John, 173–4, 177–8
Falconer, William, 213, 215–16
Farquharson, Charles, SJ, 48, 196–7
Fife, 10, 76, 87, 211
Fifteen, The, 13–14, 46, 117–18, 121, 131–2, 190
Fletcher, Andrew, of Saltoun, 190–1, 195
Forbes, John, of Corse, 144, 149n, 175–6, 209, 215
Forbes, Robert, 164, 192, 194, 213–14, 216
Forbes, William, 176, 206
Forsyth, Henry, SJ, 47–8
Forty-Five, The, 13–14, 120–1, 189–204
Franciscans, 4, 25–9, 39, 53–69
Fullarton (Fullerton), John, 130–1, 173, 179, 181, 187

Gadderar, James, 12–13, 119–21, 124n, 135, 164, 172–3, 179–81
Garden, George, 12, 86–7, 90, 93, 120–1, 138–53
Garden, James, 12, 86, 93–4, 115, 138–53
    Comparative Theology (1700), 86, 94, 142, 148
George I, 117, 119, 122, 131
George II, 119, 122, 191, 193

Glamis Castle, 97–100, 104
Glasgow, 3, 8, 10, 12, 23–4, 38, 70, 71–2, 80, 82, 130–1, 134, 194
Glenlivet, 47, 193, 196
    Battle of, 38, 50n
Good, William, SJ, 39–40
Gordon, James, 116, 133
Gordon, James, Bishop, 5, 46, 48
Gordons of Huntly, 4, 43, 46–8, 56, 103, 116, 193–4
Grabe, John Ernest, 155, 157–8, 164
Greenshields, James, 11, 112, 114, 128–30

Haddington, 22, 26–9, 195
Hanoverians, 10–11, 117, 120–1, 189, 190–1, 194, 198
Harper, William, 120, 195
Hegarty, Patrick, OFM, 60, 66–7
Hickes, George, 154–9, 165, 172, 183
    Two Treatises, 154–6
Holyroodhouse, 97–99, 101–4, 106
Honyman, Andrew, 121, 146

Inverness, 55, 130, 192, 194, 196
Iona, 20–1, 27

Jacobite, 5, 11, 13–14, 22, 43–5, 86, 112–13, 117–18, 120–2, 126, 131, 138–9, 145, 172, 189–204
Jacobitism, 1, 10–13, 44, 113, 117, 120–2, 127, 138–9, 142, 172, 189–92, 197–8
Jacobitism, Irish, 189–90
James IV, 19, 24, 29
James VI and I, 3, 6–7, 41, 49n, 54, 56, 63–4
James VII and II, 1, 10, 11, 14, 96–9, 102–4, 113–14, 117–18, 189
James VIII, 13, 103, 113–14, 117–18, 121, 132, 138, 145, 172
Jesuits, 4–5, 36–53, 54–7, 59–60, 62, 99–104, 106, 121, 147, 192, 194
Johnson, John, of Cranbourne, 155–16, 158–9, 163
    The Unbloody Sacrifice (1714–18), 156, 163–6

Kirk, governance of, 6, 8–9, 22, 54, 70, 75, 128, 138–40, 144
Kirk, inter-faith relations, 1–3, 6, 37, 46, 60, 63–65, 127, 147–8
Knox, John, 22, 26

Index

Laud, William, 7, 99
Leighton, Robert, 10, 71–3, 77–8, 80–3
   Exposition of the Lord's Prayer, 72–4
Leslie, John, SJ, 39, 42
liturgical tradition
  American, 14, 218–19
  Anglican, 11–14, 99, 112, 114,
    116–17, 119, 128, 132, 135–6, 145,
    148, 154–7, 159–65, 168, 213
  Calvinist, 5–8, 10, 38, 54, 93
  Celtic, 4, 21, 24
  Clementine, 13–14, 158–60, 162, 164,
    205–21
  Episcopalian, 1, 7, 11–14, 19, 69–72,
    79–83, 93–9, 104, 109, 112, 119,
    127–8, 130–6, 141, 164, 172–7,
    181–12, 189, 205–21
  Greek Orthodox, 7, 10, 12, 160, 175,
    182, 205, 211–13, 215–17
  Lutheran, 2, 5, 7
  Presbyterian, 1–2, 5–12, 63, 70–1,
    74–5, 77–83, 87, 89, 93, 96–7, 115,
    148, 175, 189
  Roman Catholic, 1–2, 4–6, 8–11,
    13–14, 19–34, 35–52, 61, 94, 97,
    99–105, 146, 155–6, 177, 189–90,
    193, 207
  usages, 12, 119, 157, 160–2, 172–5,
    177–82, 184, 186, 213
Lochaber, 13, 43, 45–6, 59, 66
Lockhart, George, of Carnwarth, 172–3
London, 8, 11–12, 64, 74, 75, 77, 81,
  100, 102–3, 105, 116, 118, 120,
  129, 132, 133, 134, 135, 145, 164,
  172, 173, 177, 179, 183, 205
Louvain, 57, 58, 59, 60, 67
Loyola, Ignatius, SJ, 38, 45–6, 56
Lyon, Robert, 192, 211

Macbreck, John, SJ, 41–2, 46–7
MacCaghwell, Hugh, OFM, 59, 66
McCann, Edmund, OFM, 39, 59–61,
  64, 66
Macdonald, Allan, 193, 196–7
Macdonald, Hugh, 5, 197
Macdonalds of Colonsay, 61, 65–6
Macdonalds of Keppoch, 42–5, 68, 69n,
  193, 196–7
Maclachlan, John, 13, 203
Mary, Queen of Scots, 38, 54
Mary of Orange, 11, 113, 132, 140,
  142–4
Mercer, Thomas, 120–1

Mitchell, David, 76, 78, 85n
Montrose, 129, 133, 194
Moray, 23, 55, 130, 180, 192
Munro, Robert, 46

Na Ceapaich, Sìleas, 37, 43–53
  An Eaglis/The Church, 45
Nicolson, Thomas, 5, 48
Nicolson, William, 127–8, 133
non-jurors, 9, 11–14, 113–14, 116,
  119–20, 126–7, 130, 135–6, 142,
  154–9, 164–5, 172, 174–6, 178–9,
  185, 190–2, 205, 214, 218

Ogilvie, John, OFM, 58–60, 66
Ogilvie, John, SJ, 3, 47
O'Neill, Paul, OFM, 60, 66, 68n

Paris, 3, 5, 25, 27, 40, 57, 197
penal laws, 3, 11, 14, 54, 97, 99, 105,
  117, 126, 131, 190
Perth, 7, 21, 25, 75, 80, 128, 192, 193
Perth, Earl of, 98, 102–3, 106
Petrie, Arthur, 172, 183
Pitsligo, Lord, 117, 120–1, 152n
Presbyterianism, 1, 6–10, 21, 69, 89, 96,
  104, 145
Presbyterians, 1, 6, 9–11, 13, 37, 70–1,
  74, 76–82, 86–7, 92–3, 96–8, 101,
  112–17, 119–21, 126–1, 135, 138,
  140, 142–6, 148–9, 176, 179, 186,
  189–91, 198–9
Privy Council, 81, 96, 99–101, 114, 128
Propaganda Fide, 4, 36, 55, 60–6
Protestantism, 1–2, 5, 7, 11, 44, 56, 94,
  99, 103, 126, 140, 146, 160, 182,
  193
Protestants, 3–5, 10, 22, 54, 56–7, 59,
  63, 67n, 76, 100–2, 104, 176, 191

Rattray, Thomas, 13, 121, 164, 172, 175,
  180, 182–3, 205–21
  Ancient Liturgy, 1744, 13–14, 164, 175,
  205–21
Reformation
  England, 2, 157
  Scotland, 1–2, 5, 8, 13, 19, 22, 30, 36,
    49, 54, 71–2, 99, 178, 180–2, 210
Restoration period, 8–10, 13–14, 70–85,
  87, 94, 96, 101, 121, 127, 140, 190
Roman Catholicism, 1–2, 4–9, 12–15,
  19–35, 36–69, 96–7, 99–105, 140,
  155, 177, 189–204, 207

Rome, 2, 4, 5, 19, 20, 30, 37, 38, 39, 40, 41, 46, 48, 49, 56, 57, 58, 59, 60, 62, 63, 64–6, 68n, 100–1, 104, 186, 194, 197
Rose, Alexander, 114, 128, 135, 177

St Andrews, 6, 21, 22, 23, 25, 27, 38, 43, 44, 46, 76
Salmerón, Alphonsus, SJ, 37, 45
Sarum texts, 23–30
Scots Catholic Colleges, 55–7
  Douai, 5, 42, 46–7, 196
  Madrid, 47, 64
  Paris, 3, 5, 46, 197
  Rome, 5, 46–7, 64, 100
Scottish Catholic Missions
  Dominican, 4, 45, 54, 56, 66–7
  Franciscan, 4, 53–69
  Jesuits, 4–5, 35–52, 53–6, 62, 67
  Scottish secular clergy, 4, 54, 66
  Vincentian, 4, 45, 47
Scottish Parliament, 2–3, 22, 37, 54, 74–5, 100
Scottish Service Book (1637), 8–9, 11–12, 14, 75, 79, 83, 98
Scougal, Henry, 10, 12, 86–95, 120, 139, 141, 146–8, 208
  Life of God in the Soul of Man, 1677, 86, 89–92, 94, 141
Scougal, Patrick, 87, 139, 146
Seabury, Samuel, 15, 164, 172
Sharp, James, 75, 77, 80–1
Sharp, John, 132, 157
Skinner, John, 172, 217
Society of Jesus *see* Jesuits
Strathmore, Earl of, 98–9

Stuart, Charles Edward, Prince, 193, 195, 197
Stuart, House of, 1, 9, 12, 14, 120, 142, 145, 190–1
Stuart, John, OFM, 58–9, 64
Sydserff, Thomas, 74–6
Synod of Dunblane (1662), 77–8

Teresa of Avila, 146
Thirty-Nine Articles, 6, 8, 9, 11, 15, 132
Treaty of Union (1707), 1, 11, 189
Trent, Council of, 2, 56–7, 64, 68, 158
Tridentine, 2, 4, 8, 14, 28, 30, 37, 49, 56–7, 63
Tyrie, John, 193–4

universities, 7, 12, 88, 190
  Aberdeen, 22, 86, 88, 116, 139
  Edinburgh, 72
  Glasgow, 6, 71, 134
  St Andrews, 6, 21–2, 38, 43–4, 46
usagers, 13, 160, 162, 172–4

Valens, Robert, SJ, 40, 42

Ward, Cornelius, OFM, 60–2, 64–6, 69n
Watson, James, 101–2, 104–7
Wesley, John, 86, 92
Westminster Confession of Faith, 8–11, 87, 96, 113, 135, 142–4, 148
Wheatly, Charles, 156, 165–6, 167n
White, Francis, CM, 45–6
William of Orange, 9–11, 113, 117, 126, 132, 140, 142–4

York, 132, 134, 157, 195

EU representative:
Easy Access System Europe
Mustamäe tee 50, 10621 Tallinn, Estonia
Gpsr.requests@easproject.com

www.ingramcontent.com/pod-product-compliance
Lightning Source LLC
Chambersburg PA
CBHW070348240426
43671CB00013BA/2441